TRADE AND TRADERS IN EARLY INDIAN SOCIETY

Highlighting diverse types of market places and merchants, this book situates the commercial scenario of early India (up to *c.* AD 1300) in the overall agrarian material milieu of the subcontinent. The book questions the stereotypical narrative of early Indian trade as exchanges in small quantity, exotic, portable luxury items and strongly argues for the significance of trade in relatively inexpensive bulk commodities – including agrarian/floral products – at local and regional levels and also in long distance trade. That staple items had salience in the sea-borne trade of early India figures prominently in this book which points out that commercial exchanges touched the everyday life of a variety of people. A major feature of this work is the conspicuous thrust on and attention to the sea-borne commerce in the subcontinent. The history of Indic seafaring in the Indian Ocean finds a prominent place in this book pointing out the braided histories of overland and maritime networks in the subcontinent. In addition to three specific chapters on the maritime profile of early Bengal, the third edition of *Trade and Traders in Early Indian Society* offers two new chapters (14 and 15) on the commercial scenario of Gujarat, dealing respectively with an organization of merchants during the early sixth century AD and with the long-term linkages between money-circulation and overseas trade in Gujarat *c.* AD 500-1500). A new preface to the Third Edition discusses the emerging historiographical issues in the history of trade in early India. Rich in the interrogation of a wide variety of primary sources, the book analyses the changing perspectives on early Indian trade by taking into account the current literature on the subject.

Ranabir Chakravarti, an eminent expert in the social and economic history of early India, is known for his enduring interests in the Indian Ocean maritime trade during the pre-modern times. A regular contributor to peer-reviewed journals and edited academic volumes in India and abroad, he has authored/co-authored and edited/co-edited the following works: *Warfare for Wealth: Early Indian Perspectives* (Calcutta, 1986); *A Sourcebook of Indian Civilization* (Hyderabad, 2000); *Trade in Early India* (New Delhi, 2001); *Indo-Judaic Studies in the Twenty First Century: A View from the Margins* (New York, 2007); *Exploring Early India up to c. AD 1300* (New Delhi, 2016); *History of Bangladesh: Early Bengal in Regional Perspectives up to c. 1200 CE* in two volumes (Dhaka, 2018). He also contributed to the annotation of the English translation (by Giles Constable) of a 14th century Latin Crusade tract, *How to Defeat the Saracens* (Washington DC, 2012). He has also written three books in Bangla on early Indian history. Dr. Chakravarti was elected to preside over the section on Ancient Indian History by Indian History Congress in 2011.

Trade and Traders in Early Indian Society

(Third Revised and Enlarged Edition)

RANABIR CHAKRAVARTI

MANOHAR

Third edition published 2021
by Routledge
2 Park Square, Milton Park, Abingdon, Oxon OX14 4RN

and by Routledge
52 Vanderbilt Avenue, New York, NY 10017
Routledge is an imprint of the Taylor & Francis Group, an informa business

First edition published by Manohar Publishers 2002
Second edition published by Manohar Publishers 2007

British Library Cataloguing-in-Publication Data
A catalogue record for this book is available from the British Library

Library of Congress Cataloging-in-Publication Data
A catalog record for this book has been requested

ISBN: 978-0-367-52978-9 (hbk)
ISBN: 978-1-003-08412-9 (ebk)

Typeset in Times New Roman 10.5/12.5
by Ajay Arts, New Delhi 110 002

MANOHAR

To Professor B.N. Mukherjee
as a mark of my indebtedness to him
and for inspiring me by his
indefatigable spirit of the quest
for knowledge

Contents

Preface to the Third Edition

Mixed feelings of joy, anxiety and trepidation are simultaneously at work as I write this Preface to the third edition of my book, *Trade and Traders in Early Indian Society* (original edition 2002, second edition 2007). When Ramesh Jain, the helmsman of Manohar Publishers & Distributors, expressed his wish to reprint or bring out a revised edition of the book, I told him my preference for the latter option. It is matter of joy for this author that his publisher found this book worthy of a third edition. I personally never thought the volume would go beyond its second edition. In the current thrust and vogue for social and cultural history I was hesitant about the viability and acceptability of a book on economic life in the subcontinent during a remote past. As this book is ready for re-appearing, like the proverbial cat with nine lives, my publisher is perhaps more assured than its author about its future. I record my heartfelt thanks to Mr. Jain for his initiative to bring out the third edition of this book.

The element of anxiety at writing the Preface is largely due to the bleak future of historical studies and also of the calling of History in India. There is an alarming chasm between the excellence of historical researches in and on India done by professional practitioners of the past and the recent claims and utterances on History pronounced by those—including politicians--who have little or no skill and training in this field of knowledge. The use and abuse of the past, often with majoritarian, supremacist and muscular nationalist programmes, have been made time and again to gain political mileage; this has resulted in the terrible shrinkage of space for professional debates on and also dissent from a number of ill-bred notions about the past. As a historian, I am at a deep unease to find how legal luminaries, in the context of pronouncing significant judgments, have paid lip-service to historical researches and findings, but ended up by annulling the respect for history at the altar of the majority's religious faith and sentiments which, under no circumstances, are compatible with the lived plural traditions and practices in India. History as a subject of enquiry is meant for explaining pasts and such explanations would naturally never remain static. If and when the discipline of History becomes a tool for glorification of 'us' and vilification of 'them', then the driving force is hate, at the root of which is the fear of the different. And hate is not a mental state; it is an ideology designed and let loose to serve majoritarianism. Those who, during recent decades, have been misusing and abusing history for current and future political agenda, are farthest from historiography which is the forte of a qualified and trained historian. Embedded in historiography, the historian can generate, check and verify what historical evidence is and distinguish it from legends and myths. That is the building block of the historian's explanations of the pasts which are indeed varied as perceptions and historical paradigms too shift. Sinister motives and designs are on the anvil to stifle the multiple voices of pasts which are recovered, at least partially, by those who are qualified to be admitted to the calling of history. And the calling of history cannot be allowed to be taken over by self-styled dabblers in history.

The trepidations arise out of my own intellectual shortcomings which stare at me as I go through the earlier editions of this book. Some of my ideas and evidences are admittedly dated now. But I decided not to discard them, but kept them as markers of my limitations which I try my best to overcome in the third edition. That is why I thought of adding two new chapters to this edition; the Bibliography and the Index have also been updated in the light of the new material placed and discussed. The Bibliography and the Index were refreshed respectively by Devdutta Kakati and Dev Kumar Jhanjh, both doctoral students at the Centre for Historical Studies, Jawaharlal Nehru University, New Delhi. I am thankful to them for taking up my request.

The two new essays included here were first published in the following sources:

'Three Copper Plates of the Sixth Century AD: Glimpses of Socio-Economic and Cultural Life in Western India', in Ellen M. Raven, ed., *South Asian Archaeology 1999*, Groningen: Egbert Forsten, 2008: 395-9. This publication is now with the publisher, E.J. Brill, Leiden, as per the information from Professor Ellen M. Raven.

'Gujarat's Maritime Trade and Alternative Moneys (*c.* 550-1500

CE)', in Susmita Basu Majumdar and S.K. Bose, eds., *Money and Money Matters in Pre-Modern South Asia: Essays in Memory of Nicholas G. Rhodes*, New Delhi: Manohar, 2019: 221-38.

I record here my most sincere thanks and appreciation to the editors and publishers of these two essays for their kind consent which enabled me to include these two pieces.

The proposal from Mr. Jain and my preliminary ideas to include the two essays, stated above, coincided with my sojourn, to San Diego in the USA in the month of September 2019. My wife, Dr. Tutul Chakravarti, who is a Glaucoma specialist, was awarded a Fulbright-Nehru Fellowship for her Glaucoma researches for one academic year at Hamilton Glaucoma Centre, University of California, San Diego. I decided to go to San Diego with her as a co-passenger, since the United States-India Educational Foundation takes care of the overseas travel and stay of an accompanying spouse. Initially I had no other agenda but to while away my time in southern California; at this juncture came the request from Mr. Jain. It so happened that just on the eve of our departure from India, Professor Catherina Gere, head of the Department of History, UC San Diego, very generously made me a Visiting Scholar to her Department. This provided me with access to the libraries and other resources at the UC San Diego. All these factors, almost manifesting the Buddhist theory of the Chain of Causation (*Paticcasamuppada/Pratityasamutpada*), combined to push me out of my slumber and carried me back to the desk. My wife, along with Professor Catherina Gere, the USIEF and the University of California, San Diego have contributed in their own ways in the making of this edition: my sincere thanks to them.

Even with these opportunities handed out to me, this edition was prepared in the midst of a deep void. There is no chance for me now to hand over the third edition to Professor B.N. Mukherjee, my mentor, as I had done on the two previous occasions. His passing away on 4 April 2013 after prolonged illness has robbed me of his precious presence in my life, enriching me enormously with his monumental knowledge of India's past. He is no more but remains an inspiration to me. This edition is my tribute to his indelible memory.

II

I owe an explanation to readers regarding the choice of essays added to this edition. First, both the chapters relate to the commercial and social situations in Gujarat: the first on a very compact period of about two decades (*c*. 53-19 CE) and the second on the linkage of trade and money matters in Gujarat over nearly a millennia (*c*. 550-1500). There will be some inevitable overlaps in these two essays. With the inclusion of these two pieces as chapters 14 and 15 of the third edition, both Bengal and Gujarat, situated on two flanks of north India, have six chapters between them. Both these regions offer crucial outlet to the seas for the land-locked north India plains. If Bengal is noted for the largest delta in the world – the Ganga delta – Gujarat possesses one delta, that of the Narmada. Gujarat also has a few estuaries of prominent rivers. These riverine networks were and still are crucial to the maritime networks of Bengal and Gujarat. Moreover, both the new chapters offer images about activities of actual merchants, either in their individual or collective capacities, in the context of Gujarat. Taking a close look at merchants and their operations at diverse market places is indeed one common theme in this collection to which the two new chapters may fit. The chapters also highlight the importance of the transactions in agrarian products, often in bulk. That trade in daily necessities, including edible and commercial crops and salt, was an inseparable ingredient of commerce, both within and beyond the subcontinent by overland and maritime networks alike, has been argued for in the book.

The inclusion of the essay on the three sixth century CE copper plates, throwing light on a body of merchants (*vaṇiggrāma*) is primarily prompted by my recent and very fruitful discussions with Professor Walter Slaje, a leading Indologist at the Martin Luther University, Halle-Wittemberg and Professor Harald Wiese of the University of Leipzig in June 2019 (thanks to a generous invitation by Professor Annette Schmiedchen to Humboldt University, Berlin, under the auspices of the German Academic Exchange Service or the DAAD). Professors Slaje and Wiese drew my attention (and in fact, gifted me a copy) to the latest and full length study (in the form of a monograph) of the famous charter of Viṣṇuṣeṇa, dated 592 CE, who ruled in the Kathiawad peninsula of Gujarat. This charter is indispensable for the study of the *vaṇiggrāma*. Harald Wiese and Sadananda Das have given us a wonderful text of the inscription, now freshly edited and translated anew with exemplary meticulous detail. In fact, the method and approach of Wiese and Das to the editing and translating of an epigraphic text with elaborate explanatory notes provide an excellent example and platform to emulate in similar in-depth interrogations of epigraphic texts in future.[1] While I am neither an epigraphist nor a Sanskrit scholar, I was, however, a bit surprised that this latest discussion on the *vaṇiggrāma*, the main purport of the charter of 592 CE, did not address the existence of another *vaṇiggrāma* in Gujarat itself, which was functional at least about nine decades before the charter of 592 CE.[2] For reasons unknown to me, neither Wiese nor Das seems to have been aware of a previous *vaṇiggrāma* in Gujarat, preceding the homonymous merchants' body in the late sixth century CE almost by a century. It is not merely the earlier references to an operational *vaṇiggrāma* in 503 and 506 CE in Gujarat that encouraged me to bring the chapter (no. 14) in this collection, but the scholarly contributions from Wiese and Das helped me understand that the two early sixth century copper plates were indicators of the shapes of things to come in a more mature form in the closing decade of the same century. The longevity of this professional body of merchants for more than a century in Gujarat is beyond any doubt. Certain patterns of the development of this professional body would emerge as and when one compares the famous Viṣṇuṣeṇa charter with its two predecessors of 503 and 506 CE. In fact these points did not occur in my essay published in 2008 and are included here. These are afterthoughts emanating from the new readings of the Viṣṇuṣeṇa charter. That is why the present statement in the Preface is deemed necessary. This assumes some significance in the context of the situation of merchants' vis-à-vis the state society.

In addition to giving explicit names of individual merchants (as members of the *vaṇiggrāma*) and the places they hailed from, the records especially those of 503 and 506 CE highlight two place-names. The first is Sangamapallikā, identified with modern Sanjeli (the find spot of the three copper plates), in the Panchmahal district, Gujarat. The second place is Vadrapāli (identified with Vadphali, also in Panchmahal district, Gujarat) which was the issuing centre of the three copper plates of the early sixth century CE and where merchants from disparate places assembled. Vadrapāli was clearly a market place and an administrative centre at a locality level (in the district or *viṣaya* of Śivabhāgapura). It will also be impossible to miss that the merchants' body, by arranging for the voluntary levy of cess – in both cash and kind, on the commodities its members dealt in – assumed administrative responsibilities and functions at a locality level tier of administration. Thus one may plead here for a case of merchants' participation in locality-level tiers of administration, especially in resource gathering. No less significant are the two place names Sangamapallikā and Vadrapāli, both having name-endings analogous to *pallī*. It sounds logical to argue that the transformation of a few hamlets (*pallī/pallikā/pāli*), perhaps of non-agrarian character, into a state society was facilitated by an association of merchants. The itinerant nature of merchants, evident from the epigraphic reference to non-local merchants (*vaideśya/caturdiśābhyagāta*) probably was conducive in transforming non-agrarian hamlets to a locality-level administrative tier and an exchange centre, along with the circulation of metallic money. The expansion of the complex state society in the subcontinent into areas, marked by pre-state polities and relatively simpler societies, gains considerable visibility from *c*. 400 CE onwards, largely in the light of the issuance of copper plate charters in favour of brāhmaṇas and other religious donees. The brāhmaṇas are perceived as the principal agents of the state society to penetrate into the habitats of non-sedentary groups like the hunter-gatherers and pastoralists. The gift of landed properties to brāhmaṇas not only led to the expansion of agriculture into non-sedentary zones, but also paved the way for the consolidation of the *varṇa-jāti* structure in a relatively simpler society with less sharp differentiation and hierarchy. The copper plates of 503, 506 and 519 CE and the charter of Viṣṇuṣeṇa of 592 CE, when read together, cannot but leave a strong impression that merchants, especially as a professional body, were no less effective an agent than brāhmaṇas in incorporating a non-sedentary zone and the people thereof into a complex and sedentary state society. The merchant, essentially itinerant by nature, was ideally suited to interact with and penetrate into the hamlets (*pallī*) of non-sedentary groups, like the hunters-gathers and pastoralists.

This impression gains further ground if one pays a close look at the very opening section of the charter of Viṣṇuṣeṇa in 592. At the request of the body of merchants, the *vaṇiggrāma*, Viṣṇuṣeṇa 'graciously issued (his) own charter of statutes for the protection and settlement of people that were (here) before and those that were not (here) before (*mayā bhūtapūrvvasya janapadasyābhūtapūrvvasya ca* ... *sthitipātraṁ prasādīkṛtam*, Text V 3-4).[3] While there was no categorical mention of the creation of a settlement in the copper plates of 503/506 CE, this record, nearly nine decades later, explicitly states about the creation of a new settlement by bringing a body of merchants there. The striking point here is the almost verbatim reproduction of a key passage in the *Kauṭilīya Arthaśāstra*, strongly recommending the creation of new agrarian settlements or *janapadaniveśa* (duly noted by Wiese and Das), in a late sixth century charter. The significant point of departure in the charter of Viṣṇuṣeṇa from the *Arthaśāstra* model is the application of the *janapadaniveśa* policy to facilitate a new settlement for merchants (in an organized body) and not agriculturists by the Maitraka realm in Valabhī (in Gujarat).[4] The much greater elaborate statement, in the form of 72 statutes in Viṣṇuṣeṇa's charter of 592, suggests the maturation of the institution of *vaṇiggrāma* from its incipient stage, encountered in the three Sanjeli copper plates of the early sixth century.

This, however, does not imply a sharp separation of the agrarian sector from its non-agricultural counterpart in the political economy of western India in the sixth century CE. The copper plates of early sixth century and that of Viṣṇuṣeṇa also demonstrate the clear awareness of the importance of transactions of paddy (*dhānya:* statutes 26 and 59), possibly at a locality-level administrative-cum-exchange centre. Edible spice cultivation is writ large in Viṣṇuṣeṇa's charter in the form of references to cumin (*kanikkā*), coriander (*kustambarī*) and black mustard (*rājikā*) in its statute nos. 62-5. Similarly sugar cane was grown for producing molasses, mentioned in the copper plate of 503 CE, as a commodity for transaction. This may have some linkage with the process of 'brown sugar boiling' (*ḍheṅkukaḍḍhaka*, statute 19 of Viṣṇuṣeṇa's charter, following Kosambi's interpretation). Kosambi's interpretation seems to be more plausible in the light of a reference to a sugar cane grove (*ikṣuvāṭaka*, statute 49). The importance of a non-cereal crop, namely indigo (*nīla*), is underlined in the 592 CE charter at least twice (statutes 19 and 48). Indigo production and the use of the indigo vat in western India in the late sixth century has a distinct bearing upon the presence of the female dyer (*chimpikā*, statute 71). The use of this important dyeing agent cannot be divorced from the textile production for which Gujarat was famous for centuries. The other point of note is the continuity of some terms of weights and measure, like *setika/setinika*, for more than a century in the records from Sanjeli and the charter of Viṣṇuṣeṇa. The significant development is the repeated use of the term *śulka*, tolls and customs or commercial levy, in the charter of 592; it does not occur in the three Sanjeli plates of the early sixth century. This once again strengthens our idea of the maturation of the commercial system from its initial phase in the early sixth century to the last decade of the sixth century. In fact the very last section of the charter of 592 proclaims that the statutes, engraved in the reign of Viṣṇuṣeṇa, was endorsed by a *sāmanta*, a subordinate or intermediary ruler, named Avantī from Darpapura, thereby giving an assurance to the effectiveness of the clauses in favour of the *vaṇiggrāma* and the group's trading activities; it also cautioned that no hindrance to the statutory arrangements, laid down in the charter, should be caused in future (*eṣāṁuparilikhitasthitipātravyavasthayā prativasātāṁ svapaṇyena cātmanāṁ varttayatāṁ na kenacit paripanthana kārayeti*).[5] The endorsement was done on year (*samvat*) 357, *karttikabā* 7. If *samvat* 357 refers to the Kalacuri era of 248 CE, then the endorsement was done on 29 October, 606 CE; if however the year referred to the Gupta-Valabhī era of 319-20 CE, then it is to be dated in 3 November 676 CE.[6] In other words, the statutes in favour of the organization of merchants seem to have remained in force either for another 14 (606 CE) years or as many as 84 years (676 CE). The sustained presence of the *vaṇiggrāma* in Gujarat from early sixth century to the third or last quarter of the seventh century – that is for nearly 170 years – is unmistakable.

At the beginning of the sixth century CE Vadrapāli, the site of the activities of the *vaṇiggrāma*, was possibly a locality-level administrative centre that witnessed the convergence of local and non-local merchants for professional reasons and also for the acts of their cultural patronage to a Vaiṣṇava shrine. As we argued before, the mutation in the nature of the settlement at Vadrapāli can be accounted for by the presence of merchants. On the other hand, the site of the settlement in 592 CE (also in subsequent times), clearly marked as the residence of the merchants' body (*vāsaka*), was Lohaṭagrāma. Apparently this was a village where the *vaṇiggrāma* was facilitated with a regular settlement by an order from the political authority. But was it really a village, as Wiese and Das in their latest translation of the document described it?[7] The site was steeped in exchange related activities in which the state's interests were palpable. This is best evident from the several references to the levy of tolls and customs (*śulka*). Such levy of tolls and customs can rarely be associated with a rural settlement. We shall later return to the trading activities at Lohaṭagrāma. Besides artisanal activities related to dyeing and molasses making, the record of 592 CE enlists the following artisans: the blacksmith (*lohakāra*), the carpenter (*rathakāra*) and the potter (*kumbhakāra*: all in statute 72). The levy (*ādāna*), imposed on some manufactured items, would be evident from the mention of 'a workshop producing mechanical equipment' (*yantrakuṭi*: statute 51). One can hardly lose sight of the manufacturing and sale of wine and liquor (*madya* and *surā*: statutes 42-7) figuring prominently in

Viṣṇuṣeṇa's charter, along with a reference to large fermenting vessel (*bhājana*). This fits well with the reference to some kind of carriage for transporting wine (*madyavāhanaka*: statute 66) which, once again, was subject to taxation. The mentions of shops (*āpaṇa*: statutes 9 and 21) further speak of retail trade which further suggests that Lohaṭagrāma was a non-rural settlement, notwithstanding the suffix *grāma* attached to it.

No less striking is the provision for imposing *śulka* on water-vessels or *vahitras*. The term *vahitra* figures twice in our record of 592 CE: first in the context of transportation of 'trade-goods' (*bhāṇḍa*) and the second referring to the transportation of bamboos (*vaṁśa*). The term *vahitra* has been taken in the sense of a boat by Wiese and Das (statutes 53 and 61). While the terms *vahitra* and *nau* may be used as synonyms, at least as per dictionary usage, the term *vahitra* may refer to a large sea-going vessel, distinct from an ordinary boat. This is illustrated by the use of the term *vahitra* in the context of ports in the inscription of the Śilāhāras of the Konkan coast. A close perusal of these inscriptions of the eleventh century will also show that the large sea-going vessel (*vahitra*) was distinguished from coasting vessels, presumably smaller than the *vahitra*. The coasters were known in the Śilāhāra inscriptions as *pravāhana*.[8] One is, therefore, tempted to equate the term *vāhana* (a carriage) in the charter of 592 with the coasting vessels (*pravāhana*) of Konkan. Seen from this light Lohaṭagrāma appears to have been visited by both large ships (*vahitra*) and coasting vessels (*vāhana/pravāhana*). This, in its turn, prompts us to consider Lohaṭagrāma as a coastal site, probably offering port facilities. It can hardly be considered as a rural settlement in spite of the suffix *grāma* attached to Lohaṭa. A contextual analysis of relevant statutes cannot but speak of multiple and complex functions there, which are not expected to have taken place in a *grāma*. One may go a bit further as one closely examines Kosambi's translation of statute 52: 'Merchants who have come from a foreign region) only for shelter through the rainy season, are not to be charged import duty (and immigration tax), but export duty and emigration tax are to be charged on leaving' (*varṣaparyuṣita vaṇijāḥ prāveśyaṁ śulkātiyātrikaṁ nadāpanīyaḥ, nairggamikaṁ deyam*).[9] First, the port facilities at Lohaṭagrāma looms large by the use of the term 'crossing' — obviously of the sea (*atiyātrika*) which was generally subject to the imposition of tolls and customs. If the term *atiyātrika* is juxtaposed with *samyātrika*, meaning voyaging passengers, the sense of crossing the sea becomes more apparent. In this context

Kosambi's translation of the statute 52 is a possible pointer to the well-established custom of prolonged sojourning at an Indian Ocean port, waiting for a favourable alteration in the monsoon wind system. It is also well known that most traditional ports on both the sea-boards of the subcontinent would remain closed—or least activities there will be dull—during the fury of the rainy season. The presence of *vahitras* and *vāhanakas*, when read in the light of the statute no. 52, offer some glimpses of the coastal location of and port functions at Lohaṭagrāma. The maritime orientation of Lohaṭagrāma, situated in the Kathiawad peninsula, has been missed by Wiese and Das.

Moreover, the explicit mention of a royal storehouse (*rājakīyagañja*: statute 51) at Lohaṭagrāma and regular references to the realization of various taxes would once again underline that Lohaṭagrāma was no village. At this locale commercial and administrative functions came together. It is possible that it had originally emerged as a village (*grāma*). B.D. Chattopadhyaya has made us aware that villages were neither isolated, nor undifferentiated; nor were they self-sufficient and enclosed.[10] In sum, the active presence of the *vaṇiggrāma* at both Vadrapāli and Lohaṭagrāma would strongly portray that villages morphed and had the capacity to absorb multifarious functions, firmly located in the non-agrarian sector of the economy in the sixth and the seventh century Gujarat.

A close look at the 710 CE Anjaneri CP may be in order here.[11] Situated not far away from Nashik, old Govardhana which was a thriving artisanal and commercial centre in the early historic times, was an old town of Sāmagiripattana. The suffix *pattana* is a firm marker of the urbane character of the settlement. The old town somehow fell into disuse and became deserted (*utsāditam*); it was resettled at the initiative of the ruler Pṛthvīcandra Bhogaśakti. It seems that the management of the municipal affairs was then entrusted with a merchants' body (*nagaram*) by two *śreṣṭhīs*, Ela and Karapuṭa. The resuscitation of the deserted city was attempted through a commercial rejuvenation there and is the reason for the prominent role of the merchants at the resettled Sāmagiripattana. Kosambi rightly pointed out that the term *nagara* stood for both an urban centre and a merchants' body in charge of the municipal administration. The residing merchants at Sāmagiripattana were granted perpetual remission from the payment of tolls and customs. This was surely done to offer inducement to settling merchants at a rejuvenated city. But no less significant is the presence of three hamlets (*pallikā*) at the outskirts of Sāmagiripattana.

These were Ambeyapallikā, Sāvaneyapallikā and Maureyapallikā. The association of merchants/merchants' body with non-agrarian *pallikā*, in the context of the emergence of a new exchange centre and that of a locality-level tier of administration, is once again illustrated by this record. All the inscriptions related to merchants and their bodies, so far examined here, demonstrate the state's preference for and interests in creating exchange centres in non-sedentary areas where mature trade centres would gradually emerge. A distinct pattern is discernible and it cannot be dismissed as merely co-incidental.

The presence of merchants, in their individual or collective capacities, at emergent market places needs a serious examination, in the light of available evidence, for assessing not only the relevance of the exchange-related activities and networks, but also for situating the merchants' as an instrument for the furtherance of the state society. The consolidation of the state system would certainly be conducive to vibrant market-place trade, which is far more complex than gift-exchange, barter and such like relatively simpler exchanges. The expansion of the state society gained pace and visibility from *c*. fourth century CE. To attribute the narrative of the spread of monarchical polity primarily to agrarian expansion, through the agency *agrahāras*, will run the historiographical risk of ironing out complexities and diversities in locales away and different from agrarian terrains in the subcontinent.[12] Here is plea for the recognition of the role of merchants in the furtherance of the state society in the crucial 'threshold times'.[13]

III

At this juncture may be taken up the inclusion of the essay on the maritime trade of Gujarat during almost a millennium, from c. 550-1500 CE. Prior to *c*. 1600 two premier ports represented the maritime profile of Gujarat, if not the whole of western India. These were Bhṛgukacchha/Bharugaccha/Barygaza/Bharuch and Stambhapura/Stambhatīrtha/Kanbaya/Cambay. Bhṛgukacchaa shone in the maritime history of the Indian Ocean, particularly its western sector, during the late centuries BCE to about 500 CE. It was past its heyday when Xuanzang reported about it in the first half of the seventh century CE. Bharugaccha was still a port of reckoning, as Xuanzang would bear it out, but was no longer the stellar port of western India. Like many other ports of pre-modern India, Bhṛgukaccha could have suffered from the siltation of the riverine channel(s) of the river Narmada. It is also possible and likely, though it may not be proved on the basis of evidence, that the crucial and protracted hinterland of Bhṛgukaccha in the Deccan and Ujjayinī in the western part of Malwa (Avantī region) was disturbed and lost on account of the long-lasting rivalry between the Rāṣṭrakūṭas of the Deccan and the Pratihāras of Kanauj. It is well known that the Malwa plateau, especially Ujjayinī, was politically coveted by – and a bone of contention between these two formidable regional powers – from *c.* mid-eighth to the late tenth century CE. The rise of the Paramāras of Malwa from the eleventh century onwards with a firm control over Ujjayinī, coinciding with the political prominence of the Caulukyas of Gujarat, seems to have ensured that Bhṛgukaccha would remain cut off from its vital hinterland located in the Avantī/Ujjayinī region. This did not possibly augur well for the port of Bhṛgukaccha.[14] Bhṛgukacchha did not, of course, die down, as several Arabic and Persian texts on travel and geography referred to it as a port.[15] In terms of its position in the western Indian Ocean Bhṛgukaccha faced the immensely greater prominence of the port of Stambhatīrtha/ Stambhapura, named as Kanbaya in Arabic and Persian accounts. This is the celebrated port of Khambat or Cambay, located in the estuary of the river Mahi, with access to the Gulf of Khambat. The efflorescence of Kanbaya/Cambay as the premier port of western India for at least six centuries – from 1000 to 1600 CE – contributed to the gradual fading out of the pre-eminence of Bhṛgukaccha which continued but functioned as a subsidiary or feeder port of Cambay.

This continuity of Bhṛgukcchha is captured in some business letters of Jewish merchants of the period from the eleventh to the thirteenth centuries. One such letter of 1097 CE has been utilized to suggest the longevity of Barus or Bhṛgukaccha in Chapter 15 of this book. Without elaborating on that particular letter, it is important to note here that Suchandra Ghosh recently has drawn our attention to a Jaina text of the twelfth century that was aware of Bhṛgupura as a port (*velākula*). The text in question is the *Moharajaparajaya*, a drama in Prākṛt, on the theme of the embracing of Jainism by King Kumārapāla (1143-72 CE), of the Caulukya house, under the influence of his preceptor and a great Jain scholar Hemacandra. In this drama figures a wealthy merchant (*setthi/śreṣṭhī*) who undertook a journey from Anahilapura to Bhṛgupura with five hundred junior merchants and boarded a vessel (*pravāhana*), obviously for a sea-voyage. Ghosh's main thrust is on the city of Anahilapura or Patan in modern Gujarat and she duly points to the overland connectivity between the Caulukya capital and the port in question. The use of the *pravāhana* for a voyage from Bhṛgupura may suggest that the port actively participated in coastal commerce along the western sea-board of India.[16] That *pravāhanas* plied for the looping trade along the western sea-board is evident from the near contemporary inscriptions of the Śilāhāras from north and south Konkan. This is a coast contiguous to the Gujarat littorals. A contextual analysis of the Śilāhāra records also bear out that the *pravāhanas* were distinct from the *vahitras* which were plying on high-sea or blue sea voyages. Ghosh has further dwelt on the business letter of 1097 CE, also cited by us in Chapter 15, to suggest the possibility of the long-distance sea-borne network between Barus/Broach and the Red Sea port of Aydhab. She has rightly pointed, as we too have argued that the Cairo geniza letters of voyaging Jewish merchants (the *India Traders* of S.D. Goitein) speak of the overseas commerce of Broach in the twelfth century. This is actually the only written source that offers an image of the continuity of Broach's overseas linkages with the Red Sea area. Otherwise Broach figures in the early medieval sources as a port for coastal voyages along the western sea-board of India. There is little doubt that it was overshadowed by Cambay during the 1000-1500 CE period.

Nearly half a century later, another letter of a Jewish India trader, written from al Manjarur or Mangalore (southernmost part of coastal Karnataka) in 1145 CE speaks of Barus/Broach. The writer of the letter is Maḥrūz b. Jacob, himself a ship-owning merchant (*nakhudā*) who wrote to his business compatriot, Abu Zikrī Kohen (who was a prominent 'India trader') in great anxiety at the news of Abu Zikrī having suffered an attack of pirates near the port of Tāna (Thana, a suburb of Mumbai, Maharashtra). Consoling him at the terrible loss of trade goods on account the piratical attack, and also thanking the Almighty for the safety of his life, Maḥrūz b. Jacob urged upon Zikrī Kohen to forthwith return to al Manjarur wherefrom the two together would go back to Egypt. Maḥrūz wrote:

> I had previously written to you at Tāna. Meanwhile, the boat escorting the ship arrived and its soldiers told us that the ship in which your excellency (i.e. Judah b. Joseph ha-Kohen), my lord travelled had been seized by pirates and I was very sad about this. Your servant had thought that your honour my lord was in Tāna and I had previously sent letters to the nakhudā Tinbū, advising him to pay to my lord 21 mithqāls. Afterwards, my lord Sheikh Abu'l Qasim ibn Qaṭṭān had told me your Excellency was in

Broach. Under all circumstances please come quickly to Mangalore.[17]

Maḥrūz urged upon Abu Zikrī Kohen to take the gold coins from *nakhudū* Tinbū, who was 'staying in Tāna'. He also stressed on the availability of 'boats' from Kanbayāt (Cambay) and Tāna for the coastal voyage down to al Manjarur. Put in the context of the piracy at Tāna, the letter underlined upon the coastal network connecting al Manjarur from Kanbayāt and Tāna. The writer also strongly recommended his brother-in-law to collect the cash (in gold currency) from an Indian ship-owner stationed at Tāna. This leaves a strong impression that even for coastal voyages between al Manjarur and Gujarat via the Konkanese port, Tāna and Kanbayāt were the preferred ports of embarkation. Even Tāna, in spite of piracy there, was considered a suitable port for a coastal voyage to al Manjarur. One needs to look closely at the advice of Maḥrūz to collect cash from an Indic ship-owner at Tāna. This implies a trip—overland or coastal—from Barus/Broach to Tāna/Thana. Seen from this light, the geniza letter does not accord prominence and importance to Barus/ Bharuch/Broach in the coastal shipping network along the western sea-board of India.

A different image of Broach emerges from a numismatic perspective. Broach has yielded a coin hoard having specimens of coins belonging to the thireenth and fourteenth centuries. This hoard was noticed by Codrington, discussed by Simon Digby and more recently re-examined, especially in the context of the maritime commerce in the western Indian Ocean, by Najaf Haider and Roxani Margariti.[18] This matter deserves a close scrutiny as our chapter here also delved into the question of money in the context of maritime trade of pre-1500 Gujarat.

This Broach hoard has brought to light coins datable from 1260 to 1382 CE. It consists of 448 gold coins and 1,200 silver species. Nearly 70 per cent of the gold coins (367 out of 448) of various types and weights were issued by the Mamluk Sultans of Egypt from Cairo, Alexandria and Damascus. These are possibly the same as the Egyptian *mithqāls* figuring in the Jewish Cairo geniza documents. The Egyptian gold coins co-existed with Italian gold coins (1339-68 CE): 33 Venetian *ducats* and 5 Genoese *quartarolo.* The significant point is, as Haider notes, that the al Karimi merchants of Egypt used *ducats* to procure commodities arriving in the Red Sea. Moreover, there were a few gold coins (half *mithqal*-s) which were issued by Mongol rulers (post-Abbasid Caliphate) and the Muzaffarids of Kirman (in southern

Iran), issued from the mints at Tabriz, Shiraz and Baghdad. These coins probably reached Broach from the Persian Gulf. The hoard also contained 46 gold coins of the Delhi Sultanate, reaching Broach in the aftermath of the conquest of Gujarat by the Delhi Sultanate in 1296 CE. In addition to the gold specimens, the hoard also consisted of silver coins from Yemen, Egypt (Mamluk coins) and Iran. The hoard strongly suggests that Broach was the destination of diverse types of gold and silver currency from both the sea-lanes of the Red Sea and the Persian Gulf, along with gold coins from the Delhi Sultanate. Does it leave an impression of the revival of the long-distance, overseas linkages of Broach/Bharuch from approximately the mid-thirteenth century onwards? This numismatic perspective is brought here as an afterthought of Chapter 15; therefore, I am not in a position here to answer this question. But, at least, it underlines the fluctuating fortunes and therefore the complexities in the past of a prominent port of pre-modern western India.

The thirteenth-fourteenth centuries hoard of precious metal coins (mostly non-indigenous) at the port of Broach/Barus/Bhṛgukacchha is symptomatic of the role of India as the 'sink pit'[19] of precious metals from the Mediterranean and West Asia. The unidirectional flow of precious metal currency in India from the West tells the story of metallic moneys moving towards areas where it would command a higher value. There was also little reciprocity in the movement of money in other direction: precious metal money hardly, if ever, moved westwards from the subcontinent across the western Indian Ocean. This implies that the subcontinent, in general, sent out more goods than it brought in. Haider rightly observes that the relatively lower demand of non-local 'imported' commodities in the subcontinent (and also in China) is an indicator of the ability of the pre-colonial economy of the subcontinent to 'meet internal needs from local and regional markets at a lower cost'. If the balance of this trade was favourable to the subcontinent in general on a longue duree basis, gold and silver currencies from overseas regions were also the 'most favoured means of settling trade balances'.[20]

Turning our attention back to Barus and the use of various types of non-indigenous currencies in (coastal) Gujarat in the light of the late eleventh century geniza documents (in Chapter 15 of this book), one has to weigh in Margariti's observation that the actual specimens of circulating non-indigenous coins of the tenth-thirteenth centuries CE phase in the subcontinent are not numerically impressive. In fact, these may appear negligible in comparison to the availability of profuse number of Roman coins during the first three or four centuries CE in the subcontinent. As only handful specimens of Fatimid coins (909-1171 CE) are actually found in India, one may logically raise doubts about the volume of monetized transactions during the period from tenth-thirteenth centuries in the context of the sea-borne commerce in coastal western India. However, the importance of the Jewish business letters in this context will be difficult to discount. These written texts, unlike the epigraphic records replete with coin-terms – largely in the context of remission of varied types of levies (both agrarian and commercial), in favour of religious donees – are unimpeachable as evidence of actual transactions of commodities in monetary terms. It is clearly discernible from the geniza letters that Indic merchants and their diverse counterparts across the western Indian Ocean were very conversant and familiar with Egyptian *mithqāls*, Yemeni Maliki *dinars*, Zabti *dinars* (issued by Zabīd, a Red Sea port rivaling Aden), Yemeni silver coins and other Islamic silver species along with Indic denominations (typical term for Indic denomination is *filī*) – an irrefutable marker of the 'mixed bag of coins' in regular circulation.[21] Margariti further highlights the distinct possibility of the incorporation of the Fatimid coins 'into local circulation zones in India, thanks to their metrological compatibility with the locally issued coins'.[22] The ready availability of an impressive sum of 21 Egyptian *mithqāls* for the piracy-stricken Judah b. Joseph ha-Kohen, stationed at Barus in 1145 CE, needs to be appreciated and understood in the light of what Margariti terms as an 'interdenominational currency zone'.[23] The geniza letters leave no room for doubt that these diverse metallic pieces were not accepted as mere bullions on Indian shore and market places, even at an exchange centre as far inland as Nahrwara (Anahilapura/Anahilapattana) in the late eleventh century. As the geniza letters let us hear the voices of merchants, who were also recorders and recipients of experiences of their trading activities in the western sea-board of India (including Gujarat), these letters also enlighten us about the expertise of merchants in handling diverse types of cash originating from dispersed areas. This prompts Margariti to correctly discern that these merchants, including the Indic players, were also possibly able to assay the intrinsic value of these diverse species.

I would like to draw upon another perceptive observation of Margariti. Her readings of both Goitein and Udovitch on the Cairo geniza papers help her demonstrate that the commercial economy in the geniza papers was one primarily of credit and not cash. This accounts for the widespread occurrence of *hawāla*, a credit instrument, in the documentary geniza. The *hawāla* probably helped keep track of debts which were cleared by the 'dispatch of merchandise, only less frequently with cash'.[24] The documentary geniza also underlines that payments in cash occurred when the Jewish merchants dealt with their counterparts belonging to other religious groups. This once again highlights the possibility of the inflow of actual precious metal currencies in the western sea-board of India, including at ports in Gujarat. If a well-monetized society in the Mediterranean world of al Mahdiya (Tunisia), Misr (Egypt) and Sicily was strongly oriented to the credit instrument of *hawāla*, the relevance of *hundikā*, *cirikā*, *ādeśa* etc., as alternative moneys and bills of exchange for transactions at local and regional circuits in Gujarat – as argued in Chapter 15 – can hardly be lost sight of.

It is plainly visible that in explaining the choice of the new chapters included in the third edition of the volume, I did not attempt at summarizing the contents of these chapters. The main purpose of this Preface is to suggest the relevance of these chapters in the light of recent contributions to the appraisals of trade and traders by several experts. My engagements with these scholars, along with my own findings, have perhaps elongated this Preface far longer than the extent of a routine and customary Preface to a new edition. If this lengthy prefatorial intervention tells on the patience of readers, I can merely pray for their indulgence.

San Diego, California, USA RANABIR CHAKRAVARTI

NOTES

1. Harald Wiese and Sadananda Das, *The Charter of Viṣṇuṣeṇa*, Halle-Wittenberg: Martin Luther University, 2019.
2. The three plates from Sanjeli during the reign of Huna ruler Tormana was first studied by R.N. Mehta and R.N. Thakkar, *The MS University Copper Plates of Toramāna*, Vadodara: MS University, 1978; it was re-edited with English translation by K.V. Ramesh, 'Three Copper Plates from Sanjeli', *EI*, XL, 1986. Extracts from the English translations are also available in Niharranjan Ray, B.D. Chattopadhyaya, V.R. Mani and Ranabir Chakravarti, *A Sourcebook of Indian Civilization*, Hyderabad: Orient Longman, 2000 (see the Appendix).

3. All references to sections and statutes and translations here are from Wiese and Das, *The Charter of Viṣṇuṣeṇa.*
4. This is not a unique instance of the use of and familiarity with the vocabulary and ideas of the *Kauṭilīya Arthaśāstra* in sixth/seventh centuries CE. Romila Thapar, 'History as Literature: The Plays of Viśākhadatta' in idem, *The Past before Us: The Historical Traditions of Early North India*, Cambridge (Mass): Harvard University Press, 2013: 353-80 demonstrates Viśākhadatta's strong grounding in the *Artha-śāstra* in the seventh century. Similarly in near contemporary Odishan inscriptions one comes across Akṣaśālin, along with Samāharttā and Sannidhātā. See Dev Kumar Jhanjh, 'Akṣaṣālika, Akṣaśālin and Suvarṇakāra as the Engravers of Copper Plate Charters of Odisha (*c.* 7th-11th Centuries CE)', *PIHC* (78th session), 2018: 117-26.
5. Wiese and Das, *The Charter of Viṣṇuṣeṇa*: 161, 166.
6. Both the dating figure in Wiese and Das, *The Charter of Viṣṇuṣeṇa*: 166
7. Wiese and Das, *The Charter of Viṣṇuṣeṇa*: 166; they have taken the word *grāma* in the literal sense of a village.
8. Ranabir Chakravarti, 'Coastal Trade and Voyages in Konkan: The Early Medieval Scenario', *IESHR*, XXXV, 1998: 97-124. Attention may also be drawn to the mention of a *vahitra* in the context of the port (*velākula*) of Dāmalipta (i.e. Tamralipta, a famous port in the Ganga delta) in the *Daśakuamāracarita* of Daṇḍin (*c.* seventh century). This *vahitra*, also called a *pota*, was described as a *yavana* vessel, having a captain (*nāvikanāyaka*). It was clearly differentiated from the boats (*naukā*) of pirates. Isabella Onians, *What Ten Young Men Did* (English translation of Daṇḍin's *Daśakuamāracarita*), Clay Series, New York: New York University Press and JJC Foundation, 2005, see sections II.51 and II.54. First, the *yavanavahitra* probably suggests a foreign vessel. A foreign vessel, visiting the port of Tamralipta, is unlikely to have been a coaster. Hence the term *vahitra* here should denote a large ocean-going ship. It is difficult, however, to understand why Onians translated the word *yavana* as 'Greek'. The term *yavana* stood for a Hellenized person from the West, including a Greek, but not merely a Greek. In the seventh century it is quite unlikely that a Greek ship should be in the vicinity of a Bengal port. On the *yavana*, see Himanshu Prabha Ray, 'The Yavanas in Ancient India', *JESHO*, XXVII, 1985; also Suchandra Ghosh, *From the Oxus to the Indus: Political and Cultural Study c. 300 BCE to 100 BCE*, New Delhi: Primus, 2018. The *bhāṇḍa* carried on board the vessels could also mean, in addition to its sense of trade goods, containers or storage jars. Such containers and storage jars are clearly visible in the famous painting of a large ocean-going ship at Ajanta. See D. Schlingloff, *Studies in Ajanta Paintings*.

9. D.D. Kosambi, 'Indian Feudal Trade Charters', idem, *The Combined Methods of Indology and Other Writings*, collected and introduced by B.D. Chattopadhyaya, New Delhi: Oxford University Press, 2003.
10. B.D. Chattopadhyaya, *Aspects of Rural Settlements and Rural Society in Early Medieval India*, Calcutta: K.P. Bagchi, 1990. Chattagrāma (Chittagong, Bangladesh) and Venugrāma (Belgaum, Karnataka), in spite of their *grāma* name-endings, would hardly appear in early medieval textual and epigraphic sources as villages. These were respectively a major port and a thriving inland trade centre.
11. V.V. Mirashi, *Corpus Inscriptionum Indicarum*, IV, pt. 1, New Delhi: Archaeological Survey of India, 1955: 150-8; also Kosambi, 'Indian Feudal Trade Charters' for its incisive analyses.
12. Discussions on the political economy of the Gupta period are minimal in the latest anthology on the Gupta: Kunal Chakrabarti and Kanad Sinha, eds., *State, Power and Legitimacy: The Gupta Kingdom*, New Delhi: Primus, 2018. In this fine collection of essays on the Gupta political culture the overwhelming thrust is on religious legitimation of a new type of kingship in India from 300 to 600 CE. Only two essays therein by D.N. Jha and K.M. Shrimali relate to material matters in the making of the Gupta power. But these two scholarly essays too focus essentially on the agrarian sector, thereby relegating the importance of trade in the making of the state society to margins. An elaborate discussion is available in Ranabir Chakravarti, 'Merchants vis-à-vis the State Society: Reflecting on Some Case Studies from Early Historic and Threshold Times', *Studies in People's History*, VI, 2019. The importance of the studies of the state and the Indian Ocean maritime history will be evident from Hermann Kulke and Bharabi Prasad Sahu, *A History of Pre-colonial India*, New Delhi: Oxford University Press, 2018; this is an indispensable work for the broad overview, historiographical issues and a rich bibliography.
13. The chronological label 'threshold times' is used here after Romila Thapar, *Early India from the Origins to c. AD 1300*, London: Allen Lane, 2002.
14. For the long-drawn conflicts between the Pratihāras and the Rāṣṭrakūṭas see R.C. Majumdar, ed., *The Age of Imperial Kanauj*, Bombay: Bharatiya Vidya Bhavan, 1966. The gradual fading out of Bhṛgukachha in southern Gujarat (Lāṭadeśa) seems to have facilitated the rise of the port of Sanjan in the northern-most fringe of Konkan coast from the ninth century onwards. For a recent overview of Sanjan (Sindan in the Arabic texts on travel and geography), incorporating the textual accounts of Sanjan and also excavated materials there (excavations by Rukshana Nanji) see, Suchandra Ghosh

and Durbar Sharma, 'The Port of Sanjan/Sindian in Early Medieval India: A Study of its Cosmpolitan Mileu', in Kenneth R. Hall, Rila Mukherjee and Suchandra Ghosh, eds., *Subversive Sovereigns of the Sea*, Kolkata: Asiatic Society, 2017: 67-88. Ghosh and Sharma, however, did not situate the rise of Sanjan in the background of the decline of Bhṛgukaccha and the loss of the dynastic hinterland of Ujjayinī for Bhṛgukaccha.

15. Elizabeth Lambourne, 'Describing the Lost Camel: Clues for West Asian Mercantile Networks in South Asian Maritime Trade (Tenth-Twelfth Centuries AD)', in Marie-Francoise Boussac, Jean-Francois Salles and Yon Bapiste, eds., *Ports of the Ancient Indian Ocean*, New Delhi: Primus, 2016: 351-407; Jean-Charles Ducene, 'The Ports on the Western Coast of India according to Arab Geographers (Eighth-Fifteenth Century AD)', in Boussac, Salles and Yon, eds., *Ports of the Ancient Indian Ocean*: 165-78; also Ranabir Chakravarti, 'Indic Mercantile Community and the Indian Ocean World: A Millennial Overview (*c.* 500-1500 CE)', in Angela Schottenhammer, ed., *Early Global Communities Across the Indian Ocean World*, Salzburg: Palgrave Mac Millan, 2019: 191-226.
16. Suchandra Ghosh, 'Anahilapura: Understanding Its Expansive Network during the Time of the Chaulukyas', *Asian Review of World Histories*, 6, 2018: 236-45. The essay is rich in empirical details, but short on contextual analyses of her evidence, especially the *Maharajaparajaya* and the geniza letter of 1097 CE.
17. S.D. Gotein and Mordechai A. Friedman, *India Traders of the Middle Ages: Documents from the Cairo Geniza ('The India Book')*, Leiden: E.J. Brill, 2008: 473-9. Quotation in pp. 476-7. This is the fully annotated English translation of the letter which first appeared in S.D. Goitein, *Letters of Medieval Jewish Traders*, Princeton: Princeton University Press, 1973; relevant extracts of this letter from the 1973 translation are also available in Ray, Chattopadhyaya, Mani and Chakravarti, *A Sourcebook of Indian Civilization* (see the Appendix).
18. O. Codrington, 'On a Hoard of Coins Found at Broach', *Journal of the Bombay Branch of the Royal Asiatic Society*, XV, 1882-3: 339-70; Simon Digby, 'The Broach Coin Hoard as Evidence of the Import of Valuta across the Arabian Sea during the Thirteenth and Fourteenth Centuries', *Journal of the Royal Asiatic Society*, 1980: 129-38; Najaf Haider, 'The Network of Monetary Exchange in the Indian Ocean Trade 1200-1700', in Himanshu Prabha Ray and Edward A. Alpers, eds., *Cross Currents and Community Networks: The History of the Indian Ocean World*, New Delhi: Oxford University Press, 2007: 181-205; Roxani Eleni Margariti, 'Monetization and Cross-Cultural Collaboration

in the Western Indian Ocean (Eleventh to Thirteenth Centuries', in Francesca Tivellato, Lear Halevi and Catia Antunes, eds., *Religion and Trade: Cross-Cultural Exchanges in World History 1000-1900*, New York: Oxford University Press, 2014: 192-215.

19. Haider, 'The Network of Monetary Exchange': 182.
20. Ibid.: 186.
21. Margariti, 'Monetization and Cross-Cultural Collaboration': 207.
22. Ibid.: 209. Significantly the geniza documents used the term *naqad* for cash; this is the same as Bengali *nagad*, also meaning cash.
23. Margariti, 'Monetization and Cross-Cultural Collaboration': 214. Margariti, however, has based her statement on the Indic currency system on J. Deyell, *Living Without Silver*, New Delhi: Oxford University Press, 1990 and largely on B.D. Chattopadhyaya, *Coins and Currency System in South India* AD *225-1300*, New Delhi: Munshiram Manoharlal, 1990. Margariti has therefore treated the Indic currency scenario from the point of dynastic coinages. It needs to be stressed here that there is a long tradition of issuing non-dynastic coins in India. The earliest metallic coins of India, the punch-marked coins, were uninscribed and did not carry an image and name of their issuers. Dynastic coinages were first introduced in India by the Greek rulers in the late third century BCE. The Harikela silver coins in the eastern part of the Bengal delta were in circulation during 600-1200 CE days, but were not dynastic coins. Similarly one comes across the evidence of silver coins (*dramma*) being manufactured by a money merchant (*Śreṣṭhī-sārtha*) at Sanjan, in the ninth century CE, then under Rāṣṭrakūṭa occupation (see. D.C. Sircar, 'Rashtrakuta Charters from Chinchani', *EI*, XXXII, 1955). Elaborate discussions are available in B.N. Mukherjee, *The Media of Exchange in Early Medieval North India*, New Delhi: Harman, 1992. For a different perspective see K.M. Shrimali, 'Monetary History of Early India: Distinctive Landmarks', in Susmita Basu Majumdar and S.K. Bose, eds., *Money and Money Matters in Pre-Modern South Asia*, New Delhi: Manohar, 2019: 177-220. Shrimali has reservations about the availability and circulation of metallic currency in India during the early medieval times, especially in the 600-1000 CE phase.
24. Margariti, 'Monetization and Cross-Cultural Collaboration': 213.

Preface to the Second Edition

A pleasant surprise awaited me as Mr. Ramesh Jain and Mr. Ajay Jain of Manohar Publishers and Distributors informed in mid-2004 that the copies of the first edition of this book had sold out. This was neither intended to be a text book nor a popular one. Given the present intellectual climate in which the study of history in general creates few opportunities and economic history in particular is somewhat less attractive with the preference for cultural and linguistic turns in historical studies, my reaction to the publisher's proposal to go for a second edition was one of hesitance and perplexity. As the second edition now goes to press, the credit should first go to my publishers for having initiated such a thought and persisting with the idea for nearly two years. The second edition is an enlarged one, with the incorporation of two more recently published essays. 'Information, Exchange and Administration: Case Studies from Early India', was presented first to the Panel on Information and Communication Technologies in India Through the Ages, organized by the Indian History Congress (Mysore session) in 2003, and subsequently published in the collection of essays, *Webs of History, Information and Communication Technology from Early to Post-Colonial India,* edited by Amiya Kumar Bagchi, Dipankar Sinha and Barnita Bagchi (New Delhi: Manohar, 2005). I am thankful to the editors and the publisher for kindly permitting me to include this piece in the present volume as chapter 12. The second essay and the last piece (chapter 13) in this volume originally appeared in the *Studies in History,* vol. 20, 2004 as a review article. My sincere thanks go to Professor Neeladri Bhattacharyya and Dr. Kumkum Roy (Members of the Editorial Board for the *Studies in History)* and Sage Publications for their generous permission to reprint this article here. I have taken this opportunity to slightly modify the two new essays mainly for the sake of maintaining uniformity in style and on some occasions for retouching a few statements. I take the cue from Professor R.S. Sharma who in a jocular vein once described all historians as revisionist: here, however, I proceed on a serious note and try to improve my shortcomings which are ever present. The second edition is in paperback with the hope that it will be accessible to a wider and larger readership than the previous one. Needless to explain, the Bibliography has also been upgraded. The second edition of this book was planned and prepared at the Institute for Advanced Study, Princeton. I would like to record my most sincere thanks to the Institute for Advanced Study for providing me with Membership and with fascinating facilities of study. The authorities of Jawaharlal Nehru University by granting me the necessary leave enabled me to avail of this opportunity. I am most thankful to the authorities of Jawaharlal Nehru University for this.

II

It will perhaps not be out of place here to tell my readers the reasons of my incorporating the two new pieces to the second edition. First, both the essays relate to the broad theme of the book, merchants in early Indian society. Second, the two pieces are connected with the history of India's maritime commerce prior to AD 1500 which has been one of themes of this volume. The third point of commonalty between the two new pieces is in the nature of sources used. In the Jewish geniza letters and the inscriptions of Tamil mercantile groups as well one hears the voice of merchants who speak about themselves, their success and failure, aspirations and frustrations, their families and their cultural and social worlds. Recent historiography has given due recognition to the role of trade and merchants in the making of the history of early India. Without diminishing the importance of the agrarian material milieu of the subcontinent over millennia, historians of late do not necessarily view the subcontinent as a landlocked area, engaged in agriculture and crafts production. That the coastal tracts also have a distinct impact on the early history of the subcontinent is gaining ground in academic circles. It is therefore in the fitness of things that recent overviews and textbooks of Indian history (including early India) have underlined the importance of trade in the 'traditional' economy and society of India.[1] The previous imbalance of viewing Indian history primarily from the 'epicentric' Ganga valley/landlocked north India has also undergone interesting shifts, resulting in considerable attention to the peninsular part which has better accessibility to coastal tracts and sea-lanes. Contrary to the Eurocentric image that the subcontinent opened out to the wider world as an outcome of the advent of the Europeans in the fifteenth century, there is an impressive body of evidence of India's trade and cultural networks with Central Asia, Southeast Asia and West Asia, also East Africa and eastern Mediterranean regions.

The economic impact of this trade was not incidental, as indeed also its imprint on various cultures and its linking of Roman, Indian and Chinese centres.[2]

These studies indeed contributed to exploding the myth of the insularity of India during the pre-modern times. Even more important is the point that the lively tradition of multi-culturalism and plurality has gained a greater visibility. This provides the context of bringing in the essay (chapter 12) on communication and exchange of information which were crucial to existing polities and the world of merchants in early India. However, the intention of the present author is to situate trade and traders (including maritime commerce) in the non-agrarian sector of early Indian economy which was indeed predominantly agrarian. The merchants, however rich they might have been, were at the fringe of a vast continental society which they were not in a position to alter substantially.[3]

The study of India's maritime trade in the Indian Ocean tries to impress upon, in this book, the crucial linkages between the vast subcontinental landmass and the coastal areas—where stood India's ports—and the connectivity of the ports with their respective forelands and hinterlands. A word on early Indian ports may be relevant here. It has recently been pronounced that in the ancient period no specific terminology for 'port' is in evidence or was for that matter required. Among others, the term *pattana* was used for both a market centre and also a riverine settlement.[4]

While ancient harbour structures associated with the port area are rarely visible in archaeological terms in India,[5] one comes across regular references to *paṭṭanam/paṭṭinam* (different from *pattana)* in Sanskrit and Tamil sources and also to *velākulas.* As Hall demonstrated long ago, *paṭṭanam/paṭṭinam*—distinct from *erivīrapaṭṭanam*—in Tamil designated ports in or near the sea-coast.[6] Contrary to the unsustainable claim made in the above quote, terms like *paṭṭanam/paṭṭinam* and *velākula,* figuring in textual and epigraphic sources, clearly denote ports. For instance, Tāmralipta (near modern Tamluk, West Bengal), the well known ancient port in the Ganga delta, figures in the *Daśakumāracarita* of Daṇḍin (*c.* AD seventh century), as a *velākula.* At this *velākula* came *vahitras* (a type of sea-going craft) of the yavanas, as Daṇḍin narrates. Similarly, the port of Ghogha in Gujarat carried the suffix *velākula* in its nomenclature; this *velākula* was regularly visited by ships from

Hormuz in the Persian Gulf *(Hurmujīvāhana)*. The association of ships *(vāhana/vahitra)* with the term *velākula* cannot but demonstrate that the term *velākula* stood for a port. Many Tamil inscriptions, especially those eulogistically describing the activities of the merchants' body—the 500 svāmis of Ayyavole—regularly speak of *velāpurams* (ports). Impressing upon the distant voyages undertaken by merchants belonging to the 500 svāmis of Ayyavole, these inscriptions describe in a standardized manner their visiting 32 *velāpurams* (ports).[7] It is therefore impossible to lose sight of the vocabulary regarding ports in Classical Indian languages like Sanskrit and Tamil.

I would also like to add here that I have used the term 'seascape' in the last essay not in the sense of seeing the land from the sea. In fact this presents a view of the maritime space—'the liquid plains of the sea',[8] to quote Braudel—from land, since the Tamil mercantile groups were not solely maritime merchants. Ayyavole or Aihole, the celebrated centre of the 500 svāmis, was very much an inland location in Karnatka. Many of the merchants, belonging to mercantile groups, were active in inland trading in Kerala, Tamilnadu, Karnataka and Andhrapradesh, as Karashima and Subbarayalu (among others) have ably demonstrated. Yet when some of these merchants voyaged in and across the Bay of Bengal, they left fascinating images of their sea-borne communications and exchanges. Early Indian inscriptions, which are mostly related to the continental society and land-oriented polities, in this case provide new vistas of the sea. In this way, Karashima, Subbarayalu and their colleagues have established new landmarks in terms of the sources and methodology of studying India's maritime commerce. Though my 'seascape' here does not deal with seamarks, the use of the word 'seascape' may not be unjustified as it provides a new perspective on how people in coastal areas actively create their identities, sense of place and histories.[9]

NOTES

1. See for example Ranabir Chakravarti ed., *Trade in Early India,* New Delhi, 2001 (paperback ed, 2005); Hermann Kulke, 'A Passage to India: Temples, Merchants and Ocean', *JESHO,* vol. XXXV, 1993, pp. 154-80; Romila Thapar, *Early India from the Origins to c. AD 1300,* London, 2003; Hermann Kulke and D. Rothermund, *A History of India,* New York, 2004 (fourth edition).
2. Romila Thapar, 'Great Eastern Trade: Other Times, Other Places', Vasant J. Sheth Memorial Lecture, 2002.

3. Cf. Ashin Das Gupta, *The World of Indian Ocean Merchants 1500-1800*, New Delhi, 2001. Himanshu Prabha Ray has recently critiqued the linking of trade with agrarian expansion and emergence of urban centres; Ray explains that such an approach is rooted to the over-reliance of historians on the social evolution model of V. Gordon Childe (This is seen in her Preamble to Himanshu Prabha Ray ed, *Archaeology of Seafaring, the Indian Ocean in the Ancient Period*, New Delhi, 1999, pp. 2-3; it is later elaborated in Himanshu Prabha Ray, *Archaeology of Seafaring in Ancient South Asia*, Cambridge, 2003). To what extent recent historiography of the formation of state and urban centres draws from Childe's model is debatable. As early as 1973, A. Ghosh in his study of the second urbanization in India (*The City in Early Historical India*, Shimla) went beyond one of Childe's major formulations that technological change leads to social change. Ghosh's line of enquiry has been subsequently followed by other historians and archaeologists. The emphasis of Childe on diffusion as an agent of change has been critiqued by many historians of early India who on the other hand have stressed on 'local formations' and development 'from within'. See for example, B.D. Chattopadhyaya, *The Making of Early Medieval India*, New Delhi, 1994; Hermann Kulke ed., *The State in India AD 1000-1700*, New Delhi, 1994. Anyway, it will be futile to delink the history of trade, urban centres and state formation in early India from the agrarian scenario.
4. Ray, 'Preamble', in *Archaeology of Seafaring, the Indian Ocean in the Ancient Period*, p. 16. (italics mine). Ray has been persisting with this argument (literally with the very sentence!), palpably wrong, also in the article 'Seafaring in Peninsular India in the Ancient Period', in David Parkin and Ruth Barnes eds., *Ships and Development of Maritime Technology in the Indian Ocean*, London, 2002, p. 67 and the monograph *The Archaeology of Seafaring in Ancient South Asia*, p. 22. Not only Ray is completely off the mark, but even stranger than this is her statement in the last mentioned book (p. 289). Here Ray cites a Rāṣṭrakūṭa inscription from northern Konkan narrating the conquest of chiefs of 'all harbours *(velākulas)*' in the neighbourhood of Sanjan. Here she finds the existence of harbours and also cites the ancient term *velākula* as a synonym of a harbour! Ray 's statements on two pages of the same book (*The Archaeology of Seafaring in Ancient South Asia*, p. 22 and p. 289) are glaringly self-contradictory which in fact suggests a lack of rigour in her handling of relevant primary source(s) and/ or source-language(s).
5. The tremendous changes brought about by European/British engineering technology of the nineteenth century in installing harbour constructions are discussed by M.N. Pearson, *The Indian Ocean*, London and New York, 2003, pp. 211-18.
6. K.R. Hall, *Trade and Statecraft in the Age of the Colas*, New Delhi, 1980.

7. Noboru Karashima ed., *Ancient and Medieval Commercial Activities in the Indian Ocean: Testimony of Inscriptions and Ceramic Sherds*, Tokyo, 2002; see also the last chapter in the present book.
8. Fernand Braudel, *The Mediterranean and the Mediterranean World in the Age of Philip II*, trn. By J. Reynolds, London, 1992, p. 65.
9. Gabriel Cooney, 'Introduction: Seeing Land from the Sea', *World Archaeology*, vol. xxxv, 2003, pp. 323-8; the quotation is from p. 323.

Acknowledgements

This book was planned roughly a couple of years back. It took me some time to give it the final shape as the stylesheet and other editorial matters of the different essays had to be standardized. In this rather tedious job the publisher of this volume, Manohar Publishers & Distributors, gave me all possible help and showed exemplary patience. I would particularly like to record my thanks to Mr Ramesh Jain for his support and to Mr B.N. Varma, the Editor, for many friendly suggestions regarding the production of the book.

I take this opportunity to dedicate this book to my mentor, Professor B.N. Mukherjee, formerly Carmichael Professor of Ancient Indian History and Culture, University of Calcutta. It has been my distinct privilege to have been his pupil not only during my days as a Ph.D. student under his supervision, but ever since 1977 which marked my cherished association with him. On each and every occasion I have discussed with him various academic issues, I invariably became enriched, my doubts removed, my errors rectified and my ideas clearer. Most important, he has always been open to debates and encouraging difference of opinion. I feel gratified to offer him this humble effort of mine as a token of my profound respect and admiration for this extraordinary scholar.

I have been fortunate enough to have received valuable advice from several senior academics and friends and academic support from a number of institutions at various stages of the preparation of essays included in this volume. My sincere and grateful thanks to Professor Romila Thapar; Dr F.R. Allchin and Dr Bridget Allchin of the Ancient India and Iran Trust, Cambridge; Dr David Washbrook, St. Antony's College, Oxford; Professor Dietmar Rothermund, South Asian Institute, Heidelberg; and Professor Hermann Kulke, University of Kiel. I pay my tribute to my teacher the late Dr N.N. Bhattacharyya who introduced me to the Manohar Publishers & Distributors. The staff of the libraries of the University of Calcutta (Alipur Campus), the Asiatic Society, Calcutta, National Library, Bodleian Library and Indian Institute Library

(Oxford) and the Library of St. Antony's College, Oxford gave me unstinted cooperation and support which is most appreciated. The index of this book was prepared by Dr. Suchandra Ghosh, Lecturer, Department of Ancient Indian History and Culture, University of Calcutta; my most sincere thanks goes to her.

I would like to acknowledge with thanks the kind permission I received from the following publishers to reprint here seven of my previously published essays:

1. 'Early Historical India: A Study in Its Material Milieu', in *History of Science and Technology in Ancient India*, ed. Debiprasad Chattopadhyaya as a project of the National Institute for Science, Technology and Development Studies; published by Firma KLM, Calcutta, 1991, pp. 345-50.
2. 'Merchants and Other Donors at Ancient Bandhogarh', *South Asian Studies*, vol. 11, 1995 (Journal of the Society for South Asian Studies), pp. 33-42.
3. 'The Putabhedana as a Centre of Trade in Early India', *South Asian Studies*, vol. 12, 1996 (Journal of the Society for South Asian Studies), pp. 33-9.
4. 'Rājaśreṣṭhī', in *Archaeology and History, Essays in Memory of Shri A. Ghosh*, vol. II, eds. B.M. Pande and B.D. Chattopadhyaya, New Delhi: Agam Kala Prakshan, 1987, pp. 671-8.
5. 'Maritime Trade and Voyages in Ancient Bengal', *Journal of Ancient Indian History*, vol. XIX, 1992 (published 1996), University of Calcutta.
6. 'Vaṅgasāgara-saṁbhāṇḍāriyaka: A Riverine Trade Centre of Early Medieval Bengal', in *Explorations in Art and Archaeology of South Asia, Essays Dedicated to N.G. Majumdar*, ed. Debala Mitra, Calcutta: Directorate of Archaeology and Museums, Govt. of West Bengal, 1996, pp. 557-72.
7. 'Trade at Maṇḍapikās in Early Medieval North India', in *Society and Ideology in India, Essays in Honour of Professor R.S. Sharma*, ed. D.N. Jha, New Delhi: Munshiram Manoharlal, 1996, pp. 69-80.

I would like to record my sincere thanks to Dr. Gautam Sengupta, Director, Directorate of Archaeology and Museums, Govt. of West Bengal for kindly giving me permission for publishing the photographs of terracotta figures, now in his Museum. Last but not the least, I must acknowledge that the very idea that a number of my published and unpublished essays on a connected and more less common theme could be brought out in the form of a monograph was suggested by my wife, Dr Tutul Chakravarti. It was her constant goading that accelerated my leisurely pace of writing and the final handing over of the manuscript to Mr Ramesh Jain of Manohar Publishers. Her involvement in the making of this book is too deep to be measured in terms of formal thanks.

Department of Ancient Indian History and Culture RANABIR CHAKRAVARTI
University of Calcutta
2 February 2001

Abbreviations

AC	*Abhidhānacintāmaṇi*
AI	*Ancient India*
AK	*Amarakośa.*
AR	*Abhidhānaratnamālā*
BEFEO	*Bulletin de l'Ecole Francaine d'Extreme Orient*
CII	*Corpus Inscriptionum Indicarum*
DK	*Daśakumāracarita*
EC	*Epigraphia Carnatica*
EI	*Epigraphia Indica*
IAR	*Indian Archaeology—A Review*
IESHR	*Indian Economic and Social History Review*
IHQ	*Indian Historical Quarterly*
IHR	*Indian Historical Review*
IMB	*Indian Museum Bulletin*
JAS	*Journal of the Asiatic Society, Calcutta*
JASB	*Journal of the Asiatic Society of Bombay*
JBRS	*Journal of the Bihar Research Society*
JEŠHO	*Journal of the Economic and Social History of the Orient*
JNSI	*Journal of the Numismatic Society of India*
KAS	*Kauṭilīya Arthaśāstra*
KM	*Kuvalayamālā*
KSS	*Kathāsaritsāgara*
LL	*Lüders' List of Brahmi Inscriptions up to* AD *400 with the exception of Those of Aśoka, being a supplement to EI, vol. 10, 1912.*
PHAI	*Political History of Ancient India*
PIHC	*Proccedings of the Indian History Congress*
SAS	*South Asian Studies*
SBE	*Sacred Books of the East*
SH	*Studies in History*
SI	*Select Inscriptions Bearing on Indian History and Civilisation* in two volumes

SII	*South Indian Inscriptions*
SK	*Samaraiccakahā*
TM	*Tilakamañjarī*
YKT	*Yuktikalpataru.*

CHAPTER 1

Introduction

The eleven chapters which give this book its present shape are the outcome of the author's sustained interests in the history of trade in early India. Seven published and four unpublished essays were written in a span of thirteen years, from 1987 to 2000, though most of them belonged to the nineties of the last century. The four hitherto unpublished chapters are the Chapter 1: 'Introduction', Chapter 7: 'Seafaring in the Bengal Coast: The Early Medieval Scenario', Chapter 10: 'The Peṇṭhā as a Centre of Trade in the Deccan *c.* AD 600-1300' and Chapter 11: 'Nakhuda Nuruddin Firuz at Somnath: AD 1264'. The very title of this book makes it amply clear that trade with its various aspects and dimensions forms the common theme of all the chapters. Considering the great dependence of Indian people on agriculture for millennia, it is hardly surprising that the principal thrust in the social and economic historiography of early India would be towards the study of its agrarian milieu. The non-agrarian sector of the economy is therefore often viewed as secondary to the mainstream agrarian economy. This does not however imply that the non-agrarian sector of early Indian economy has been marginally treated in the economic historiography. Crafts, trade and urban centres—the principal facets of the non-agrarian sector of the economy—of early India have indeed attracted sustained attention of historians. After all, early Indian thinkers themselves were certainly aware of the importance of trade or *vāṇijya* as an occupation. The academic discipline *vārttāśastra*, so called certainly because of its association with *vṛtti* or livelihood, included in it *vāṇijya* or trade along with *kṛṣi* (agriculture) and *paśupālana* (cattle keeping and animal husbandry). The *Kauṭilīya Arthaśāstra* recommends the study of *vārttāśastra* along with Ānvikṣikī (Philosophy), Trayī (Vedic literature) and Daṇḍanīti (Statecraft) for a prince who would be subsequently become a ruler (I.4.1-4).

There is a long history of lively interests of scholars in the history of trade and urban development in early India. The historiography of early Indian trade also shows a distinct preference for the study of long-distance trade—both overland and overseas—the study of exports and imports, the survey of routes of communication and the enlisting of early Indian ports, especially their possible identifications on a modern map. The other common feature in this historiography is to present urban centres almost invariably as thriving commercial centres and to hold commercial exchanges as the principal causative factor towards urbanization. Without belittling the importance of this conventional narrative approach to the history of trade, it must be emphasized that an understanding of trade and urban centres can hardly be delinked from the agrarian sector. Significantly enough, the expression 'agro-cities' has been used to characterize early Indian urban centres.

II

The present volume on trade of course takes into account trade routes, items of export and import and ports in early India. These aspects of trade are presented here not as frozen elements but rather as changing characters, and it is their variations which is strongly emphasized. A few words about the plan of the volume and thematic linkages among chapters may be in order. Some repetitions and overlaps in the treatment of these essays in such a collection as this is perhaps unavoidable. The second chapter surveys the socio-economic situation in India during nine centuries (*c*. 600 BC-AD 300) which saw extremely important changes in social, economic, political and cultural fields. It delves into the pattern of urban development which assumed a pan-Indian character during the five centuries (200 BC-AD 300), generally labelled as the post-Mauryan period. The spread of urban centres is viewed here as an indicator of growing complexities in society. The proliferation of urban centres often coincided also with the spread of territorial polities in areas which had not hitherto experienced state formation. Such a process, occurring notably in trans-Vindhyan India in the post-Maurya times, speaks of the transformation of the society from a relatively simpler to a more complex stage. The growth of cities during the second urbanization in Indian history coincided with brisk trade, especially long-distance trade of India with areas abroad. But the generation and availability of agricultural surplus seems to have been the principal causative factor for the spurt of urban centres, to which trade provided an additional fillip.

A major thrust of this book is to explore various types of market places and merchants which are often treated as undifferentiated and blanket categories in conventional economic historiography. A few words about perceptions of trade centres may be presented here. Three chapters in this book highlight the diversities of centres of exchange which are the principal arena of merchants' activities (Chapters 4, 9 and 10). Like different categories of merchants (discussed later), various types of market places also appear in our sources, like those in a *nagara* or *pura* (large urban centre), a *puṭabhedana* (literally, where boxes of commodities were unsealed), *nigama* (a market centre in between a village and a city), *pattanagāma*, *paṇyapattana/paṭṭinam*, *velākula* (a port), *maṇḍapikā* (present day *mandis* in north India), *peṇṭhā/piṇṭhā/peṁṭa* (cf. modern *peṭh* in the Deccan and south India). The Tamil Sangam literature informs us of market places held during the day (*nālaṅgāḍi*) as well as in the evening (*allaṅgāḍi*); these were located in the area between the coastal tract (*maruvurppakkam*) and the residential area (*paṭṭinappakkam*).[1] A close study of the *puṭabhedana* as an exchange centre is available in Chapter 4. It is true that the *puṭabhedana* figures mostly in literary sources belonging to the second half of the first millennium BC.[2]

Of large centres of trade in early India mention must be made of ports (*velākula* in Sanskrit and *paṭṭanam/paṭṭinam* in Tamil) which dotted both the coasts of India. Ports of early historical times, especially from *c.* 200 BC to AD 300, figure in Chapter 2 often in the context of India's long-distance seaborne commerce both with the eastern Mediterranean region and South-East Asia. A distinctive shift in the studies in seaborne trade and ports of India during the last two decades is visible in the increasing utilization of archaeological materials. Roman trade with India, for instance, was primarily studied with reference to the *The Periplus of the Erythraean Sea*, the *Natural History* of Pliny and the *Geography* of Ptolemy. Mortimer Wheeler's excavation at Arikamedu firmly introduced field archaeological materials as sources to the study of Roman trade with India. In recent times, Vimala Begley's fresh examinations of the Arikamedu materials demonstrate that the Rouletted Ware throws light actually on the network among ports along the entire length of the eastern sea-board during 200 BC-AD 200.[3] The study of amphorae also provides concrete proofs of India's trade with the Roman empire. An eloquent testimony to India's role in the trade with the Roman empire is available in a mid-second century AD loan contract document on a papyrus recording the export of Gangetic nard, excellent textile, ivory and tusks on board the ship *Hermopollon* which was lying at anchor at the celebrated port of Muziris in Malabar. All these were luxury items on which was imposed a customs duty of 25 per cent at the Roman warehouse in Alexandria. Lionel Casson who made a masterly translation and study of this loan contract document[4] has also examined afresh Pliny's account of the development of maritime-routes between India and the West. He suggests that the most improved stage of voyages brought mariners and merchants from a Red Sea port to Malabar in as quick a time as twenty days, which was earlier thought to have taken forty days.[5] There are also new developments in the study of the alterations of the monsoon wind system (known as Etasian and Hippalus wind in the Classical literature) which greatly influenced the shipping and navigation patterns in the Indian Ocean. Mazzarino shows that the commonly known *hipalus* (*hippalus*) wind, mentioned by Pliny, is actually a misreading of the term *hypalum*. His reading implied that the wind system was so named not after the Greek sailor Hipplaus, but that the term *hypalum* stood for seasonal south-west wind.[6] Profound scholarship is writ large in the textual comparison between Classical accounts and the Sangam literature on commerce between India and the Roman empire by Romanis.[7] Romila Thapar establishes the signal importance of pepper of Malabar, the black gold, in the seaborne trade with the Roman empire; this set the trend for the enormous demand for Malabarese pepper in Europe even up to the early modern times.[8]

To what extent such widespread trade contacts were conducive to urban development in India is a problem that has demanded considerable scholarly attention. It has already been stated that the five centuries spanning from 200 BC to AD 300 witnessed simultaneous growth of trade, urbanism and territorial states on a pan-Indian scale and to an unprecedented degree. The Deccan and the far south particularly experienced the formation of urban and state society in the post-Maurya period, prior to which there existed virtually no major urban centre and a *mahajanapada*-like territorial polity in trans-Vindhyan areas. The epicentre of this spread of urban and state society over the greater parts of the subcontinent is generally located in the Ganga valley, and more precisely in the middle Ganga plains, which witnessed the formation of 'primary' states and urban centres around the sixth-fifth centuries BC. The pattern of city formation and state formation seen in the Ganga valley was subsequently replicated in the trans-Vindhyan India largely on account of the penetration of the material culture of the Ganga valley into the Deccan and south India following the expansion of the Magadhan power under the Mauryas. Judged from this angle, the emergence of urban centres and territorial states in the Deccan and the far south may represent what anthropologists consider as the formation of 'secondary' states and urban centres. It has been further argued that trade, particularly long-distance commerce, plays an important role in the process of secondary urban centres and state societies.[9] Dilip K. Chakrabarti's survey of urban centres up to *c.* AD 500, largely on the basis of excavated and explored materials, highlights the role of the growth of population, settlement of specialized craftsmen and occupational groups and trade in the making of early historical urban centres. He also considers that many or even most of the major cities were leading religious centres too. Champakalakshmi argues that the spurt of urban centres in Tamilakam during the early centuries of the Christian era can be seen in the *marutam* (fertile agricultural tracts in major rivers valleys) and *neital* (coastal area) regions, the latter particularly famous for the *paṭṭinams* or ports. These ports were the principal points of long-distance trade which mainly revolved around transactions in luxury and exotic items. A thorough examination of the Sangam texts leads her to argue that daily requirements transacted at local level exchange centres were subsistence oriented and not traded in bulk. She therefore explains the growth of urban centres in Tamilakam during early historical times as a result of external stimulus. The urban process in early historic Tamilakam did not strike deep roots in the society and declined after the gradual decay of Roman trade in the third century AD.[10]

An elaborate study of ports on the Bengal coast is presented in three chapters which highlights the position of early Bengal as an active zone of maritime trade. Chapter 6 throws light on the maritime trade and voyages in the Bengal coast from *c.* third century BC to sixth century AD; while the seafaring activities in the same area during the subsequent centuries (AD 600-1300) form the discussions in Chapter 8. The main reason of selecting the Bengal coast as an area of the study of maritime trade is that Bengal is a unique *āsamudrahimācala* zone (stretching from the Himalaya to the sea) where inland riverine communication was considerably facilitated by numerous rivers in the Ganga delta. Over the last two decades many new data, largely archaeological in nature, have been discovered from Bengal and these offer many new insights into the maritime trade in Bengal. In such discussions premier ports in early historical Bengal like Tamralipta and Chandraketugarh and Samandar (possibly located near present day Chittagong in Bangladesh) of the Arabic and Persian accounts (*c.* tenth to thirteenth centuries) have naturally figured in a prominent manner. These ports are not treated in isolation, but in relation to their respective hinterland and foreland, the communication pattern, the items of exchange and the last but not the least, the shipping network and navigation in the Bay of Bengal. The principal object of these two chapters is to situate the Bengal coast in the maritime network of the Indian Ocean prior to AD 1500. The third essay on the maritime activities in the Bengal coast offers a probe into a relatively unknown riverine trade centre, Vaṅgasāgara-saṁbhāṇḍāriyaka, identified with Sabhar close to present-day Dhaka in Bangladesh, on the basis of an inscription of *c.* AD 971 (Chapter 7). Though it was certainly not an outstanding port on the coast, it probably stood on a river. Its unusual toponym strongly hints at its linkages with the Vaṅgasāgara or the Bay of Bengal and its role as a feeder port to its more illustrious counterpart at Samandar near Chittagong. It is indeed not an isolated instance of a riverine port. Prior to the rise of Vaṅgasāgara-saṁbhāṇḍāriyaka, another port, namely, Devaparvata, standing on the river Kṣīrodā (modern Khirnai) and identifiable with the archaeological site of Mainamati-Lalmai in Comilla, Bangladesh, is noted for similar riverine communications in the Bengal delta from the late seventh to the early tenth century AD. Bengal does not offer any evidence of the existence *maṇḍapikā* as a middle tier trade centre of the early middle ages. But the inland riverine ports and trade centres like Devaparvata, Vaṅgasāgara-saṁbhāṇḍāriyaka, Dvārahāṭaka and Vetaḍḍacaturaka—all belonging to the early medieval times—appear to have assumed a similar role of a middle category trade centre in a typically *nadīmātṛka* (fed by numerous rivers) region. These three studies of the maritime trade and linkages in the Bengal coast bring to light the importance of epigraphic materials including landgrants for this kind of an exercise. My understanding of the maritime trade stems from the seminal researches of Fernand Braudel on the Mediterranean. Another salient feature of our study of seafaring activities along the Bengal coast both in ancient and early medieval periods is the presentation of archaeological and literary evidence of ship-building tradition and navigation patterns.

Chapters 9 to 10 present in-depth discussions on two types of market centres which emerged and gradually proliferated in the seven centuries from *c.* AD 600 to 1300. These are the *maṇḍapikā* (modern *maṇḍi*) in north India and the *peṇṭhā* (modern *peṭh*) in the Deccan. The regional character of these two types of trade centres has been brought into focus. These two chapters attempt to situate the *maṇḍapikā* and the *peṇṭhā* in a hierarchy of market places. It has been argued that the *maṇḍapikā* and the *peṇṭhā* were usually larger than smaller, rural-level market centres and weekly marts (*haṭṭa/aḍḍa/santhe*) and periodic fairs (*yātrā*), but stood below the very large trade centre in an urban area (*nagara/pattana/ mānagaram*). In other words, one would like to see in the *maṇḍapikā* and *peṇṭhā* a middle-tier market centre which provided the vital linkages between large urban markets and their rural hinterland. My discussion strongly stresses on the interrelation between the expansion of agriculture by the creation of *agrahāras* in the early middle ages and the rise of *maṇḍapikās* and *peṇṭhās* as middle category market places and centres of grain trade. The real strength of the *maṇḍapikā* and the *peṇṭhā* lies in their being rooted to the adjacent rural areas. The lively and brisk trade at *maṇḍapikās* and *peṇṭhās*, which often provided the crucial linkages between the cities/ports and the rural hinterlands, further demonstrates that there was no crisis in the commercial life in the early medieval age. Equally significant is our finding that the *maṇḍapikā* and the *peṇṭhā* on several occasions assumed urban proportions. If the medieval period experienced the proliferation and maturation of *maṇḍis* and *peṭhs* in north India and the Deccan, the early middle age saw the beginning of the process. Studies of the *maṇḍapikā* and *peṇṭhā* strongly negate the image of languishing trade and urban decay in early medieval times, especially in the period from *c.* AD 600 to 1000, which are portrayed as symptoms of feudal social formation of India.[11] This consequently raises questions about the assumed deurbanization, figuring prominently in the historiography of Indian feudalism. It is rather strange that the proponents of Indian feudalism related the decay of urban centres of early historical times due to languishing trade, especially the decline of India's commerce with the Roman empire. The same school of scholars argue for the reappearance of cities in India after 1000, implicitly implying that urbanism picked up once again with the growing presence of Arab merchants in the Indian Ocean trade. Such a position seems to explain the peaks and valleys in early Indian urbanism in terms of external stimuli only. One may recall here that a number of historians, however, suggest that early historical urban centres could emerge around 600 BC, because of agricultural improvements and the availability of agrarian surplus. Trade, though important, seems to have played a secondary role in the formation of Indian urban centres. The remarkable spread of agricultural settlements in the early middle ages, about which there is little doubt, should be considered as a stimulant and not as a hindrance to urban growth. The perception that many early medieval cities were reduced to mere centres of religion and pilgrimage has also been recently countered. The immense popularity of sectarian Bhakti cults and the growth of temple oriented religious institutions, especially in early medieval south India, in fact fostered urban growth and also the integration of polity in regional kingdoms. Religious institutions have been portrayed as a necessary concomitant of the urban process. Religious ideology, revolving around Bhakti cults, often provided the validation of local and regional processes in social and political life in early medieval times and paved the way for institutional permanence and socio-political dominance.[12] Urban centres of the early medieval times were, however, not a mere continuation of early historical urban development. While urban centres of *c.* 600 BC-AD 300 are found to have assumed an all-India character with their epicentre in the Ganga valley, early medieval urban centres had no such epicentre and the latter were strongly rooted to their local and regioinal surroundings. It has therefore, been, described as a development from within and hence, distinguished as the 'third urbanization' in Indian history.[13]

III

In spite of obvious gaps in our knowledge of early Indian commerce, a more or less connected account of trade in India prior to the arrival of European powers and trading companies is now more or less intelligible to us.[14] Yet the merchant is only a dim figure in this tale of trade, mainly because of the virtual non-existence of any biographical literature of an early Indian merchant and/or of his lineage. The point to ponder is whether this is a problem merely of the lack of data or it indicates the indifferent attitude of a traditional agrarian society to trade and traders. There are, in fact, some historians who view that trade and traders were marginal to the mainstream of agrarian socio-economic and cultural set up of traditional India. Moreover, it has been argued that the initiatives to trade in India were not indigenous and always came from elsewhere, particularly the West.[15] This requires a close examination as it involves not only the question of trade but of the ethos of traditional Indian society.

There is a rich and growing historiography on the long-lasting and widespread (both within the subcontinent and beyond) trade contacts of the Harappan civilization (*c.* 2500-1750 BC). Though no individual Harappan merchant is known, remains of a structure from Banawali (in Haryana) have been identified as the residence of a well off trader.[16] The *Ṛgveda* (*c.* 1500-1000 BC) offers descriptions of wealthy *paṇis* undertaking distant journeys for substantial gains (*śatadhana*). Readings into the accounts of *paṇis* led D.D. Kosambi to consider them as the forerunner of regular *vaṇiks* in subsequent literature.[17] The *paṇis* continue to figure in the *Atharvaveda* and the *Vājasaneyī Saṁhitā* as prosperous persons. But the Vedic texts generally show a hostile attitude to *paṇis*.[18] The *vaṇik* in the later Vedic texts was not held in high esteem; he belonged to the vaiśya *varṇa* which seems to have experienced deterioration of ritual and social status *vis-a-vis* the brāhmaṇa and the kṣatriya. The vaiśya with his traditional functions of cultivation, cattle keeping and trade was viewed as one who was to be lived on by another (*anyasya ādyo*), who could be evicted at will (*yathākāma utthāpya*) and who could be oppressed at will (*yathākāma preṣya*).[19] This attitude hardens in the *Arthaśāstra* of Kauṭilya (IV.2) who perceived the merchant as suspect and dangerous an element as a thorn (*kaṇṭaka*) which required purification (*śodhana*, actually meaning suppression). The *Arthaśāstra* uses the term '*vaidehaka*', which stands for a petty or ordinary trader and rarely speaks of the fabulously rich *śreṣṭhī*. The unabashed distrust of merchants in the *Arthaśastra* (II.16 and II.21-2) is clearly visible in the list of their fraudalent activities which were brought under the strict surveillance of the *śulkādhyakṣa* (officer in charge of the collection tolls and customs) who should take draconian steps to curb merchants.[20] One is not sure to what extent such recommendations were put into practice during the Maurya rule; in case there were some administrative surveillance on merchants, it was limited to the metropolitan area of the Maurya empire, i.e. Magadha and adjacent territories.[21] This degree of stringent administrative control over merchants and trade is not matched in the recommendations of the early Dharmaśāstras. But the rather negative attitude to trade and traders hardly softened in this genre of normative texts. Thus Manu denounces the wealth derived from trade as an admixture of clean and unclean (*sadasat*) and a combination of truth and falsehood (*satyānṛta*);[22] the merchant or the practioner of *satyānṛta* is branded as an open thief (*prakāśyataskara*). In the list of forbidden acts during the Kali (*kalivarjya*), the worst of the ages, the Dharmaśāstra imposes maximum stricture on sea-voyages.[23] Could such an injunction act as a deterrent to maritime commerce and traders?

Yet, the ambivalence of early Indian theorists can hardly be missed because, in spite of their general disapproval of merchants, such theorists hailed commerce as the abode of the goddess of fortune (Lakṣmī). The divergent attitudes of normative treatises to trade and traders may be related to the identifiable phases of boom and slump in the history of early Indian trade.

In a sharp distinction to the brahmanical treatises, there is a positive stance to trade and traders in the two major non-brahmanical relgions of India, viz., Buddhism and Jainism. The functions of a merchant are described in the Pali canonical literature as noble (*ukkaṭṭhakamma*), fit to be followed by persons of noble lineage or pedigree (*ukkaṭṭhakula*); members of the *ukkaṭṭhakula* were khattiyas, brāhmaṇas and gahapatis.[24] There is an interesting dialogue between the Buddha and Sāriputta on the contrasts between trade and agriculture. *Kasi* or agriculture requires constant supervision and care, but it is full of uncertainties, and handsome gain from agriculture is possible only when one is very successful in it. Trade or *vaṇijjā*, on the other hand, is viewed as a less tiresome profession with a lesser responsibility; but the possibility of enormous profit from *vaṇijjā* is often in the offing. For a person engaged in trade (*vanijjāpayutta*) four possible results are envisaged: it could lead to a failure or loss (*chedagāminī hoti*), the gain may not be as much as was anticipated (*na yathābhippāya*), the earning could be as much as was estimated (*yathābhippāya*) and the outcome may far exceed the expected gain (*parābhippāya*).[25] The close linkages between the wandering Buddhist monk and the itinerant merchant are not also unknown. There is a distinct likelihood that both shared a common halting place, for instance a cave shelter lying on or in close proximity to well traversed routes, especially during the rainy season (*vassāvāsa*). The interrelation between the expansion of mercantile activities within and beyond the subcontinent and the more or less simultaneous spread of Buddhism in different parts of South Asia, Central Asia and South-East Asia calls for close scrutiny. Historians of the traditional trade of India have occasionally voiced their doubts about the adventurous and commercial spirits of Indian merchants, mainly in the light of the stricture on crossing the sea laid down in the normative texts.[26] A counterpoint to this assertion is seen in the different types of merchants figuring in various types of early sources.

This study highlights the fact that the diversity of merchants is no less impressive than that of market places, already discussed. Apart from the *vaṇik* or merchant in general, the *sārthavāha* or the carvan trader and the immensely rich *śreṣṭhī*, there were the dealer in animals—cattle, horses and elephants (*govaṇija*, *aśvaṇija*, *kudiraicetti*, etc.), *paṇika/nidu kadi ilaiyinar* (betal leaf/areca nut seller), *lohavaṇija* (iron-dealer), *pakarnar* (hawker) and *nemakavaṇija/umnar/uppuvaṇikan* (salt merchant). While the north Indian donative records generally remain silent about the specific commodity the trader dealt in, the Tamil-Brahmi inscriptions in south India (*c.* first century BC-third century AD) are more explicit on this point: *panita vaṇikan* (toddy seller), *aruvai-vaṇikan* (cloth merchant), *ponvaṇikan* (gold merchant), *maniy-vaṇṇakkan* (lapidarist) appear as distinguishable dealers in diverse commodities. The literary impressions of the import of quality horses from the north-west closely match the representation of horses and their dealers, the latter wearing non-Indian dresses, in the rock art of Chilas (Karakorum highway) which has also yielded the epigraphic evidence of the presence of Sogdian and Chinese merchants.[27] The merchant in early Indian society was therefore neither an undifferentiated entity nor merely a pedlar.[28] Tamil-Brahmi inscriptions (*c.* late first century BC to third century AD) discovered from the Red Sea area clearly record the names of merchants who undertook distant voyages across the sea. Another Brahmi inscription found in Egypt, palaeographically assigned to the second century AD, records the names of merchants, probably hailing from the Deccan.[29]

In Chapter 3 I have tried to highlight how various types of merchants converged at a relatively isolated place like Bandhogarh in eastern part of Madhya Pradesh during the early centuries of the Christian era. A very special type of merchant, viz., the *rājaśreṣthī* or the royal merchant figures in our discussions in the fifth chapter. Interestingly enough, the *rājaśreṣthī* appears frequently and prominently in inscriptions of the Deccan and south India in the post-1000 AD days, though the earliest known textual reference to such a royal merchant goes back to about third century AD. The last chapter focusses principally on one single merchant, viz., Nuruddin Firuz, a rich ship-owner (*nakhuda*) from the famous Persian Gulf port of Hormuz, who came to Somanātha in 1264 and patronized the construction of a mosque at Somanātha with the active help of local 'Hindu' merchants. A unique bilingual inscription, in Arabic and Sanskrit, furnishes considerable details of the social and cultural scenario at Somanātha, a great centre of Śaivism in Gujarat and also an active port in the Gujarat coast in the early middle ages.

IV

A study of merchants of early India has also to address the problem of the formation of mercantile associations or professional organizations of merchants. As early as second century BC a particular body of merchants, *vaṇiggrāma* (*vaṇig* = merchant and *grāma* = collection) figured in an epigraphic record from Karle.[30] Their first appearance is noted in the context of the western Deccan; but in early sixth centuries AD such *vaṇiggrāmas* attained much greater prominence in western India. This is known from a recently discovered inscription from Sanjeli (Gujarat), dated in regnal year 3 of the Hūṇa ruler Toramāna (*c.* AD 503).[31] The list of traders, belonging to the *vaṇiggrāma*, consists of both local (*vāstavya*) merchants at Vadrapāli, the issuing centre of the copper plate, and the non-local traders who came from many places (*caturdiśābhyāgataka-vaideśya*). Their names and the places they hailed from figure in the record in the context of their having agreed to pay voluntary cesses on certain commodities in favour of a temple. They are:

1. Gomika of Daśapura (Mandasore)
2. Pitṛyaṣa Cirāyuṣa of Kānyakubja (Kanauj in the Ganga-Yamuna doab)
3. Gduṣuyebhaṣṣam of Ujjaiyinī (Ujjain in western Malwa)
4. Droṇosoma Bhakkala of Varuṇodarī
5. Bhannitīya Dhruvabhākṣana Agniśarmma of Mahishradaka
6. Bhakkura of Pracakāśa (Prakasa on the Tapi)
7. Rudradatta from Gaṇyatara
8. Bharana Bhaṭṭīśa Śarma from Priyajñarayasa
9. Kalayottikabhaṭṭi of Saṅgaḍhyaka
10. Datta Gujjara of Rivasulavāṇijaka
11. Bhaṭṭi Mahattara
12. Svāmika Maheśvara Mallaka
13. Koṭṭadeva of Sadgama.

These merchants met at the house (*gṛhavāstuveti*) of another merchant (*vāṇijaka*) Ṣaṣṭhī. The merchants who are mentioned without any reference to their respective areas, may safely be assumed to have been local (*vāstavya*) traders at Vadrapālī. Ṣaṣṭhi's residence would certainly make him a local merchant at Vadrapālī, a point further strengthened by the gifting of his own house (*svadīyagṛhavāstu*) in favour of a Viṣṇu temple (*paramadevatābhagavatāyatana*), the donation being recorded in the second charter from Sanjeli, dated to the year 6 of Toramāna (*c.* AD 506). That the importance of the *vaṇiggrāma* continued to grow in western India is amply evident from the famous inscription of Viṣṇuṣeṇa, dated to AD 592. This inscription is an official charter recording the settlement (*ācārasthitipatra*) of the members of the *vaṇiggrāma* at Lohāṭagrāma (in modern Kathiawad) at the initiative of Viṣṇuṣeṇa, the terms and conditions of the settlement of merchants being laid down in seventy-two clauses.[32] The *vaṇiggrāma* rose to considerable prominence in early medieval south India under the name *maṇigrāma*. The same area simultaneously witnessed the rise of two other important bodies of merchants, viz., the 500 *svāmīs* of Ayyavole and the Nānādeśī.[33]

A graphic account of a *vaṇik-meli* or a congregation of merchants from different places at the port of Suppāraka in the western Deccan is available in the Prakrit text *Kuvalayamālā* of Udyotanasuri (*c.* eighth century AD). The narrative may provide us with some images of the sharing and exchange of information, often verging on what amounts to commercial intelligence, among merchants. Some narrated their experience of the sale of horses in Kośala, the transaction in betel nuts in Uttarāpatha, the demand for conchshells from Dvārāvatī, pearls and the trade in superior cloth from Persian Gulf areas; there are of course tales of voyages to Suvarṇadvīpa and Dvārāvatī in South-East Asia. There are many fantastic elements in this account which is not based on real situations, but nevertheless the story betrays familiarity with the world of early Indian merchants. In this text there is also another tale of the young son of an established merchant. The young merchant was keen on undertaking a distant overseas journey. His father was naturally very anxious and apprehensive of the safety of his son in course of such a long and risky voyage. The father pointed to the difficulties of journeying to a distant land (*duradesāntara*), marked by tortuous roads (*visamapanthā*), crooked persons (*niṭṭhura-loo*), many bad elements (*bahue dujjanā*) and very few honest people (*viralāsajjanā*). All these hindrances were projected by the father to somehow dissuade his son from undertaking a risky voyage.[34] On the other hand, the Bodhisattva in the *Suppāraka Jātaka* was himself a master mariner who was an expert in bringing in (*āharaṇa*) and out (*apaharaṇa*) ships from harbours.[35] Interestingly enough, the Buddha is given the epithet Dipaṁkara (= Dvīpaṁkara in Sanskrit), literally meaning a mariner expert in sailing to overseas destinations.

V

It is significant to note that the merchant in early India prominently figures as a donor to religious institutions and as a patron of diverse cultural activities, particularly in the context of the history of Buddhism and Jainism which required sustenance and support from the relatively richer community. This will be evident from the large number of donative inscriptions (*c.* second century BC to third century AD) recording the munificience of many merchants to Buddhist and Jaina organizations in many parts of India. One has to appreciate that Buddhist texts speak not only of the trader's generosity to the Buddhist monastery, but also of his conscious efforts to aspire for a distinct and exclusive social entity.[36] The orthodox Brahmanical texts, generally unfavourable to the merchant however, urges him to use his wealth in works of public charities (*pūrttakarma*), especially during pilgrimages. During the early medieval phase of Indian history (*c.* AD 600-1300) can be seen the proliferation of sectarian Brahmanical cults and the increasing importance attached to the building of structural temples by kings and well off persons. Several inscriptions of the twelfth-thirteenth centuries, recording the donations of merchants to religious institutions, contain a genealogy and family history of the merchant donor. This was aimed at legitimizing his claim to high pedigree and social exclusivity.[37] A case in point is seen in the donations made to some temples at Siyadoni (in modern Bulandshahr district, UP), a prominent *maṇḍapikā* in the ninth century by a merchant. The donor in question was a salt dealer (*nemakavaṇija*) who followed this profession on a hereditary basis. At the end of a list of all his donations to temples the donor describes himself not merely as a *nemakavaṇija*, but as belonging to *nemakajāti*.[38] In such claims for social exclusivity by the merchant may be discerned his attempt to invest a part of his wealth (something tangible) to gain social status (something intangible).

It is in the twelfth and thirteenth centuries that biographical texts about very prosperous and outstanding merchants began to surface on the literary scene. Two such preeminent merchants in Gujarat were Vastupāla and Jagaḍu who were heroes of the *māhātmya* or *carita* type of texts woven around their multifarious achievements. Vastupāla was not merely a great merchant but became a celebrated *mahāmātya* or high ranking administrator too. Both were lauded for their immense wealth and for being great patrons of Jainism as well. An interesting point is that they became central characters of a particular type of literary creations which were primarily composed as a distinct literary genre eulogising foremost royal heroes. The *Harṣacarita*, the *Rāmacaritam* and the *Vikramāṅkadevacaritam* are well-known illustrations of the royal life-histories. The merchant therefore at least on certain occasions could be considered a character or a personality important enough to be projected as the principal character of a tale. Such texts are so far found only in north India. On the other hand, in several inscriptions from the

Deccan and south Indian of the post AD 1000 days the network of merchants' operations, their donations and patronage to religious and cultural activities form subjects of epigraphic narrations and on certain occasions even eulogies.

VI

Early India not only witnessed many indigenous merchants, but also non-Indian merchants from neighbouring and distant areas. Contrary to the bias of ancient theoretical treatises against merchants in general, the same normative texts (e.g. the *Arthaśāstra*) clearly recommended the ruler to encourage the arrival and settlement of traders from abroad in his kingdom.[39] During the first three centuries of the Christian era there developed a number of trading stations of Graeco-Roman merchants on both the sea-boards of south India. Excavated sites like Arikamedu and Karur (to cite only two prominent examples) and the mention of a temple of Augustus at the port of Muziris in the *Tabula Peutangariana* are clear pointers to the presence of Graeco-Roman merchants.[40] The Sangam texts and the two later Tamil epics (the *Silappādikāram* and the *Maṇimekalai*) speak of the presence of *yavanas* in the famous port city of Kāverīpaṭṭinam (in the Kaveri delta).[41]

The same impression is available in the medieval times when the spread of Islam resulted in the intimate commercial linkages between India and the western Indian Ocean areas. The Arab writers' impressions of the amiable attitude of many Indian political authorities to Arab Muslim merchants in different coastal areas of India are matched by inscriptions from the west coast referring to regular settlements of Arab merchants who not only maintained friendly relations with the local political authorities, but were also present at important social and cultural occasions in the coastal society. There is a remarkable convergence of epigraphic data and Arab accounts on the excellent relations between various Arab merchants settled in the Konkan coast and the Rāṣṭrakūṭa rulers (*c.* ninth-tenth centuries) who are highly praised by Arab authors.[42]

Similar cooperative spirit is amply borne out by a number of Jewish business letters of eleventh and twelfth centuries. Many Jewish traders were interested in the trade with India and maintained regular commercial ties with it in an overseas network, spanning from Egypt to the Malabar coast via the Red Sea. Abraham Yishu, a Jewish merchant hailing from Tunisia, lived in the port town of al Manjrur or Mangalore in northern Malabar from 1132 to 1149. A large number of letters received by Yishu throw immense light on the operations of Jewish merchants in India and more importantly, their excellent relations with Arab Muslim merchants and Indian Hindu traders. When a Jewish merchant was a victim of piracy at Thana, he was sent 21 *mithqals* or Egyptian gold coins from Mangalore through an Indian ship owner Tinbu. Tinbu was considered as the best person to help the unfortunate Jewish merchant as between the writer of the letter (himself a Jewish merchant) and Tinbu 'there are *bonds of inseparable friendship and brotherhood*' (italics mine). No less interesting is another letter to Abraham Yishu sent from Aden. The writer of this letter not only sends his regards and best wishes to Abraham Yishu, but also the same to Bama, the Hindu slave and business agent of Abraham Yishu. In fact in one letter to Abraham Yishu, Bama is referred to as 'brother Bama'.[43]

Perhaps the most eloquent testimony of the accommodation of foreign merchants in the coastal society comes in the shape of the bilingual inscription from Somnath which is probed in-depth in Chapter 11. There are clear data to show that Somanātha continued to flourish in the twelfth and thirteenth centuries as a famous Śaiva religious centre even after the devastations carried out by Ghaznavid raids in 1026/7. That it was a leading centre of the Pāśupata sect of the Śaivas becomes absolutely clear from the inscriptions of 1264 and 1287. It is in this cultural setting that the construction of the mosque by Nakhuda Nuruddin Firuz at Somanātha with the active cooperation and patronage of local Hindu merchants, Hindu ruler and administrators and Pāśupata *ācāryas* is to be situated. There is little doubt about Somanātha's importance as a trade centre and port in addition to its being a celebrated sacred centre in the second half of the thirteenth century. The spirit of religious tolerance and amity reaches its noblest level when Allah is lauded in the Sanskrit record as Viśvarūpa (Universal), Viśvanātha (Lord of the Universe), Śūnyarūpa (Formless, i.e. Aniconic) and Lakṣyālakṣya (simultaneously Visible and Invisible).[44]

It is not easy to explain why the foreign merchant was generally given preferential treatment *vis-a-vis* the indigenous merchant of India. In view of the rather low estimation of trade and traders in early Indian theoretical treatises, the likely explanation is that the so-called 'dirty job' was considered by orthodox theoreticians to be best left to the 'other' non-indigineous communities. There is little doubt that the political authority in ancient India was well aware of the revenue bearing potential of trade (including foreign trade), which must have supplemented the primary agricultural resource base of the state. There is clearly no standardized image of the merchant in early India. There is an unmistakable difference in the attitude of brahmanical treatises from that in the Buddhist and Jaina texts, the latter undoubtedly upholding the role of the merchant in a more positive manner. The image of the merchant in early Indian theoretical treatises does not match the portrayal of merchants as heroes and eminent personalities in creative literature. Śūdraka appears to have had little hesitation in projecting Cārudatta as the hero of his famous drama, *Mṛcchakaṭikam*; Cārudatta, one cannot forget, was a *vipra-sārtha*, i.e. a brāhmaṇa following the profession of a merchant. Similarly, there was little difficulty on the part of the priest or manager of a Sun temple at Indrapura (Indore in Bulandshahr district, UP) to accept a perpetual donation in cash (*akṣayanīvi*) from two merchant brothers in AD 466 who were kṣatriya-vaṇiks.[45] Such brāhmaṇas and kṣatriyas did not apparently take to trade as an *āpaddahrama* which allowed deviations from strict *varṇa-jāti* rules in the wake of some calamity (*āpad*). No such *āpad* or calamity is either explicitly stated nor implied in the relevant sources. In other words, the normative literature does not provide us with an all-purpose key to understand the complexities of the world of merchant in early India.

In a predominantly agrarian country like India merchants must have been numerically fewer than the vast multitude of agriculturists. Foreign merchants residing in India as diasporic communities were therefore an even tinier minority. The study of the settlements of foreign traders in different areas of India, especially in coastal tracts, offers extremely valuable data on cultural synthesis and coexistence among Graeco-Romans, Persians, Arab Muslims, Hindus of India and Jewish 'India traders'. The most significant message the history of trade and traders in early India beckons to the present situation lies in the images of social and cultural accommodation of and the spirit of tolerance to several minority groups. The enquiry into merchants and their pursuits in early India strongly drives home the importance of recognizing the role of minority communities in the flowering of a plural and complex society like India not only of remote past, but also of recent experience.

NOTES

1. R. Champakalakshmi, *Trade, Ideology and Urbanization: South India c. 300 BC to AD 1300*, New Delhi, 1996.
2. See the chapter on the 'Puṭabhedana as a Centre of Trade in Early India' in this volume. The term '*puṭabhedana*' is used to underline commercial

character of *peṇṭhā*. It also figures as a synonym of *pura/nagara* in the *Nāmaliṅgānuśāsana* of Amarasiṁha, belonging to the Gupta period.

3. Vimala Begley and Richard Daniel de Puma, eds., *Rome and India, the Ancient Sea Trade*, New Delhi, 1992; V.D. Goghte, 'The Chandraketugarh-Tamluk Region of Bengal: Source of the Early Historic Rouletted Ware from India and Southeast Asia', *Man and Environment*, XXII, 1997, pp. 69-85.
4. Lionel Casson, 'New Light on Maritime Loans: P. Vindob G 40822', *Zeitschrift fur Papyrologie und Epigraphik*, Band 84, 1990, pp. 195-206; the English translation of this important document is also incorporated in Niharranjan Ray, B.D. Chattopadhyaya, Ranabir Chakravarti and V.R. Mani, *A Sourcebook of Indian Civilization*, Calcutta, 2000, pp. 607-9.
5. Lionel Casson, 'Ancient Naval Technology and the Route to India', in Vimala Begley and Richard Daniel de Puma, eds., *Rome and India*, pp. 8-11.
6. S. Mazzarino, 'The Hypalum of Pliny', in Federico de Romanis and A. Tchernia, eds., *Crossings, Early Mediterranean Contacts with India*, Delhi, 1997.
7. Federio de Romanis, 'Rome and the Notia of India: Relations between Rome and Southern India from 30 BC to the Flavian Period', in Romanis and Tchernia, eds., *Crossings*, pp. 80-160.
8. Romila Thapar, 'Black Gold: South Asia and Roman Maritime Trade', *South Asia*, vol. XV, 1992, pp. 1-28.
9. Sudarsan Senaviratne, 'Kalinga and Andhra: The Process of Secondary State Formation', in H.J.M. Claessen and P. Skalnik, eds., *The Study of the State*, The Hague, 1981, pp. 317-38.
10. Champakalakshmi, *Trade, Ideology and Urbanization*, pp. 92-174.
11. For a recent statement on this see Ranabir Chakravarti, 'Between Cities and Villages: Linkages of Trade in India *c.* AD 600-1300', in Georg Berkemer, Tilman Frasch, Hermann Kulke and Jurgen Lütt, eds., *Explorations in the History of South Asia: Essays in Honour of Dietmar Rothermund*, New Delhi, 2001, pp. 99-120.
12. Chamapakalakshmi, *Trade, Ideology and Urbanization*, pp. 37-69.
13. B.D. Chattopadhyaya, *The Making of Early Medieval India*, New Delhi, 1994, especially the chapter entitled, 'Urban Centres in Early Medieval India: An Overview'; also Chamapakalakshmi, *Trade, Ideology and Urbanization*.
14. Ranabir Chakravarti, ed., *Trade in Early India*, New Delhi, 2001.
15. Such a position is taken by E.H. Warmington, *The Commerce between the Roman Empire and India*, London, 1974 (2nd edn.).
16. An overview of Harappan trade is available in Shereen Ratnagar, 'Harappan Trade in Its World Context', *Man and Environment*, XIX, 1994, pp. 117-27; also see R.S. Bisht, 'Excavations at Banawali', in Gregory L. Possehl,

ed., *Harappan Civilization, a Contemporary Perspective*, Delhi, 1993, pp. 117-18.

17. D.D. Kosambi, *The Culture and Civilisation of Ancient India in Historical Outline*, London, 1966.
18. For references to *panis* in the Vedic literature, see A.A. Mcdonnell and A.B. Keith, *The Vedic Index of Names and Subjects*, II, London, 1910.
19. See R.C. Majumdar, ed., *The Vedic Age*, Bombay, 1951; R.S. Sharma, *Material Culture and Social Formation in Ancient India*, Delhi, 1983, for discussions on these epithets of the vaiśya found in the *Aitareya Brāhmaṇa*.
20. Vide U.N. Ghoshal, *A History of Indian Public Life*, vol. II, Bombay, 1966.
21. Romila Thapar, *The Mauryas Revisited*, Calcutta, 1987.
22. *Manusmṛti*, IV.6; tr. G. Buhler, *Sacred Book of the East*, XXXV, Oxford, 1886.
23. P.V. Kane, *History of Dharmaśāstra*, vol. V, Poona, 1962.
24. *Vinaya Piṭaka* IV.6; N. Wagle, *Society at the Time of the Buddha*, Bombay, 1966.
25. N. Wagle, *Society at the Time of the Buddha*.
26. E.H. Warmington, *The Commerce between the Roman Empire and India*, p. 1.
27. Karl Jettmar, ed., *Antiquities from Northern Pakistan*, vol. I in 2 parts, Munchen, 1989.
28. A more exhaustive treatment of this point is made by Ranabir Chakravarti, 'The Role of the Mercantile Community (*c.* 150 BC-AD 400)', *Encyclopaedia Britannica* (in press).
29. R. Saloman, 'Epigraphic Remains of Indian Traders in Egypt', *Journal of the American Oriental Society*, 1991, pp. 731-6.
30. The importance of the *vaṇiggrāma* was first appreciated by D.D. Kosambi, 'Dhenukākaṭa', *JBAS*, vol. XXX, 1955, p. 66.
31. R.N. Mehta and A.M. Thakkar, *The M.S. University Copper Plate Grants of Toramana*, Baroda, 1978; also K.V. Ramesh, 'Three Early Charters from Sanjeli', *EI*, vol. XL, 1986, pp. 175-86.
32. An elaborate discussion is made by Ranabir Chakravarti, 'Three Copper Plates of AD Sixth Century: Glimpses of Socio-Economic and Cultural Life in Western India', to be published in *South Asian Archaeology*, XV, Leiden; for a masterly analysis of the contents of the charter of Viṣṇuṣeṇa see D.D. Kosambi, 'Indian Feudal Trade Charters', *JESHO*, vol. 2, 1958, 281-93.
33. Meera Abraham, *Two Medieval Merchant Guilds of South India*, New Delhi, 1988.
34. A.N. Upadhyaye, ed., *The Kuvalayamālā of Udyotanasuri*, Varanasi, 1969.
35. V. Fausboll, ed., *The Jātaka*, IV.436 The story with some modifications also appears in the *Jātakamālā* of Āryaśūra (*c.* seventh century), tr. J. Speyer, in the *Sacred Books of the Buddhists*, vol. I, London, 1895, pp. 124-5.

36. Romila Thapar, *Ancient Indian Social History*, Delhi, 1978; particularly the essay on 'Social Mobility in Ancient India with Special Reference to Elite Groups'; Himanshu Prabha Ray, *Monastery and Guild: Commerce under the Satavahanas*, New Delhi, 1986; Ranabir Chakravarti, 'Merchants and Others Donors at Ancient Bandhogarh', in this volume.
37. Chattopadhyaya, *The Making of Early Medieval India*, especially the essay 'Markets and Merchants in Early Medieval Rajasthan', therein.
38. *Epigraphia Indica*, vol. I, 1892: 112-18.
39. This is clearly seen in the chapter on the *Paṇyādhyakṣa* in the *Arthaśāstra* (II.16).
40. There is a recent spurt in the publications on commerce between the Roman empire and India. The archaeological perspective of this trade is available in Vimala Begley and Richard Daniel de Puma, eds., *Rome and India*. The re-examination of literary data is offered in Romanis and Tchernia, eds., *Crossings*.
41. Champakalakshmi, *Trade, Ideology and Urbanization*.
42. G.F. Hourani, *Arab Seafaring*, Beirut, 1951; S. Maqbul Ahmed, *Early Arabic Accounts of India and China* (translations of the accounts of Sulaiman and ibn Khurdadbeh), Shimla, 1989; Ranabir Chakravarti, 'Monarchs, Merchants and a Maṭha in Northern Konkan (900-1053 AD)', *Indian Economic and Social History Review*, vol. XXVII, 1990: 189-208; V.K. Jain, *Trade and Traders in Western India 1000-1300*, New Delhi, 1989.
43. The immense importance of Jewish documents, found from a *genizah* in Cairo, is best illustrated in the celebrated studies by S.D. Goitein. See his *Letters of Medieval Jewish Traders*, Princeton, 1973; also Shaul Shaked, *A Tentative Bibliography of the Genizah Documents*, Paris, 1964; analyses of these business letters for the study of Indian maritime trade are made by Ranabir Chakravarti, 'Coastal Trade and Voyages in Konkan: The Early Medieval Scenario', *Indian Economic and Social History Review*, vol. XXXV, 1998, pp. 97-123. Amitav Ghosh, *In an Antique Land*, New Delhi, 1990 has written a novel on the life of Abraham ben Yiju by a superb combination of historical data from the *genizah* business letters and literary imagination.
44. How Somnath began to surface in the colonial and nationalist historiography has been highlighted by Romila Thapar, *Narrative and Making of History*, Delhi, 2000, pp. 24-50.
45. D.C. Sircar, *Select Inscriptions Bearing on Indian History and Civilization*, vol. I, Calcutta, 1965, pp. 318-20.

CHAPTER 2

Early Historical India: A Study in its Material Milieu (*c.* 600 BC-AD 300)

Researches in early Indian history over the last three decades show a major change in historical vision: the earlier emphasis on dynastic chronicling is increasingly being replaced by the historian's penchant for understanding the economy, society, polity and culture of early India. Historians appear now to have been less interested in what Kosambi termed as 'episodic history'[1] and engage themselves in unravelling the changing character of early Indian history and also identifying the possible agents of such changes. One such formative stage of Indian history is termed 'early historical' which spans from sixth century BC to third century AD and which succeeds the proto-historic/pre-literate phase in the history of the subcontinent.

The period witnessed the rise of territorial powers (*janapadas/mahājanapadas*) in place of lineage-based polities (*janas*); it also saw a continuous struggle between the urge for imperial unity and the love for local autonomy (expressed mainly by the 'republican'/oligarchic or *gaṇa-saṁgha* type of polities).[2] The most important change in the economic life was the emergence of agriculture as the mainstay of the material life of the people first in the Ganga valley and then gradually over the whole of the subcontinent. The agrarian economy when firmly rooted naturally provided enough surplus to maintain whole-time craftsmen of diverse types. As production increased both in the spheres of agriculture and crafts, trade developed in a natural sequence. The early centuries of the Christian era ushered in a glorious phase of Indian commerce which was drawn into the network of international trade, both overland and maritime. The new generative forces must have helped in transforming an essentially lineage-based and more or less egalitarian society into a stratified society. Symptoms of a complex society are discernible in the form of sharpening of *varṇa-jāti* differentiation and in the emergence of classes. These broad developments, spanning over about nine centuries, can hardly be expected to have occurred in a uniform and unilinear manner in a vast spatial unit like the Indian subcontinent.

There is however a major point of unity in the changing socio-economic and cultural scene and that is the process of urbanization. Though the earliest cities appeared in the subcontinent as far back as the days of the Harappa civilization (*c*. 2300-1750 BC)[3] urban centres virtually vanished from the scene between 1500 and 600 BC. It is from the sixth century BC onwards that the historian encounters a spurt of urban centres, first in the middle Ganga basin and then gradually throughout the subcontinent.[4] The question is so far undecided whether urbanization in the Ganga basin was a survival or revival of Harappan urbanism; but the majority of present-day scholars view urbanization in the early historical period as independent of its proto-historic counterpart.[5] The difference between the two urbanisms is not merely temporal but also visible from the point of view of its socio-economic, political and cultural milieu.

This requires an exhaustive discussion. But one should try to understand at the outset what is a city.

There are several definitions of an urban centre. Despite the multiplicity of such definitions and concepts of a city, the city can best be seen as a unit of human settlement sharply distinct from a village. The difference between a city and a village is marked by the 'oldest and most revolutionary division of labour: between the work in the fields on the one hand and activities described as urban on the other'.[6] The essential hallmarks of a pre-industrial, if not pre-historic, city were summed up by Gordon Childe in 1950.[7] These are:

1. A city is much more extensive and densely populated than any previous human settlement.
2. Though peasants were often found just outside the city, the main inhabitants of the city essentially consisted of non-food-producing people, i.e. full-time specialist craftsmen, merchants, priests, rulers and administrative officers, who were supported by the surplus produced by peasants.
3. The primary producer is to pay a tiny part of the agricultural surplus to a deity or divine king. The concentration of this surplus is essential for the emergence of cities.
4. Construction of true monumental buildings is a distinctive mark

of city life; it is also indicative of the concentration of social wealth.

5. Among the non-food-producing population of an urban centre, priests, civil and military leaders and officials enjoyed a position of pre-eminence. They claimed the major share of the concentrated surplus and that led to the formation of ruling class.

6-7. Invention of writing, rise of a community of clerks and the elaboration of exact and predictive sciences—arithmetic, geometry and astronomy—are inseparably associated with the emergence of an urban centre.

8. Other specialists gave a new direction to artistic expressions. Artist-craftsmen, sculptors, painters, seal cutters, etc., began to practise their craft according to conceptualized and sophisticated styles.

9. A part of the concentrated surplus is meant for paying for the importation of raw materials. Trade and market and especially long-distance trade are closely linked up with city life.

10. The specialist craftsmen in a city is provided with raw material and guaranteed security in a state organization based on residence rather than kinship. The city is a community to which a craftsman can belong both economically and politically.

These criteria when closely examined would show that the basic motivating factor behind the process of urbanization was the betterment of technologies which paved the way for the production of the vital surplus. This surplus not only sustained the non-food-producing population of the city but also the ruling group.

Significant changes took place in the fields of production of surplus and the methods of channelization of the surplus from the days of the Harappan civilization to those of the urban development during the early historical period. The Harappan civilization depended on bronze and stone implements for agrarian production. We are still in the dark regarding the nature of the ruling class in the Harappan civilization, but a considerable number of scholars are of the opinion that some kind of a sacerdotal authority controlled the affairs of the Harappans.[8] It has also been suggested that the exact sciences (arithmetic, geometry and astronomy) which were inseparably associated with the emergence of the first urbanization were also intermixed with magico-religious beliefs and practices, obviously to the advantage of the priestly community.[9] Attention has also been paid to the relative scarcity of offensive weapons and defensive body armours during the Harappan civilization. D.P.

Chattopadhyaya argues, taking the cue from D.D. Kosambi and Joseph Needham, that in the absence of true implements of coercion the ruling groups took recourse to magical and superstitious beliefs which were intertwined with exact sciences.[10] Chattopadhyaya hints at a distinct possibility that[11] this religious ideology was the main instrument in Harappan culture for the purpose of policing the state. Thus the exact sciences at once facilitated the growth of urbanism and instead of emancipating people from superstitions went hand in glove with the latter for controlling the ruled and for channelizing the social surplus.

The period between the fall of the Harappan and the emergence of the Gangetic urbanism witnessed no cities. Moreover the Dharmasūtras speak of definite hostility towards cities and the *Ṛgveda* shows that a pastoral economy prevalied from *c.* 1500-1000 BC. The subsequent period of the later Vedic literature signalled the expansion of the Vedic people from the Punjab towards the east, south and south-east. The most important aspect of this migration was the settlement of sedentary agricultural communities, distinct from the pastoral people of the early Vedic period in the upper, and then gradually, in the middle Ganga basin. The transformation of the pastoral Ṛgvedic society into a fully agrarian community during the later Vedic phase is one of the most significant developments in the economic history of early India. While definite facts about the growth of agriculture are known in this period, the idea of private property and the growth of royal power can also be noticed from a study of the later Vedic literature. To this one can add some progress in crafts and industries and the beginning of the use of iron.[12]

This is the period which marked the growing ritualization in social and religious life which consequently led to the increasing importance of the priestly community, the brāhmaṇas, at the cost of the vaiśyas and śūdras.[13] Attention may be drawn in this connection to the alliance between the brāhmaṇas and the kṣatriyas for their mutual benefit. This can best be illustrated by the performances of royal sacrifices like the Rājasūya, Vājapeya and Aśvamedha which signified the growth of royal power and at the same time the greater influence of rituals and their organizers in social and even political life.[14]

Interestingly enough, iron which appeared for the first time during this period seems to have been used at the initial stage for military purposes. Excavations at several sites included within the erstwhile kingdoms of Kuru, Pañcāla, Matsya, Madra and particularly at the archaeological site at Atranjikhera have yielded profuse iron weapons.[15]

This may amply demonstrate the improvement in the military technology which in turn intensified the coercive authority of the ruler and facilitated extraction of agricultural surplus. Under such circumstances, it may be reasonably presumed that the growth of secular power would gradually relegate the importance of rituals and religious performances as a means of social and political control. Judged in this light, the growth of military technology would pave the way for the emergence of a standing army and as a result a process of secularization of the political and social life would begin.

The impact of these changes was clearly visible with the arrival of the early historical period from the sixth century BC onwards. The rise of *mahājanapadas* not only coincided with the rise of protestant religions like Buddhism and Jainism, but also lessened the importance of the priestly community in statecraft. The early historical period had the potential to question the ritual supremacy of the religieux and emphasize on the material basis of life. This could be amply demonstrated by the Kautiliyan idea of the elements (*prakṛti*) of the state:[16] there one does not encounter the priest or the *purohita* in the list of elements of the state (the *purohita*, however, is included by Kauṭilya in the list of the highest paid officers of the realm).

This discussion may drive home the fact that at the turn of the sixth century BC there was an overall challenge against the old orthodoxy in the air. Judged from this angle, one may appreciate that fresh grounds were being broken in almost all walks of life.

The renewed emergence of cities is to be studied against the background of this changing situation and the challenge against orthodoxy. Cities of the early historical period are not to be regarded as a loose agglomeration of traits (i.e. exchange and administrative centres), but should be viewed as a manifestation of a process which transformed the society from a more or less egalitarian phase into a sharply class-differentiated one. The historian doubtless faces an uphill task, but is on a relatively surer ground as the chronological framework is at present reasonably clear. The proverbial paucity of data which plagues any student of early Indian history is somewhat less. Diverse types of evidence—literary (indigenous, foreign, popular, theological and theoretical literature), epigraphic, numismatic and archaeological (mainly stratified evidence from excavations)—can profitably be used for the study of the socio-economic conditions during the period of nine hundred years of our study.

II

As the scene opens in about 600 BC the geographical focus is on the middle Ganga valley which seems to have relegated the importance of the upper Ganga valley and parts of the Punjab (the area known as Brahmāvartta/Brahmarṣideśa lying between the Sarasvatī and Dṛṣadvatī rivers). The *Aṅguttara Nikāya* enumerates sixteen territorial powers (*mahājanapadas*) embracing a region from Gandhāra in the north to Aśmaka in the south and from Avantī in the west to Aṅga in the east.[17] The visibly greater concentration of *mahājanapadas* in the middle Ganga basin, i.e. in modern eastern UP and Bihar would unmistakably point this region as the 'area of attraction'.[18] Significant and prosperous human settlements were not necessarily confined to the area termed as *śiṣṭadeśa* in the sacerdotal Brahmanical literature. In fact the expansion of settlements from the Punjab area to the east, south and south-east had begun since *c.* 1000 BC. The enlarging geographical horizon of the later Vedic literature and the distribution of the Painted Grey Ware sites (which are more or less coeval with the later Vedic literature) amply demonstrate the process of gradual penetration in the Ganga valley by people from the Punjab.[19] This movement of people not merely signalled change of habitat, but was linked up with the transformation of the pastoral life of the Ṛgvedic period (*c.* 1500-1000 BC) into a fully sedentary agricultural society of the later Vedic times (*c.* 1000-600 BC).[20]

The impact of this process was effectively felt from 600 BC onwards when a large number of agrarian settlements emerged in the middle Ganga basin. It has been suggested that the regular use of iron tools (from *c.* 800/750 BC onwards) held the key to the successful clearance of dense forests of the Gangetic valley by widespread tree felling.[21] The area, one of the most fertile tracts of the subcontinent due to profuse rainfall and the presence of life-giving streams from the Himalayan glaciers, began to be regularly exploited for agriculture.

The most suitable crop was of course rice which had appeared during the later Vedic period.[22] R.S. Sharma suggests that transplantation of paddy began from *c.* 600 BC which definitely improved production of rice; a new variety of rice namely *śāli* also emerged in this period.[23] Interestingly enough, Trevor Ling points to the distinct possibility of higher fertility rate in rice-eating areas like the middle Ganga valley.[24]

Apart from rice, sugar cane and cotton figured among cultivated crops. Cultivation of these two cash crops, as distinct from cereals, clearly points to an agrarian development.

The most tangible proof of the growth of settlement in the riparian tracts of the Ganga valley is provided by archaeological evidence of a new kind of ceramic tradition, viz., Northern Black Polished Ware (NBPW).[25] This new pottery type is subsequent to and technologically more advanced than the Painted Grey Ware. The chronological position of the NBPW is now fairly clear (*c.* 600-100 BC). Though the NBPW is unearthed from some sites in the upper Ganga basin like Ropar and Ahicchatra and even beyond the Ganga valley in Ujjayini, the heaviest concentration of the NBPW sites is in the middle Ganga basin. The alluvial tracts on the southern as well as northern side of the Ganga have yielded around 450 NBPW sites between Allahabad (the region represented by the *mahājanapada* of Vatsa) and Bhagalpur (the region represented by the *mahājanapada* of Aṅga).[26] This is precisely the area where existed three of the four principal monarchical powers, viz., Vatsa, Kośala and Magadha. Available literary sources are replete with references to agricultural operations and particularly iron ploughshares. It has been suggested that iron was probably used with increasing regularity for ploughing, because the heavier and thicker alluvial soil of the middle Ganga valley could be ploughed much more effectively with an iron share than by one made of copper, the latter being suitable for light, loamy type of soil in the upper Ganga valley.[27]

Archaeologically, however, only two iron ploughshares have been found from NBPW phases at Kauśāmbi and Vaiśālī[28] (in the later phase of NBPW). Nevertheless, archaeological evidence may point to the presence of more iron tools for production than those unearthed from the earlier PGW phase. Though the extent of the use of iron tools in cultivation and the impact of iron technology on agriculture in general are as yet not fully ascertained, it is quite likely that the alluvial tracts of the middle Ganga basin considerably helped enrich the agrarian economy. Early Pali canonical texts occasionally refer to *gahapatis*, a term originally meaning a householder or head of the family, but denoting in the sixth-fifth centuries BC an agriculturist/peasant.[29]

According to the *Baudhāyana Dharmasūtra*, assignable to *c.* fifth century BC an arable plot, ideally suitable to maintain a family, should measure 5 *nivartanas*.[30] On the other hand, estates as large as 500-1000 *kariṣas*, also figure in early Pali texts;[31] these are apparently too big to be cultivated by the peasant himself, and therefore slave labour and hired labour are employed to till such bigger plots.

As success in agriculture in India was, as it still continues to be in modern times, a virtual gamble with the monsoons, the agrarian community had to depend on irrigation projects. The middle Ganga valley, endowed with reasonably regular amount of annual rainfall and perennial rivers of glacial origin, appears to have been relatively less dependent on irrigation. The *Kuṇāla Jātaka*, probably preserving an earlier tradition, narrates an impending clash between two republican clans, the Śākyas and Koliyas, over the first use of the water of the river Rohiṇī to irrigate their respective fields.[32] The story underlines the importance of irrigation in the middle Ganga valley.

Development in agriculture seems to have been beneficial for the rise of crafts and various other occupations. The later Vedic literature, particularly the *Yajurveda* contains some information on the rise in the number of crafts.[33] But it is in the early Pali canonical texts (e.g. *Vinaya Piṭaka*, the first four *Nīkayas* of *Suttapiṭaka*, viz., *Dīgha*, *Majjhima*, *Saṁyutta* and *Aṅguttara Nikāyas* and the *Suttanipāta*) that an unmistakable proliferation of crafts is clearly seen. Weavers, carpenters (*vaḍḍhakīs*), smiths (*kammāras*), leather workers (*cammakāras*) are repeatedly mentioned in these sources. Along with these crafts catering mainly to daily necessities, mention may be made of ivory work which is of course a luxury item meant for moneyed people. Two of the most significant crafts were iron works and pottery. Iron objects are found in considerable number from sites in UP, e.g. Kauśāmbī, Prahladpur, Banaras, and Mason and in Bihar, e.g. Chirand, Vaisali, Patna, Sonpur and Champa.

These include axes, adzes, knives, razors, nails, sickles, many of them being intimately associated with agricultural operations. The definite improvement in iron tools in this period must have been due to the easy access to the richest iron ore deposits in south Bihar area. Some iron artifacts of NBPW phase from Banaras are found to have contained the same impurities as noticed in the iron ores of Singhbhum and Mayurbhanj. This goes to show the importance of iron mines of south Bihar and adjoining areas giving greater fillip to the growth of iron-based industrial activities.

Another significant development in the craft economy was the beginning of organization of industries under the names *śreṇī*, *gaṇa*, *pūga*, *saṁgha*, all loosely translated as guild. These terms occur in Pāṇini's *Aṣṭādhyāyī*[34] and early Buddhist canons. To what extent a guild organization became an integral part of craft economy cannot be ascertained at the present state of our knowledge. But the *Gautama Dharmasūtra* not only speaks of professional organizations among cultivators, traders, moneylenders and artisans, but also allows them to 'lay down rules for their respective classes'.[35] This implies a gradual evolution of guild laws which would control and guide activities of these professional bodies.

A well-established agrarian base sustaining diverse types of craftsmen also encouraged exchange of commodities. The *Aṣṭādhyāyī* of Pāṇini was aware of the essential elements in trade, viz., *krayavikraya*, i.e. purchase and sale.[36] The same text would also suggest differentiations among merchants on the basis of commodities they dealt in and also areas they hailed from.[37] Early Pali texts highlight the position of rich merchants (*seṭṭhis*) with traditionally 80 crores of wealth (*asīti koṭivibhava*) and of caravan traders (*sātthavāhas*) often driving a large number of wagons from the eastern to the western limit (*pubbanta-aparānta*). Though regular exchange networks had arrived in the middle Ganga valley by the later Vedic period, commerce began to be definitely linked up with a flourishing money economy from the sixth century BC onwards. The earliest coins of India, viz., punch-marked silver types, began to be circulated throughout the Ganga valley and tended to spread beyond it.[38] It is rather unlikely that these coins were struck by existing political authorities; these were probably minted by different merchant groups.

As a flourishing economy was spreading over greater parts of northern India, political consolidation can also be noticed in the shape of the rise of four major monarchical powers (Kośala, Vatsa, Avantī and Magadha) and one non-monarchical clan (the Licchavis), thereby reducing the previous number of rival political powers from sixteen to five. The ensuing struggles for supremacy among these five ultimately paved the way for political paramountcy of Magadha in north India.[39] The need of the hour was the creation of a well-exercised, regularly paid and properly maintained standing army. Such a permanent armed force, distinct from militia forces of pre-600 BC times, could best be maintained by a regular system of appropriation of surplus. Political developments of this period show a definite inclination towards greater concentration of coercive powers in the hands of the king who was now in a position to claim various levies from agrarian, industrial and commercial activities. A king of Kāśī is described in the *Mahāvagga* as very wealthy and with a full treasury and storehouse (*mahaddhano paripuṇṇa kośakoṭṭhāgāla*).[40] Similarly the *Suttanipāta* states that Kośala was rich in vigour and prosperity (*dhanaviriyeṇa sampanna*).[41] While Bimbisāra had under him a large number of royal officers,[42] early Pali canonical texts refer to settlement officers (*rajjugāhakāmaccas*) who were definitely associated with revenue assessment and collection. Extraction of the agrarian surplus held the key to the growth of political power of rulers and also to the process of urbanism which will be discussed later.

This now brings us to the process of urbanization which reappeared in Indian scene almost after a millennium since the decline of the Harappan towns. Available literary sources are full of descriptions of towns and cities, numbering sometimes as much as sixty. This is in strong contrast to literary evidence of earlier periods which rarely referred to cities. Of outstanding cities belonging to the early phase of the second urbanization were six, viz., Campā, Rājagaha, Sāvatthi, Vārāṇasī, Kauśāmbī and Kusinara.

They are usually depicted as having huge ramparts, moats, gateways, lofty palaces, busy streets full of merchants and artisans and royal residences. The descriptions are often stereotyped and to be taken with a grain of salt.[43] All these six cities are intimately associated with the life and activities of the Buddha. The Buddha and his followers repeatedly emphasized upon their preference for *dāna* (gift) to *saṁgha* to *dakṣinā* (sacrifical fees for priests). The concept of gift of alms fits in well into an urban milieu than a rural surrounding, as townsmen with more surplus at their disposal were in a position to patronize Buddhists more effectively. This should be appreciated in the background of the well-known support of the trading community to the *saṁgha*.

Many of the urban sites, including the six major ones, are excavated, and literary data may therefore be compared with the archaeological. The major problem here is that most of early historical urban sites were vertically excavated, mainly with a view to determining their chronology. But only regular horizontal diggings could really unravel the structure, layout and life in such urban centres. At Atranjikhera the PGW layer spread over 650 sq. m while the succeeding stratum of NBPW measured 850 m x 550 m.[44] This indicates growth of the site and demographic increase. One may infer breaking of new grounds in the site concerned which almost assumed urban dimensions. One of the most distinctive features of an urban site, namely fortification wall, has also been unearthed from excavations. The most enormous fortification wall is reported from the Kauśāmbī excavation (circuit over 6.5 km).[45] The fortification wall, according to G.R. Sharma, the excavator, was erected in *c.* 1000 BC. This is considered to be too high an overdating by A. Ghosh who, however, assigns it a date prior to the arrival of NBPW.[46] Pre-NBPW fortifications were raised at Eran, Ujjayini and Rajghat (Vārāṇasī). In Eran and Ujjayini imposing fortifications of mud bricks were erected in 700 BC and 750 BC.[47] The huge mud rampart at Rajghat is placed around 600 BC.[48] A stone fortification also protected the urban site of Rājagṛha (over a circuit of 40 km.), which is traditionally associated with Magadhan rulers Bimbisāra and Ajātaśatru.[49] While these fortifications were built in or before 600 BC other urban centres had their fortifications subsequently, between 400 and 200 BC.

Though excavated materials do not admittedly tally with the glorified accounts of cities in Buddhist texts, one had to take into serious consideration the emergence of a large number of non-rural settlements where people earned their livelihood by various professions other than cultivation. Many of these sites were either situated on navigable rivers or at points of convergence of overland routes. Several urban sites were simultaneously craft and commercial centres and also political headquarters of *mahājanapadas*. The presence of a newly moneyed class can be inferred from the use of a deluxe black polished pottery which appears to have been beyond the reach of ordinary persons. Excavations at Śrāvastī (Period I, 600-300 BC) yield beads of precious and semi-precious stones.[50] Apart from the fairly high degree of manufacturing skill which sustained such a craft, it also presupposes the existence of an urbane rich community which required such luxury items.

The picture of a burgeoning economy and the beginning of urbanization in the Ganga valley is more or less agreed upon by historians. But there are sharp differences of opinion regarding the key factor behind urbanization. The role of social surplus without which the city can hardly exist is rightly stressed. R.S. Sharma underlines the major change in production process, mainly due to the advent of iron technology in agriculture and crafts. According to Sharma, regular use of iron implements helped clear the dense forest and till the heavy alluvial soil. The resultant agrarian surplus was then appropriated by political authorities who were rapidly growing in power. This surplus played a vital role in the emergence of non-rural settlements functioning as manufacturing, commercial and political centres. Sharma thus highlights the role of technology in bringing about socio-economic changes of far reaching consequences.[51] This view is countered by A. Ghosh[52] and George Erdosy[53] who give priority to the social need/political demand for surplus rather than to the capacity to produce the surplus as a result of technological innovations. In other words they argue in favour of the greater role of a power structure (here in the shape of political authorities of the *mahājanapadas*) without which a surplus could not appear the moment it is asked for.

It is not easy at the present state of our research to indicate which factor—technological change or the rise of a power structure—played a greater role in the emergence of cities in the Ganga valley. There would be, however, little hesitation to conclude that cities could hardly exist and prosper without the combination of the two.

The rapid survey in this section is admittedly confined to north India. A contrasting pattern is seen in the trans-Vindhyan regions. Archaeological excavations/explorations have brought to light the practice of agriculture, presence of Black and Red Ware, use of iron and megalithic burial customs in contemporary Deccan.[54] But no major urban settlement is reported from archaeological findings. Keeping abreast with this development, absence of territorial powers in contemporary Deccan is also interesting. It is not unlikely that lineage-based polities held sway over the region in question. Social stratification was apparently less noticeable in the Deccan than in the north. All these seem to have precluded production and appropriation of a social surplus from agriculture and non-agrarian sources in spite of the prevalence of iron technology. The lack of an ongoing process of the emergence of a state structure probably thwarted the growth of urban centres in the Deccan. And this may go in favour of Ghosh's argument. The other important point is that despite the rise of various cities in the Ganga valley, Pāṭaliputra stays in the background. In fact the greatest city of the ensuing centuries was only known as Pāṭaligāma and dubbed as a *puṭabhedana*[55] (literally, meaning a place where lids of merchandise were opened). The Buddha nevertheless prophesied its future greatness.[56] He seems to have rightly assessed the economic importance of a trade centre at the confluence of three rivers and with an extensive hinterland in the vast plains; to this should be added the strategically better location of Pāṭaligāma than Rājagṛha, particularly since the beginning of Magadha's territorial expansion during Bimbisāra's and Ajātaśatru's reigns.[57]

III

The economic and political developments during the age of the Buddha resulted in the gradual dissolution of the near autarchic situation of pre-600 BC days. The developments, no doubt of great importance, were however essentially confined to north India. A pan-Indian situation could be visualized only since late fourth century BC with the establishment of the Maurya empire. The Mauryas ruled over a vast territory, extending from Afghanistan in the north to northern Karnataka in the south and from Kathiawad in the west to Kalinga in the east, due mainly to the aggressive designs of Candragupta Maurya and Aśoka.[58] The maintenance of this vast territory could be effectively achieved by a huge standing army and a very substantial bureaucracy. The army and bureaucracy in turn could function smoothly only if the ruling authority marshalled enough resources to maintain them. This was the need which prompted the arrival of a managerial state during the Maurya period. The Mauryas not merely founded a centralized state, but the imperial government participated in production and distribution of commodities, parallel to private enterprises.[59] The result was the creation of a tremendous expansion of the scope of state activities which were guided strongly by economic considerations. This would logically encourage strong, realistic and pragmatic views in the matters of statecraft. This is best exemplified by the *Kauṭilīya Arthaśāstra* which invariably champions the economic interests of the political authority.[60] Kauṭilya attaches foremost importance to material well-being, on which rests the ideals of religious practices and pleasures (*arthaiva pradhānam, arthamūlaṁ dharmakāmāviti*).[61]

The key to the Maurya policy of state control of the economy lies in the highly successful exploitation of the agrarian surplus. The Mauryas were the first political authority to have exercised control over both the Indus and the Ganga river systems which supported the major agrarian communities. The state appears to have under it extensive crown lands (*sītā*) which were brought under constant supervision of the *Sītādhyakṣa* (Director of Agriculture over crown lands).[62] Hired labourers were employed by the state to cultivate the crown land; arrangements were there to provide the cultivator with cattle and other agricultural implements.[63]

But the most important policy was the one of creation of settlements (*janapadaniveśa*) in areas where no agrarian villages existed before or there were previous settlements but now deserted *(bhūtapūrvama-bhūtapūrvaṁ vā)*.[64] Kosambi suggested that Aśoka probably carried away (*apavūḍha*) prisoners of war from Kalinga and settled them in new *janapadas*.[65] The untapped resources—particulary agricultural—of these *janapadas* had to be fully exploited and negligence to cultivate land in a newly settled area led to confiscation of the plot.[66] The *Arthaśāstra* prescribes the ruler to provide agricultural advance in the form of cash, cattle and seeds to new settlers.[67] This appears to have been a forerunner of modern agricultural loan provided by the state. The loan had to be paid back to the royal treasury, as otherwise the entire policy would be detrimental to the enrichment of the treasury (*kośopaghātaka*).[68]

The period also marks the political authority's definite interests in irrigation projects without which agriculture could hardly prosper in India. Megasthenes speaks of government officials, Agoranomoi, who looked after, among other things, sluice gates on rivers in order to ensure distribution of irrigational waters to tillers.[69] The most eloquent testimony to state initiative in irrigation is provided by the lake Sudarśana in Kathiawad. It was launched during Candragupta's reign; Aśoka not only maintained it but also 'decorated' it with conduits (*praṇālībhiralaṁkṛtam*) which definitely helped distribution of water to nearby arable areas.[70] The *Arthaśāstra*, as one expects, brings all irrigation projects (*setu*) under governmental supervision and recommends levy of irrigation cess (*udakabhāga*). The irrigation cess was not levied at a flat rate but according to the manner of procurement of water.[71] Besides this, Kauṭilya directs the *sītādhyakṣa* to install a rain-gauge (*varṣamānakuḍya*)[72] so that irrigation facilities could be provided to relatively dry and arid zones.

In the fields of craft and industry the initiative of the state is also clearly visible. The *Arthaśāstra* rightly emphasizes the role of mines and minerals over which state monopoly is claimed.[73] According to Kauṭilya, treasury emerges out of mines; and the army is born out of treasury (*ākaraprabhavaḥ kośaḥ, kośāḍḍaṇḍa prajāyate*).[74] The *Ākarādhyakṣa* along with a number of subordinate offices thoroughly supervises all the stages of mineral production, right from extraction of minerals from ores to sending them to appropriate royal factories (*karmāntas*) and finally to the sale of metals through official channels.[75] It is significant that the southernmost headquarters of the Mauryas named Suvarṇagiri was situated very near the famous Kolar gold fields. Allchin discovered traces of very old workings of gold and diamond fields in Karnataka and western Andhra Pradesh. These, according to him, could possibly go back to the days of the Mauryas.[76] Megasthenes' accounts would suggest overall supervision of all industrial activities.[77] This is to some extent confirmed by the *Arthaśāstra* which discusses about state textile factories, breweries, arms factories and state manufacturing of standardized weights and measures.[78]

The Mauryas showed lively interests in trade and commerce. The *Astynomoi* of Megasthenes maintained a strict vigilance over activities of merchants.[79] The Mauryas are said to have maintained roads by providing them with distance signals.[80] This account of Megasthenses is strikingly confirmed by the evidence of a royal road (*karapathi*) in the Laghman area in Afghanistan. Two Aramaic edicts of Aśoka from Laghman which speak of this royal road also contain information about distance of several places from Laghman.[81] In the *Arthaśāstra* scheme of things, management of commerce is assigned to the director of trade (*paṇyādhyakṣa*)[82] and director of market place (*saṁsthādhyakṣa*). The *paṇyādhyakṣa* arranges for the sale of commodities produced in royal farms and factories, and devises suitable policies to control distribution of commodities in the market.[83] The profit is fixed at 5 per cent for indigenous traders and 10 per cent for foreign merchants. Maintenance of a strict price line is considered to be one of the major functions of the *paṇyādhyakṣa*.[84] This officer is also in charge of trade abroad and is advised to send trade missions to foreign countries. The *Arthaśāstra* however categorically instructs him that he should go wherever there is profit and avoid absence of the same (*yatolābhastatogacchet, alabhāṁ parivarjayet*).[85]

The brief summary of the state-controlled economic activities may impress upon us the fact that the Mauryas were able to build up a remarkable resource base. To this should be added the revenue machinery of the Mauryas which was aimed at appropriating the surplus from almost every sphere of the economy. The *Arthaśāstra* shows that land revenue was by far the most important source of income, the usual rate being $^1/_6$ or $^1/_4$ of the produce. Besides *bhāga* (share), *bali* and *udakabhāga* were also imposed.[86] The government also levied various taxes on crafts and commerce. Moreover the *Arthaśāstra* prescribes very stringent measures for emergency financing.[87] All kinds of force and fraudulent practices are upheld by the theoretician to replenish the state treasury facing financial stringency.

The ability of the Mauryas to extract the surplus from agriculture and other spheres of the economy and the growth of a truly imperial political structure with several political centres strewn over the subcontinent, provided further impetus to urban development.

The most important urban centre was of course Pāṭaliputra, the Maurya capital. Megasthenes' accounts impress upon us the effective management of a large urban centre.[88] Apart from administrative interest in crafts and commerce in Pāṭaliputra, Megasthenes reports about official supervision over foreigners (the presence of foreigners is hardly surprising in view of the Mauryas' intimate connections with West Asian rulers) and population pattern.[89] The *Arthaśāstra* provides the first systematic theoretical discussions on urban layout. The text in question views the urban centre as a fortified site (*durga*) and differentiates between its habitational, administrative, and commercial sectors.[90] The importance of urban centres is amply borne out by the *Arthaśāstra* which not only emphasizes the revenue potentials of a city, but also includes it in the list of elements of the state.[91]

The Mauryas appear to have encouraged urban growth beyond the middle Ganga valley where urban sites had first flourished in *c.* 600 BC. Thus the Bhir Mound at Taxila reveals stone houses in the city along with a road.[92] While no defence walls are seen in the ruins of Taxila and Puṣkalāvatī (present Charsadda), these appear in Śravastī (phase II)[93] and Ahichhatra (phase II).[94] A metalled road is reported from Kauśāmbī assignable to *c.* 350 BC.[95] A definitely planned urban lay-out is evident from the excavations at Sisupalgarh in Orissa, which seems to have come into existence in *c.* 300 BC.[96] Soakage jars at Kauśāmbī and wide distribution of ring wells at various urban sites would point to betterment in civic sewage and public drainage systems.[97] A new urban site that began to make its presence felt in the doab was Mathurā. This city in the erstwhile Śūrasena *mahājanapada* was looked down upon in the *Aṅguttara Nikāya* as dusty, with uneven grounds, infested with fierce dogs and even for dearth of alms.[98] The period between 400-200 BC not only witnessed mud fortifications around the city,[99] but also a flourishing textile industry.[100] Excavations at Sonkh point to a prosperous bead industry.[101] A very interesting development is the diversity in secular house planning—square, oblong and even circular.[102] This leads us to infer about the varied tastes of builders and/or their financiers in the urban complex of Mathurā. The changing character of Mathurā can be appreciated from a passage in the *Mahābhāṣya* of Patañjali. The text recognizes the inhabitants of Mathurā as more cultured than the citizens of Saṅkāsya and Pāṭaliputra (*Saṅkāsyakebhyaśca Pāṭaliputrakebhyaśca Mathurā abhirūpatarā iti*).[103]

IV

The state-controlled economy of the Maurya period ended with the political collapse of the Maurya power (*c.* 187 BC). But the dynastic upheaval did not adversely affect the economy. A major change, however, occurred: private enterprise began to dominate the economic scene, in agriculture, crafts and commerce alike, replacing the state-managed economy of the Maurya period.

As is expected, the vast state farms under the control of the *sītādhyakṣa* gave way to smaller agricultural holdings which came mostly under private proprietorship. The early legal literature, represented by the *Manusmṛti*, the *Yājñavalkyasmṛti* and the Śāntiparvan of the *Mahābhārata* strongly uphold private ownership of land. This is clearly corroborated by epigraphic evidence of gift/sale of plots to religious groups and persons. Usabhadāta (or Ṛṣabhadatta), son-in-law of the Western Kṣatrapa ruler Nahapāna, had to purchase a plot of land from a Brāhmaṇa owner and then donated it to the Buddhist *saṁgha.*[104] The incident leaves unmistakable evidence of private ownership in land and double transfer of a particular plot, first by sale and then by gift. The Mauryas seem to have carried to trans-Vindhyan India the pattern of agriculture, based on iron ploughshare and irrigation. Several new crops appear on the scene, along with the traditional ones. These include two major cash crops, coconut (grown for the first time in northern Konkan)[105] and pepper[106] (in the Malabar coast). Excavations at different sites indicate cultivation of wheat, rice, barley, millet and lentils. That the riparian tracts between the Godavari and Krishna became particularly prosperous for rice cultivation is borne out by the name Dhānyakaṭaka (literally, rice bowl).

Considerable attention was paid to irrigation. Political authorities were probably more interested in launching and maintaining supra-local irrigation projects than having overall control over all hydraulic projects. The most famous example in this regard is undoubtedly the repair and renovation of the Sudarśana lake by Rudradāman I.[107] This is closely matched by Coḷa Karikāla's attempts to prevent the Kāverī delta, the core area of the Coḷas, from flooding.[108] One of the most remarkable feats of hydraulic engineering is seen in the large brick-built storage tank unearthed from the excavation at Sringaverapura near Kauśāmbī. This tank had two chambers of varying depth and was connected with the Ganga by a brick-built channel. Water from the Ganga was allowed to enter the deeper chamber first where sediments were deposited and then the cleaner water passed into the second chamber from the first through an interconnecting channel.[109] That hydraulic techniques had considerably improved in the early centuries of the Christian era will be evident from the epigraphic reference to hydraulic mechanics (*odayantrikas*)[110] and reference to water wheel with pot garland (*rahaṭṭa ghadiyas*) in the *Gāthāsaptaśatī.*[111]

The most remarkable feature of economic life was, however, proliferation of crafts and expanding trade. The period under review yields for the first time epigraphic evidence of a large number of craftsmen who left their names, traces of their occupation and religious leanings in the course of making donations to various religious groups and persons. Such records are particularly available from western Deccan caves, Buddhist sites of Bharhut and Sanchi and from Mathurā.[112] Sifting through the epigraphic evidence one comes across carpenters (*vaḍḍhakī*), bamboo-workers (*vasakāra*), reed-makers (*konācika*), braziers (*kāsakāra*), potters (*kulārika*), weavers (*kaulika*), perfumers (*gaṁdhika*), clothmakers (*prāvarika*), oilmen (*tilapiṣaka*), garland-makers (*mālākāra*), jewellers (*maṇikāra*), ivory workers (*dantakāra*), goldsmiths (*suvarṇakāra*), blacksmiths (*lohikakāruka*). The list includes products of daily necessities and also luxury items. Most of the latter were urban crafts. Many of these crafts and artisans are also mentioned in Jātaka stories which are assigned by modern scholars to the early centuries of the Christian era.[113] One of the foremost industries must have been textile; textile products flourished particularly in the Deccan obviously because of the facilities of cotton plantation in the black soil there. The *Periplus of the Erythraean Sea* (assignable to late first century AD) speaks of two active textile centres in central Deccan, namely Tagara (Ter) and Paithan (Pratiṣthāna, the Sātavāhana capital).[114] Excavations at Ter have yielded a number of vats for dyeing cloth[115] which seems to confirm the evidence of the *Periplus*. Similar dyeing vats are also reported from the excavations at Arikamedu (near Pondicherry).[116] One of the most famous textile products, viz., muslin, is repeatedly mentioned in the Classical accounts, and the *Periplus* considers muslin of the Gange country (in lower deltaic Bengal) as the best and costliest type.[117]

Crafts production, like production in agrarian economy, is characterized in this phase by lessening control of the state and growing private enterprise. There was perhaps one sector in industrial production where the state authority seems to have retained its interests: it was mining industry. Legal literature of this period advocates royal monopoly over all mines and minerals. Epigraphic and literary materials, when studied along with the *Geographike Huphegesis* of Claudius Ptolemy (*c.* AD 150), may indicate that the Kuṣāṇas took initiative to work out diamond mines in eastern Malwa (variously called Daśārṇa, Ākara, Purva Malava and Cosa).[118] These diamond mines later seem to have been controlled by Rudradāman I (AD 150).[119] The *Periplus* (also Ptolemy's *Geography*) mentions pearl fisheries in the Pāṇḍya kingdom of far south India.[120] These fisheries in the Kolchic Gulf (probably the Gulf of Mannar) were located at Kolchi (present day Korkai, dt. Tirunelveli, Tamil Nadu) and were under the monopoly control of the local Pāṇḍya rulers. The *Periplus* narrates that captives of war, awarded capital punishment, were used here as deep-sea divers. While the procurement area was in Kolchi, pearls were distributed under government control only from Argarus (Uragapura of the Saṅgam literature and present-day Uraiyur in dt. Tiruchirappalli, Tamil Nadu).[121] Recent excavations at Korkai have brought to light remains of pearl oysters from various levels,[122] confirming thereby the description in the *Periplus*. Mining operations in early India also included salt manufacture. While theoretical treatises would advocate salt manufacture under royal control, epigraphic evidence, however, suggests prevalence of private enterprise in salt-making against the payment of a salt tax to the state. This is proved in a round-about way by epigraphic references to remissions from salt tax (*aloṇakhātakam*, i.e. *alavaṇakhādakam*) known from the Sātavāhana records of the early centuries of the Christian era.[123] The *Naturalis Historia* of Pliny (dedicated to Titus, the son of Vespasian in AD 77) contains a significant passage in this connexion: referring to the practice of salt quarrying in Mt. Oromenus (Salt Range in Pakistan), the author says that political authorities derived greater revenue from salt mines than from even those of gold and pearls.[124] The importance of salt manufacture has been rightly assessed from the point of its revenue yielding potentials. We have stated at the outset that there was a lesser degree of state control on craft and industry than that prevalent under the managerial state of the Mauryas. Political authorities, however, appear to have been interested in deriving levies out of industries and crafts mainly run by private enterprise. This is clearly illustrated by the imposition of levies on craftsmen (*kārukara*) in the Sātavāhana territory.[125] In view of the steady growth of crafts and industries in the western and central Deccan during the period in question, the attempt of the Sātavahana rulers at realizing revenue out of them sounds quite logical.

One of the salient features in industrial life was the growing importance of guilds (mostly called *śreṇīs*). Almost every industrial activity and major profession were organized under their respective guilds. Large number of epigraphic documents from western, eastern and central Deccan, central India and Mathurā leave little room for doubt about their economic importance which is also clearly recognized in diverse literary sources, e.g. the Jātakas, Avadānas, *Milindapañho*, *Manusmṛti*, *Yājñavalkyasmṛti*, *Mahābhārata*.[126] The legal literature throws valuable light on the cooperative character of these organizations and also on the guild laws. While early Buddhist literature knew of the members of a guild and their president/leader (*jeṭṭhaka*, *pamukha*, etc.), legal literature of this period adds to it the executive officers (*kāryacintakas*),[127] indicating thereby growing complexities and expanding functions of guilds.

An eloquent testimony to the expanding scope of activities of guilds is seen in the new function of guilds as banks. Inscriptions from western, central and eastern Deccan and Mathurā record a number of cases where guilds accepted permanent deposits of money (*akṣayanīvi*) on condition that the principal would be kept intact and only the interest would be utilized (*vṛddhibhojyam*).[128] The guild thereby provided the vital capital to expanding craft activities. These guilds also played a vital role in contemporary trade network to which we shall come later.

This proliferation of crafts was equally matched by a trade boom from the first century BC onwards. The vast subcontinent provided a market large enough for consumption of growing agricultural and industrial commodities. But the most significant aspect of commercial activities of this period is the brisk participation of India in long distance international exchange network—both overland and maritime—particularly with the Roman empire.[129] The Roman empire had definite interests in commerce with the East which at the outset took the form of trade links with China. There was a great craze for Chinese silk in Roman market which was supplied with that commodity and other items along the famous overland Silk Road. However, the presence of the Parthians or Arcacids (An-hsi of early Chinese texts) of Iran as an unavoidable commercial and political intermediary between China in the east and Rome in the west created considerable obstacles for the free flow of merchandise. There was a need for an alternative and less extortionate intermediary. This need was fulfilled by the foundation of the Central Asiatic empire of the Kuṣāṇas who extended their rule over vast territories of north India including the Indus delta and Kathiawad peninsula (first century AD).[130]

To this period is also assigned the discovery of south-western monsoon winds and its increasing utilization in high sea trade between India and Rome via the Red Sea.[131]

The *Periplus* (section 64) describes how Chinese silk trade was diverted through Bactria to Kabul area and from there to Peshwar-Rawalpindi area, and thence to Mathurā in the Ganga-Jamuna doab.[132] From Mathurā merchandise was brought to Barygaza, the most important port on western seaboard of India,[133] via Sanchi and Ujjayini.

The silk was shipped to Rome from Barygaza. The *Periplus*, Ptolemy's *Geography*, Pliny's *Natural History*, Strabo's *Geography*—all unequivocally refer to the very prosperous and brisk Indo-Roman trade. Pliny discusses the gradual development of the sea routes in four stages, the latest and most developed phase of which brought a ship from a Red Sea port to Muziris (Cannanore) in the Cera country, the most important port in Malabar, within forty days.[134] Strabo noted (in *c.* 19 BC) that previously only four or five ships undertook voyages to India; but during the reign of Augustus no less than 120 ships sailed to Indian ports annually from Alexandria.[135]

The two seaboards of India, particularly the western seaboard, were dotted with a number of ports and harbours. The outstanding ports were Barygaza, Muziris[136] on the west coast and Khaberos and Poduca on the east coast.[137] Some ports have been termed *emporion* by Ptolemy. The term '*emporion*' is used by Ptolemy in a very restricted sense. It seems to have denoted 'an oriental market town lying in or near the seacoast and beyond the imperial frontiers of Rome. In such emporia permanent lodges of western traders were established definitely under formal agreements with appropriate Indian rulers.'[138] Regular settlements of foreign merchants possibly grew up at Muziris (where a temple of Augustus was erected according to the *Tabula Peutengariana*[139]), and at Poduca (as is evident from the excavations at Arikamedu), an Indo-Roman trading station near Pondicherry. All major political powers of the subcontinent, namely the Kuṣāṇas, Śakas, Sātavāhanas, Coḷas, Ceras and Pāṇḍyas are found to have actively encouraged long-range trade in or through their respective territories.[140]

Several trade missions between the Roman emperor and Indian powers have been well-known to students of Indo-Roman trade, thanks to Warmington's researches.[141]

The most eloquent testimony of this trade is supplied by the presence of a considerable number of Roman coins in several hoards in India.[142] Most of such coins are found from south India, indicating that the area had closest commercial links with Rome. Roman coins were mostly used as bullion in India. The impact of trade on the currency system appears to have been considerable. Monetization was fairly extensive. Major powers like the Kuṣāṇas and Sātavāhanas expectedly had their impressive coinage;[143] but even non-monarchical clans also minted their own coins.[144] Another significant aspect of coinage was the availability of a large number of copper coinage (along with gold and silver coinage). As copper coins were generally utilized for daily transactions as against gold and silver coins, mainly used for international transactions in valuables, there was an impact of monetization even on the daily life of the common people.

Under such circumstances it is hardly surprising to find merchants enjoying considerable eminence. Available literary and epigraphic materials are replete with names and activities of wealthy merchants (*seṭṭhis*, *gahapatis*, *rājaśreṣṭhīs*[145] or royal merchants). The merchants are often found to have been organized under commercial guilds (e.g. *vaṇiggrāma* in a Karle inscription).[146] These occupational and commercial guilds are known to have maintained close links with religious establishments.[147] Himanshu P. Ray has effectively demonstrated the role played by the monastery and guild in the Sātavāhana territory in the expansion of commerce. The linkage patterns among mercantile guilds, Buddhist *saṁgha* and rulers have also been highlighted. Ray views monasteries of western Deccan 'as pioneers and as centres providing information on cropping patterns, distant markets, organization of village settlements and trade. They also helped established channels of communication in newly-colonized regions and those channels could then be used by the state to enforce its authority.'[148]

The above survey of the economic condition of the period from *c.* second century BC to third century AD gives an impression that there was all-round development in agriculture, trade and crafts. The development was not confined to the Ganga valley or north India, but spread more or less over the entire subcontinent though with varying patterns. The political scene also speaks of expansion of monarchical system over greater parts of the subcontinent. The rise of large empires under the Kuṣaṇas and the Sātavāhanas provided the required political structure without which economy could hardly prosper.

The economic and political climate seems to have paved the way for brisker rate of urban growth which reached its peak between the second century BC and third century AD. While urban centres in previous periods were mainly confined to northern Indian plains, they became in this period an all-India phenomenon. It will be quite impossible to do justice to the emergence and growth of urban centres all over the country within the relatively short space of this paper. Hence only some salient features may be highlighted here.

In Taxila, one of the foremost urban sites of the north-west, the excavations at Sirkap shows considerable growth from its previous stage represented by the materials in the Bhir mound. Founded by the Indo-Greeks, Taxila (Sirkap) was extended and fortified by masonry wall by Indo-Parthian rulers. It was a fully planned city, with spinal streets spreading from the north gate to the entire length of the city. The main street was interlinked with smaller lanes and streets spreading from the north gate to the entire length of the city. The main street was interlinked with smaller lanes and streets which met at right angles. Residential houses were laid out in a well-defined manner. Such planned urban centres are a novelty in the general Indian scene and the influence of foreigners is quite unmistakable.[149] A. Ghosh aptly remarked, 'foreign in origin and conception, Sirkap is not a representative Indian city'.[150] In Ahicchatra a concrete road was found from a layer assignable to about 200 AD.[151] In north-eastern Bihar, Vaiśālī, the stronghold of the Licchavis witnessed three successive fortifications between the second century BC and second century AD.[152] The Orissan urban complex at Sisupalgarh which has already figured in our discussion in a previous section underwent a process of elaboration. A massive mud rampart was raised in the phase ranging from 200-100 BC and this was later reinforced by brick revetments. The most impressive feature was, however, a magnificent gateway complex.[153] A remarkable growth is seen at Mathurā which came under Scytho-Parthian first and Kuṣāṇa rule later. As both the powers had strong links with and orientations to north-western borderland of the subcontinent, Mathurā became, as it were, a part of the north-west. Archaeological materials unearthed from levels 23 and 24 at Sonkh (assignable to the Kṣatrapa age) reveal that houses were irregularly placed and streets looked crooked in comparison to earlier periods. B.N. Mukherjee draws our attention to 'the use of stone in the projected sections of buildings at street corners, probably to ensure protection against damages by vehicles'.[154] This is rightly interpreted as a sign of increase in the volume of traffic and consequently that of merchandise and traders. This was followed by the seven levels of Kuṣāṇa occupation at Sonkh.

The ground plan of level 16 shows the most systematic and developed phase of urban layout.[155] Residential houses were built not only of mud bricks but also burnt bricks. Fortifications at Mathurā were revived, enlarged, and repaired. An inner mud enclosure or fortification of smaller size was raised, which seems to have provided security to the administrative headquarters.[156] One may remember that Mathurā emerged as one of the political centres of the Kuṣāṇa empire.[157] The city of Mathurā, which was an object of scorn and hatred in the *Aṅguttaranikāya*, a Buddhist source of *c.* fourth century BC, is eulogized in the *Lalitavistara*, another Buddhist text of *c.* third century AD as prosperous, large, beneficial, with easy availability of alms and abounding in population (*iyaṁ Mathurā nagarī ṛddhā ca sphītā ca kṣemā ca subhikṣā cākīrṇā bahujanamanuṣya ca*).[158]

Several urban sites are reported from the western and central Deccan of which Nevasa,[159] Ter and Satanikota[160] are of outstanding importance. A few words may be said here about Satanikota. This fortified site in the Kurnool district is situated on the right bank of the Tungabhadra. The site has been assigned to a period ranging from first century BC to third century AD. The urban centre was protected not only by a rampart wall constructed of Cuddapah slabs, but also by a moat all round it. It has a facing of burnt brick and the southern part of the site is dominated by an elaborate gateway complex. A flourishing bead industry seems to have existed there. The spurt of urban centres in the Sātavāhana territory is well reflected in epigraphic records which name towns and refer to *nagara* (urban centres) and *nigma* (market centres). The eastern Deccan which from the time of Gautamīputra Sātakarṇi became an integral part of the Sātavāhana empire also came under the impact of growing urbanism. Several excavated sites like Amaravati, Bhottiprolu, Salihundam, Nagarjunakonda, all situated in the Krishna delta, show urban dimensions and Buddhist association.[161] This area figures prominently under the name Maisolos/Masalia in the *Periplus*[162] and Ptolemy's *Geography*.[163]

The combined testimony of the Classical accounts, archaeological materials, epigraphic and numismatic evidence proves beyond doubt the existence of a flourishing economy. The proximity of the area to the eastern seaboard with a few important ports (for example Kontakossylla, Allosygne emporia)[164] dotting the coast, further enhanced the importance of the zone. The site of Dhānyakaṭaka (lit. rice bowl) served as an inland port town, up to which the Krishna was navigable. Excavations have revealed the existence of a navigational channel connected with the river. The prosperous commercial economy is well attested to by epigraphic evidence of merchant guilds.[165] One of the most impressive sites is Nagarjunakonda which was naturally fortified by surrounding hills on three sides. A fortified area within the site is identified with royal residence. Nagarjunakonda incidentally was the capital of Ikṣvākus who ruled from *c.* AD 225 to 330.[166]

All residential structures were situated outside the fortified area and concentrated in the eastern part. Broad roads, cross-roads and bylanes do underline the impressive layout of the city. The site also contained religious structures of Buddhist and Brahmanical people. One of the most important urban structures was the amphitheatre with tiered gallery accommodating no less than 1,000 spectators.[167]

The far south, dominated by the Coḷas (in the Kaveri delta), the Pāṇḍyas (near Madurai) and the Ceras (in Kerala), also came within the scope of urbanization. The Saṅgam poems, the earliest Tamil literature, contain graphic, but often stereotyped, accounts of towns and cities.[168]

Excavations at several sites have recently revealed growth of urban centres, though the material remains do not often tally with the flourishing condition of cities described in early Tamil literature.[169] One of the most significant centres was Kāverīpaṭṭinam (Khaberos emporium of the Classical authors) which was the Coḷa capital. The Saṅgam texts and the two epics, the *Maṇimekalai*[170] and the *Śilappādikāram*[171] eloquently describe the city. Archaeological remains would confirm the existence of the site from *c.* third century BC to fifth century AD. A brick structure identified with a wharf suggests its importance as a port. Several public tanks/baths, frequently described in literary accounts, may be seen in the remains of semi-circular brick structures with water reservoir and an inlet channel connected with the Kaveri.[172] The well known site of Arikamedu, often identified with Poduca emporion of Ptolemy seems to have been occupied from the first to third century AD. Its distinctive features as a trading station is evident not only by its closeness to the sea but also by the remains of a large warehouse. The presence of Graeco-Roman merchants at this site is inferred from typically Graeco-Roman intaglio designs on two gems, a red-glazed ware and Roman lamps and glass wares.[173]

The foregoing discussions may highlight the fact that the most distinctive feature of the material milieu of early historical India is the process of urbanization. This second urbanization had its primary manifestation in the middle Ganga valley, but it gradually assumed a pan-Indian character. The spread of urbanism from north Indian plains to the Deccan and far south went through two corridors, one in the western Deccan and the other through the forests of central India across the Andhra coast towards the Tamil country. It would be extremely difficult to discern the single dominant factor in the process of second urbanization. Despite the multiplicity of and controversies about the definition of an urban centre, there may be some consensus in the view that a city is essentially populated with a non-agricultural community which depends for its livelihood on crafts, trade, various services and administrative functions. It is not therefore surprising that many authorities would ascribe greater importance to growth of trade and commerce and rise of administrative centres as contributing factors to urbanization. But it may be rightly argued that the non-food producing community of an urban centre cannot survive without an agricultural surplus which was grown in its rural hinterland. The extraction of the surplus from agriculture was no less important than its production; the gradual consolidation of a power structure could demand and realize the collection of surplus through a regular machinery. It was not merely an historical accident that led to the first appearance of cities in early historical India in the middle Ganga valley in *c.* 600 BC. That area in question had the potential to produce the surplus and to generate and sustain forces conducive to urban growth.

The same area also showed a definite inclination towards the formation of state power in place of lineage-based polities. A strong agrarian base which was ably exploited by an increasingly crystallized power structure appears to have provided the foundation of the emergence of cities in early historical period. Though proliferating crafts and the steadily developing trade (particularly foreign trade) were responsible for lending maturity to the urban process, these are to be assigned a position secondary to the agrarian growth.

This pattern is first seen in north Indian plains though not necessarily confined to it. The Deccan witnessed urban growth subsequent to that in the north. Whether it was the western Deccan or eastern Deccan, urban growth there is primarily linked with agrarian expansion. This point has been demonstrated by Himanshu P. Ray[174] and more emphatically by H. Sarkar.[175] Sarkar argues very forcefully that archaeological and literary evidence of urban development in Andhradeśa highlights that most cities were agrarian ones, i.e. 'the market for selling and exchanging agricultural products', and they 'far outnumber other types'.[176] He is aware of the presence of a number of flourishing centres of trade on the Andhra coast, but maintains that most 'early cities of Andhradeśa depended heavily on plant and animal products'[177] and assigns to industry a rather secondary position as a factor behind urban growth in the area concerned. Like the Ganga valley, the Godavari valley was very much suited to rice cultivation and it is precisely in this area where most urban centres sprang up.

It is quite clear that the agrarian potential could not best be exploited in the Deccan before the emergence of a consolidated political authority. While the interrelation between urban growth and state formation in north India is more or less accepted, the picture is hardly clear in the Deccan. It is quite evident that the rise of the Sātavāhanas as the first imperial power of the Deccan played a crucial role in urbanization thereof. But the passage from pre-state polity to the emergence of the Sātavāhana monarchy is not as yet clearly understood. B.D. Chattopadhyaya makes an interesting attempt to identify the process 'of the emergence of what we may call localities'.[178] These localities may correspond, in the absence of a suitable term in the context of the

Deccan, to north Indian *janapadas*. Chattopadhyaya suggests that 'the transition from the phase of uninscribed coins to that of inscribed of local rulers' may indicate the 'political profile' of 'emergent localities across the Deccan'.[179] The process reached its culmination obviously in the pan-Deccan empire of the Sātavāhanas in subsequent times.

The crystallization of a state-society in the Deccan seems to have facilitated demanding and then realizing the surplus from the agrarian sector, which in turn led to the emergence of cities in trans-Vindhyan India.

It would be unfair if all cities of early historical times were put into one straightjacket of agro-cities. The coastal towns, especially of far south, could hardly have grown to such great proportions but for the impact of Indo-Roman trade. In the plains of north India the city of Mathurā presents an interesting departure from the general pattern. Mathurā is not known to have been situated in an area famous for its fertility and neither capable of raising an agricultural surplus. The *Āvaśyakacūrṇī* and *Bṛhatkalpabhāṣya* explicitly state that Mathurā's prosperity depended not on agriculture but on trade.[180] Moreover, this trade at Mathurā was hardly based on terminal trade, because Mathurā could really boast of only one commodity of her own, i.e. its textile products. Mathurā appears to have thrived on transit trade. It prospered because of the growth of Indo-Roman trade and also because it emerged as a nodal point where several important overland routes converged.

Urbanization as a social and cultural process manifests the tendencies of the transformation of a simpler society into a more complex one. This was more or less valid in the case of second urbanization also. The population in an urban centre was not only more dense than in a rural settlement, but was heterogenous too. As early historical India witnessed arrival of a large number of foreigners in the wake of migration, invasion and trade, the urban society was bound to be heterogenous. Culturally speaking, the arrival of new people and their admixture with local populace would lead to acculturation and synthesis. As barriers of thoughts would be lowered down in such a situation, new forms of cultural expression would assert themselves.[181] The urban centre, being by nature more open to the intermixing of peoples and ideas of varied types, would be the ideal theatre for the interplay of diverse cultural elements. This would automatically encourage freshness of thought and a spirit of enquiry and along with that a protest against earlier orthodoxy. One cannot possibly miss the fact that the early historical period marked not only the emergence and growth of cities, but is also considered as one of the most creative ages in Indian history.[182] Apart from the voluminous creative literature, this age produced medical treatises like the *Caraka-saṁhitā*, the *Suśruta-saṁhitā*, astrological treatises like the *Romakasiddhanta* and the *Yavanajātaka* of Sphujidhvaja, the vast legal literature (Dharmaśāstras) and the great treatise on pōlity, the *Kauṭilīya Arthaśāstra*.[183]

The spirit of enquiry and freedom of thought must be seen in the social background where patrons of religious and cultural movements rarely referred to their *varṇa* affiliations but indicated their occupational standings.[184] A marriage between a jeweller and ironmonger was hardly frowned upon,[185] though it violated the orthodox Brahmanical norm. How open the society was can best be appreciated from the fact that a courtesan could offer a donation to a Jaina religious organization without renouncing her profession or suppressing her mother's profession which was the same.[186] The growth of urbanism, expansion of trade, and increasing monetization seem to have relegated the importance of birth as a determinant of social status. The *Aṅgavijjā* refers no less than four times, and in at least four different ways, to existing social groups. First it enumerates the traditional four *varṇas*. Then it speaks of social status being determined by birth as well as occupation (e.g. a bamhana-vessa, i.e. brāhmaṇa by birth and vaiśya by profession). In the third place the society is said to have been divided into two: *ayya* (*ārya*) or nobles and *milikkhu* (*mlecchas*) impure. The last description divides the society into two: *ayya* (*ārya*) or free men and *pessa* or servile community. The text categorically states that the sudda could also belong to *ayya* group.[187] This indicates that (1) society was divided into broad classes: freemen and slaves, and (2) social position was not determined by birth alone but also by the occupation of the person concerned. In other words it implies that a *śūdra* could raise himself to the status of an *ārya* by improving his economic condition, despite his 'low' birth. The impact of wealth appears to have put the age-old, traditional, orthodox, Brahmanical social norms to severe strain. Thus to Caraka the motivating factors behind all human actions were 'desire for life, desire for riches and desire for future life'. He further adds that the physician's wealth was not only made of the goodwill generated by the relief given by him to his patients, but also by material wealth and patronage secured by him from kings (*īśvarāḥ*) and wealthy persons (*vasumantāḥ*).[188] Only the latter factors could provide him with an easy and comfortable life. The epitome of the changed attitude and lifestyle was best expressed in the urban milieu. That is why the *Kāmasūtra* has the *nāgarka* (citybred man) at the centre of the lifestyle it advocates.[189] One may also recall the famous passage of Kālidāsa that nobody should take a gem to a village for assessment when a city (*pattana*) is available.[190]

But this, however, is only one version of the story. The orthodox Brahmanical view could hardly tolerate the relatively open attitude of cities. The city became, as it were, almost a by-word of aversion and contempt to *śāstrakaras*. As early as the days of the *Gautama Dharamasūtra* the city is damned because of perpetual *an-andhyāya* (non-recital of Vedas).[191] The injunction continues in the *Manusmṛti*[192] and *Vasiṣṭha Dharmaśāstra*.[193] A kind of ruralism permeates the attitude of law-givers who looked askance at cities. Sociologists opine that a high degree of tension generally exists between the urban and provincial lives. It is true that these two elements are interdependent but are separated by a gulf of mistrust, suspicion and contempt. Yet, there was a remarkable penchant for urbanism in early historical India which seems to have echoed a German maxim '*stadtluft macht frei*' (the city air makes you free).

NOTES

1. D.D. Kosambi, *An Introduction to the Study of Indian History*, Bombay, 1956, p. 1.
2. H.C. Raychaudhuri, *Political History of Ancient India, with a Commentary by B.N. Mukherjee*, New Delhi, 1996 (8th edn.), pp. 166-9.
3. Bridget Allchin and Raymond Allchin, *The Rise of Civilization in India and Pakistan*, Cambridge, 1982.
4. Harappan cities mark the first stage of urbanization followed by the one in the Ganga valley after about a millennium, the latter being known as the 'second urbanization' in India.
5. A. Ghosh, *The City in Early Historical India*, Shimla, 1973.
6. Fernand Braudel, *The Structures of Everyday Life*, London, 1985, p. 479.
7. V. Gordon Childe, 'The Urban Revolution', *The Town Planning Review*, vol. XXI, 1950, pp. 3-17. Childe's formulations were based on the evidence of the emergence of first cities in the ancient Near East, Mesopotamia and Indian subcontinent. Several modern sociologists and urban historians have questioned his formulations. Gideon Sjoberg, *The Pre-industrial City of Past and Present*, Glencoe, Ill, 1960; Lewis Mumford, *The City in History, Its Origins, Its Transformations and Its Prospects*, London, 1961.
8. It is extremely difficult to pass any final judgement about the nature of authority in the Harappan civilization, as no written material can be used for this purpose. There is however, considerable evidence to show that priests did play an important role in the management of affairs in Egyptian and

Mesopotamian civilizations, the two near contemporaries of Harappan civilization. According to Childe, 'magic and religion constituted the scaffolding needed to support the rising structure of social organization and of science. Unhappily the scaffolding repeatedly cramped the execution of the design and impeded the progress of the permanent building. . . . The principal beneficiaries from the achievements of farmers and artisans were priests and kings. Magic rather than science was thereby enthroned and invested with the authority of the temporal power.' V. Gordon Childe, *Man Makes Himself*, Harmondsworth, 1965, p. 236.

9. Childe, *Man Makes Himself*, p. 236.
10. Debiprasad Chattopadhyaya, ed., *History of Science and Technology in Ancient India*, vol. I, Calcutta, 1986, pp. 336ff.
11. Chattopadhyaya, ed., *History of Science and Technology*, vol. I, p. 350.
12. There is some controversy regarding the beginning of the use of iron in ancient India. Though the term *ayas*, often taken in the sense of iron, figures in the *Ṛgveda*, it is difficult to prove the existence of iron tools, on the basis of archaeological findings, prior to BC 1000 considers the beginning of iron as early as BC 1000 which became more frequent around BC 800. Excavations at Noh and Jodhpura (Rajasthan), at Bhagawanpura and Dadheri (Haryana), at Atranjikhera, Lal Qila, Jakhera (UP) yielded Painted Grey Wares and 'fairly commonly' iron during the period of BC 900-500. N.R. Banerjee, *The Iron Age in India*, New Delhi, 1965. See Allchin and Allchin, *Rise of Civilization*, p. 318.
13. The *Aitareya Brāhmaṇa*, one of the major texts of the later Vedic times, shows that the vaiśya could be evicted at will (*yathā-kāma utthāpya*), oppressed by others at will (*yathā-kāma preṣya*—VIII.29.4) and the śūdra could even be put to death at will (*yathā-kāma vadhya*).
14. For a general description of these royal sacrifices, U.N. Ghoshal, *A History of Indian Political Ideas*, Bombay, 1966; Raychaudhuri, *Political History*, pp. 145-54.
15. Earliest iron artefacts, more or less coeval with PGW, mainly comprise spearheads, arrowheads, hooks, etc. These were mainly meant for warfare—both offensive and defensive purposes. The use of furnaces and hearths provided with bellows is reported from the excavation at Suneri (Jhunjhunu dt., Rajasthan). R.S. Sharma, *Material Culture and Social Formation in Ancient India*, New Delhi, 1983, p. 59; For iron artefacts unearthed from Atranjikhera, R.C. Gaur, *Excavations at Atranjikhera*, New Delhi, 1983.
16. *KAS*, VI.1. The seven limbs (*aṅgas*) or elements (*prakṛtis*) of the state are enumerated as follows: (1) svāmī (king/head of the state), (2) *amātya* (bureaucracy, including ministers), (3) *janapada* (populated territory), (4) durga (fortified towns including the capital city), (5) *kośa* (treasury), (6) *bala/daṇḍa* (standing army), and (7) *mitra* (ally). The limbs are enumerated according to their graded importance in the body politic.
17. The term *janapada* literally means 'feet of the tribe'. Actually it denotes a

territorial state as distinct from a lineage-based polity. The *Aṅguttaranikāya* (IV. 252, 256, 260) enlists sixteen such territorial states (*mahājanapadas*): (1) Kāśi (modern Varanasi), (2) Kośala (Lucknow-Gonda-Faizabad area), (3) Aṅga (Bhagalpur region, eastern Bihar), (4) Magadha (Patna-Gaya region, southern Bihar), (5) Vajji/Vṛji (area around Vaisali, north Bihar), (6) Malla (ancient capital Pava in northern UP), (7) Cedī (eastern part of modern Bundelkhand, ancient capital Suktīmatī), (8) Vatsa (area around Allahabad in UP), (9) Kuru (near modern Delhi), (10) Pañcāla (Rohilakhand and central Doab), (11) Matsya (near Jaipur, Rajasthan), (12) Śūrasena (area around Mathurā in UP), (13) Assaka/Aśmaka (on the banks of the river Godavari), (14) Avantī (area around Ujjayini, MP), (15) Gandhāra (Taxila-Peshawar, Rawalpindi area, Pakistan) and (16) Kamboja (Hazara dt., Pakistan).

18. B. Subbarao, *The Personality of India*, Baroda, 1958, pp. 85-106.
19. The *Aitareya Brāhmaṇa* (VIII. 14) was aware of no less than five principal regions, east, west, north, south and the central quarters. The central quarter, called *Dhruvā-madhyamāpratiṣṭhādiś* (from which later emerged the more common term '*Madhyadeśa*') was situated in the upper Ganga valley and considered as the land par excellence. This clearly indicates an increasing awareness of the geographical horizon of the Vedic people whose principal habitat had definitely shifted from their erstwhile settlement in the land watered by the river Indus, the Sarasvatī and the tributaries of the Indus (i.e. the area known as *Saptasindhava* in the *Ṛgveda*).
20. The *Ṛgveda* contains more references to cattle rearing and cattle wealth than to agriculture. The term '*go*' literally meaning cow or cattle stands for wealth (*rayi*) and a wealthy man is called *gomat* (lit. possessing cattle wealth) in the *Ṛgveda*. Even the term for war in the *Ṛgveda* is '*gaviṣṭi*' (literally meaning desire for cattle). There are, of course, some references to agriculture, but most of these are found in the interpolated sections of the text (e.g. Maṇḍala X of the *Ṛgveda*). The *Ṛgveda* at best speaks of the process of transition from pastoralism to sedentary agriculture. R.S. Sharma, *Perspectives in the Social and Economic History of Early India*, New Delhi, 1983, pp. 110-14; Ranabir Chakravarti, *Warfare for Wealth: Early Indian Perspective*, Calcutta, 1986, pp. 7-25.
21. Iron tools like axes and adzes seem to have been used for tree-felling. Deforestation could also have been possible by burning the dense forest in the Ganga valley. The story of Videgha Māṭhava in the *Śatapatha Brāhmaṇa* (I.4.1.14-17) may indicate such a process. Māṭhava undertook a journey from the banks of the Sarasvatī in the west to that of the Sadānīrā in the east (i.e. in Mithilā or Videha region in north Bihar) with the sacred fire in his hand. The account probably symbolizes Brahmanical expansion from the upper to the middle Ganga valley after having cleared the dense forest in the Ganga valley by burning.
22. The term for rice is *vrīhi* which is not found in the *Ṛgveda* in this sense.

23. Sharma, *Perspectives*, p. 122.
24. Trevor Ling, *The Buddha*, Harmondsworth, 1980, pp. 42-3.
25. Allchin and Allchin, *The Rise of Civilization*, pp. 319-20, 323-4.
26. Allchin and Allchin, *The Rise of Civilization.*
27. It is not unlikely that due to this heavier and thicker alluvial soil in the middle Ganga valley, four, six, eight, sixteen and sometimes even twenty-four oxen were attached to the plough. See *Maitrāyaṇī, Kaṭhāka Saṁhitas* and *Pañcaviṁśa Brāhmaṇa.*
28. Sharma, *Material Culture*, p. 95, p. 112n. Pāṇini knew iron ploughshares as *ayovikāra kusī* (IV.1.42). The *Suttanipāta* calls it *phāla* (*Kokālika Sutta*) while a later Pāli synonym for the same was *ayonāṅgala*. T.W. Rhys Davids and Wiliam Stede, *Pali English Dictionary*, London, 1921.
29. The term '*gahapati*' (Skt. *Gṛhapati*) not only meant an agriculturist householder, but in later times was also used as a status symbol in association with a very rich person, often a merchant. N. Wagle, *Society at the Time of the Buddha*, Bombay, 1966.
30. Sharma, *Perspectives*, p. 123.
31. Sharma, *Perspectives*, p. 123.
32. V. Fausboll, ed., *The Jātakas*, in 6 vols., London, 1877-97; Jātaka, no. 523.
33. A large number of crafts are mentioned in the description of Puruṣamedha sacrifice in the *Yajurveda*.
34. V.S. Agrawala, *India as Known to Pāṇini*, Lucknow, 1953.
35. *Gautama Dharmasūtra* XI. 21.
36. Agrawala, *Pāṇini.*
37. Agrawala, *Pāṇini: aśva-vaṇija, go-vaṇija, Madra-vaṇija, Kāśmīra-vaṇija* and *Gandharī-vaṇija.*
38. Punch-marked coins which are the archaeologically earliest metallic medium of exchange in India are found over greater parts of the sub-continent. Early punch-marked coins are, however, found from the middle Ganga valley which emerged as the most important region in the subcontinent during the period from the sixth century BC to the second century BC. See, P.L. Gupta, 'A Bibliography of Punchmarked Coins of Ancient India', *JNSI*, vol. XVII, 1955, pp. 1-23.
39. Chakravarti, *Warfare for Wealth*, pp. 26-76.
40. *Mahāvagga*, X, 2, 3.
41. *Suttanipāta, Pavajjasutta.*
42. According to Buddhist tradition Bimbisāra had under him no less than 80,000 villages and their respective headmen (*grāmikas*). Raychaudhuri, *Political History*, p. 208.
43. The doubt about the actuality of the literary descriptions of early historical towns has rightly been raised by A. Ghosh, *The City.*
44. Ghosh, *The City*, p. 60.
45. G.R. Sharma, *Excavations at Kauśāmbī, 1949-50*, Delhi, 1969.
46. Ghosh, *The City*, p. 11.

47. *IAR*, 1956-7, p. 24.
48. A.K. Narain and T.N. Roy, *The Excavations at Rajghat, Varanasi*, Benares, 1976; also see *IAR*, 1960-1, p. 37.
49. Ancient Rājagṛha, present Rajgir, was the capital of Magadha prior to the rise of Pāṭaliputra. Being surrounded by five hills, it is naturally fortified. Muhammad Hamid Qureshi, *A Visit to Rājagṛha* (revised by A. Ghosh), Delhi, 1939; A. Ghosh, 'Rajgir, 1950', *AI*, vol. VII, 1951, pp. 66-78.
50. K.K. Sinha, *Excavations at Śrāvastī 1959*, Varanasi, 1969.
51. R.S. Sharma, 'Iron and Urbanisation in the Ganga Basin', *IHR*, vol. I, 1974, pp. 98-103; R.S. Sharma, 'Material Background of the Origin of Buddhism', in Mohit Sen and M.B. Rao (eds.), *Das Kapital Centenary Volume—A Symposium*, Delhi, 1968.
52. Ghosh, *The City*, Chapter III, section 2.
53. George Erdosy, 'The Origin of Cities in the Ganges Valley', *JESHO*, vol. XXVIII, 1985, pp. 294-325.
54. Allchin and Allchin, *The Rise of Civilization*, pp. 325-46; also A.K. Narain, ed., *Seminar on the Problems of Megaliths in India*, Varanasi, 1969.
55. *Dīgha Nikāya*, edited by T.W. Rhys Davids and J. Estlin Carpenter, London, 1890-1911, II.72. The *Kauṭilīya Arthaśāstra* (II.3) uses the term *paṇya-puṭa-bhedana*, thereby making its commercial nature more explicit.
56. *Dīgha Nikāya*, II.72.
57. Chakravarti, *Warfare for Wealth*, pp. 32-9.
58. The extent of the Maurya empire can be best determined on the basis of the internal and external evidence of the edicts of Aśoka. Aśoka calls the territories within his empire *vijita*, *rājaviṣaya*, etc. (i.e. conquered territory, royal domain), while those outside his empire—both within the subcontinent and beyond—were designated as *aṁta avijita* (unconquered frontiers). The Maurya empire included in it parts of Afghanistan. This was possibly due to the cessation of territories, viz., Arachosia (Kandahar), Paropanisadae (Kabul) and Gedrosia (southern Baluchistan) to Candragupta Maurya from Seleucus. That Aśoka retained his hold over these areas in Afghanistan is unmistakably proved by his edicts found in Afghanistan. B.N. Mukherjee, *Studies in the Aramaic Edicts of Aśoka*, Calcutta, 1983.
59. Sharma, *Perspectives*, pp. 128-36; Romila Thapar, *Aśoka and The Decline of the Mauryas*, London, 1961, pp. 54-93; Chakravarti, *Warfare for Wealth*, pp. 49-60.
60. We have used here the critical edition of the *Kauṭilīya Arthaśāstra* edited by R.P. Kangle in three parts. Though T.R. Trautman's statistical analysis of the text indicates that the *Arthaśāstra* assumed its present shape in first/second centuries AD, the kernel of the text, namely Book II, has been assigned to the third century BC and hence to the Maurya period.
61. *KAS*, I.19, 35.
62. *KAS*, II.24.
63. *KAS*, II.24.2-3. One of the most controversial topics of agrarian history of

the Maurya period is the one concerning the ownership of land. Megasthenes and three later Classical authors (Arrian, Diodorus and Strabo who give excerpts of Megasthenes' *Indika*) tend to convey the impression that the Maurya ruler was the sole owner of all lands in the state and no private person was allowed to hold land. The accounts of Diodorus and Strabo mention that cultivators tilled the land of the king on condition of paying respectively one-fourth and three-fourths share of the produce. A study of early Indian land system would on the other hand indicate the existence of a distinct sense of individual ownership of land. Though the king owned vast stretches of crown land (*sītā*), this did not go against the individual ownership of land. See U.N. Ghoshal, *The Agrarian System in Ancient India*, Calcutta, 1972; G. Bongard Levin, *Mauryan India*, New Delhi, 1985, pp. 138-53.

64. *KAS*, II.1.1.
65. D.D. Kosambi, *The Culture and Civilisation of Ancient India in Historical Outline*, New Delhi, 1972, p. 149.
66. *KAS*, II.1.10.
67. *KAS*, II.1.13, 114, 16.
68. *KAS*, II.1.14, *kośopaghātakau varjayet.*
69. Strabo, *Geographikon*, Book XV.1, sec. 50.
70. *SI*, vol. I, pp. 175-80.
71. *KAS*, II.24.18; the rate of water-cess was 1/5, if water was set in motion by own hands of cultivators, 1/4 if set by shoulder, 1/3 when set flowing in channels by a mechanism (*srotoyantra*) and 1/4 when lifted from rivers, lakes and wells.
72. *KAS*, II.5.7.
73. *KAS*, II.12.
74. *KAS*, II.12.37.
75. B.C. Sen, *Economics in Kauṭilya*, Calcutta, 1967.
76. F.R. Allchin, 'Upon the Antiquity of Gold Mining in Ancient India', *JESHO*, vol. V, 1962, pp. 195-216; F.R. Allchin, 'Antiquity of Gold Mining in the Gadag Region of Karnataka', in M.S. Nagaraja Rao, ed., *Madhu*, New Delhi, 1981, pp. 81-2.
77. The city commissioners (*astynomoi*) of Pāṭaliputra were divided into six boards each consisting of five members. The first board supervised everything regarding industrial arts. Classical authors also state that all artisans (comprising the fourth 'caste') had to pay taxes to the state, except the shipbuilders and armour-makers who were employed by the government.
78. *KAS*, II.18 (*Āyudhagārādhyakṣa*—superintendent of the armoury); *KAS*, II.19 (*Tulāmānapautavaṁ*—standardization of weights and measures); II.23 (*Sūtrādhyakṣa*—superintendent of yarns); II.25 (*Surādhyakṣa*—controller of spirituous liquors).
79. This will be evident from a study of the functions of the *astynomoi*. See Strabo, *Geographikon*, XV.1, sec. 57.

80. Megasthenes states that this was one of the functions of the *agoranomoi*, officers in charge of the countryside. According to him, distance signals on highways were erected after every 10 stadia.
81. The epigraphic evidence of a royal road during the Maurya period is also corroborated by the account of Eratosthenes (death in *c.* 255 BC) who spoke of a royal highway connecting Palimbothra (i.e. Pāṭaliputra) with the north-western borderland of the subcontinent. Mukherjee, *Aramaic Edicts*, pp. 9-22.
82. *KAS*, II.16 and II.21-2. The term *Saṁsthādhyakṣa* occur in IV.2.1.
83. *KAS*, II. 16.1 and 4.
84. *KAS*, IV.2.28. The passage is to be studied in the context of the general subject matter of the chapter concerned. This chapter is known as *Kaṇṭakaśodhana*, literally purification of thorns (to the state). In this chapter one of the sections is *Vaidehakarakṣaṇa*, i.e. protection from (dishonest) traders. It implies that in the *Arthaśāstra* scheme of things a trader is viewed as a thorn to the state. The merchant in the *Arthaśāstra* is simply called a *vaidehaka* (an ordinary trader) and not given the prestigious epithet *śreṣṭhī*.
85. *KAS*, II.16.25.
86. U.N. Ghoshal, *Contributions to the History of Hindu Revenue System*, Calcutta, 1972; that the Maurya state imposed both *bhāga* (share of the produce) and *bali* (an obligatory payment) is amply borne out by the Rummindei Pillar Inscription of Aśoka.
87. *KAS*, V.2.
88. Pāṭaliputra, according to Megasthenes, was 90 stades (9½ miles) in length and 15 stades (1¾ miles) in breadth. It was surrounded by a moat and a fortification wall, the latter having 570 watch towers and 64 gates. See R.C. Majumdar, *The Classical Accounts of India*, Calcutta, 1960. The management of the municipal affairs was entrusted to the astynomoi, divided into six boards, who jointly looked after ports, marts and temples also.
89. The second of the six boards of city commissioners was entrusted with matters concerning foreigners at Pāṭaliputra. In the event of their illness and death, information was sent out and their property taken care of and protected. The fourth board was in charge of what may be called a forerunner of modern census. Megasthenes explicitly states that the census was carried on with a view to preparing assessment of revenue.
90. *KAS*, II.4 for the urban layout, II.36 for the recommendations on the management of the municipal affairs.
91. *Durga* or the fortified area is the fourth element of the state. It is significant that while discussing the functions of the *Samāharttā* (Collector General, II.6), *durga* or fortified areas (i.e. urban centres) is placed ahead of *rāṣṭra* (i.e. countryside) in the list of sources of revenue. While the sources of income from *durga* number twenty, those from *rāṣṭra* are thirteen (*KAS*, II.6.1-3).

92. John Marshall, *Taxila, an Illustrated Account of Archaeological Excavations Carried out at Taxila under the Orders of the Government of India between the years 1913 and 1934*, Cambridge, 1951, p. 92.
93. Sinha, *Excavations at Śrāvastī*.
94. A. Ghosh and K.C. Panigrahi, 'The Pottery of Ahichchhatra', *AI*, vol. I, 1945, pp. 38-9.
95. Sharma, *Excavations at Kauśāmbī*, pp. 24-6; G.R. Sharma, *Excavations at Kauśāmbī, the Defences and the Śyenaciti of Purushamedha*, Allahabad, 1960.
96. B.B. Lal, 'Sisupalgarh 1948: An Early Historical Fort in Eastern India', *AI*, vol. V, 1949, pp. 37-9.
97. Sharma, *Excavations at Kauśāmbī*, pp. 37-9. These soak wells/or jars could have also been used for irrigation purposes. See, Sharma, *Perspectives*, p. 159; Marshall, *Taxila*, p. 94, for the sewage system in Taxila (Bhir Mound).
98. *Aṅguttara Nikāya*, pt. III. ccxx, 256.
99. *IAR*, 1974-5, p. 49.
100. *KAS*, II.11.115. Textile products of Mathurā are mentioned here along with those of Aparānta, Kaliṅga, Kāśī, Vaṅga, Vatsa, and Mahiṣa.
101. H. Hartel, *Excavations at Sonkh*. See particularly the findings from levels 16-22, assignable to the Maurya period.
102. Hartel, *Excavations at Sonkh*; B.N. Mukherjee, *Mathurā and its Society*, Calcutta, 1981, p. 104.
103. *The Mahābhāṣya of Patañjali*, edited by F. Kielhorn, Bombay, 1892-1909; V.3.57.
104. *SI*, vol. I, pp. 169-70.
105. *SI*, vol. I, pp. 164-67; Nasik inscription of Nahapāna, yrs. 41, 42, 45, speaks of plantation of no less than 8,000 seedlings of coconut trees (*śiśunārigela mūlāṇi*) at a village named Cikhalapada (= Skt. Citkhalapadra) in Kapurahāra (= Karpūrāhāra; *āhāra* = district). Similarly 3200 coconut trees were planted in village Nanaṁgola, Nasik inscription of Nahapāna, *SI*, pp. 169-70.
106. The availability of pepper in Malabar is reported in the *Periplus of the Erythraean Sea* (sec. 56), and Pliny's *Natural History*.
107. This reservoir, originally built by Candragupta Maurya and well maintained by Aśoka, suffered a huge breach due to a terrible storm in the very first regnal year of Rudradāman I. It was repaired in a short time (*anati-mahatākālena*) and required huge expenditure from the treasury of Rudradāman I (*svasmāt kośāt mahatādhanaughena*). *SI*, vol. I, pp. 175-80.
108. K.A. Nilakanta Sastri, *A History of South India*, Bombay, 1966.
109. B.B. Lal and K.N. Dikshit, 'Sringaverapura: A Key Site for the Proto-history and Early History of the Central Ganga Valley', *Puratattva*,

vol. X, 1978-9, pp. 1-8; B.B. Lal, 'A 2000 Year Old Feat of Hydraulic Engineering in India', *Archaeology*, vol. XXXVIII, 1985, pp. 48-53.
110. *Odayantrikas* or *Udakayantrikas*, i.e. hydraulic mechanics are referred to in the Nasik inscription of Ābhira Īśvarasena, *EI*, vol. VIII, pp. 82-3.
111. *The Gāthāsaptaśatī of Hāla*, edited and translated by R.G. Basak, Calcutta, 1971, verse 90.
112. *EI*, vol. II, pp. 79-116. H. Lüders, *Mathurā Inscriptions* (edited by K.L. Janert), Gottingen, 1961; James Burgess and Bhagawanlal Indraji, *Inscriptions from the Cave Temples of Western India*, Delhi, 1976 (rpt.).
113. It is difficult to assign any definite date to Jātaka stories. Though some of the stories could have originated in a period prior to the Buddha, most of them are of later date. The Jātakas appear to have reflected the social condition of the period commonly known as the Śaka-Kuṣāṇa-Sātavāhana phase.
114. *Periplus*, sec. 51.
115. B.N. Chapekar, *Report on the Excavations at Ter, 1958*, Poona, 1969.
116. R.E.M. Wheeler, A. Ghosh and Krishna Deva, 'Arikamedu: An Indo-Roman Trading Station on the East Coast of India', *AI*, vol. II, 1946, pp. 17-124.
117. *Periplus*, sec. 63. For the trade and urban centres of early Bengal, Amita Ray, Presidential Address, sec. I, *PIHC*, Goa session, 1987.
118. *Geographike Huphegesis of Ptolemy*, tr. E.L. Stevenson, New York, 1932; B.N. Mukherjee, *The Economic Factors in Kushāṇa History*, Calcutta, 1970; Chakravarti, *Warfare for Wealth*, pp. 94-6.
119. Rudradāman I is described as the lord of many areas including Ākara, i.e. eastern (*pūrva*) part of Malwa which came under his possession after the heyday of the Kuṣāṇas. His treasury is said to have been overflowing with minerals, gems and precious objects including diamond (*vajra*), *SI*, vol. I, pp. 175-80; B.N. Mukherjee, 'Revenue, Trade and Society in the Kushāṇa Empire', *IHR*, vol. VII, 1980-1, pp. 24-53.
120. *Periplus*, sec. 58; *Geographike Huphegesis*, VII. 10.
121. *Periplus*, secs. 58-9.
122. R. Nagaswamy, 'Excavations at Korkai', *Damilica*, vol. I, 1970, pp. 50-4.
123. *SI*, vol. I, pp. 198-200, 208; D.C. Sircar, *Indian Epigraphical Glossary*, New Delhi, 1966.
124. Pliny, XI.11.1.
125. Karle Cave inscription of Vāsiṣṭhīputra Pulumāvi, *SI*, vol. I, p. 202.
126. R.C. Majumdar, *Corporate Life in Ancient India*, Calcutta, 1925; A.N. Bose, *Social and Rural Economy of Northern India*, vol. I, Calcutta, 1967.
127. Majumdar, *Corporate Life*, pp. 36-7.
128. Nasik inscription of Nahapāna, yrs. 41, 42, 45, *SI*, vol. I, pp. 165-6.
129. There are many books and research papers on various aspects of Roman trade. E.H. Warmington, *The Commerce between the Roman Empire and*

India, London, 1974 (rpt.); M.I. Rostovzeff, *The Social and Economic History of the Roman Empire*, 2 vols., Oxford, 1957; R.E.M. Wheeler, *Rome beyond the Imperial Frontier*, London, 1954; U.N. Ghoshal, 'Economic Condition', in K.A. Nilakanta Sastri, ed., *A Comprehensive History of India*, vol. II, Bombay, 1957, pp. 430-57; L. Bulnois, *The Silk Road*, London, 1966; M.G. Raschke, 'New Studies in Roman Commerce with the East', *Aufstieg und Niedergang in der Romischer Welt*, vol. IX, Berlin, 1978, pp. 601-1356.

130. B.N. Mukherjee, *Rise and Fall of the Kushāṇa Empire*, Calcutta, 1989.
131. The discovery of the south-west monsoon wind is generally ascribed to a Greek sailor, Hippalus, after whom the wind was often called the Hippalus wind. *Periplus*, sec. 57, Pliny, Book VI.26.104. The discovery of the monsoon winds was one of epoch-making significance in the history of the Indian Ocean trade.
132. *Periplus*, secs. 48, 64.
133. For a description of Barygaza, see *Periplus*, secs. 43, 44, 49.
134. Pliny, Book VI.26.104; Chakravarti, *Warfare for Wealth*, pp. 91-2.
135. Strabo, *Geographikon*, II.5.12.
136. *Periplus*, secs. 54-7, Ptolemy, VII.8.
137. Ptolemy, VII.13 and 14.
138. Mukherjee, *Economic Factors*, p. 47.
139. K. Miller, ed., *Peutengerische Täfel*, Munich, 1962, segment XIII.
140. Chakravarti, *Warfare for Wealth*, pp. 105-12.
141. Warmington, *Commerce*, pp. 35ff.
142. R.S. Sharma, *Urban Decay in India (c. AD 300-c. AD 1000)*, New Delhi, 1987, p. 136 says that there are 129 sites in India yielding Roman coins. His figure is based on the unpublished article of Mansfield G. Raschkey, 'Roman Coinfinds in the Indian Subcontinent: A Catalogue and Analysis'; also see R.E.M. Wheeler, *My Archaeological Mission to India and Pakistan*, London, 1976, p. 38.
143. B.N. Mukherjee, *Kushāṇa Coins in the Land of Five Rivers*, Calcutta, 1979; B.N. Mukherjee, *Kushāṇa Silver Coinage*, Calcutta, 1982; Ajay Mitra Sastri, ed., *The Coinage of the Sātavāhanas and Coins from Excavations*, Nagpur, 1972.
144. K.K. Dasgupta, *A Tribal History of Ancient India: A Numismatic Approach*, Calcutta, 1976.
145. Richard Fick, *Social Organization of North-Eastern India during the Buddha's Time*, Calcutta, 1920; Bose, *Social and Rural Economy*, vol. II, Chap. I; Ranabir Chakravarti, 'Rājaśreṣṭhī', Chap. 5 of this volume.
146. Our attention to the mercantile organization named *vaṇiggrāma* was first drawn by D.D. Kosambi, 'Dhenukākaṭa', *JBAS*, vol. XXX, 1955, pp. 50-71. Activities of such a *vaṇiggrāma* are found in an inscription of AD 592. *EI*, vol. XXX, pp. 163-81. This organization became particularly prominent in erly medieval south India under the name *maṇigrāmam*.

147. Himanshu Prabha Ray, *Monastery and Guild: Commerce under the Satavahanas*, New Delhi, 1986.
148. Ray, *Monastery and Guild*, p. 89.
149. Marshall, *Taxila*.
150. Ghosh, *The City*, p. 61.
151. Ghosh, *The City*, p. 62.
152. B.P. Sinha and Sitaram Roy, *Vaiśālī Excavations 1958-62*, Patna, 1969, pp. 5-6.
153. Lal, 'Sisupalgarh', pp. 62-105.
154. Mukherjee, *Mathurā*, p. 116.
155. Mukherjee, *Mathurā*, p. 116.
156. Mukherjee, *Mathurā*, p. 118.
157. Mukherjee, *Rise and Fall*.
158. *Lalitavistara*, edited by P.L. Vaidya, Chap. II, p. 15.
159. H.D. Sankalia, *From History to Prehistory at Nevasa*, Poona, 1960.
160. N.C. Ghosh, *Excavations at Satanikota*, New Delhi, 1986.
161. H. Sarkar and B.N. Mishra, *Nagarjunakonda*, New Delhi, 1972; H. Sarkar and S.P. Nainar, *Amarāvatī*, New Delhi, 1973.
162. *Periplus*, sec. 62.
163. Ptolemy, VII.15.
164. Ptolemy, VII.15.
165. R.P. Chanda, 'Some Unpublished Amaravati Inscriptions', *EI*, vol. XV, pp. 257-78.
166. The Ikṣvāku rule in the Krishna-Godavari valley and the Krishna delta followed that of the Śātavāhanas. Four rulers of the Ikṣvāku family are known from their epigraphic records. A century of the Ikṣvāku rule, with each of the four rulers being assigned an average period of 25 years, in the Krishna delta is not unlikely. The Ikṣvāku rule terminated when Ābhira Vasuṣeṇa (Nagarjunakonda Inscription of Ābhira Vasuṣeṇa) conquered the area in question in or around *c.* AD 330.
167. Sarkar and Misra, *Nagarjunakonda*.
168. R. Champakalakshmi, 'Archaeology and Tamil Literary Tradition', *Puratattva*, vol. VIII, 1975-6, pp. 110-22.
169. Champakalakshmi, 'Archaeology and Tamil'.
170. S.K. Aiyangar, *The Maṇimekalai in its Historical Setting*, London, 1938.
171. *Śilappādikāram*, translated by V.R.R. Dikshitar, Madras, 1939.
172. *IAR*, 1962-3, p. 13; *IAR*, 1963-4, p. 20.
173. Wheeler, Ghosh and Deva, 'Arikamedu', pp. 17ff.
174. Ray, *Monastery and Guild*, particularly the Chapter on 'Agrarian Expansion and Trade'.
175. H. Sarkar, 'The Emergence of Cities in Early Historical Andhradeśa', in B.M. Pande and B.D. Chattopadhyaya, eds., *Archaeology and History*, vol. II, New Delhi, 1987, pp. 631-42.
176. Sarkar, 'Emergence of Cities', p. 635.

177. Sarkar, 'Emergence of Cities', p. 639.
178. B.D. Chattopadhyaya, 'Transition to the Early Historical Phase in the Deccan', in B.M. Pande and B.D. Chattopadhyaya, eds., *Archaeology and History*, vol. II, New Delhi, 1987, p. 728.
179. Chattopadhyaya, 'Transition', p. 729.
180. Mukherjee, *Mathurā*, p. 195, n. 200.
181. B.N. Mukherjee, Presidential Address, sec. I, *PIHC*, Bodhgaya session, 1981.
182. The period between the fall of the Mauryas and the rise of Gupta empire is viewed as one of disintegration, a 'Dark Age' by S. Chattopadhyaya, *Early History of Northern India*, Calcutta, 1958.
183. B.N. Mukherjee, ed., *India in World Wisdom*, Calcutta, 1986.
184. This is best illustrated by the large number of donative records of the early centuries of the Christian era when donors almost invariably recorded their occupations/professions, but very rarely their caste (*varṇa/jāti*) status.
185. Lüders, *Mathurā Inscriptions*, p. 383, Inscription no. 4.
186. LL, inscription no.102.
187. *Aṅgavijjā*, edited by Muni Punyavijayaji, Chap. II, secs. 40-6, 101-3; Chap. 57, sec. 218; Chap. 24, sec. 149; Mukherjee, 'Revenue, Trade and Society'.
188. Mukherjee, Presidential Address, *PIHC*.
189. *Kāmasūtra of Vātsyāyana*, edited by K.R. Aiyangar, Lahore, 1924; H.C. Chakladar, *Social Life in Ancient India, Studies in Vātsyāyana's Kāmasūtra*, Calcutta, 1929.
190. This famous verse occurs in Kālidasa's *Mālavikāgnimitram*, Act. I.
191. *Gautama Dharmasūtra*, XVI.43.
192. *Manusmṛti*, IV.107.
193. *Vasiṣṭha Smṛti*, XIII.1.

CHAPTER 3

Merchants and Other Donors at Ancient Bandhogarh

INTRODUCTION

The discovery of many new historical data—both literary and archaeological—and the re-examination of the already known data with new tools of analyses over the last five decades have considerably enlivened the study of early Indian history (up to AD 1200). There has also been a growing recognition that early India did have its agents of and capacities for change. These forces of change, when studied in juxtaposition to the obvious and well-known forces of continuity in Indian history, may sharpen our understanding of the contours of historical development in the subcontinent. The present historiographical position hardly allows one to cling to the much cherished notion of the changelessness of Indian history over millennia. Hence it seems unsatisfactory to club the entire period from the earliest times to AD 1200 into a single and simple chronological entity—'ancient India'. Early Indian history up to AD 1200 may better be appreciated in terms of a number of stages or phases:

(a) prehistoric and proto-historic phase (occasionally designated as the pre-literate period), up to 600 BC;
(b) early historical period (*c.* 600 BC-AD 300);
(c) late ancient from *c.* AD 300 to 600 (widely known as the classical phase or the Gupta period); and
(d) early medieval (*c.* AD 600-1200).[1]

The present chapter is related to the early historical period of Indian history. The availability of diverse types of data (though largely fragmentary and hardly adequate)—literary, epigraphic, numismatic, art historical and field archaeological evidence from explored and excavated sites—has facilitated a better understanding of these nine centuries. The period brought about changes of far-reaching consequences in the political, material, socio-religious and creative activities in the subcontinent.[2] As the dynastic history of these nine hundred years is now better known, recent historiography naturally indicates a shift of focus from dynastic upheavals to an integrated study of socio-economic, political and cultural conditions of the period under review. The change in the orientation to historical studies would of course imply a change in the orientation of the use of available source materials. The historian therefore shows a preference for the combination of archaeological (including epigraphic, numismatic and art historical) and literary evidence (indigenous as well as 'foreign'), and does not take for granted the information provided solely by literature, without, however at all diminishing the importance of the last named source.[3]

The most conspicuous watershed in the nine centuries of early historical India is undoubtedly the Mauryan epoch (*c.* late fourth century BC to *c.* 185 BC) which not only marked the creation of a nearly pan-Indian empire for the first time, but also signified the culmination of the process of the rise of Magadhan power from the middle Ganga valley to the greater part of the subcontinent. The decline of the Mauryan empire (first quarter of the second century BC) brought several new elements, including the advent of foreigners as invaders, rulers, migrants and merchants, to the Indian scene. But the disintegration of the empire did not necessarily result in any major political, socio-economic and cultural catastrophe. In fact the second half of the early historical period, i.e. from *c.* 200 BC-AD 300 (the post Maurya period) is known for being one of the most creative phases of Indian history.

These preliminary remarks may help to orient the content of the present study which deals with sources belonging essentially to the second half of the early historical period. A hallmark of the period under review was the large number of donations of movable and immovable objects, including gifts in cash, to Buddhist *saṁghas* and *vihāras* and Jaina monasteries by people from different walks of life. Hundreds of small donative inscriptions have so far been discovered in Bodhgaya (middle Ganga valley), Mathurā (Ganga-Yamuna doab), Sanchi, Bharhut (central India), large parts of the western Deccan (Nasik, Karle, Bhaja, Junnar to name only a few sites) and also the eastern Deccan in the deltas of the Godavari and the Krishna. These inscriptions not only mention the object of donation to a particular religious organization, but also record names of donors/patrons along with their near relatives and occasionally preceptors too, their places of origin and the purposes of their donations.[4] An interesting feature of these donative records is the relative rarity of examples of royal donations to religious institutions, though donors occasionally (but not regularly) refer to reigning kings with a view to accurately dating their respective acts of patronage. Thus, out of a total number of 631 donative records at the celebrated stupa at Sanchi only three refer to royal donations.[5] Sanchi, Bharhut, Mathurā, Nasik, Karle, Junnar and Amaravati among other being famous religious and art centres and also yielding a profusion of donative records, it is only natural that researches on early historical donations (*dāna*) have concentrated on the wealth of information gleaned therefrom.

The focus of the present discussion is however not on these renowned centres, but on a less familiar place Bandhogarh, situated in Rewah in present Madhya Pradesh (23° 40' N lat. and 81° 3' E long.). Rewa is known for its steep-sided plateau which is a major feature of 'the country between Bundelkhand and the Son'.[6] Though the annual average rainfall is 40-50 in. (1,016-1,270 mm) and the fertile black loamy soil is suitable for wheat cultivation, the 'whole area is extremely isolated and backward'.[7]

N.P. Chakrabarti discovered about twenty donative records in Bandhogarh as early as 1938, although he published them later.[8] These records were found engraved in a number of artificial caves of soft sandstone rocks in and around Bandhogarh. The early history of the area is very dimly known. During early medieval times Bandhogarh and the area around it seem to have been under the Kalacuris of Ratanpur. A marriage alliance between the Vāghela chief Karṇadeva and the Kalacuris led to the presentation of Bandhogarh as a dowry to the Vāghelas in the thirteenth century. From then onwards Bandhogarh became known as a Vāghela stronghold. During medieval times it was generally known as Bandhu.[9]

Some light however is shed on the early history of Bandhogarh by the epigraphic records, discovered by Chakrabarti. These records are dated to a particular era which Chakrabarti equates with the Śaka era (also known as the Kaniṣka era after the homonymous Kuṣāṇa ruler). Although the exact beginning of the Śaka era in terms of the Christian era has been a matter of long scholarly debate, a large number of historians including N.P. Chakrabarti, place the first year of this era in AD 78.[10] The records from Bandhogarh, according to Chakrabarti, are assignable to the second century AD on palaeographic grounds. The records under review not only contain information about donations, but also names of the rulers, precise dates in the Śaka era, season of the year and exact days. Interestingly enough there is no reference to months of the year; but three seasons appear frequently. These are *giṁha* (*grīṣma* = summer), *vāsa* (*varṣā* = rainy season) and *hemanta* (= winter).

Each season therefore comprised four months. Each season appears to have divided into eight *pakhas* (= *pakṣas* or fortnight). In this way the Bandhogarh records bear a distinct affinity with similar donative records from Mathurā which during the early centuries of the Christian era was definitely under the occupation of the Kuṣāṇas who established a seat of power at Mathurā.[11] The rulers figuring in the records from Bandhogarh are:

(1) Mahārāja Vāsiṭhīputa Siri Bhīmasena, year 51 (i.e. 51+78 = AD 129) who is generally identified with a homonymous ruler mentioned in the Gunji inscription of 52, i.e. AD 130.[12]
(2) Mahārāja Kochiputa Poṭhasiri with known dates in 86, 87 and 88 (i.e. AD 164, 165 and 166). In at least one record he is described as the son of Bhīmasena (*Mahārāja Bhīmasenaputa*).[13]
(3) Mahārāja Bhaṭṭadeva with one known date, year 90 (= AD 168). he is described as the son of Poṭhasiri and also the son of Kosikī (*Mahārāja Kosikiputasa* and *Mahārāja Poṭhasiriputasa Siri Bhaṭṭadevasa*).[14]

It appears that Bhīmasena, Kochiputa Poṭhasiri and Bhaṭṭadeva ruled in dynastic succession from 51 to 90 (i.e. AD 129-68). Two other rulers whose identities cannot be ascertained also figure in our records. They are Vāsiṭhīputa Siri Citasena (Śrī Citrasena) and Vaiśravaṇa, son of Mahāsenāpati Bhadrabala (*Mahāsenāpater Bhadrabalasya putra*). The fragmentary nature of the records does not allow us to read their known dates. Vaiśravaṇa, however, is thought to have been identified with a ruler of the same name who figures as a ruler of Kauśāmbī in a record dated 107 (AD 185). The empire of the Kuṣāṇas at the zenith of their power under Kaniṣka embraced areas to the east of Mathurā as far as Vārāṇasī. There is however little evidence of the continuation of the political hold of the Kuṣāṇas over the area to the east of Mathurā during the rule of successors of Kaniṣka.[15] It may not be impossible therefore that the rulers figuring in the Bandhogarh records came to power with the gradual disappearance of the Kuṣāṇa hold in the middle Ganga valley in the days after Kaniṣka (year 1-23, i.e. AD 78-101).

THE DONORS OF BANDHOGARH

Now to the study of the actual donors and donations on the basis of ancient inscriptions found at Bandhogarh. It may be stated at the outset that the records here are studied chronologically, while Chakrabarti published them and numbered them on the basis of their findspots. The maximum number of donations relate to the gift of what has been variously called *lātā-ghara*, *lāta*, *lātāni*. Chakrabarti takes these terms to denote rock-cut cave shelters, caused to be excavated by their respective donors. D.C. Sircar, commenting on Chakrabarti, points out that 'in many of the inscriptions *na* often has a form that closely resembles *ta*. It is not impossible that the intended reading of what has been read as *lāta*/*lātā* is *lāna* or *lānā*'.[16] *Lāna* or *lānā* clearly corresponds to Prākṛt *lana*, i.e. Sanskrit *layana*, meaning a cave shelter. In fact one Bandhogarh record does clearly read *[la]yo(ya)na* = *layana*.[17] The practice of engraving dedicatory records on the walls of the *lāta*/*layana* was widely prevalent in the contemporary Deccan, particularly the western Deccan.

The earliest gift was that of a *lātāghara* or cave dwelling donated in 51(= AD 129) during the reign of Mahārāja Vāsiṭhīputa Bhīmasena on the eighth day of the fifth fortnight of the rainy season (*Mahārāja Vāsiṭhīputasa Siri Bhīmasenasa savachare ekapane 50 1 vāsa pakhe pacame 5 divase aṭhame*). The donation was made by a *goṣṭhī* or committee consisting of *negama* Phagusena (Phalgusena), *negama* Mada (= *Madra*), *suvaṇakāro* Balamita (= Balamitra), *negama* Sivaśaka (Śivaśakra), *Kāṭhikārika-kammāra* Śaka (= Śakra), *negama* Ceti (= Cedī), *vāṇijaka* Śivadhara, and *vāṇijaka* Tīra.[18]

The epithets of the donors now may be examined. The term *suvarṇakāra* clearly stands for a goldsmith. The epithet *kāṭhikārika-kammāra* is a combination of two terms, *kāṣṭhīya-kārika* (one working in wood) and *kammāra* (blacksmith). Chakrabarti takes him to be a 'carpenter-blacksmith'.[19] But the meaning of carpenter is generally covered by the term *vaḍhaki*/*vardhaki*, so frequently seen in many donative records and the Jātaka stories. Hence *kāṭhikārika* may better be taken to denote a wood-worker, as distinct from a carpenter. Chakrabarti's rendering noted above may also imply that Śaka or Śakra was simultaneously a wood-worker and a blacksmith. Such a craftwise combination is rarely met with in early Indian sources. Is it possible that the person was primarily a blacksmith who also engaged wood-cutting? The two more frequently used epithets in the record are *negama* and *vāṇijaka*, translated by Chakrabarti as merchant and trader respectively. One gets the impression that the two terms were generally synonymous and interchangeable. But as the two terms appear simultaneously in the same inscriptions (they figure in other records from Bandhogarh too), a differentiation in their categories was probably intended. The word *vāṇijaka* is a generic/blanket term to denote any trader; but generally a *vāṇijaka* is not as prominent or wealthy as the *seṭṭhi/śreṣṭhī*, the merchant par excellence. *Vāṇijaka* may therefore be taken to mean a petty or ordinary trader, somewhat akin to the *vaidehaka* of the *Arthaśāstra*. The other epithet *negama*, i.e. Sanskrit *naigama* is obviously derived from *nigama*. The term *nigama* has variously been translated as a city, district, large village, bigger economic unit, a ward in a city, etc.[20] Although the term *nigama* occasionally figures along with *gāma* (i.e. village), a *nigama* is generally viewed as a non-rural settlement.[21] The word *nigama* also stands for a corporate body of persons following a common craft or trade (cf. the expression *kulikanigama*, in the sense of a professional body of artisans, figuring on seals of the Gupta period from Vaiśāli.[22] The *nigama/naigama* type of merchant (distinct from a *vaidehaka*) may therefore be taken as being a trader belonging to a certain guild-like body of merchants.[23] In the record under review we come across more merchants as donors than artisans. But the merchant and the artisan combined into a *goṭhikā/goṣṭhī*, i.e. a group for the sake of donation. Following Romila Thapar,[24] this may be considered as an evidence of 'collective patronage'. Such collective patronage was often used to underline the cohesion of the community making the gift.

Significantly enough, no donative record is available at Bandhogarh between the years 51 and 86. The silence regarding patronage is broken during the reign of Bhīmasena's son and successor Kochiputa Poṭhasiri (Kautsīputra Prauṣṭhaśrī) whose known dates have already been discussed in the Introduction. Kochiputa's reign is marked by the maximum number of donations following in quick succession. No less than nine donative records belong to his reign; of these seven are dated to the year 86.

In the year 86 during the reign of Poṭhasiri, on the tenth day of sixth fortnight of the summer season (*gimha*, abbreviated in the record as *gi*), a cave shelter for habitation was donated by the minister Bhabatha, who was the son of *negama* Ujha (*Negamasa Ujhasa putena amaca-Bhaḅathena ketana-lātāghara kārāpitā*).[25] The royal master of *amaca* (i.e. *amātya*) Bhabatha, is not mentioned by name, but he was in all probability Poṭhasiri himself. The remarkable point about this donor is that he originally belonged to a mercantile family and changed his profession from trade to administration, which provides unmistakable evidence of the occupational mobility of this particular donor. The economic well-being of the *negama* family could well have paved the way for Bhabatha's entry into the administrative circle. As one's actual status is expected to have risen with one's appointment as a minister, Bhabatha's case may illustrate upward social mobility.[26]

In the same year, exactly a month after Bhabatha's donation, another donor appears (on the tenth day of the seventh fortnight of summer in the year 86 of Poṭhasiri). He is Magha, an *amaca* (= *amātya*) or minister of Koshiputa Poṭhasiri and also serving him as the minister in charge of war and peace (*saṁdhivigahi-vavaṭena* = *sandhivigrahi-vyāpṛtena.*) Magha's father Cakora is described to have been an *amaca* too, though the name of the ruler whom he served is not stated in the record. Thus Magha belongs to a family of ministers, and therefore must have been a member of what may be called an 'elite group'. This record also furnishes the earliest possible epigraphic evidence of a *sandhivigrahika*, i.e. a minister in charge of war and peace or external affairs. *Amaca* Magha caused two inscriptions to be engraved to record his gifts. In each record an identical donation is mentioned: two tanks (*vāvi* = *vāpi*), two cave dwellings (*lātāghara*) and a garden (*ārāma*). In all therefore four tanks, four cave dwellings and two gardens were donated.[27]

There are five more records of the year 86 during the reign of Poṭhasiri. All these refer to donations by two individuals, Rakhita (= Rakṣita) and Cela. Rakhita has been described as the son of Phaguhathika, i.e. Phalguhasti (profession unstated) and the grandson of Cakaka (Cakra) who was a *negama*, i.e. a merchant belonging to a guild-like professional group. Cakaka hailed from Kauśāmbī (*Kosambeyasa*), one of the most important urban centres of the Ganga valley and among the foremost archaeological sites of early historic times.[28] The other donor along with Rakhita is Cela, who was the son of Datika (= Datti) and grandson of Chamika (= Kṣamin). Both Datika and Chamika were *negamas*. Thus both the donors belonged to a family of *negama* merchants. Although the donors' own occupational credentials have not been explicitly stated, the records underline their social category as *negamas*. As members of a professional group like *negama* merchants would not normally change their calling, it is likely that Rakhita and Cela too followed their hereditary profession. The five records also point to the possible contacts between Kauśāmbī and the ancient Rewa region, contact being maintained through the present Chunar-Mirjapur-Vindhyachal areas. As Kauśāmbī stood at the juncture of the middle Ganga valley and the Ganga-Yamuna doab, contacts with Kauśāmbī could have facilitated further linkages of ancient Bandhogarh with areas in the doab too.

Rakhita and Cela gave, as evident from their five records, gardens (*ārāmas*), cave dwellings (*lātāni*) and a vessel/bowl/cask (*chagavaro*, *chaṅgavara* in Pali). In one record the *lāta* or cave dwelling is said to have had a hall (*maḍava* = *maṇḍapa*) also. Altogether the two donors are credited with donations of five *lātāgharas* and five *ārāmas*, in addition to several *chagavaras* or bowls/caskets. All donations of this group were made on a single date, i.e. 'on the fifth day of the first fortnight of *Hemanta*' in the year 86 during the reign of Mahārāja Kochiputa. (*Mahārājasa Kochiputasa savachare chāsite 80 6 hemanta pakhe paṭhame 1 divase pacame 5*).[29]

The next donation was made by another merchant (*negama*), Pusa (i.e. Puṣya), a resident of Pavatha (= Parvata) and son of Āyāsaka (= Āyāsa). In the monsoon season (*vāsa*) of the year 87 during the reign of Kochiputa he donated a tank (*vāpi*) cave dwelling (*lātāghara*) and a gymnasium (*vāyāmasālā* = *vyāyāmaśālā*).[30] This is undoubtedly an exceptional donative record, as no where else does one come across the gift of a gymnasium. This is also the earliest known and, at the same time, a unique epigraphic reference to a *vyāyāmaśālā* in India. In fact, a gymnasium has well known relevance to Hellenic cultural context, but is hardly to be expected in an Indian situation and that too in an area of relative isolation like Bandhogarh. Though there is now no physical trace of this *vyāyāmaśālā*, the existence of such a structure in the second half of the second century AD can be taken for granted in view of the explicit epigraphic reference to this sporting arena. That the *vyāyāmaśālā* was meant for recreation purposes can hardly be doubted.[31] The actual residence of the merchant donor, namely Pavatha, cannot be identified satisfactorily. Chakrabarti points out on the basis of the commentary of the *Suttanipāta* to the existence of *Pabbataraṭṭha* (i.e. *Parvata-rāṣṭra*) in the centre of *Videha-raṭṭha*, i.e. in north Bihar.[32] A much later source of evidence, the travels of the Chinese pilgrim Hsüan Tsang, speaks of Po-fa-to (= Parvata) located near Mūlasthāna or Multan in present-day Pakistan.[33] In the absence of any other corroborative data one cannot conclude whether Parvata was situated in north Bihar or Multan in Pakistan. However, the typonym may suggest that it was situated in a mountainous region. It may therefore be conjectured, but by no means proved, that Parvata could have also denoted the Vindhyachal area, a hilly tract not far from Rewa.

The last known record of the reign of Poṭhasiri is dated in the fifth day of the second fortnight of Hemanta, in the year 88 (= AD 166). This speaks of the donation of the cave shelter (*lāta*) and a well (*kūpi*) by a *vāṇijaka*, Gahavudhi, son of Suhita (= Suhṛta) and grandson of Jīvanaka, a *vāṇijaka* of Mathurā.[34] The donor is once again a merchant who seems to have followed his family profession. The *vāṇijaka*, as distinct from a *negama*, was in all probability a petty trader. While his grandfather was a resident of Mathurā, a leading urban centre and a major cultural centre of early historical times, Gahavudhi came to ancient Bandhogarh from Saptanairika. The identification of Saptanairika is unknown, but the inscription clearly indicates a shift of residence of this merchant family. The reference to Mathurā in this record may suggest possible linkages between the Ganga-Yamuna doab and the Rewa plateau. In addition to the *kupi*, Gahavudhi also donated *raju* (= *rajju* = rope) and *ghaṭikā* (a vessel) obviously for fetching water from the well. There is also a reference to the construction of *sodheya* (= *saudheya*) or a structure. The term *saudheya*, as distinct from *lātallayana*, may donate a sophisticated building rather than a rock-cut cave.

Attention now may be drawn to two records of the year 90 (= AD 168) engraved during the reign of Bhaṭṭadeva, son and successor of Poṭhasiri. One record marks the donation of a *layana* (cave shelter) by *negama* Dhanamitaka (= Dhanamitra), son of Vesākha (Vaiśākha) and grandson of *negama* Ajnataka.[35] Once again one encounters here a *negama* following his family occupation of mercantile activities, possibly continuing over three generations. The other record belonging to the reign of the same ruler, mentions a person, described as being the grandson of Vasumita. The name of the donor and his social/occupational credentials cannot be read because of the fragmentary nature of the record. The unnamed donor also gave a cave shelter.[36]

The two undated donative records may be examined now. In one of the records the name of the reigning king Vāsiṭhīputa Siri Citasena is mentioned, but his identity cannot be established. The donor is the same in two records, namely Phagu (= Phalgu). It is suggested therefore that both donative records may have been inscribed during the reign of Citasena.[37] The interesting point about the donor is that he was the grandson of Pusaka (i.e. Puṣya) and resident of Pavatha (= Parvata). One is immediately reminded of Pusaka, a resident of Pavatha and the donor of the *vyāyāmaśālā*, discussed earlier. As the two Pusakas appear to have been identical, his grandson seems to have also visited Bandhogarh and made donations. But Pusaka was a *negama*, his grandson Phagu was a *vāṇijaka*. Does this indicate some changes in the status of this merchant family?

Finally we take up two donative records mentioning a ruler named Vaiśravaṇa, son of Mahāsenāpati Bhadrabala. As Chakrabarti tends to identify him with the homonymous ruler mentioned in an inscription of Kauśāmbī, dated year 107 (= AD 185), his reign may be assigned to the final phase of the second century AD. Here one encounters a ruler whose father was a general. But the more significant point is that the donor was the ruler himself, a fact not seen hitherto in the context of Bandhogarh. He donated two cave dwellings.[38] If Vaiśravaṇa is considered as a ruler of Kauśāmbī, his donations may speak of the continuation of the earlier linkages between the middle Ganga valley and the Rewa plateau.

SOCIAL ANALYSIS

Ancient Bandhogarh witnessed an assemblage of various types of donors in the second century AD, ranging from *c.* AD 129 to at least AD 185, that is, a period of over fifty years. There was an apparent gap in donations between AD 129 and AD 154, the reason of which is unknown to us. One notes a more or less continuous presence of diverse types of donors from the year 86 (= 154) to the year 107 (= 185). It is significant that the first two gifts in the year 86 were made by two ministers, who were followed by merchant donors. In view of a gap of nearly twenty-five years in donations, one is tempted to suggest that the merchant donors took the lead from the administrators' patronage. Donors at Bandhogarh were essentially merchants (*vāṇijaka* and *negama*) and various craftsmen. Such social categories are also present in numerous donative records in many parts of India. Only two of the twenty records speak of the direct royal patronage. This is a feature that also matched with tendencies elsewhere in India.

These are the features of donations in ancient Bandhogarh that are shared with other Indian areas: there are also a number of distinguishing characteristics of the donations at Bandhogarh. In the donative records under review the absence of *gahapati* (moneyed people whose wealth came primarily from their landed property)[39] and *seṭṭhi* (the merchant par excellence) as categories of prosperous donors can hardly be missed. The *negama* and the *vāṇijaka*, who were the major donors at ancient Bandhogarh did not probably enjoy the prosperity and prestige generally associated with a *gahapati* or a *seṭṭhi*. Female donors, quite prominent in votive inscriptions from many other places, are conspicuous by their absence at ancient Bandhogarh. The Bandhogarh inscriptions are also silent about the presence of *śreṇīs* or occupational guilds who are quite prominent in donative records elsewhere.

But the most distinctive feature of donations at Bandhogarh is the complete absence of reference to any religious group/institution/establishment to which these donations were made. Donations in a pan-India context were generally given to the Buddhist *saṁghas* or *vihāras* and Jaina monasteries by lay devotees and/or disciples. But no such group or institution figures in our records from Bandhogarh as recipients of donations. The area has also failed to yield any contemporary image of a divinity. Chakrabarti also notes that inscriptions are silent about any religious leanings or preference of donors. He however found the name Śivabhakta (literally a devotee of Śiva) engraved in cave no. 6.[40] This leads him to argue that at Bandhogarh the 'earliest rock cut caves were dedicated to Śaiva worship'. It must however be pointed that all early historical donations were invariably associated with Buddhist and Jaina monasteries and practically never with Brahmanical practices. In fact Brahmanical religious practices were largely oriented towards the performance of sacrifices following Vedic prescriptions to which the institution of *dakṣiṇā* (payment of sacrificial fee to officiating priest or priests) was more relevant than that of *dāna* which was characteristic of Buddhist and Jaina monastic life. In view of this it would indeed be difficult to see any Śaiva association with Bandhogarh on the basis of a single occurrence of the proper name Śivabhakta. Donors desire that let *dhama*, i.e. *dharma* and *puṇya* (merit) be increased (*vadhatu*). The desire is of course that merit be accrued to the patron as a result of his patronage or *dāna*. Few can deny that an act of the patronage like *dāna* is inseparably associated with the acquisition of merit in exchange of a donation of tangible goods. The term *dhama/dharma*, though generally taken in the sense of a particular religious belief, may not stand here for any specific sectarian creed—Brahmanical, Buddhist or Jaina. It may rather be taken to denote righteousness, since the donors here never spoke of their religious leanings.

Acts of *dāna* in the early historical context are largely performed by various types of craftsmen and merchants. Donative records, including those at Bandhogarh throw much light on various occupational groups and social categories, but rarely refer to donors' *varṇa-jāti* affiliations. These leave an unmistakable impression that occupation was used to indicate the donor's actual status which may not necessarily correspond to the ritual status according to the strict sastric codes. It is also clear that the act of patronage, which required tangible wealth, resulted in the enhancement of the status and prestige of the patron (something intangible). One may note here that contemporary socio-religious treatises—Brahmanical as well as non-Brahmanical ones—repeatedly emphasized the importance of *dāna*. The Buddhist text *Saddharma-puṇḍarika* translated into Chinese (as early as the third century AD) urged both monks and lay devotees to communicate with the Buddha only through worship and donation, as the text considered that it would be impossible for Buddhists to approach the Master through proper understanding. The text also marks the great religious prominence of Avalokiteśvara Bodhisattva who appeared as even more compassionate than the Buddha and as a saviour of people in trouble, including those in endangered caravans.[41]

In Brahmanical texts the concept of *dāna* is often intermixed with *iṣṭapūrtta-dharma*. While the term *iṣṭapūrtta* figures as early as the *Ṛgveda* and the Upaniṣads, it is in the early Dharmaśāstras that the concept is really highlighted. *Iṣṭa* generally stands for sacrifices, as per Vedic prescriptions while *pūrtta* would mean meritorious work of public utility (e.g. digging of a well or a tank—*khātādikarmma*). The general sastric view is that while the *dvijas* (i.e. those belonging to the three higher *varṇas*) were entitled to both Vedic sacrifices and participating in meritorious work (*pūrtta*), the śūdra could only perform *pūrtta*. It is interesting to find that a Puranic passage glorifies *pūrtta* as something even higher than *iṣṭa* or Vedic sacrifices: a man secures only heaven (*svarga*) by *iṣṭa* but *pūrtta* brings him salvation (*mokṣa*).[42]

Acts of patronage seen at ancient Bandhogarh and at many other religio-cultural centres of early historical times may logically be brought to the category of *pūrttadharma*. Patrons of *pūrttadharma* were by and large people from different walks of life who did not necessarily enjoy very high ritual status as per *jāti-varṇa* norms. There is hardly any room for doubt about the popularity of the institution of *dāna* among agri-culturists, craftsmen and merchants. The desire for the increase of *dhama* (*dharma*), expressed in the Bandhogarh records, may therefore refer to the augmentation of *pūrttadharma* which cut across sectarian barriers. An increase in *pūrttadharma* in its turn could ensure an increase in *puṇya* for the donor/patron. This would logically result in the augmentation of his actual social status and prestige. For a donor who did not belong to a high *jāti-varṇa* status, *dāna* could provide an alternative means of improving his actual status in society. Certain worldly considerations seem to have encouraged donors to patronize acts of *pūrttadharma*. '*Dāna* cannot be treated as an exclusively religious institution divorced from the social and economic tenor of life'.[43] The institution (of *dāna*) all along had firm roots in the material culture of India.[44] These arguments may also indicate a similar orientation to the acts of *pūrttadharma* by diverse donors at ancient Bandhogarh. As no religious groups or institutions are known to have received these donations and as the religious affiliations of donors do not figure in our records, the Bandhogarh donative records may be considered as examples of 'secular' gifts. This will be particularly highlighted by the donation of a *vyāyāmaśālā* or gymnasium. It is highly significant that one of the cave shelters is labelled as *sārtthikalāta*, i.e. a *lāta* or cave-dwelling meant for caravan traders (*sārthikas/sārthavahas*, etc.).[45] These once again strengthen our suggestion that 'secular' and not religious donations were made at Bandhogarh.

CONCLUSION

Why did donors—merchants, craftsmen and administrators—choose to come to Bandhogarh? Bandhogarh could hardly be considered a religious or cultural centre like Mathurā, Sanchi and Nasik. Economically speaking the area was not known for agrarian prosperity or as a centre of crafts and commerce. In fact epigraphic records from Bandhogarh do not give us an impression that there were regular settlements in and around the area. A rock near the Bandhogarh caves, on the other hand, bears figures of several animals and also an inscription. The inscription reads '*mugave selo*' i.e. *mṛgayā-śaila*.[46] Thus the area was in a hilly and forest tract, fit for hunting expeditioins. This once again presents the enigma: why did donors—none of the them being explicitly stated as being local residents—come to Bandhogarh to make donations?

The inscriptions under review may provide some indirect clues to this riddle. The palaeography of these records, once again according to Chakrabarti, shows some correspondence to the Kuṣāṇa epigraphs from Mathurā and also bears some affinity with inscriptions of western India (under the Kṣatrapas) and the western Deccan. 'The dating system of the Bandhogarh records—giving a date in Śaka year, season, fortnight and the day—are clearly inspired by the Mathurān system during the Kuṣāṇa period.' This then logically suggests cultural penetration (and hence cultural contacts) from the Ganga-Yamuna doab through the middle Ganga valley into the Rewa area. Such a possibility will further be strengthened by the evidence of the arrival of donors from Kauśāmbī at Bandhogarh. The name of Mathurā too was not unheard of in the Bandhogarh records. Epigraphic and palaeographic features may lead us to conclude that Bandhogarh in Rewa was so situated as to be apaproachable both from the Ganga valley and the western Deccan.

Literary evidence like the story of Baveru throws light on the arterial route from Pratiṣṭhāna in the central Deccan to Śrāvasti in the northern part of the middle Ganga valley. The route passed through western Malwa (Māhiṣmatī or Ujjayinī), eastern Malwa (Vidiśā) and central India (Tumbavana or Tumain in Madhya Pradesh, also known as Vanasabhaya) to Kauśāmbī whence it went up to Śrāvastī. This route must have passed through the ancient Rewa region which had well known linkages with the middle Ganga valley. The discovery of Northern Black Polished Ware at Jhar in Rewa district (though numerically not impressive) may indicate penetration of some salient features of the material life in the middle Ganga valley into central India.[47] The discovery of Aśokan inscriptions at Rupnath (near Jabbalpur) and Panguraria[48] once again highlights the presence of elements of the Ganga valley culture in this region. The Aśokan inscription at Panguraria leaves little room for doubt that eastern Madhya Pradesh became an area important enough to be brought under the administrative supervision of a *kumāra* (a prince of the Maurya family) in the third century BC. One may also recall, on the basis of the Jogimara Cave inscription of the second century BC, the presence of a sculptor (*lupadakha*) of Vārāṇasī in what is at present Surguja district in eastern Madhya Pradesh.[49] All these scattered pieces of evidence may at least underline that the proximity of the Rewa region both the middle Ganga plains and central India facilitated its contacts with both regions. There is a distinct likelihood that Bandhogarh was situated on or near the famous Pratiṣṭhāna-Śrāvasti route. But despite its location on this route Bandhogarh on its own did not offer much economic opportunity; yet the presence of donors over nearly half a century at Bandhogarh may be explained if we logically surmise that is provided *vāṇijakas*, *negamas* and *sārtthas* with some facilities of an intermediate halting station on a long overland route and in a rather inhospitable area. This probably necessitated excavation of cave dwellings, tanks and wells and a gymnasium at Bandhogarh for itinerant merchants. This study thus attempts at explaining the peculiarities of Bandhogarh as an unique site yielding 'secular' donative records.

NOTES

1. The possibility of change in early Indian life is argued mostly in Marxist historiography of early India. See Kosambi, *Culture and Civilization*; Sharma, *Material Culture*; Sharma, *Perspectives*.
2. For a general introduction to this period see R.C. Majumdar, ed., *The Age of Imperial Unity*, Bombay, 1968; Nilakantha Sastri, ed., *A Comprehensive History*, vol. II. Major trends in socio-economic life are discussed by

Chakravarti, 'Early Historical India: A Study in its Material Milieu (*c.* 600 BC-AD 300)', included in this volume, Chap. 2. Two outstanding features of material life, viz., the emergence of urban centres and territorial state, of the period under review are studied in depth; see for example, Romila Thapar, *From Lineage to State*, New Delhi, 1984; Dilip K. Chakrabarti, *Theoretical Issues in Indian Archaeology*, New Delhi, 1988; G. Erdosy, *Urbanization in Early Historical India*, Oxford, 1988; F.R. Allchin, 'City and State Formation in Early Historic South Asia', *SAS*, vol. V, 1989, pp. 1-16; F.R. Allchin, 'Patterns of City Formation in Early Historic South Asia', *SAS*, vol. VI, 1990, pp. 163-73.

3. There has been a notable growth of archaeological knowledge through many excavations and explorations of early historical sites. For a general survey and reference see A. Ghosh, ed., *An Encyclopaedia of Indian Archaeology*, 2 vols., Delhi, 1989. D.C. Sircar is known for his wide use of epigraphic materials to glean data on economic life, though he himself did not specialise in the economic history of early India.
4. H. Lüders, 'A List of Brahmi Inscriptions up to AD 400 with the exception of Those of Aśoka', being a supplement to *EI*, vol. 10, 1912.
5. Vidya Dehejia, 'Collective and Popular Bases of Early Buddhist Patronage: Sacred Monuments', in Barbara Stoller Miller, ed., *The Powers of Art: Patronage in Indian Culture*, New Delhi, 1992, pp. 35-45.
6. O.H.K. Spate and A.T.A. Learmonth, *India and Pakistan: A General and Regional Geography*, London, 1967, p. 628.
7. Spate and Learmonth, *India and Pakistan*, p. 628.
8. N.P. Chakrabarti, 'Brāhmī Inscriptions from Bandhogarh', *EI*, vol. XXXI, 1955, pp. 167-86.
9. V.V. Mirashi, *CII*, vol. IV in two parts, Ootacamund, 1955; P.K. Bhattacharyya, *Historical Geography of Madhya Pradesh*, New Delhi, 1977.
10. Scholarly debates on assigning the beginning of the Kaniṣka era in terms of the Christian era are still unabated. The following possibilities are suggested: AD 78, 128, 144 and 248; see in this context A.L. Basham, ed., *Papers on the Date of Kaniṣka*, Leiden, 1968. The theory of AD 248 as the beginning of the Kaniṣka era has nowadays gone out of serious consideration. Mukherjee, *Rise and Fall*, p. 621 makes a review of the controversy.
11. Mukherjee, *Rise and Fall.*
12. Chakrabarti, 'Brāhmī Inscriptions from Bandhogarh', p. 169.
13. Chakrabarti, 'Brāhmī Inscriptions from Bandhogarh', p. 181.
14. Chakrabarti, 'Brāhmī Inscriptions from Bandhogarh', p. 183.
15. Mukherjee, *Rise and Fall.*
16. D.C. Sircar's comments appear as footnote 1 in Chakrabarti, 'Brāhmī Inscriptions from Bandhogarh', p. 169.
17. Chakrabarti, 'Brāhmī Inscriptions from Bandhogarh', p. 182.
18. Chakrabarti, 'Brāhmī Inscriptions from Bandhogarh', p. 177.

19. Chakrabarti, 'Brāhmī Inscriptions from Bandhogarh', p. 178.
20. M. Monier Williams, *Sanskrit English Dictionary*, Delhi, 1979 (rpt.), p. 545.
21. Ghosh, *The City*, pp. 46-7.
22. Majumdar, *Corporate Life*.
23. In discussions on early Indian commerce merchants often appear as a generic category without their specific types being clearly pointed out. Blanket terms like 'trader', 'merchant', '*seṭṭhi*', etc., are not enough to show different categories/levels of merchants. An attempt to discern various types of merchants in the context of the early medieval Konkan has been made by Ranabir Chakravarti, 'Merchants of Konkan', *IESHR*, vol. XXIII, 1986, pp. 208-15.
24. Romila Thapar, 'Patronage and Community', in Barbara Stoller Miller, ed., *The Powers of Art: Patronage in Indian Culture*, New Delhi, 1992, pp. 19-34.
25. Chakrabarti, 'Brāhmī Inscriptions from Bandhogarh', p. 182.
26. Romila Thapar, *Ancient Indian Social History*, New Delhi, 1978, explores in an essay the possibilities of upward mobility in early Indian society.
27. Chakrabarti, 'Brāhmī Inscriptions from Bandhogarh', p. 181.
28. Sharma, *Excavations at Kauśāmbi 1957-59*; Sharma, *Excavations at Kauśāmbi 1949-50*; Erdosy, 'The Origin of Cities'; Erdosy, *Urbanization*.
29. Chakrabarti, 'Brāhmī Inscriptions from Bandhogarh', pp. 177-8.
30. Chakrabarti, 'Brāhmī Inscriptions from Bandhogarh', p. 185.
31. For a more elaborate discussion on this *vyāyāmaśālā* see, Ranabir Chakravarti and Suchandra Dutta Majumder, 'An Ancient Gymnasium at Bandhogarh', *Monthly Bulletin of the Asiatic Society*, July 1992, pp. 1-7.
32. Chakrabarti, 'Brāhmī Inscriptions from Bandhogarh', p. 172.
33. T. Waters, *On Yuan Chwang's Travels in India*, New Delhi, 1961, pp. 255-6.
34. Chakrabarti, 'Brāhmī Inscriptions from Bandhogarh', p. 180.
35. Chakrabarti, 'Brāhmī Inscriptions from Bandhogarh', p. 182.
36. Chakrabarti, 'Brāhmī Inscriptions from Bandhogarh', p. 183.
38. Chakrabarti, 'Brāhmī Inscriptions from Bandhogarh', p. 186.
39. Wagle, *Society at the Time of the Buddha*, pp. 151-5 and Uma Chakravarti, *Social Dimensions of Early Buddhism*, New Delhi, 1987, pp. 65-94 amply demonstrate on the basis of the Pali texts that the *gahapati* was fabulously rich person and that he should not be confused with Sanskrit *gṛhapati*, a householder. It is surprising that Dehejia, 'Collective and Popular Bases of Early Patronage', continues to designate the *gahapati* simply as a householder. Early Buddhist texts clearly distinguish a *gahapati* from an ordinary householder who is called a *gihī* (*gṛhi*) and a *gahaṭṭha* (*gṛhastha*).
40. Chakrabarti, 'Brāhmī Inscriptions from Banghogarh', p. 183.
41. Prosperous agriculturists and merchants, including ship-owners, prominently figure in recently discovered Kharoṣṭī-Brāhmī documents from West

Bengal, palaeographically assignable to the first four centuries of the Christian era. See, B.N. Mukherjee, 'Kharoṣṭī and Kharoṣṭī-Brāhmī Inscriptions from West Bengal, India', *IMB*, vol. XXV, 1990. Despite the presence of moneyed men ancient Bengal has so far not yielded any donative record. These epigraphic documents, significantly enough, speak of a cultural life steeped in the Vedic tradition. There is little reference in these documents to Buddhist and Jaina practices. This may offer some clues to the problem of the absence of donative records in ancient Bengal.

42. Xin Ri Liu, *Ancient India and Ancient China AD 1-600*, New Delhi, 1988, pp. 94 ff.
43. P.V. Kane, *History of Dharmaśāstra*, vol. V, pt. 2, Poona, 1962, pp. 947-9.
44. Vijaya Nath, *Dāna: Gift System in Ancient India (c. 600 BC-AD 300): A Socio-Economic Perspective*, New Delhi, 1987, p. 255.
45. Chakrabarti, 'Brāhmī Inscriptions from Bandhogarh', p. 178.
46. Chakrabarti, 'Brāhmī Inscriptions from Bandhogarh', p. 172.
47. Nayanjyot Lahiri, *The Archaeology of Ancient Indian Trade Routes*, New Delhi, 1992, pp. 316, 330.
48. D.C. Sircar, *Asokan Studies*, Calcutta, 1979, pp. 94-103.
49. Lüders, 'A List of Brahmi Inscriptions', p. 93, Inscription no. 921.

CHAPTER 4

The Puṭabhedana as a Centre of Trade in Early India

INTRODUCTION

The economic historiography of early India (*c.* up to AD 1300) understandably has a distinct thrust towards agrarian condition and relevant issues. The remarkable dependence on agriculture as the mainstay of material life is known for its continuity over millennia down to the present time. The profusion of crops, both cereals and cash crops, and their immense diversity over the greater part of the subcontinent, provide an excellent platform for the non-agrarian sector of the economy to prosper side by side with the flourishing agriculture. There may be seen among economic historians of early India a growing awareness of the importance of the study of crafts, commerce and urban centres, without however losing sight of the predominantly agricultural material milieu. Probings into the crafts, trade and urban life of early South Asia are now integrally linked up with researches in agrarian history.[1]

Recent studies of pre-modern societies by anthropologists, sociologists and historians highlight the distinction between exchange and trade. While the former is often located among the redistributive activities and gifts in relatively simpler societies, trade is generally viewed as a more complex system marked by the availability of exchangeable surplus, growing monetization, formation of the state, urban society and administrative structures.[2] In other words, one has to be aware of the process (or processes) leading from the stage of exchange to that of commerce and also of the possibility of their mutual overlapping, especially in the context of the well-known regional disparities in South Asian history.[3] The other problem which the economic historian of early India has often to face is the frequent use of such terms as merchant (cf. *śreṣṭhī*) and mart (*pattana*) as blanket categories. Such a perspective rarely takes into account the possibility of the existence of different types of merchants and market places in early India. A number of efforts of late in these directions help sharpen our understanding of the non-rural sector of the economy, mainly with the help of textual and epigraphic data.[4] Field archaeological materials from explored and excavated sites, when juxtaposed with textual and epigraphic evidence, give a distinct impression of the hierarchies of settlements of non-rural nature belonging to early historical times.[5] In the light of the foregoing discussions the present chapter proposes to take a close look at a particular type of trade centre, known as *puṭabhedana* in early India.

THE EARLY HISTORICAL SITUATION

The earliest known occurrence of the term *puṭabhedana* is found in the *Mahāparinivvānasuttanta* of the *Vinayapiṭaka*, one of the most important canonical texts of the Buddhists assignable to pre-Maurya times (i.e. before the fourth century BC). Describing the final days in the life of the Master, the text gives an account of his visit to Pāṭaligāma which is called a *puṭabhedana* within the *mahājanapada* of Magadha (generally identified with southern Bihar). The term *puṭa* stands for covered boxes (of merchandise); so the term *puṭabhedana* is logically taken to mean a place where lids of the boxes or packages of merchandise were broken (i.e. opened, *bhedana*). This is also borne out by the *Sumaṅgalavilāsinī* of Buddhaghoṣa, the commentator on the *Vinayapiṭaka* (*c.* fifth century AD), who explained the term as *puṭa-bhedanaṭṭhānam* and *bhāṇḍa-bhāṇḍikānāṁmocanaṭṭhānam*.[6] The term *puṭabhedana* thus clearly denotes a centre of trade. In the context of its reference to Pāṭaligāma it was logically translated as 'a centre of interchange of all kinds of ware'. The *puṭabhedana* in question stood at the confluence of the Ganga and the Son, a location which must have facilitated riverine commerce and communication. This is further indicated by the mention of a ferry point (*tiṭṭha*, i.e. *tīrtha*), *Dīgha Nikāya* II, 90-1 which the Buddha used for proceeding to Koṭigāma in the non-monarchical *mahājanapada* of the Vajjis in north Bihar.[7] The Buddha is said to have taken note of the *vanippatho* (*vaṇikpatha*) or overland routes at the *puṭabhedana* of Pāṭaligāma. The most significant aspect of this trade centre was its fortification which was being constructed at the time of the Buddha's visit by two Magadhan ministers, Vassakāra and Sunīdha, under the instruction of the Magadhan king Ajātaśatru. This was done, according to the text, in view of Ajātaśatru's preparations of military assaults on the non-monarchical Vajjis. The importance of the *puṭabhedana* was thus clearly realized by the Magadhan ruler, known for his militant stance against neighbouring powers. The textual description speaks of the gateway (*dvāra*), ferry point (*tiṭṭha*), overland trade routes and fortification at Pāṭaligāma, but there is no account of a *koṭṭhāgāra* offering storage facilities of merchandise. Interestingly enough, this *puṭabhedana* does not figure in the list of principal cities (*mūlanagara*) nor as a subsidiary town (*śākhānagara*) existing in the Ganga valley during the days of the Buddha. The place, though commanding commercial importance and hence political attention, did not probably attain urban proportions in the lifetime of the Buddha. This seems to have led Kosambi[8] to designate it as a 'stockade' (in the sense of a trade centre with fortification) and Allchin to label it as a 'wharf'.[9]

The location and present identification of the *puṭabhedana* has been made easier for us by the Buddha himself who did not fail to forecast the future greatness of the place under the new name Pāṭaliputra. Pāṭaliputra was to become in the Buddha's prophesy the foremost city (*agganagara*). Political history of ancient India tells us that the Magadhan capital was shifted from Rajagṛha (modern Rajgir, south Bihar) to Pāṭaliputra (modern Patna) during the time of Udayi in the post-Ajataśatru days and the city remained the premier political centre of India at least up to the middle of the sixth century AD.[10]

Pāṭaliputra as the Mauryan capital and also as a great urban centre seems to have retained its commercial importance. This will be evident from the *Indika* (now lost and preserved only in excerpts and summaries of later Calssical writers) of Meghasthenes, the Seleukidian ambassador at the capital of Candragupta Maurya, the founder of the Maurya dynasty. Members of at least three of the six boards of city officials (*astynomoi*), entrusted with the municipal administration of the Mauryan capital, supervised commercial activities at Pali(m)bothra, i.e. Pāṭaliputra.[11]

This logically brings us to an examination of the relevant data in the *Kauṭilīya Arthaśāstra*, the earliest stratum of which namely the *Adhyakṣapracāra* section (Book II) has been assigned to the third century BC, i.e. contemporary to the Maurya period.[12] This celebrated text on early Indian polity stands out for giving primacy to economic/financial matters in the management of the state. In the chapter concerning the making of fortified (urban) centres (*durganiveśa*), the theoretician recommends the establishment of a *paṇyapuṭa-bhedanam*.[13] The commercial character of a *puṭabhedana* has already been discussed. Kauṭilya further highlights the same by using the prefix *paṇya* to *puṭabhedana*. In the section dealing with the functions of the *śulkādhyakṣa* (director of tolls and customs) the term *paṇyapuṭa* occurs (II.21.20) to denote a package of commodities. The *paṇyapuṭa* would have to he sealed with an appropriate stamp (*mudrā*) of the authority, as and when the *śulkādhyakṣa* received the *śulka* or tolls and customs.[14] The merchant could break the sealed package of commodities for transaction at a trade centre which is therefore called a *paṇya-puṭabhedana*. The *Arthaśāstra* lays down that such a centre of trade should be established within a *sthānīya* or administrative headquarters over eight hundred villages having a revenue collection centre too (*samudayasthāna*). Kangle suggests that the *sthanīya* figuring in the *durganiveśa* section should actually stand for an important urban centre, if not the capital city itself. The *paṇyapuṭabhedana* should ideally be approachable both by overland (*aṁsapatha*) and water (*vāripatha*) routes. This has some obvious correspondence to the account of Pāṭaligāma mentioned earlier. But Kauṭilya's *paṇyapuṭabhedana* is marked by greater complexities than its counterpart at Pāṭaligāma. It is closely integrated to a politico-administrative centre (*sthānīya*) and its revenue bearing potentials (including revenue from trade) are duly underlined. The *paṇyapuṭabhedana* of Kauṭilya therefore seems to have had a more pronounced urban orientation.

An even more elaborate description of the *puṭabhedana* is seen in the account of Sāgala with which opens the *Milindapañho*, datable to *c.* second-first century BC.[15] The capital of Milinda, identified with the Indo-Greek ruler Menander, was at Sāgala which is generally agreed to be the same as Sialkot in Punjab. Sāgala is clearly described both as an urban centre (*nagara*) and a *nānāpuṭabhedana*. The prefix *nānā* appears to have indicated the fact that at the trade centre (*puṭabhedana*) at Sāgala diverse commodities and merchants from different places converged. There is also a clear reference to its storehouse (*koṭṭhāgārā*) which must have had arrangements of warehousing. According to the *Milindapañho*, the city of Sāgala in the Yona or Yavana country was endowed with a defence, gate (*gopura*), archways (*toraṇa*), rampart (*pākāra*), moat (*parikhā*), royal palace (*antepura*), streets (*vīthi*), squares (*caccara*), crossroads (*catukka*) and shops (*āpaṇa*). If there was really any commercial centre at Sāgala, its urban character can hardly be doubted. One cannot deny that this graphic literary account has as yet little archaeological corroboration. Historians of early Indian urbanism are therefore not always impressed by such stereotypical and hyperbolic descriptions.[16] The text in this case nevertheless offers us some ideas about the perceptions of early Indians of a flourishing commercial centre in an urbane setting. This is perhaps why Sāgala, irrespective of its neglect by archaeologists, finds a place in a recent discussion of ancient Indian cities with a specific thrust towards archaeological evidence.[17]

A continuity in the image of a commercial centre in an urban setting can be discerned in the famous Sanskrit lexicon, the *Nāmaliṅgānuśāsana* of Amarasimha (more popularly known as the *Amarakośa*). Generally ascribed to the Gupta period and not later than the eighth century AD,[18] the text in question gives a number of synonyms of *pura/purī* (urban centre). One of these is *puṭabhedana*, equated also with a *pattana*. The interchangeability of these terms in the lexicon is a clear pointer to a definite correlation between a *puṭabhedana* (with or without prefixes like *paṇya* and *nānā*) and a urban centre by the end of the early historical period (*c.* AD 600).

THE EARLY MEDIEVAL SITUATION[19]

The textual and epigraphic data, pertaining to early medieval times (*c.* AD 600-1300), throw admittedly less light on *puṭabhedanas*. One may therefore be tempted to suggest that the *puṭabhedana* probably did not continue to enjoy its vantage position in the material life of that period. This also sets a suitable stage for the proponents of the idea of Indian feudalism to argue that the *puṭabhedana* could not survive in an age marking the decline of trade, lessening use of coins, urban decay and the emergence of a self-sufficient and closed rural society.[20]

Contrary to this dominant historiography, the term *puṭabhedana* is found in the description of commerce at a *peṇṭhā* in the *Yaśastilakacampu* of Somadeva Suri. A major Jaina writer, Somadeva explicitly describes himself as a contemporary of the Rāṣṭrakūṭa king Kṛṣṇa III (AD 939-65). A close perusal of the text suggests that Somadeva was well aware of the realities of socio-economic life in the early medieval Deccan.[21] In a story highlighting the terrible results of theft (*steyaphala*), the account of the establishment of a *peṇṭhā* is clearly described as a *paṇya-puṭabhedana*. One cannot therefore miss the commercial nature of a *peṇṭhā*. Before proceeding to the features of this trade centre it should be pointed out that the historical actuality of Śrībhūti and that of the *peṇṭhā* founded by him for commercial purposes cannot be established from the story. One should remember that Somadeva told this story to draw certain morals. He in fact places the story in *Prayāgadeśa*, located in and around present Allahabad in UP where the existence of a minister named Śrībhūti is not known, nor a market place labelled as *peṇṭhā* is encountered. There are grounds to believe that he was describing features of a *puṭabhedana* somewhere in the Deccan. The important point is that the text seems to have contained reflections of socio-economic realities of a trade centre belonging to the tenth century Deccan.

Let us now examine the features of the *puṭabhedana* after *Yaśastilakacampu.*[22] The *peṇṭhā* had many well laid out apartments (*vibhaktānekāpavarakaracanāśālinī*) and large storage areas for merchandise (*mahābhāṇḍavāhīnī*). The place was provided with drinking facilities, eating houses, assembly halls and roads (*prapāsattra-sabhāsanāthavīthiniveśana*). Merchants from various directions and countries flocked there to carry on business (*nānādigdeśopasarpaṇa-yūjaṁvaṇijām*). This fits in well with the description of a cattle-shed at the *peṇṭhā* which is said to have been provided with water, fodder and firewood. Arrangements for guards to protect boxes with excellent items of trade were made as storage of the same began at the *peṇṭhā* (*bhāṇḍanārambhodhaṭabharīrapeṭakapakṣarakṣāsāram*). The trade centre embraced an area of about a couple of miles (*gorutpramāṇa*) and was marked by ditches (*kulyāḥ*), a rampart (*vapra*), fortification (*prākāra*) and a moat (*parikhā*). This speaks of the impressive size of the commercial centre and also the steps taken to ensure protection of the area. Śrībhūti is credited with establishing the custom of collecting tolls, shares and rent at a moderate rate at the *peṇṭhā* (*praśāntaśulkabhāṭaka-bhāgahāravyavahāramacīkarat*). The rent must have been collected by Śrībhūti for letting out spaces in storage areas to merchants. The idea to levy tolls at a moderate rate may imply inducements offered to merchants to come to this newly created *puṭabhedana*. Measures were further taken to drive away from the *peṇṭhā* gamblers, jesters, dancers, masseurs and whoremongers. This was done probably with a view to ensuring unhindered commercial transactions of merchants who were to be prevented from indulging in the entertainment and vice.

This is an excellent pen-picture of brisk trade and associated life at a *puṭabhedana* with the epithet *peṇṭhā*. But with no known historicity or actuality of the account, does it have any validity in our understanding of the *puṭabhedana*? Fortunately an answer in the affirmative looks likely on the basis of other sources belonging to the early medieval period. Somadeva in his other well-known treatise on policy, the *Nītivākyāmṛtam*, speaks of the *piṇṭhā* which is further described as a *paṇyapuṭabhedinī*.[23] There is little room for doubt about the identity between *peṇṭhā* and *piṇṭhā* in two separate works by the same author who describes them as *puṭabhedana* or *paṇyapuṭabhedinī*. The *Nītivākyāmṛtam* further considers *piṇṭhā* as a *śulkasthāna* or a point of collection of tolls and customs.

This is elaborated in the following recommendation that the *piṇṭhā*, maintained judiciously, would bring endless wealth to the king like a *kāmadhenu* (*nyāyena rakṣitā puṭabhedinī piṇṭhā rājñākāmadhenu*). The close correspondence between the two texts on the revenue bearing aspects of the *peṇṭhā* cannot but be taken into consideration. There is however one major difference in the two works of Somadeva. While the *Nītivākyāmṛtam*, like the *Arthaśāstra* of Kauṭilya, recommends the supervision and management of the *puṭabhedana*(*nī*) under the ruling authority, the *peṇṭhā* in the *Yaśastilakacampu*, appears to have been personally owned and managed by Śrībhūti.

The term *peṁṭa*, significantly enough, figures regularly in a number of inscriptions of the Kākatīyas, a formidable regional power is eastern Deccan ruling from the latter half of twelfth to the early part of the fourteenth century AD. These epigraphic records impress upon us the commercial activities at the *peṁṭas*. They are variously called *suṁka-peṁṭas*. The term *suṇka*/*suṇga* in Telugu and Tamil denotes tolls and customs, in other word *śulka*.[24] Further, there should not be much difficulty in suggesting discernible similarities among words like *peṇṭhā*, *piṇṭhā* and *peṁṭa*. All three were centres of trade, though the inscriptions do not call *peṁṭas* explicitly as *puṭabhedanas*. These words appear to have survived in the modern word *peth* which is suffixed to many place names, and especially trade centres, in present day Maharashtra, Andhra Pradesh and Karnataka. The *peṇṭhā* can logically be seen as a Deccanese counterpart of *puṭabhedanas* described in texts with a predominantly north Indian association.[25]

CONCLUSION

The *puṭabhedana* thus had a distinct ethos as a centre of trade in early Indian economic history. An obvious difficulty in this study is our relative lack of knowledge about historical *puṭabhedanas*, barring the instance of Pāṭaligāma (Pāṭaliputra) and Sāgala. The epigraphic evidence, being absent regarding *puṭabhedanas*, further frustrates the economic historian. Encouraging results may be in the offing, if inscriptional references to *peṇṭhās* in the Deccan—suggested to have been more or less the same as *puṭabhedanas*—are systematically tapped. Notwithstanding the sketchy and disparate data on the *puṭabhedanas*, some general features of this type of trade centre are apparent. As centres of commerce their revenue generating capacities are recognized in sources from the Maurya period onwards. Starting from the *Arthaśāstra* onwards, textual evidence indicates the *puṭabhedana* to be a point of convergence of merchants, routes and exchangeable products. This may explain why our data since the fourth-third centuries BC describe storage facilities at *puṭabhedanas*. One does not have to stretch one's imagination to appreciate why politico-administrative structures would be a regular feature associated with *puṭabhedanas*. The hinterland and the foreland of the *puṭabhedana* cannot be worked out at the present state of our knowledge. Nevertheless, trade and realizable tolls and customs therefrom did attract the attention of politico-administrative authorities. The combination of these socio-economic and political factors probably resulted in the transformation of at least some of the *puṭabhedanas* or their equivalents into urban centres of early India.

NOTES

1. Romila Thapar, ed., *Recent Perspectives of Early Indian History*, Bombay, 1995.
2. Cyril Belshaw, *Traditional Exchange and Modern Markets*, New Jersey, 1965, Chap. III.
3. In-depth and ongoing researches on early Indian trade and traders have dispelled an earlier perception of the economic condition in ancient India, a typical example of which can be seen in an following quotation:
   'The moving force from first to last came from the West, the little changing people of the East allowed the West to find them out. We have then, on the one side India of the Orient, then as now a disjointed aggregate of countries but without the uniting force of British rule which she now has a while open to commerce content generally to remain within her borders and engage in agriculture.' Warmington, *Commerce*, pp. 1-2.
4. Ghosh, *The City*; B.D. Chattopadhyaya, *The Making of Early Medieval India*, New Delhi, 1994; F.R. Allchin et al., *The Archaeology of Early Historic South Asia, the Emergence of Cities and States*, Cambridge, 1995; Chakravarti, 'Merchants of Konkan'; Chakravarti, 'Merchants and Other Donors at Ancient Bandhogarh', *SAS*, 11, 1995, pp. 33-42 (included in this volume as Chap. 3).
5. Erdosy, Urbanization; Dilip K. Chakrabarti, *The Archaeology of Ancient Indian Cities*, New Delhi, 1995.
6. T.W. Rhys Davids and J.E. Carpenter, eds., *Sumaṅgalavilāsinī*, London, 1931, pp. 540-1.
7. T.W. Rhys Davids and J.E. Carpenter, eds., *Dīgha Nikāya*, London, 1903, vol. II, pp. 90-1.
8. Kosambi, *Introduction*, p. 153.
9. Allchin et al., *The Archaeology of Early Historic South Asia*, p. 195.

10. Dilip K. Chakrabarti has argued that Pāṭaliputra (formerly Pāṭaligāma) came to great prominence because of its immense potential as a trade centre, especially riverine trade. The first Magadhan capital, Rājagṛha, was not advantageous for trade in general and riverine in particular (*Ancient Indian Cities*, p. 209). Without at all diminishing the commercial significance of Pāṭaligāma/Pāṭaliputra, its rise to political prominence was determined probably because of its more northerly and hence strategic location than that of Rājagṛha. The Magadhan conquest of Kośala and the non-monarchical Vajjis during the reign of Ajātaśatru resulted in the expansion of the Magadhan power over the extensive tracts to the north of the Ganga, while Magadhan territories originally had its base to the south of the Ganga (Raychaudhuri, *Political History*; Chakravarti, *Warfare for Wealth*).
11. Majumdar, *The Classical Accounts*. The archaeological scenario of Pāṭaliputra (modern Patna in Bihar) does not match the wealth of literary descriptions about it in Indian and Classical texts. For a general survey of the archaeological excavations conducted there see Ghosh, *Encyclopaedia*, vol. II, pp. 334-6; Chakrabarti, *Ancient Indian Cities*, pp. 209ff.
12. T.R. Trautman, *Kauṭilya and Arthaśāstra, a Statistical Investigation of the Authorship and the Evolution of the Text*, Leiden, 1971.
13. *KAS*, II.3.
14. The *Arthaśāstra* dictum shows that the packages of merchandise had to be sealed by using the appropriate *mudrā* which authenticated the product(s) fit for transactions and also ensured that necessary tolls and customs had been collected by some administrative authorities. The clear archaeological proof of this is best illustrated by the large number of seals and sealings which often also carried cord marks. This practice goes back as early as the days of the Harappan civilization (*c.* 2300-1750 BC). The connections of seals with administrative and trade mechanisms have been discussed by Allchin and Allchin, *The Rise of Civilization*; K.K. Thaplyal, *Studies in Ancient Indian Seals*, Allahabad, 1972. Plaster jar plugs, used for sealing the mouths of jars, have been found from the Red Sea site of Leukos Limen; these have been assigned to the heydays of Roman trade with India (*c.* late first century BC to the middle of AD third century). See Steven E. Sidebotham, 'Ports on the Red Sea and Arabia-India Trade', in Vimala Begley and Richard Daniel de Puma, eds., *Rome and India, the Ancient Sea Trade*, New Delhi, 1992, pp. 31-2.
15. C.A.F. Rhys Davids (tr.), *The Questions of King Milinda*, Oxford, 1890; V. Trenckner, ed., *Milindapañho*, London, 1928.
16. Ghosh, *The City*.
17. Chakrabarti, *Ancient Indian Cities*, p. 183.
18. H.D. Sharma and N.G. Sardesai, eds., *Nāmaliṅgānuśāsana of Amarasiṁha*, Poona, 1941; R.C. Majumdar, ed., *The Classical Age of India*, Bombay, 1970.
19. The expression 'early medieval', though variously defined, nowadays is

generally taken by most scholars to denote the period from *c.* AD 600 to 1300. The early medieval period in Indian history is thus placed between the early historical and medieval. The lively debate on the principal features of this period may be considered a major landmark in Indian historiography, particularly since the 1950s. For a recent statement on the ethos of this phase see Chattopadhyaya, *The Making of Early Medieval India*.

20. R.S. Sharma, *Indian Feudalism, c.* AD *300-1200*, Delhi, 1980 (2nd edn.); B.N.S. Yadava, *Society and Culture in North India during the Twelfth Century*, Allahabad, 1973; D.N. Jha, ed., *Feudal Social Formation in Early India*, New Delhi, 1987.
21. This will be evident from Somadeva's graphic account of a cattle-shed in Karahāṭaka, present Karhad in Maharashtra. See K.K. Handiqui, *Yaśastilaka and Indian Culture*, Sholapur, 1968 (2nd edn.).
22. Sivadatta and K.P. Parab, eds., *Yaśastilakacampu*, Bombay, 1901-3, pp. 344-9, especially 345; VIII.27.
23. Sushil Kumar Gupta, tr., *Nītivākyāmṛtam*, Calcutta, 1987, XIX.21.
24. P.V. Parabrahma Sastry, *The Kāktīyas of Warangal*, Hyderabad, 1978, pp. 230-1, 234-6, 247-9.
25. A brief notice on the importance of the description of the *peṇṭhā* in the *Yaśastilakacampu* has been made by Ranabir Chakravarti, 'Commercial Activities at a Peṇṭhā: Gleanings from the *Yaśastilakacampu*', *Quarterly Bulletin of the School of Historical and Cultural Studies*, vol. I, no. 1, 1994. A more elaborate analysis appears in this volume in chapter 10, 'The Peṇṭhā as a Centre of Trade in the Deccan'. It will be difficult to agree with Handiqui, *Yaśastilaka and Indian Culture*, pp. 119-20, who considers the *peṇṭhā* simply as a 'mart', a term which is too generic and without any specificity. One may also question its identification with a 'fair' (V.K. Jain, *Trade and Traders in Western India* AD *1000-1300*, New Delhi, 1989, pp. 139-40). The fair has unmistakable connections with trade, but takes place at a given period or in a specific season or at specific intervals. Periodicity is one of the hallmarks of a fair. In medieval and early modern Europe there were not many shops in the fair; shops were 'installed evidently for amusement of the public rather than for serious business' (Fernand Braudel, *The Wheels of Commerce*, London, 1985, p. 88, also pp. 82-94). The description of the *peṇṭhā* does not show it to be a periodic affair, but a regular centre of trade with a complex and well developed organization. The earliest epigraphic reference to a *peṭha* (certainly the same as *peṇṭhā/piṇṭhā/peṁṭa* of early medieval sources) is seen in the Khoh inscription of Samkṣobha of AD 529 (Gupta era 209). This record found from the present Bundelkhand area speaks of a place named Maṇināgapeṭha in the kingdom of Dābhala (around modern Jubbalpur, Madhya Pradesh) which was included in the eighteen forest kingdoms (*aṣṭādaśāṭavirājyābhyantaram*). See J.F. Fleet, *CII*, vol. III, Calcutta, 1888, pp. 112-16, especially pp. 115 and 116).

CHAPTER 5

Rājaśreṣṭhī

An important element in the world of early Indian merchants was the *śreṣṭhī*, usually a merchant of immense wealth and/or leader of the mercantile community. Among various types of *śreṣṭhīs* the one who was particularly significant was the *rājaśreṣṭhī* or the royal merchant, who may have been appointed by and/or was closely associated with the ruler. The affluence of this merchant is indicated by his epithet *śreṣṭhī* and his royal connections must have made him a merchant of outstanding importance. This paper is an attempt at understanding the functions and position of the *rājaśreṣṭhī*.

The close contact between the trade and the ruler is seen in the description of the *seṭṭhis* and their activities in the Pali canonical texts and the Jātaka stories.[1] In these sources the *seṭṭhi*, as the leader of the mercantile community, appears as one of the closest friends and associates of the king, but does not figure in the list of *rājabhoggas*, i.e. king's paid officers. It is difficult of specify the reason(s) for the special position of the *seṭṭhis* vis-a-vis the king. He may have functioned as a liaison between the ruler and the mercantile community, helped the ruler in formulating commercial policies of the realm and rendered financial assistance in time of need.[2]

II

The importance of the *seṭṭhi* underwent a significant change with the establishment of the Maurya empire. The Mauryas created a managerial state which participated in industrial and commercial activities parallel to the private enterprises. Classical accounts and the edicts of Aśoka contain interesting information regarding governmental supervision and control over traders' activities.[3] At this juncture a study of the *Kauṭilīya Arthaśāstra* may be worthwhile. A thinker of the foremost rank of the royalist school, Kauṭilya hardly allows any one other than the king himself to take initiatives in economic affairs which, according to him, is the source of success in all spheres of life. The *Kauṭilīya Arthaśāstra,* traditionally assigned to the Maurya period, takes a more stringent view and considers traders (*vaidehakas*) as thorns (*kaṇṭakas*) to the well-being of the kingdom.[4] The text strongly urges royal control over trade and constant vigilance over mercantile activities.

For the inspection and regulation of trade and commerce the king was to appoint *paṇyādhyakṣa* (director of trade) a high ranking officer.[5] He was to look after trade in his own country (*svabhūmija*) and abroad (*parabhūmija*). The *paṇyādhyakṣa* was entrusted, among other things, with the distribution and sale of commodities produced in the royal farms and factories through a single channel or centre (*rājapaṇyamekamukhaṁ vyavahāraṁ sthāpayet*).[6] The recommendation of distributing royal goods through a single channel was significant, because that would probably have minimized the competition with other products and their producers.

As an alternative arrangements to this method, Kauṭilya suggested that 'traders should sell royal goods in many places with the price fixed. And they should pay compensation in accordance with the loss sustained' (*Bahumukhaṁ vā rājapaṇyaṁ vaidehakāḥ kṛtārghaṁ vikriṇīran. Chedānu-rupaṁ ca vaidharaṇaṁ dadyuḥ*).[7] Thus, traders were entrusted with selling royal goods under certain conditions laid down by the state. Since these private traders apparently functioned as commissioned agents of the king, they may be categorized as royal merchants. As these traders had to sell the royal goods through many channels, they also faced some competition. At the same time the price of royal goods were fixed, so that the royal trader could not make any extra profit even in the face of keen competition. On the other hand, the royal merchants had to pay a compensation fee if they suffered any losses in dealing with the royal products. This implied that the state was not prepared to tolerate any loss in the sale of royal goods, and any loss incurred due to the actions of the commissioned royal agents had to be made good. Moreover they had to pay to the state some surcharge probably on the profit made by them in the sale of the royal goods. 'One sixteenth part is the surcharge in measure by capacity, one twentieth part in measure by weighing, one eleventh part of commodities sold by counting (*Śoḍaśabhāga mānavyājī viṁśatibhāgastulāmānam gaṇyapaṇyānamekā-daśabhāgaḥ*)'.[8] The royal merchants dealing in royal goods, therefore, appear to have functioned under great restrictions and supervision of the political authority.

The foreign trade was also supervised by the *paṇyādhyakṣa*.

In a foreign territory, however, he should ascertain the price and the value of the commodity (taken out) and the commodity (to be brought) in exchange and should calculate the profit after clearing expenses for duty, road cess, escort charges, picket and ferry dues, food, fodder and share (*Paravişaye tu—paṇyapratipaṇyayorarghaṁ mūlyaṁ cāgamya śulkavartaṇyā ti vāhika-gulmataradeya bhaktabhāgayyaya śuddhaṁ udayaṁ paśyet*).[9]

The *Paṇyādhyakṣa* was here entrusted with exploring the profit potential out of transactions with countries abroad, after clearing all costs. In case no profit was earned abroad he had to assess whether export or 'bringing in goods in exchange for goods' was more advantageous to the state (*Asatyudaye bhaṇḍanirvāhānena paṇyaprati-paṇyanāyanena vā lābhaṁ paśyet*).[10] B.C. Sen considers that the *paṇyādhyakṣa* used to undertake trade missions or assign members of a mercantile community to explore, negotiate and execute transactions under the instructions of the state authority. Following B.C. Sen, it appears that prominent private traders were sent as representatives in the state trade missions.[11] Once again there was a distinct possibility that private merchants were employed as commissioned agents of the king. Kauṭilya further urged that during such trade missions in foreign territories contacts should be established with forest chieftains, frontier officers and chiefs in cities and the countryside to secure their favour and to facilitate a smooth commercial intercourse.

The royal merchant in the *Arthaśāstra* was not a supplier of goods to the king, but was supplied with royal goods produced in the royal farms and factories. It was not unusual in an ancient managerial state to utilize the expertise of prominent traders in addition to government officials for the promotion, sale and distribution of royal products. The *Arthaśāstra*, however, proposed severe restrictions on the activities of the royal traders. He was not given the prestigious epithet *rājaśreṣṭhī* or even *śreṣṭhī*, but simply called a *vaidehaka*, which usually denote just an ordinary trader. The *Arthaśāstra* state did not give any quarter to the royal merchant and actually bossed over him.[12]

III

The degree of economic control of the king on trade and traders lessened in the post-Maurya phase. This phase marks a great expansion of trade within the subcontinent and beyond. The most salient feature of commerce of this period was the trade between the Roman empire and India.[13] The merchant seems to have enjoyed a better position vis-a-vis the ruler in this period.

In the *Acts of Thomas*,[14] the Syriac version of which is assignable to the third century BC, there is reference to a man called Ḥabban, 'the merchant of Gudnaphar'. Gudnaphar may be identified with the Indo-Parthian king Gondophares I (variously referred to in coins as *Gudavharasa/Guduvharasa/Gudravharasa*). Gondophares I was one of the prominent rulers of the Indo-Parthian dynasty which is known to have ruled over the north-western part of the subcontinent before the arrival of the Kuṣāṇas. Gondophares assumed the title *Mahārāja Rājātirāja Mahata* and is believed to have ruled from *c.* AD 20/1 to at least AD 45/6.[15]

In the account of the first Act of Judas Thomas, the Apostle,[16] Lord Jesus entrusted Judas with the task of preaching in India. But the Apostle was rather reluctant to go there. At that time 'a certain merchant, an Indian whose name was Ḥabban' and who was 'sent by king Gudnaphar that he might bring to him a skilful carpenter'[17] came to Jerusalem. Knowing that Ḥabban was in search of a skilful carpenter, Jesus asked the merchant whether he would like to purchase Thomas as a slave and carpenter. The Lord 'bargained with him for twenty (pieces) of silver (as) his price, and wrote a *bill of sale* thus: "I Jesus the son of Joseph the carpenter, from the village of Bethlehem, which is in Judaea, acknowledge that I have sold my slave Judas Thomas to Ḥabban, the merchant of king Gudnaphar." '[18]

This text, often legendary in character but not entirely devoid of a substratum of truth, leaves little doubt that Gondophares I employed a merchant to procure a skilful carpenter. So, Ḥabban may be described as the royal merchant of Gondophares I. This is the earliest known definite information regarding a 'royal merchant'.

While on board the ship during the return journey to India, 'Ḥabban the merchant saith to Judas, "What is thy art which thou art skilled in practising?" Judas saith to him "Carpenting and architecture—the business of the carpenter." Ḥabban further asked him what he knew to make in wood and also in hewn stone. Judas saith to him: "In wood I have learnt to make ploughs, yokes and oars for ferry boats, and masts for ship; and in stone, tombstones and monuments and temples and palaces for king." Ḥabban replied that "I was seeking just such on artificer".'[19] Ḥabban thus seems to have verified whether Judas would fit the requirements of the king. He should have been amply satisfied because the carpenter was skilled and/or experienced in building royal palaces.

'And when Judas had entered into the realm of India with the merchant Ḥabban, Ḥabban went to salute Gudnaphar, the king of India, and he told him of the artificer whom he had brought for him.'[20] The act of saluting the king by the merchant further underlines the fact that being the royal merchant he was responsible to the king. Gudnaphar then asked Judas about his skills and qualifications to which the latter answered in almost the identical manner as he did to Ḥabban. Gudnaphar was evidently satisfied and asked him to build a palace.

Judas accepted the king's order and promised to complete it in due time. The carpenter was provided with a large sum of money for building the palace. But Judas the Apostle actually spent the amount in charity and missionary activities. When Gudnaphar was informed about the alleged misappropriation of funds meant for building a royal palace, he summoned both Judas and the merchant who had brought him. When Gudnaphar asked Judas to show the palace he was assigned to build, Judas replied, 'Thou canst not see it now, but when thou hast departed from this world.'[21] 'Then the king became very furious in his anger and commanded that Thomas and the merchant who had brought him, being bound, should go to prison. . . . And the king was considering by what death he should kill Judas and the merchant; and he took the resolution that he would burn him, after being flayed, with the merchant his companion.'[22] The king naturally felt cheated. He was furious not only with Judas but also with Ḥabban who failed to satisfy his requirements as a royal merchant.

This episode shows that the royal merchant had to face serious consequences in case he could not fulfil the specific need of his master either intentionally or otherwise. Interestingly enough the king now considered Ḥabban as the 'companion' of the carpenter, whereas in the earlier paragraphs Ḥabban was described as the 'merchant who had brought him'. Gudnaphar was probably convinced that his merchant not only brought him an inefficient and cheat carpenter but was also party to the plot of misappropriating royal money.

Nepal also has a tradition of employing *rājaśreṣṭhīs*. The Thimi inscription, assignable probably to the reign of Śivadeva (AD 687-703), has an interesting passage which refers to the annual payment of a levy in cash (in silver *purāṇas*) by villagers in connection with *viṣṭimanuṣya* which would be raised by *rājakulīyavyavasāyīs* (. . . *Viṣṭi manuṣya-sambandhena prativarṣam yat purāṇaśataṁ . . . bhya eva grāmīnair dātavyaṁ rājakulīyavyavasāyibhistu na kadācidanyathā kartavyam*). The expression *rājakulīyavyavasāyī* stands for a merchant employed by or associated with a royal family. Thus it is not substantially different from the *rājaśreṣṭhī* or royal merchant. These royal merchants of Nepal were empowered to raise a levy called *viṣṭimanusya*, i.e. forced labour in the form of man (i.e. human physical labour). Since this *viṣṭi* was closely associated with royal merchants, it, therefore, seems to have been raised to facilitate the activities of the royal merchants.

This inference is further strengthened by the Lagan Tole inscription, issued by Śivadeva (AD 697).[24] In this regard *vyavasāyīs* are authorized to procure annually five load-carriers from a revenue free village on account of *Bhoṭṭaviṣṭi* (*asminagrahāre bhoṭṭaviṣṭihetoḥ prativarṣam bhārikajanāḥ pañca 5 vyavasāyibhīr grāhitavyā*). Once again there is evidence of merchants being authorized to impose a particular type of forced labour. Judging from the similarity in the two Nepalese records, the term *vyavāsayī* appears to have been a concise form of the word *rājakulīyavyavasāyī*. The term *Bhoṭṭaviṣṭi* probably means forced labour procured in connection with journeys made to Tibet. The forced labour is said to have been rendered by load-carriers who undoubtedly bore the load of the merchandise belonging to the royal merchants of Nepal. *Bhoṭṭaviṣṭi*, therefore, is not very much different from *viṣṭimanuṣya* which was imposed for more or less similar purposes.

The two epigraphs give us the following information: (a) employment of royal merchants in the seventh-eighth century Nepal, (b) royal merchants carrying on trade at least between Nepal and Tibet, and (c) royal merchants enjoying some administrative rights. The item or items of commerce they dealt in cannot be specified on the basis of these two inscriptions. As these merchants were commissioned by the king, it may be logically argued that they mainly dealt in costly and choice goods coveted by the ruling authority.[25]

Explicit references to royal merchants are not regularly available in the subsequent periods. A record of the Coḷa emperor Rājendra Coḷa (AD 1012-44) was found from Hunsur taluq in Karnataka.[26] The inscription dated in the seventh regnal year of Rajendra (AD 1020) states that 'one Barama gavuṇḍa in Te. . . . nāḍ fell upon Rājendra-Coḷa-Seṭṭi of that nāḍ as a result of which Rājendra-Coḷa-Seṭṭi died. Hulimadda, son of Alasabandhi, Rājendra Coḷa's chief in that nāḍ put to death Maḍḍyya who had lightly slain Coḷa-Seṭṭi'. Terms like Rājendra-Coḷa-Seṭṭa, Coḷa-Seṭṭi, etc., point to a merchant employed by the Coḷa emperor Rājendra Coḷa. Since the Coḷa royal merchant is not specifically mentioned by his personal name, it appears that the epithet refers to a post to which the Coḷa emperor appointed him. The record speaks of the assassinated merchant as the Rājendra-Coḷa-Seṭṭi of a particular *nāḍ*, i.e. *nāḍu* or a territorial division. This implies that Rājendra Coḷa may have employed several royal merchants and placed them over different territorial divisions. What could have been the function(s) of the Coḷa royal merchants cannot be ascertained at the present state of our knowledge.

It may not be out of place to mention that the Coḷas from the tenth century onwards maintained regular commercial contacts with the Khmers of Angkor, the Burmese at Pagan, the Ly in northern Vietnam, the Sung dynasty in China and with the Arabs in the west.[27] Commercial embassies were sent from the Coḷa court to China during the reign of Lo-tsa-lo-tsa or Rajaraja.[28] In view of the widespread overseas contacts of the Coḷas, it is possible that the Coḷa royal merchants could have been assigned to, among other things, diplomatic-cum-commercial missions to foreign countries.

Attention may now be drawn to another record from the Krishanarajapet taluq in Karnataka, dated AD 1125. It introduces to us 'one Nolabi-seṭṭi who was the Poysaḷa-seṭṭi, the promoter of the Vīra-Balañjadharma, adorned with many qualities from the five hundred *vīra-śāsanas* and the Paṭṭanasvāmī of Dorasamudra'.[29] The very name Nolabi-śreṣṭhī shows that he was a merchant. Poysala-seṭṭi is the same as Hoysala-seṭṭi, i.e. a *śreṣṭhī* or merchant of the Hoysala dynasty. The expression *vīra-balañjadharma* corresponds to the *vīra-vaṇija dharma* or the code of conduct of heroic traders. Actually *vīra-balañja* was the name of a very important mercantile body of the Deccan and south India throughout the early medieval period. The other epithet *paṭṭanasvāmī* is also significant. *Paṭṭana* may denote any urban centre including ports and marts.[30] In more or less contemporary Tamil inscriptions *paṭṭinam* actually stands for ports located on or near the sea-coast, in contradistinction to *erivīra-paṭṭinam* meaning a port or mart of the interior.[31] The *paṭṭanasvāmī* would therefore mean an administrative head of a port or a trade centre on or near the coast; it may also denote a leader of a mercantile community. The epithets of Nolabi-seṭṭi point to his prominent position as a rich merchant. His affluence based on his commercial success was probably instrumental in his obtaining close contacts with the Hoysala ruler and in his appointment as the royal merchant. In his capacity as the *paṭṭanasvāmī* this royal merchant appears to have also assumed certain administrative functions at Dorasamudra, an important urban centre and one of the capital cities of the Hoysalas.[32]

A contemporary Western Cālukya ruler, Jagadekamalla II had a royal merchant named Sovi-seṭṭi. Two inscriptions dated AD 1142 and AD 1147 state that Sovi-seṭṭi traded in jewels with Jagadekamala II.[33] It seems that the merchant procured for his royal client costly and choice stones, gems, etc.

Several *rājaśreṣṭhīs* figured in the Hoysala court during the twelfth and the thirteenth centuries. Two of them belonged to the reign of Viṣṇuvardhana (AD 1110-52); they were Hoysala-seṭṭi and Nemi-seṭṭi.[34] Kammaṭa Caṭṭi-seṭṭi was the royal merchant of Hoysala Vīra-Ballāla II (1173-1220). He figures in the inscription as having imported horses, elephants and pearls for the king.[35] All these were very valuable items of trade. Horses and elephants were indispensable for military purposes and in constant demand in the rulers' circle. The horse was in greater demand, since Indian horses were known to be poor quality in comparison to the Arab horses.[36] Here the merchant acted as a supplier of important as well as luxury items for the king. Dāmodara-seṭṭi, son of Govinda, appears as a trusted royal merchant of Hoysala Narasiṁha III (1220-38) in two records (1232 and 1234).[37] His functions are however not known.

Attention will now be shifted to royal merchants employed by the Śilāhāras of Kolhapur. The Kolhapur record of Gaṇḍarāditya (AD 1136)[38] enlists a large number of merchants who made voluntary donations of some taxes and levies in favour of Tīrthaṅkara Pārśvanātha. One of them was Vesappayya-seṭṭi, the royal merchant of Gaṇḍarāditya (*Gaṇḍarādityadevasa rājaśreṣṭhī Vesappayyaseṭṭiyarum*). The epithet *rājaśreṣṭhī* is also given to Boppanayya in the Miraj inscription of Vijayāditya (AD 1143),[39] son and successor of Gaṇḍarāditya (*Miriñjeya Boppanayya rājaśreṣṭhī*). It is not explicitly stated which king employed Boppanayya as his royal merchant. However, he appears to have been appointed by Vijayāditya since the inscription belongs to his period of reign.

One may remember that in 1136 the royal merchant was Vesappayya and not Boppanayya of 1143. So the appointment of a new royal merchant can be seen as Vijayāditya succeeded Gaṇḍarāditya. This is more evident from the fact that the same Vesappayya seṭṭi no longer appears as *rājaśreṣṭhī* in the Miraj inscription of Vijayāditya but as a *mahā-vaḍḍuvyavahārī* (i.e. a great senior merchant).[40] It can also be argued that the *rājaśreṣṭhī* did not probably enjoy a permanent employment in the royal court. Though Boppa-nayya-seṭṭi is so named only in the Miraj inscription, the Kolhapur record includes one Boppi-seṭṭi of Miriñji. Considering the phonetic affinity between Boppanayya and Boppi, and taking into account that both of them hailed from Miraj, the two names probably refer to the same person.

In the same Kolhapur record of 1136 figures Bommi-seṭṭi, of Maṇḍaleśvara's (= Nimbadevarsa's) household. Maṇḍaleśvara Nimbadevarasa is described in the same record as the *sāmantaśiromaṇi* or the principal vassal of Gaṇḍarāditya. This is further evidence of the appointment of an important merchant by a member of the ruling group. But significantly enough, Bommi-seṭṭi, in spite of being attached to a feudatory ruler's household, is not given the prestigious epithet *rājaśreṣṭhī*. One may infer that only those merchants who were directly employed by sovereign and independent rulers were called *rājaśreṣṭhīs*.[41]

These data regarding the *rājaśreṣṭhī* are admittedly scattered, spatially and temporarily. Though the antiquity of the royal merchants in India goes back to the fourth-third century BC, references to their appointments became more numerous and regular in the early medieval times, particularly in the Deccan and south India. Documents are often not explicit about the range and nature of their activities. They occasionally acted as supplier/procurers of luxury items and war animals for rulers. It cannot be fully ascertained whether they collected revenue for the king from particular trade centres. But this possibility cannot be set aside, because they enjoyed certain administrative rights as Paṭṭanasvāmī and could also impose forced labour. All these contributed to their special position in the community of the early Indian merchants.

NOTES

1. Bose, *Social and Rural Economy*, vol. II, pp. 9-14.
2. An *Avadāna* story narrates that a merchant advanced loans to Kośalan king Prasenajit during his war against Magadha. Though this is evidently a late source, it probably retains an earlier tradition. See, D.N. Jha, *Revenue System in Post-Maurya and Gupta Times*, Calcutta, 1967, pp. 109-10.
3. Megasthenes and other Classical writers refer to six boards, each consisting of five officers, who were entrusted with the administration of Pāṭaliputra. At least three of these boards invigilated the commercial activities. See J.W. McCrindle, tr. *Ancient India as Described by Megasthenes and Arrian*, Calcutta, 1921, pp. 87ff. Two Armaic edicts of Aśoka discovered at Laghman (Afghanistan) clearly show the Mauryan government's concern for maintaining a royal road (*kārapathi* or royal highway). See, Mukherjee, *Aramaic Edicts*, pp. 9-22.
4. Kauṭilya devotes an entire section to the suppression of fraudulent traders (*vaidehakarakṣaṇam*) in course of his discussion on the purification of thorns (to the kingdom), i.e. *Kaṇṭakaśodhana*, *KAS*, IV.2.
5. *KAS*, II.16.
6. *KAS*, II.4.

7. *KAS*, II.16.8.
8. *KAS*, II.16.10.
9. *KAS*, II.16.18.
10. *KAS*, II.16.18-24.
11. Sen, *Economics in Kauṭilya*, pp. 27-8.
12. In the eighteenth century Martanda Varma of Travancore imposed severe restrictions on traders' activities. Pepper trade was brought under the complete monopoly of the king and trade in other commodities was also controlled by the royal merchants of Travancore were reduced to employees of the state. See Ashin Das Gupta, *Malabar in Asian Trade 1740-1800*, Cambridge, 1967, pp. 33-72.
13. Warmington, *Commerce*; Wheeler, *Rome Beyond*; Bulnois, *The Silk Road*.
14. *The Acts of St. Thomas*, tr., A.F.J. Klijn, Leiden, 1962; B.N. Mukherjee, *An Agrippan Source, A Study in Indo-Parthian History*, Calcutta, 1969 has also referred to it.
15. Mukherjee, *An Agrippan Source*, pp. 183-98.
16. *The Acts of St. Thomas*, p. 66, para 1.
17. *The Acts of St. Thomas*, p. 66, para 2.
18. *The Acts of St. Thomas*, p. 66, para 2.
19. *The Acts of St. Thomas*, p. 67, para 3.
20. *The Acts of St. Thomas*, p. 74, para 17.
21. *The Acts of St. Thomas*, p. 75, para 21.
22. *The Acts of St. Thomas*, p. 75, para 21.
23. R. Gnoli, *Nepalese Inscriptions in the Gupta Characters*, pt. I, Rome, 1956, pp. 106-9, Inscription no. LXXVII; Dhanavajra Vajracharyya, *Lichhavi-kalka Abhilekaha*, Kathmandu, 1978, pp. 527-9.
24. Gnoli, *Nepalese Inscriptions*, pp. 107-8, Vajracharyya, *Abhilekha*, pp. 514-18.
25. Ranabir Chakravarti, 'Bhoṭṭaviṣṭi: Its Nature and Its Collection', in B.N. Mukherjee, D.R. Das, S.S. Biswas and S.P. Singh, eds., *Dineśacandrika*, New Delhi, 1983, pp. 203-8 has discussed the nature of this forced labour and how it was imposed.
26. *EC*, vol. IV, p. 83, Inscription no. 10.
27. K.R. Hall, 'International Trade and Foreign Diplomacy in Early Medieval South India', *JESHO*, vol. XX, 1978, pp. 75-98; K.R. Hall, 'Khmer Commercial Development and Foreign Contacts under Sūryavarman I', *JESHO*, vol. XVIII, 1975, pp. 313-30. It is significant that in the third quarter of the eleventh century Kulottuṅga (1070-1120) renamed the port of Viśākhapaṭṭanam as Kulottuṅgacoḷapaṭṭanam. He seems to have developed friendly relationship with Pagan through which one could reach China. Kulottuṅga is also known to have exempted tolls and custom duties obviously to encourage foreign trade. See, Ranabir Chakravarti, 'Kulottuṅga and the Port of Viśākhapaṭṭinam', *PIHC*, vol. XLI, 1981, pp. 142-5.
28. K.A. Nilakanta Sastri, *The Coḷas*, Madras, 1955, p. 219.

29. *EC*, vol. IV, p. 99, Inscription no. 3.
30. Sircar, *Epigraphical Glossary*, p. 246.
31. Hall, 'International Trade', pp. 80-1.
32. See W.H. Moreland, 'The Shahbandar in the Eastern Seas', *JRAS*, 1929. S.D. Goitein, *Letters of Medieval Jewish Traders*, Princeton, 1973, p. 188.
33. *SII*, vol. XV, Inscription nos. 24 (AD 1142) and 35 (AD 1145).
34. *EC*, vol. II, p. 137.
35. *EC*, vol. V; *AK*. 22.
36. Wassaf, Al Rashiuddin and Marco Polo wrote extensively on the poor quality of Indian horses. The Pāṇḍya king of Madura alone purchased no less than 10,000 Arab horses every year. Not only were these extremely costly, as a result of poor veterinary facilities most of the horses did not survive for more than a year. This forced the ruler to place a fresh order for ten thousand horses. The horse trader amassed considerable fortune and the king had to maintain cordial relations with him. Simon Digby, *Warhorse and Elephant in the Delhi Sultanate*, Oxford, 1971. It is significant that a horse trader (*kudiraiceṭṭi*) brought the news to the Coḷa ruler Rājendra that conditions in Ceylon were ripe for a Coḷa invasion.
37. *EC*, vol. V, *AK*. 82, *EC*, vol. XV, p. 217.
38. *CII*, vol. VI, pp. 229-35, Inscription no. 49.
39. *CII*, vol. VI, pp. 241-6, Inscription no. 52.
40. Chakravarti, 'Merchants of Konkan'.
41. Chakravarti, 'Merchants of Konkan'.

CHAPTER 6

Maritime Trade and Voyages in Ancient Bengal

INTRODUCTION

A relatively new area in Indian historical studies is the maritime history of India or more precisely India's role in the maritime activities in the Indian Ocean. With the focus of power gradually shifting from Europe since the 1940s the Eurocentric view of history has slowly taken a backseat. The emergence of new nations in the 'Third World', following decolonization, has encouraged scholars to appreciate the role of non-Europeans in the historical developments of these countries including the Indo-Pak subcontinent. In view of the location of a very large number of these new nations in Asia and Africa, it has been also recognized that the sea or seas in this region can be considered as a major point or factor of unity among nations of Asia and Africa. This has given a great fillip to the study of the Indian Ocean which in terms of activities of the people of Asia and Africa has been of tremendous significance. It is doubtless that the Indian Ocean dominates the seaface of Asia. One may in fact say, following Franz Broeze, that a long-term perspective—for instance over the last two millennia—would project Asia and not Europe as the leading maritime continent of the world.[1] Such a perspective would naturally highlight the significance of the Indian Ocean in the maritime history of the pre-modern world.

The geographical area of the maritime space called the Indian Ocean has to be defined at this juncture. The map of the Indian Ocean, published by the National Atlas and Thematic Mapping Organisation, places it up to the Cape of Good Hope in the west, to the Antarctica in the south, includes the Red Sea, the Persian Gulf, the Arabian Sea and the Bay of Bengal in it, but leaves out the Java and the China Seas.[2] A proper appreciation of the geography of the Indian Ocean is crucial in this context as it holds an important key to our understanding of the movement of people and cultural contacts across the maritime space. The distance of over 10,000 km from South Africa to South Australia certainly impresses upon us the vastness of the Indian Ocean. But it actually extends over only a fifth of the world's total maritime surface, a fact that would on the other hand point to the relative smallness of this ocean. One cannot also lose sight of the fact that this relatively small maritime space connects no less than thirty-seven countries, where inhabit a third of the world's population. This sheer numerical fact endows the Indian Ocean with a special status. The 'relative smallness, which facilitates communications, explains, why the Indian Ocean has been, more than any other ocean, the vehicle of the most varied human contacts, with very rich consequences'.[3]

The other inescapable geographical fact is the more or less central position of the Indian subcontinent (including Sri Lanka) among countries of the Indian Ocean. The two long coastlines of India, washed by the Arabian Sea and the Bay of Bengal on the west and the east respectively, jut out into the Indian Ocean and provide ample scope of maritime contacts along the two coasts and also with countries overseas. This has considerably encouraged maritime historians to take a close look at India and the India Ocean.[4] Two types of thrusts of maritime historical studies of India can broadly be identified: (a) the situation from 1500 to 1800 with the help of varied types of European documents, and (b) the relatively greater attention to the west coast of India than to its eastern seaboard. While the gradual and growing supremacy of Europeans in the Indian Ocean from the sixteenth century onwards (mainly by 'guns and sails') is unmistakable, the ethos of seafaring traditions in the Indian Ocean countries and particularly in India must be given its due recognition and importance.

SCOPE AND METHODS

It will be impossible to divorce the research in early seafaring along the Bengal coast from the broader understanding of the Indian Ocean studies, with particular emphasis on India and the Indian Ocean. The maritime historian of India and the Indian Ocean appears to have been largely inspired by the seminal researches of Fernand Braudel on the Mediterranean Sea.[5] The study of maritime history does not merely involve a particular sea or ocean, but also integrate the understanding of the connected land with that of the given sea. 'Its (i.e. the sea) history can no more be separated,' writes Braudel, 'from that of the lands surrounding it than the clay can be separated from the hands of the potter who shapes it.'[6] The maritime historian of India, taking this cue from Braudel, looks at the Indian Ocean or part(s) thereof not from the point of view of naval battles and tactics or from nationalistic stance, but urges upon the overall unity between the land and the sea. This is also the approach followed in the present study of seafaring in the Bengal coast up to seventh century AD.

It must be clearly pointed out that there was no Bengal as such in ancient times. Ancient Bengal, for the sake of convenience, may be taken to denote the areas embracing modern West Bengal in India and Bangladesh. This area in ancient days included in it four major sub-regions: (i) Puṇḍravardhana (north Bengal, Rajshahi, Bogura, Dinajpur areas); (ii) Rāḍha (areas to the west of the present Bhagirathi); (iii) Vaṅga (traditionally located in the central deltaic Bengal, i.e. Dhaka, Vikrampur, Faridpur areas of present Bangladesh); and (iv) Samataṭa (areas to the east of the Meghna covering Noakhali, Comilla and Chittagong of Bangladesh).[7] As the littorals of ancient Bengal were included in Vaṅga and Samataṭa, greater attention will be paid to these two regions. Our understanding of Vaṅga—both geographical and historical—has undergone considerable changes as a result of the discovery of new evidence. A more elaborate discussions on the Vaṅga region will be made in a following section.

A major hindrance to the researchers in the maritime history of India, particularly during the pre-1500 days, has been the acute shortage of evidence. The well-known trade between the Indian subcontinent and the Roman empire during the early centuries of the Christian era probably resulted in references to seaborne trade with India in Classical texts, which are of immense value for our purpose. The evidence of early Chinese texts, though far from being adequate, may also throw some interesting light on the topic of discussion. But the non-indigenous sources of information can at best provide only a rudimentary knowledge of the Bengal littorals, the adjacent maritime space and the life of the coastal communities. The vast and volumnious indigenous literature, both Sanskrit and non-Sanskritic, occasionally refers to the sea and maritime activities. But these mostly appear in a stereotyped poetical manner and rarely enlighten us on seafaring in a matter of fact way. Moreover, the validity of theoretical treatises on shipping and ship-building technologies like the *Yuktikalpataru* of Bhoja—widely used by pioneering researchers in this field[8]—has also recently been questioned. This problem of the paucity of data is to some extent offset by the discovery of archaeological materials, mainly from various coastal sites in India, through explorations and excavations.[9] One of the most dependable archaeological sources is inscriptions which contain occasional passing—but significant—references to shipping and ship-building, etc. In this context mention must be made of the large number of seals and sealings found from south-western parts of West Bengal. B.N. Mukherjee's startling identification and decipherment of the Brāhmī-Kharoṣṭī script, that appears on most of these seals and sealings, has broken fresh grounds in the study of the maritime history of the Bengal coast. Palaeographically assignable to the first four or five centuries of the Christian era, these seals and sealings (of private individuals, and also of official and semi-official nature) are inseparably associated with the material and cultural life of the people of ancient Vaṅga.[10] In fact this essay attempts for the first time to use these seals and sealings to reconstruct the history of the early seafaring in the Bay of Bengal. Thus a judicious juxtaposition of literary, field-archaeological, epigraphic and numismatic data may provide us with valuable information—though very much fragmented and partial—for the study of seafaring in ancient Bengal. The data, available from these sources, are also essentially impressionistic and rarely offer any reliable statistical information. The importance of the maritime affairs in the Bengal coast cannot be properly appreciated in isolation, i.e. by focusing solely on the Bengal coast, but by situating it in the general background of India and the Indian Ocean and more particularly in relation to the eastern seaboard.

THE MARITIME SPACE

The primary unit of the maritime space in the context of the present study is obviously the Bay of Bengal. The significance of the Bay of Bengal, the most important segment of the eastern Indian Ocean, in the Indian Ocean studies has been given a belated and gradual recognition.[11] A few words about the early name(s) of this Bay may not be irrelevant here. B.N. Mukherjee has recently drawn our attention to a statement of Pliny (d. *c.* AD 79) who appears to have been the first to designate the term Indian Ocean (*mari Indicum*).[12] 'Here begins the Indian race, bordering not only on the eastern sea, but on the southern also, which we have designated the Indian Ocean.'[13] As Pliny differentiated the southern sea (equated by him as *mari Indicum*) from the eastern sea (i.e. the Arabian Sea) his definition of the Indian Ocean is not the same as that of the Indian Ocean nowadays. While Pliny makes no explicit reference to the eastern sector of the Indian Ocean, the first clear connotation of this maritime space was given by Claudius Ptolemy in his *Geographike Huphegesis* (around the middle of the second century AD) under the name of 'Gangetic Gulf'.[14] This is obviously the same as the Bay of Bengal. But the Classical authors in general make few, if any, observations about the Bay of Bengal, as the shippers and sailors from the West had much closer contacts with the western segment of the Indian Ocean than with its eastern sector. Indigenous literary texts also leave for us two blanket terms: *pūrva* (eastern) and *paścima* (western) *samudra/jaladhi* (sea), referring respectively to the Bay of Bengal and the Arabian Sea. Interestingly enough, an inscription of the Candra dynasty of south-eastern Bengal, dated AD 971 mentions *Vaṅgasāgara*.[15] This is nothing but the *sāgara* or sea of Vaṅga and hence may safely be assumed as the base of the later coining of the term 'Bay of Bengal'. The term 'Vaṅgasāgara' in the Bengal inscription may closely correspond to the expression *bahr Harkand* or the Sea of Harkand/Harkal (= Harikela, south-easternmost Bengal), found in several Arab texts of early medieval times and notably in the *Hudud al Alam* of AD 982.[16] In fact *bahr Harkand/Harkal* stands for the eastern sea of India and therefore may easily be equated with the present Bay of Bengal.

THE COAST

One of the salient features of the geography of the subcontinent is the two long coastlines washed respectively by the Arabian Sea and the Bay of Bengal. The basic difference between the two littorals is to be seen in the presence of several deltas in the eastern seaboard, while on the west coast no other river except the Indus has a delta.[17] Of the deltas on the east coast, the most important is the Bengal or Gangetic delta, the largest in the world. Geographers find three distinct categories within this delta: (i) moribund delta—covering Nadia, Murshidabad and 24-Parganas districts (North) in West Bengal and the Jessore and Khulna areas in Bangladesh; (ii) mature delta—parts of 24-Parganas district and Khulna, and (iii) active delta in the marshy lands eastward of Calcutta, the Sunderbans and between the Madhumati and the Meghna.[18] The importance of innumerable rivers—both tributaries to and branches of the Ganga—in this deltaic region can hardly be over-estimated in terms of inland riverine communications which provide the vital linkage between the coast and the interior. The study of the history of navigation in the Bengal coast therefore does not remain confined to the littorals only, but has to take into serious consideration the situation in the interior in the light of its contacts with the coast and the maritime space.

The coast in question and the Bengal delta in broader terms comes to prominence in the history of seafaring in the Indian Ocean from first century AD onwards. *The Periplus of the Erythraean Sea* informs us: 'After this (i.e.the country of Dosarene located in the Kalinga coast) . . . you reach the Ganges region and in its vicinity the farthest part of the mainland towards the east, Chryse. There is a river near it that is itself called the Ganges, the greatest of all rivers in India. . . . On it is a port of trade with the same name as the river Ganges.'[19] The *Periplus* doubtless speaks of the Ganga delta, and particularly the lower Bengal area. The country and the principal port thereof have been named after the most important river flowing through it. Claudius Ptolemy in the middle of the second century AD was also aware of the same port which he located in the country of the Gangaridai.[20] Thus, like the anonymous author of the *Periplus* Ptolemy also named the country after the Ganga and located it in more or less the same region. Juxtaposing the Classical textual evidence with the Chinese literary materials, B.N. Mukherjee shows that: (1) in the early centuries of the Christian era, a part of deltaic Bengal was named after the Ganga, and (2) that the Chinese equated the Ganga country with Vaṅga.

The combined testimony of the Chinese and the Classical accounts and the historical geography and early cartography of deltaic Bengal led B.N. Mukherjee to suggest the following limits of Vaṅga in the first four or five centuries of the Christian era. 'It should have included the area, now in the 24-Parganas (North and South), Hooghly, Howrah, Midnapore and parts of Burdwan (and also Birbhum, Bankura and Nadia?)'.[21] These areas have also yielded major early historical archaeological sites. More significantly, a handsome number of documents inscribed in Kharoṣṭī and/or Kharoṣṭī-Brāhmī (mixed script) have recently been found from what was ancient Vaṅga or the Ganges country.[22] The area which came into limelight in the first four or five centuries AD is located within present West Bengal. The coastal area of Bangladesh or areas adjacent to the littoral, though initially less prominent, attained considerable importance from fifth-sixth centuries onwards.

PRODUCTS

As the navigational activities in the Bengal coast during the ancient times are studied to understand the life and conditions of communities in and around the coast, there will be a socio-economic thrust in this survey. Relevant to such an orientation will be an understanding of the products and nature of products which were available and transacted.

It is only natural that a region such as the one under discussion here was very much suited to agricultural activities as ancient Bengal was both a *devamātṛka* (endowed with profuse rainfall) and a *nadīmātṛka* (watered with rivers) country. The irrefutable proof of a flourishing agrarian economy in the Bengal coast is furnished by a number of Kharoṣṭī and Kharoṣṭī-Brāhmī inscriptions. Several seals/seal-impressions bear stylized depictions of stalks of grain often emerging out of a vessel.[23] The most important crop was of course paddy (*dhānya*) which was shown on a seal from Hadipur.[24] A *yakṣī* called Jirāmbi (i.e. a spirit protecting *jira* or cumin seed) figures on another terracotta object from Chandraketugarh,[25] indicating thereby the possibility of the cultivation of cumin seed. A vessel is *Vapayakoṣa*,[26] i.e. a vessel for a sower. Such vessels must have contained a specific amount of seed of a particular grain to be sown on a given amount of land. A seal impression from Bangarh not only depicts stalks of grain but also the vessel containing grain. The vessel is categorically described as one for containing grain (*saśyādi-dhṛtasthālī*).[27] Another terracotta seal from Chandraketugarh informs us of *a koḍihālika*, an epithet to designate a person possessing a core of (actually many) ploughs.[28] Another person Yaśa is described as rich as a Yakṣa in grain (*saśye yakṣaṣya*).[29] The last two pieces of evidence are clear pointers to the presence of very rich agriculturists. In this context it must be mentioned that many terracotta seal/sealings discovered from lower Bengal also speak of transportation of grains by maritime voyages. The destinations of such voyages are not known. This is a point which would be taken up for more elaborate discussion in a subsequent section. But such data leave little room for doubt that grains—especially paddy—were grown in large amount which paved the way for the transportation of a part of the produce by overseas voyages.[30] That the coastal areas of Bengal continued to be agriculturally prosperous in the first half of the seventh century is amply demonstrated by Hsüan Tsang (travels in India from AD 629 to 645). The pilgrim was considerably impressed by the luxuriant crops grown in San-mo-ta-ta (= Samataṭa) and Tan-mo-li-ti (= Tāmralipta).[31] Hsüan Tsang however does not specify whether grain was transported overseas also in the seventh century.

The regular references to excellent cotton textiles of ancient Bengal (a topic to be discussed more elaborately later) point to the distinct likelihood of cotton cultivation in the area concerned.

Among other products the textile is extremely important. The *Periplus* speaks of the availability of 'cotton garments of the very finest quality, the so-called Gangetic',[32] which was exported from the port of Gange. Through the same port were also 'shipped out malabathrum, Gangetic nard, pearls'.[33] The *Periplus* also mentions about the trade in Chinese (Thina) 'silk floss, yarn and cloth' which went to Limyrike (or Damirica, i.e. the Drāviḍa country in far south India) via 'the Ganges river'.[34] Thus, the Bengal coast appears to have catered to the demands in the 'West' for textile products and spices. Of these the trade in cotton garment is terminal in nature, while the export of the Chinese silk to south India was transit trade. From south Indian ports these items appear to have been shipped to the West. These products therefore were integrated with the movement of commodities in the Bay of Bengal and finally with the Indian Ocean and Mediterranean Sea trade.

The discovery of Kharoṣṭī/Kharoṣṭī-Brāhmī biscriptual documents from lower parts of the present-day West Bengal has thrown new lights on the transaction of another commodity, namely horses—a fact which is not known from other existing sources. A terracotta seal impression, now in the collection of the State Archaeological Museum, Calcutta (No. D.A. W.B. CKG. 180)—originally found from the famous archaeological site Chandraketugarh [24-Parganas district (North)], 35 km north-east of Calcutta)—'displays with a circular border a masted ship, a *svastika* symbol and a marginal legend', palaeographically assignable to the third century AD, according to B.N. Mukherjee.[35] A further examination of this object by Ranabir Chakravarti shows a figure of a horse on the right hand field and the right edge of the ship. The horse is shown in profile with its head towards the mast; its mouth, an eye and an ear also are clearly visible. The horse has a somewhat elongated neck; its torso—especially the hind leg and the tail—also appear on the seal impression. The artist/craftsman seems to have deliberately enlarged the figure of the horse, in relation to the overall composition of the scene in the seal, to draw attention to the animal. Below the figure of the horse and partly covering the forepart of the animal can be seen the figure of a man (probably seen from behind) whose right hand touches the body of the horse. The human figure may further reveal that the person in question wears a tall and flat-top cap. Such a cap is hardly indigenous to this part of ancient Bengal. There is a distinct possibility of this being a Scythian cap and its user a north-westerner of non-Indian origin. One is tempted to suggest that he is a horse-dealer though this cannot be readily proved.[36] The seal is an irrefutable proof of transaction in horses in early Bengal, more so, because a seal of this type has to be associated with the process of authentication of a transaction. It also provides the earliest evidence of the shipment of horses from an Indian harbour.

But the horse is not native to Bengal. In fact, the horse and especially good quality war horse, was always a rarity in India and had to be regularly imported into India from the north-western borderland of the subcontinent.[37] The availability of horses in Bengal can therefore be explained as an import from the north-west to the deltaic Bengal through the Ganga valley. But where was the horse sent to by maritime trade, as is clearly evident from the Chandraketugarh seal impression? An answer to this has been provided by B.N. Mukherjee on the basis of the Chinese account of Kang-tai (AD 249-50) who informs us that the 'Yueh-chih merchants are continually importing them (horses) to the Ko-ying country by sea'.[38] While the Yüeh-chih traders were either Kuṣāṇa merchants and/or dealers in the vast Kuṣāṇa realm,[39] Ko-ying is located in Malay peninsula. Kang-tai thus clearly mentions about overseas voyages to South-East Asia to transport horses from the Indian mainland. Attention has also been drawn to a copper drum (found in the island of Sangeang in South-East Asia) which has an engraved scene depicting two men in typical Yüeh-chih dresses along with a horse. The availability of Kharoṣṭī/Kharoṣṭī-Brāhmī documents in Bengal and also in Oc-eo (Vietnam) and U-thong (central Thailand, the document is now in the Lopburi Museum, Thailand) would strongly emphasize upon contacts between the Bengal littorals and South-East Asia. Such contacts must have been maritime in nature and can logically be associated with the transportation of horses to South-East Asia.[40] The horse also had a regular demand in far south India, as is evident from the Sangam texts.[41] As the horse is now known to have been sent overseas from Bengal by the *trappaga* type of ship, which in all probability was used in coastal voyages, the horse could have been shipped from a Bengal port to ancient Tamilakam by a coastal voyage.

The products involved in the maritime voyages of Bengal were therefore grains, textile products, spices of diverse types and horses. Of these the 'Gangetic' muslin, spices and horses must have been extremely precious commodities. The transaction in grain speaks of trade in an essential commodity by seaborne voyages, though the volume of this trade cannot be ascertained. While grains and muslins were exported as local products of Bengal, the horse appears to have been shipped to South-East Asia as an item of transit trade, after the demand for the horse was met in Indian mainland.

WATER TRANSPORT (SHIPS) AND SHIPPING

One of the core themes of maritime history is the study of the vessels and shipping technologies of the past. In the case of early Indian maritime studies this is a challenging task in view of the extreme paucity of data. Remains of ancient Indian ships and/or boats have so far not been found by archaeologists. The other alternative source has been the visuals of vessels depicted in paintings, sculptures, coins and occasionally seals.[42] Though these representations may not be actual or accurate—since the artist/craftsmen, if himself not a sailor, may not depict different components of the vessel in proper way or order—they provide more concrete data regarding early Indian ships than the stereotypical textual descriptions in literary works and sastric treatises.

In this context the Kharoṣṭī/Kharoṣṭī-Brāhmī seals, recently deciphered, hold a valuable clue. As the seals are doubtless integrated with trade, the information supplied by them has a direct bearing on transaction of commodities. Significantly enough some of these seals/sealings/seal impressions bear figures of water transports. Inscriptions engraved on these seals throw further light on these vessels. The data available are expected to break many new grounds in the maritime studies of early India.

A terracotta round seal (slightly damaged), found at Berachampa, 24-Parganas district (North), shows a boat with a mast placed near the fore-end or bow which is marked by a projected prow. The single mast appears to have been fitted with a banner. The stern shows an oar, the longer portion of which is below the boat and the shorter portion is projected up on board. The Kharoṣṭī-Brāhmī inscription reads *Bhajotha dijri* (or *jri*) *ssudhoradho* (*Bhajatha dvijeṣu udadhau*) meaning, 'you take resort into the Brāhmins (while) at sea'.[43] The inscribed label may suggest that it could have been used in sea-voyages, though it may not have been meant for high-sea journeys.

Next comes the seal impression from Chandraketugarh showing a ship and a horse on it (already mentioned Fig. 1). The legend in Kharoṣṭī-Brāhmī script read, '*Tasvodajana Hovaji (no) na Trapyagasa*' which means, according to B.N. Mukherjee, 'of [the ship of the class of] *trapyaka* belonging to (i.e. owned by) the power conquering (i.e. powerful) Tasvodaja family'.[44] The craft is therefore labelled *trapyaka*. This immediately reminds us of a class of ship named trappaga mentioned in the *Periplus of the Erythraean Sea* (first century AD). The *Periplus* leaves behind an account of trappaga in the context of the description of Barygaza (Bhṛgukaccha or Broach), the celebrated port on the western seaboard. According to the *Periplus*, trappagas along with the kottymba class of vessels were employed by king Nambanus (=Śaka Kṣatrapa Nahapāna) to pilot foreign ships to Barygaza, since the passage of entrance to this harbour was extremely difficult to negotiate. Trappagas used to go 'as far as Syrastrene to meet vessels and guide them up to Barygaza'.[45] Syrastrene probably stands for Saurashtra on the southern part of the Kathiawad peninsula. The trappaga was therefore a type of craft meant for coastal voyages. Their journeys between the South Kathiwad peninsula and the mouth of the Namados (the Narmada) on which stood Barygaza indicate their ability to undertake long voyage *along the coast* (italics mine). The trappaga under a slightly variant name of *tappaka* also figures in the *Aṅgavijjā*, a Jaina text of the fourth century AD, but possibly relating to earlier traditions. The *tappaka* along with the *Kottimba* (cf. Kottymba of the *Periplus*) and *saṁghāḍa* is classified in this text as a vessel of the middle variety, higher than crafts like *kaṭṭha* and *velu*. The *tappaka* and other crafts of the 'middle category' are further differentiated from the *pota* or larger ship (suitable for high-sea voyages?) which is described as having greater space (*mahāvakāśa*).[46]

All these help us identify '*trapyaka*' of our seal with the nearly homonymous crafts mentioned in the *Periplus* and the *Aṅgavijjā*. The trappaga/*trapyaka* therefore must have been in operation not only in the west coast or parts thereof, but also in the eastern seaboard and the deltaic areas of ancient Vaṅga. The *trapyaka*, besides piloting vessels from abroad to an Indian port, seems to have been in operation for transportation of commodities including as precious an item as the horse. The seal in question gives us for the first time some clues about how the trappaga/*trapyaka* could have looked like. The left half of the hull is longer, raised to a considerable height and also probably pointed at the end. One can also notice at least three vertical and parallel bands between the port and starboard sides of the vessel. At the centre of the vessel stands a single mast with a tripod[47] base and the stylized figure of a flag atop. Near the top of the mast may be seen a rectangular object from which a pair of parallel ropes come down on each side of the mast. These may be tentatively suggested as the ship's stays, though no sail is clearly visible. From the lower half of the mast (on the left hand side) an object projects out horizontally; a rope hangs down from it; at the end of the rope is an oval shaped thing which appears to have been lowered down below the ship. The oval shaped object appears to have been an anchor. B.N. Mukherjee draws our attention to a gap between the letters *ji* and *na* (see the field near lower rim of the seal on the right hand side). According to him the space between the two letters is filled up by a rope at the end of which is another anchor.[48] There might have been two anchors,[49] indicating the ship's stationary position, probably at a port.

The third specimen comes from Chandraketugarh, once again (Fig. 2). The round terrocotta seal impression bears the figure of a craft having a single mast (with a flag atop) in the foredeck. Beams are also shown, though crudely. The bow and stern are both curved upwards; an oar is fitted to the raised stern. As the boat is shown in profile, there could have been another oar (not depicted in the sealing on the other side). The Kharoṣṭī-Brāhmī mixed script reads *Jemdhas' jujusya* (= *Jayanta-Shāhi-Jujoḥ*), i.e. 'of Juja, the conquering king'.[50] The identity of this ruler cannot be established at the present state of our knowledge. But this ship is surely a royal one. It would be therefore logical to infer considerable interests of a ruler(s) in maintaining his own fleet for commercial purposes. A few Jātaka stories indicate that members of royal families took interests and initiatives in maritime voyages for trade to distant countries, including Suvarṇabhūmi.[51] The seal in question furnishes the earliest definite knowledge of a 'royal ship' in India.

Chandraketugarh also yields another terracotta (nearly round) seal impression (D.A. WB. CKG. 184, Fig. 4). The bow and stern of the vessel are both curved upwards; the stern is fitted with an oar. Beams are clearly shown on the relief. A tripod mast is erected at the foredeck and a banner is flying at the top of the mast. About the three-quarter height of the mast is a rectangular object with four holes, two on each side of the mast.[52] It is difficult to identify this object. But D. Schlingloff finds on a Sātavāhana 'ship type' coin the figure of a ship with two masts and a thick wad visible at the mast-head.[53] Though the ship on the Bengal seal and that on the Sātavāhana coin are not identical, the rectangular object near the mast-head of the first one could have been, following Schlingloff, the representation of a furled sail. The terracotta seal also has a Kharoṣṭī-Brāhmī legend (palaeographically of the third century AD), reading *Jidhatradhana Jusatrasa tridesojātrā*. This means, according to B.N. Mukherjee, 'the journey to (or in) three directions of (i.e. by) Yaśoda who has earned food-wealth' (i.e. whose wealth is earned by selling food) (*Jitatradhana-Yaśodasya trideśa-yātrā*).[54] Yaśoda therefore must have amassed wealth by transporting grains on ship (i.e. food) in 'three directions', i.e. to distant destinations. This will be further supplemented by the representation of a stylized stalk of grain in the right hand field of the seal. The message is unmistakable; the product or the principal product the ship carried was depicted on the seal, which is primarily a trade document.

An almost similar scene is depicted on another terracotta seal (nearly round) found from Chandraketugarh and now in the collection of the Indian Museum, Calcutta (IM. 90/181, Fig. 3). The seal impression shows the figure of a ship with a single mast on the foredeck and clear representations of beams. At the centre is depicted a rather disproportionately large basket from which stylized stalks of grain come out. This impresses upon the fact that the ship carried grains. This is further supplemented by the accompanying Kharoṣṭī-Brāhmī inscription: '*Soridhajasa Dijammasa Jaladhisakla* (= *Suṛddhavaśa Dvijanmasya Jaladhiśakra*)'.[55] This has been translated as '(the ship called) Jaladhiśakra (i.e. Indra of the Ocean) of [i.e. belonging to] Dvijanma who is as famous as wealthy'.[56] The stern is fitted with a steering mechanism which does not resemble an oar, seen on other representations of ships on the Bengal seals. The steering mechanism is represented by a vertical straight line which is crossed at the centre by another long horizontal line. One is not sure, but could this have been a steering oar fitted with a horizontal handle to control the movement of the ship?

A few more comments on the last two types of ships may be made at this juncture. The first was capable of undertaking *tridesayātrā*, i.e. distant voyages; the second, being named Indra of the Ocean (*jaladhiśakra*), must have also been fit for overseas voyages. They stand apart from the category of coastal vessels in the Bengal littorals, e.g. the trappaga/*trapyaka* in another seal from Chandraketugarh. Thus the Bengal seaboard had both coastal and high-sea vessels. Interestingly enough, both the high-sea ships are found to have been used for transportation of grain. Can they be equated with the *mahāvakāśa* type of large ships mentioned in the *Aṅgavijjā*?

Some more indications of the maritime transportations are available from coins found at Chandraketugarh. Three punch-marked billon coins depict (on the left hand field of coins) single-masted ships.[57] The mast is located on the foredeck, while the stern is raised high and straight. An elongated object attached to the stern could have meant a pole used as a steering mechanism. Attempts have been made to depict beams of these vessels by the use of two or three parallel horizontal strokes on the top of hulls of these vessels. Another punch-marked billon coin,[58]

Figure 1: Inscribed seal from Chandraketugarh showing the figure of *trapyaga* ship carrying a horse.

Figure 2: Inscribed seal from Chandraketugarh showing a ship 'of Juja, the conquering king'.

Figure 3: Inscribed seal from Chandraketugarh showing a ship called *Jaladhiśakra.*

Figure 4: Inscribed seal from Chandraketugarh showing a ship for *Trideśa-yatra.*

once again from Chandraketugarh, shows a vessel with a cabin, represented by two parallel horizontal lines, topped by a long vertical line. This is unique in the representation of vessels in early Bengal. The stern is raised high (but not straight), giving the vessel the shape of a crescent. On the top right of the stern may be seen portion of a pole to steer the vessel. The absence of the depiction of an oar on these vessels may suggest that they were not used in sea-voyages, but plied on riverine routes.

Among early literary texts the *Arthaśāstra* throws some lights on shipping. Laying down the ideal functions of the *nāvadhyakṣa* (director of shipping),[59] the *Arthaśāstra* uses a generic term *nau/nauka* to denote a water craft. Sea-voyages apparently did not find enough attention of the thinker who mainly dealt with riverine traffic, largely from the point of view of revenue collection. The *Arthaśāstra* however distinguishes the *mahānau* (large craft) from a small one (*kṣudrikā*). The former was employed on large rivers (*mahānadīṣu*) having enough water even during the summer and autumn (*hemantagrīṣma-taryasu*); the kṣudrikā was to ply on rivers fordable only during the monsoons (*kṣudrikāsu varṣāstra vinisu*).[60] The *Arthaśāstra* is more explicit on the components and crew of the larger vessel (*mahānau*). They are *śāśaka* (captain), *niryāmaka* (or *niyāmaka*?), i.e. the navigator, *raśmīgrāhaka* (holder of the string, i.e. one who controlled riggings by pulling or adjusting the ropes attached to the mast; is it possible to infer that ropes had to be pulled or released to manoeuvre the sail/s?); *dātragrāhaka* (the sickle-holder, i.e. the crew who would cut the ropes with a sickle during a storm) and *utsecaka* (one who bailed out water from the hold of the craft).[61]

More elaborate information is available in the *Amarakośa of Amarasiṁha*, assignable to the fifth/sixth centuries AD.[62] Various terms are found to designate different categories of crafts. While rafts are called *udupa*, boats are known by several synonyms: *nau*, *taraṇī*, *tarī* and *droṇī*. The term *pota* may stand for a larger vessel or ship. A *potavaṇik* or merchant vessel[63] carried passengers (*saṁyātrika*). The mast was known as *guṇavṛkṣa* or *kūpaka* and the oar was called *aritra*.[64] The term *naukādaṇḍa* may denote a rod or a log to assess the depth of water for safe navigation of the ship. The *sekapātra* must have been a container or bucket to bail out water, seeping into the hold of the ship. Among the crew of the *pota*, were the *nāvika* (navigator/sailor), *niyāmaka* (pilot) and *karṇadhāra* (operator of the *karṇa* or the steering oar or rudder).[65] It may not be out of place here to refer to *mahānāvika* Buddhagupta of Raktamṛttikā who figures in a fifth century fragmentary stone inscription found from the Malay peninsula.[66] The term *mahānāvika* may mean a senior or leading mariner or may also be interpreted, following D.C. Sircar, as 'captain of *mahānau*'[67] (large ship). Raktamṛttikā, wherefrom Buddhagupta hailed (*Raktamṛttikāvāsa*), must have been the same as Rangamati (*c*. 19 km south of Murshidabad, West Bengal). Raktamṛttikā was situated close to Karṇasuvarṇa, the capital of the famous Gauḍa king Śaśāṅka (*c*. AD 600-37) as will be evident from the accounts of Hsüan Tsang and the archaeological excavations carried out there.[68] This leaves little room for doubt about the overseas shipping between the Bengal littorals and the Malay peninsula.

It is difficult to present a definitive account of the shipbuilding technology in ancient Bengal. Like pre-modern ships of India and Asia, ships of Bengal must have been made of wood and without the application of iron nails. Ancient crafts in general evolved from the dug-out canoe. On each side of the keel, wooden planks were raised to form the hull. The planks were fastened together generally by stitching them with ropes, usually made of coconut coir. Such type of vessels are known to have been built by the 'sewn-plank' technique. The so-called sewn boats have widespread distribution over the Red Sea, the Persian Gulf and the rest of the Indian Ocean also.[69] Schlingloff on the basis of early depictions of boats and ships from Sanchi and Bharhut suggests that 'planks are secured with wooden dowells and not cord'.[70] He further cites the instance of an ancient Malayan river boat (assigned to the second half of the first millennium AD) which had both cords and wooden dowells.[71]

A remarkable feature of shipping in the Indian Ocean during the pre-modern period is the influence of the monsoon winds on the movements of the ship. The more or less regular and hence predictable movements of two monsoon winds in alternate directions (June-September: south-west monsoon; October/November-March/April: north-east monsoon) must have deeply influenced overseas shipping. The knowledge of the monsoon winds appears to have been possessed by ancient Indian mariners. But the increasingly intelligent and more developed utilization of the wind-system can definitely be seen from the late first century AD. This is the time when the Indo-Roman seaborne trade was at its zenith.[72] The south-west monsoon, known as Etasian or Hippalus wind, was regularly used by Western mariners to reach the western littorals of India from the Red Sea ports. The same wind system could be used by ships sailing in the Bay of Bengal, voyaging from the Coromandel or the Andhra coast, to the Orissa or Bengal coast or South-East Asia.

Ptolemy speaks of an *aphaterion* in the Andhra coast or the departure point of a ship bound for Chryse Chora/Chryse Chersonesis (i.e. Suvarṇabhūmi or Suvarṇadvīpa).[73] The voyage from the Bengal coast to south Indian littorals and/or South-East Asia must have been made with the onset of the reverse monsoon (i.e. north-east monsoon). This is strikingly confirmed by Fa-hsien's return sea-voyage to China. Fa-hsien started his journey from the port of Tāmralipta (in present Midnapur district), the famous international harbour in the Bengal littoral. 'He embarked in a large merchant-vessel and went floating over the sea to the south-west. It was the beginning of winter, and the wind was favourable; and after fourteen days, sailing by day and night, they came to the country of Singhala (i.e. Sri Lanka). The people said that it was distant (from Tāmralipta) about 700 *yojanas*.'[74] Thus the sea-voyage from Tāmralipta to Sri Lanks was undertaken during the time of north-eastern monsoon. On the other hand the journey which brought Itsing (AD 673-95) from Malay to Tāmralipta[75] must have been made during the south-western monsoon.

PORTS

A discussion on sea-voyages may logically be followed by one on ports and harbours. It must be stated that ancient ports were rarely on the open roadstead or sea and largely situated in the estuary of a river or in the delta of a river. This is also true of the eastern seaboard, including the Bengal littorals. The eastern coast is less indented than the western seaboard which consequently is better endowed with natural harbours.[76]

Names of harbours of ancient Bengal are only a few. It is also extremely difficult to suggest their exact locations in antiquity, as the hydrography of Bengal has undergone considerable changes in ancient and modern times. The identification and fixing the location of ports of ancient Bengal has been a subject of keen controversy among scholars.

An early port mentioned in the Classical sources is Gange, so named because of being situated in the Gange country, certainly named after the river Ganga.[77] Gange is also mentioned by Ptolemy as a mart.[78] It may be located at or near Deganga in 24-Parganas district (North),[79] through which flowed the Jamuna, a branch of the Ganga which ultimately emptied itself into the Bay of Bengal.

The representations of ships/boats on terracotta seal(s) and seal impressions found from Chandraketugarh, strongly suggest that it was a major port of early historical Vaṅga. Situated on the banks of the

Vidyadhari river, Chandraketugarh, a famous archaeological site, may safely be designated as a riverine port having facilities of both coastal and long distance high-sea voyages. Enormously rich in surface finds, Chandraketugarh covers an area of 3 sq. miles. Excavations conducted here from 1956-7 to 1967-8 show a continuous sequence from pre-Maurya to Pāla times, divided into six periods. Material evidence of transaction may be inferred from the discovery of NBPW and copper punch-marked coins from the Maurya level. The next phase (designated late Suṅga) has yielded, among other things, cast copper coins. Numerous terracotta figurines of great beauty and charm, model toy carts drawn by various animals, beads and coins are among the notable antiquities discovered from this site.[80] This riverine port is known only from archaeological materials, though attempts have been made to equate it with the Gange port of the *Periplus*.

The port par excellence in this area was Tāmralipta, generally equated with Tamluk (in the Midnapur district), situated on the right bank of the Rupnarayan. It is probably the same as Tamalites of Ptolemy and Taluctae of Pliny.[81] P.C. Dasgupta finds no less than fifteen textual references to Tāmralipta in ancient literary texts.[82] It was at its height when Fa-hsien and Hsüan Tsang visited Tāmaralipta respectively in the fifth and seventh centuries AD. While Fa-Hsien left India from this port for Sri Lanka, Hsüan Tsang was highly impressed by the availability of precious items at this port. The international maritime contacts of Tāmralipta will further be evident from the disembarkation of Itsing at this port from the Malay peninsula. The very epithet *velākula* affixed to Tāmralipta (variously called Dāmalipta, Tāmralipi, Tāmraliptika, etc.)[83] clearly shows it to be a port. Excavations carried out at Tamluk in 1954-5 indicate that the site was under occupation from the neolithic to modern times. The 'Maurya-Suṅga phase' (Period II) has yielded NBPW and black slipped ware, red-ware, terracotta figurines with cast copper coins of 'pre-Christian times'. Period III (first-second centuries AD) witnessed the advent of Rouletted Ware and Red-Polished Ware, which are indicative of long-distance, if not foreign, contacts. A brick-built stepped tank and ringed soak-well throw light on the structural activities in this phase. Period IV (Kuṣāṇa-Gupta) is marked by terracotta figurines; urban scenes are depicted on terracotta plaques found from this phase which has also yielded coins and semi-precious beads.[84]

It must be pointed out that the excavated materials are not impressive enough to match the literary data that highlight the prosperous and brisk trade carried at this port. Surface finds from Tamluk and neighbouring areas (within the present Tamluk-subdivision)—now in the collection of Tamluk museum and other private owners and agencies—are quite impressive, but the provenance of these objects are not always recorded correctly.

Recent archaeological explorations in the coastal areas of the Midnapur district amply bear out that there are a number of early historical sites not far away from Tamluk, e.g. Bahiri, Tikasi, Tilda, Panna, Amritberia, Natshal, Badur, Nandigram, Latpatia, etc. Of these Bahiri, Tikasi and Tilda deserve special mention.

Sites like Bahiri, Tilda and Tikasi may indicate that these were in ancient times connected with riverine and ultimately the seaborne trade of south-western Bengal. By no means can these be compared with Tāmralipta. But their riverine contacts and ultimate access to the sea may underline their significance as smaller ports which could have acted as supporting or feeder ports for a much larger harbour nearby like Tāmralipta.[85]

It is hardly surprising that Tāmralipta practically overshadowed these smaller harbours. But there were other ports which were less prominent than Tāmralipta but certainly played a role in the maritime tradition of Bengal. A study of available Chinese evidence strongly suggests that around seventh century Samataṭa area (Noakhali-Comilla region in Bangladesh) gradually began to emerge as point of contact for coastal as well as long-distance voyages in the Bay of Bengal. Only few names survive among ancient harbours of Samataṭa. One, however, is known from epigraphic source. This is Devaparvata, identified with Mainamati-Lalmai in Comilla (Bangladesh). The earliest epigraphic evidence of Devaparvata is furnished by the Kailan C.P. of Śrīdharaṇarāta (*c.* AD 665-75).[86] Devaparvata is described to have been encircled by the river Kṣīroda (i.e. modern Khira/Khirnai), both banks of which were decorated by boats and in which elephants bathed. Devaparvata is also given the epithet *sarvatobhadra*, meaning that it was approachable from all four sides (by river?) or it had gates on all four sides (*atha matta-mātaṅgaśatasukhavigāhyamāno vividha tīrthyā naubhiraparimitabhi-ruparacitakulāya parīkṣitad-abhimatanimnagāminyā Kṣirodayā sarvvatobhadrakād-Devaparvvatāt*). This unmistakably shows Devaparvata to be a riverine port in Samataṭa, not far away from the Bay of Bengal. Around Devaparvata were also three *naudaṇḍakas* or boat parking stations. The inscription in question also mentions a *villabhaṅga* (cf. the Bengali word *bil*, moss covered with water) which was associated with *niṣkrānta praviṣṭaka* (facilities for entry and exit of vessels?).[87]

ROUTES OF MARITIME CONTACTS: HINTERLAND-FORELAND

A port does not stand in isolation in a given area; its activities are linked up not only with areas inland (often urban and political centres), but also with other harbours in various littorals, far and near. In other words a major port must have a regular hinterland inland and a foreland overseas for catering to the needs thereof and also for being supplied with items of trade. Regular routes of contacts, maritime as well as overland, are indispensable for the prosperity of a port.

A glance at the map of north India would immediately show that for the greater part of the Ganga valley—especially the middle Ganga valley—the Bengal delta provided the only outlet to the sea. This clearly impresses upon us the importance of the harbours on the Bengal coast for the 'landlocked' north India. As the littorals in question come into prominence in the late first century BC or first century AD, the Jātaka stories are replete with anecdotes (perhaps stereotypical) of voyages by merchants from Vārāṇasī or Campā (near Bhagalpur) to Suvarṇabhūmī or Suvarṇadvīpa.[88] Such merchants seem to have first undertaken a riverine journey along the Ganga to the Bengal coast, wherefrom a sea-voyage was next made to South-East Asia. The recent discovery of Kharoṣṭī documents in ancient Vaṅga has thrown new light on the extensive hinterland of coastal Vaṅga. Kharoṣṭī was largely known to have been in use in the north-western areas of the subcontinent. But of late Kharoṣṭī inscriptions are found near Chunar, in the heart of the Ganga valley, and Vaṅga.[89] This would clearly suggest overland linkages of north-western India with the middle Ganga valley and finally with the Bengal littorals. This extensive hinterland immensely facilitated the trade in horses from the north-west to Vaṅga wherefrom a part of this consignment was shipped to South-East Asia.

The information in the Classical sources regarding the availability of malabathrum at the port of Gange on the Ganges leads one to infer that the product was brought to Gange from elsewhere and was not a product locally available. B.N. Mukherjee hints at the possible source of malabathrum (*tamāla patra/tejpātā*) in 'inter alia Khasi and Jaintia hills'.[90] Seen from this light the hinterland of Gange spread as far north-east as the mountains of Assam. The north-eastern borderland must also have furnished from Thine (China) 'silk floss, yarn and cloth' that brought to the river Gange (i.e. obviously to a port on the Ganges) and then shipped to Limyrike or south India.[91]

More concrete information is available regarding Tāmralipta. The visit to the port in question by Fa-hsien by an overland journey from Campā (in eastern Bihar) highlights the connection between port and the hinterland far inland. Similarly I'tsing, having disembarked at Tāmralipta after his sea-voyage from the Malay peninsula, proceeded overland to Magadha via a route which was, according to him, also traversed by large number of merchants. Attention may also be focused on Hsüan Tsang's travels in Bengal. The pilgrim proceeded from Nalanda to Ka-chu-wen-kie-lo (Kajaṅgala, near the Rajmahal hills), then to Pun-na-fa-tan-na (Puṇḍravardhana or north Bengal), followed by his journey to Ka-mo-lu-po (Kāmarūpa in Upper Assam) wherefrom he came down to San-mo-ta-ta or Samataṭa. From Samataṭa he went to Tan-moh-li-ti or Tāmralipta and thence to Kie-la-na-su-fa-la-na or Karṇasuvarṇa (in the present Murshidabad district).[92] Two coastal areas, viz., Samataṭa and Tāmralipta were thus interlinked by overland routes, which also connected the coast with Kāmarūpa and Rāḍha. Moreover, Hsüan Tsang's journey from Karṇasuvarṇa to Orissa must have been undertaken through the present Midnapur district which included in it the port of Tāmralipta. Hsüan Tsang also did not fail to observe that 'the water and land'[93] embraced each other at Tāmralipta, impressing upon the reader thereby that at Tāmralipta both land and sea-routes converged. This must have been instrumental in bringing the port in question to prosperity and prominence. Tāmralipta seems to have declined as an international port around the eighth century. The last known reference to Tāmralipta is furnished by the Dudhpani inscription.[94] According to this record, three merchant brothers hailing from Ayodhyā came to Tāmralipta where they earned considerable money by trading. This once again points to the long-distance connection between the port and its hinterland.

Now to the possible maritime routes of contact. The *Periplus*, as has already been pointed out, clearly shows shipping of merchandise from the port of Gange to Limyrike, i.e. south India and more precisely the Coromandel coast harbours. Such shippings must have followed the coastal route along the eastern seaboard. Epigraphic records from the coastal Andhra region and dated to the third century AD tell us about the presence of Buddhist monks at Veṅgi, hailing from many countries, including Vaṅga.[95] This once again may suggest coastal contacts between Vaṅga and Veṅgi. Archaeological corroboration of this contact is also available. The discovery of Rouletted Ware at numerous sites all along the eastern seaboard has to be duly weighed in: Alaganakulam, Kaveripattinam, Nattamedu, Arikamedu, Vasavasamudram, Kanchipuram (in Tamilnadu), Amaravati, Salihundam and other sites in coastal Andhra, Sisupalgarh in Orissa, Tamluk and Chandraketugarh in West Bengal. The discovery of RW should be appreciated from the point of view of a definite pattern of distribution and transaction. The recent re-examination of RW materials at Arikamedu by Vimala Begely leads to revised dates of this ware. The distribution of RW begins from about second century BC and continues up to AD 300.[96] This implies that the RW need not have to be looked at from the point of view of Indo-Roman Mediterranean source. All these would firmly establish the coastal network of communication along the entire length of the eastern seaboard. This is an indigenous coastal network system which had its own dynamism and need not been seen from the angle of external contacts. To this may be added the discovery of Kharoṣṭī and Kharoṣṭī-Brāhmī documents not only in ancient Vaṅga but also from the excavations at Manikpatnam (near Chilka Lake) in coastal Orissa.[97] This doubtless demonstrates, once again, coastal network between ancient Vaṅga and Kalinga.

The discovery of Kharoṣṭī and Kharoṣṭī-Brāhmī documents in Thailand and Vietnam adds to the dimension of our knowledge of Vaṅga's overseas contacts with South-East Asia. It appears that such voyages were initially coastal in character from the delta of the Ganga to that of the Irrawaddy or lower Burma and Thailand. The Isthmus of Kra provided a suitable and easy overland passage from west to east, whence the Gulf of Siam could then be approached. From the fifth century onwards. Tāmralipta's long-distance contacts with Sri Lanka and thence to the Malay peninsula through the Malacca Strait are well attested to by Chinese textual evidence.[98]

Interestingly enough, Hsüan Tsang draws our attention to the commercial activities in Samataṭa at a time when Tāmralipta was already at its zenith. The pilgrim records his impression, albeit faint and inadequate, about the knowledge of six areas which had contacts with Samataṭa. These are Shi-li-cha-ta-lo (Śrīkṣetra in Burma with its capital at Prome on the Irrawaddy), Kia-mo-land-kia (Kāmalaṅka, identified with Pegu and the Irrawaddy delta in Burma). To-lo-po-ti (Dvārāvatī, the famous Burmese kingdom in Sandowe region), I-shung-na-pu-lo (Īśānapura to the east of Dvārāvatī), Mo-ho-chen-po (Mahācampā in Vietnam) and Yen-nio-na-chen (Yamanadvīpa, identification uncertain).[99] There is a clear hint that contacts between Samataṭa and these regions in South-East Asia had already started by the first half of the seventh century, probably by maritime voyages. This suggests the gradual emergence of Samataṭa as a maritime zone of considerable importance.

CONCLUSION

A few things should be pointed out in this concluding section. Despite the widely-held notion that the Bengal coast had regular contacts with the Roman traders/sailors, it will be well nigh impossible to furnish concrete proof in favour of this hypothesis. The 'emporia' in India as enlisted by Ptolemy indicate settlements of Roman traders/sailors at places in or near the seacoast under the encouragement of the rulers thereof. The northernmost limit of the distribution of such 'emporia' of Ptolemy along the eastern seaboard is the Andhra coast.[100] The absence of 'emporia' in the Kalinga and Vaṅga coast cannot but be interpreted that these two littorals had no direct participation in Roman trade.

The importance of the Bengal coast, both in West Bengal and also the Samataṭa area in Bangladesh, for maritime voyages along the eastern seaboard and also with South-East is enormous. The port par excellence in ancient Bengal was of course Tāmralipta. But we have demonstrated already how Samataṭa was gradually making its presence felt, although slowly, in the affairs of the Indian Ocean, since the seventh century AD.[101] The decline of Tāmralipta in *c.* eighth century immensely enhanced the importance of the Samataṭa-Harikela country. From the eighth century onwards the major area of seaborne contacts between Bengal and other countries in the Indian Ocean became Samataṭa-Harikela where Samandar (near Chittagong) emerged as a great port.[102]

ACKNOWLEDGEMENT

A considerable part of the contents of this paper is based on the research work on 'Indigenous Traditions of Navigation in the Indian Ocean (Bengal Coast)', a project carried under the auspices of the Council for Scientific and Industrial Research. The author wishes to thank Professor B.N. Mukherjee, Carmichael Professor, Department of Ancient Indian History and Culture, Calcutta University; Dr. Gautam Sengupta, Director, Department of Archaeology, Government of West Bengal, Sri Pratip Kumar Mitra, Officer-in-charge, State Archaeological Museum, Government of West Bengal and Dr. Asok Datta, Lecturer, Department of Archaeology, Calcutta University for their valuable cooperation and help.

NOTES

1. Franz Broeze, ed., *Brides of the Sea*, Kensington, 1989, p. 8.
2. Ashin Das Gupta and M.N. Pearson, eds., *India and the Indian Ocean 1500-1800*, Calcutta, 1987, pp. 9-10.
3. Charles Verlinden, 'The Indian Ocean in the Ancient Period and the Middle Ages', in Satish Chandra, ed., *The Indian Ocean: Explorations in History, Commerce and Politics*, New Delhi, 1987, p. 27.
4. For a general appreciation of this subject the following recent publications are of considerable help: Das Gupta and Pearson, eds., *India and the Indian Ocean*; Chandra, ed., *The Indian Ocean*; K.N. Chaudhuri, *Trade and Civilization in the Indian Ocean from the Rise of Islam to 1750*, Cambridge, 1985; K.N. Chaudhuri, *Asia before Europe, Economy and Civilization in the Indian Ocean from the Rise of Islam to 1750*, Cambridge, 1990.
5. Fernand Braudel, *The Mediterranean and the Mediterranean World in the Age of Phillip II*, in 2 vols., London, 1972.
6. Braudel, *The Mediterranean*, vol. I, p. 17.
7. A. Bhattacharyya, *Historical Geography of Ancient and Early Medieval Bengal*, Calcutta, 1977.
8. R.K. Mookerji, *Indian Shipping: A History of Seaborne Trade and Maritime Activities of Indians from the Earliest Times*, Bombay, 1912, p. 57.
9. Begley and de Puma, eds., *Rome and India.*
10. Mukherjee, 'Kharoṣṭī and Kharoṣṭī-Brāhmī Inscriptions'.
11. There is a definite thrust of historical researches on the western seaboard which has better contacts with West Asia and the Mediterranean world. The eastern littorals have recently received its due recognition, but mostly for the period after AD 1500. Vide P.J. Marshall, *East Indian Fortune: The British in Bengal in the Eighteenth Century*, Oxford, 1976; Om Prakash 'European Trading Companies and the Merchants of Bengal', *IESHR*, vol. III, 1964; S. Arasaratnam, *Merchants, Commerce and Companies in the Coromandel Coast 1650-1740*, Delhi, 1986; Sanjay Subrahmanyam, *Improvising the Empire*, New Delhi, 1990; Ashin Das Gupta, *Vangopa-sagara* (in Bengali), Calcutta, 1989 who equates the Bay of Bengal with the eastern Indian Ocean, gives us a brief but clear understanding of the nature of maritime activities in this area in the post-1500 days.
12. B.N. Mukherjee's Bengali article in *Desh*, 5.12.92; 23-9 discusses the evolution of the connotation of the term Indian Ocean.
13. Pliny, *Naturalis Historia*, tr. J. Rackham, London and Cambridge, Mass, 1942, p. 381; the text reads: '*Indorumque gens incipit, non Eoo tantum mari adiacens verum et maridiane quod indicum appellavimus*'.
14. *Geographike Huphegesis*, VII.1.16.
15. The record was first edited with translation by R.G. Basak, *EI*, vol. XXVIII, pp. 57-68; it was subsequently commented upon by D.C. Sircar, *EI*,

vol. XXVIII, pp. 337-9. Sircar correctly assigned the record to the regnal year 46 of Śrīcandra, i.e. AD 971.

16. For an elaborate discussion see Ranabir Chakravarti, 'Vaṅgasāgara-saṁbhāṇḍāriyaka: A Riverine Trade Centre of Early Medieval Bengal', included in this volume as Chap. 7.
17. Spate and Learmonth, *India and Pakistan.*
18. Spate and Learmonth, *India and Pakistan.*
19. *Periplus of the Erythraean Sea*, ed. and tr., Lionel Casson, Princeton, 1989, secs. 62-3.
20. Ptolemy, *Geographike Huphegesis*, VII.1.81.
21. Mukherjee, 'Kharoshṭī and Kharoshṭī-Brāhmī Inscriptions', p. 66.
22. Mukherjee, 'Kharoshṭī and Kharoshṭī-Brāhmī Inscriptions', Appendix I: A List of Select Inscriptions (hereinafter List), pp. 42-62.
23. Mukherjee, 'Kharoshṭī and Kharoshṭī-Brāhmī Inscriptions', List, nos. 5, 9, 10, 14, 21, 29 and 37.
24. Mukherjee, 'Kharoshṭī and Kharoshṭī-Brāhmī Inscriptions', List, no. 60.
25. Mukherjee, 'Kharoshṭī and Kharoshṭī-Brāhmī Inscriptions', List, no. 39.
26. Mukherjee, 'Kharoshṭī and Kharoshṭī-Brāhmī Inscriptions', List, no. 2.
27. Mukherjee, 'Kharoshṭī and Kharoshṭī-Brāhmī Inscriptions', List, no. 9.
29. Mukherjee, 'Kharoshṭī and Kharoshṭī-Brāhmī Inscriptions', List, no. 35.
30. Mukherjee, 'Kharoshṭī and Kharoshṭī-Brāhmī Inscriptions', List, nos. 10 and 6.
31. Hsüan Tsang, *Ta-Tang hsi-yü Chi*, tr., Samuel Beal, New Delhi, 1983 (rpt.), pp. 199-200.
32. *Periplus*, sec. 64.
33. *Periplus*, sec. 64; Malabathrum was probably not a product of Bengal proper and grown in the north-east frontier areas wherefrom it must have been brought to the port of Gange for further shipment. B.N. Mukherjee, *The External Trade of North-Eastern India*, New Delhi, 1992.
34. *Periplus*, sec. 64. The trade from Gange to Limyrike must have been maritime, following the eastern littorals.
35. Mukherjee, 'Kharoshṭī and Kharoshṭī-Brāhmī Inscriptions', List, no. 11.
36. Ranabir Chakravarti, 'Maritime Trade in Horses in Early Historical Bengal: A Seal from Chandraketugarh', *Pratnasamiksha*, vol. I, 1992, pp. 155-60.
37. Mukherjee, 'Kharoshṭī and Kharoshṭī-Brāhmī Insçriptions'.
38. L. Peteche, *Northern India According to the Shui Ching Chu*, Rome, 1950, p. 53.
39. Mukherjee, *Economic Factors*, pp. 37-8.
40. Mukherjee, 'Kharoshṭī and Kharoshṭī-Brāhmī Inscriptions', Pl. XLI, Figs. 59, 61 and 62. Significantly enough Chinese evidence of the celebrated voyages of Zheng He in the fifteenth century, records the export of horses from the Bengal coast to China. See Haraprasad Ray, *Trade and Diplomacy in India-China Relations: A Study of Bengal during the Fifteenth Century*,

New Delhi, 1993, pp. 118-20. This may suggest a continuity of a much earlier tradition of the shipment of horses from the Bengal coast to South-East Asia and China, though the details of this trade over the millennia are not known.

41. Himanshu Prabha Ray, 'Seafaring in the Bay of Bengal in the Early Centuries AD', *SH*, vol. VI, 1990, p. 11.
42. For the reconstruction of the history of shipping in Europe visual representations of sea-going vessels on seals, medallions, etc., have been used. Vide Charles Singer et al., eds., *A History of Technology*, vol. II, Oxford, 1979, pp. 563ff. Jean Deloche, 'Konkan Warships of Eleventh-Sixteenth Centuries as Represented by Memorial Stones', *BEFEO*, vol. 82, 1987, pp. 165-84, demonstrates how sculptural depictions can be used for studying the shipping of past. D. Schlingloff has made incisive enquiries of early Indian ships on the basis of the Ajanta paintings. D. Schlingloff, *Studies in the Ajanta Paintings*, New Delhi, 1988.
43. Mukherjee, 'Kharoshṭī and Kharoshṭī-Brāhmī Inscriptions', List, no. 51.
44. Mukherjee, 'Kharoshṭī and Kharoshṭī-Brāhmī Inscriptions', List, no. 11.
45. *Periplus*, sec. 44.
46. Chakravarti, 'Maritime Trade in Horses'.
47. Ray, 'Seafaring in the Bay of Bengal', p. 6 cites evidence of the use of tripod masts in the depiction of early ships of South-East Asia.
48. Mukherjee, 'Kharoshṭī and Kharoshṭī-Brāhmī Inscriptions', List, no. 11.
49. Chakravarti, 'Maritime Trade in Horses'.
50. Bose, *Social and Rural Economy*, vol. II.
51. Mukherjee, 'Kharoshṭī and Kharoshṭī-Brāhmī Inscriptions', List, no. 13.
52. Mukherjee, 'Kharoshṭī and Kharoshṭī-Brāhmī Inscriptions', List, no. 6.
53. Schlingloff, *Ajanta Paintings*, p. 200.
54. Mukherjee, 'Kharoshṭī and Kharoshṭī-Brāhmī Inscriptions', List, no. 6.
55. Mukherjee, 'Kharoshṭī and Kharoshṭī-Brāhmī Inscriptions', List, no. 10.
56. Mukherjee, 'Kharoshṭī and Kharoshṭī-Brāhmī Inscriptions', List, no. 47.
57. Chittaranjan Roy Chowdhury, *A Catalogue of Early Indian Coins in the Asutosh Museum, Calcutta*, Calcutta, 1962, Plate X.
58. Roy Chowdhury, *A Catalogue of Coins*, Plate VIII.
59. *KAS*, II.28.
60. *KAS*, II.28.13.
61. *KAS*, II.28.13.
62. *Amarakośa of Amarasiṁha*, ed. A.D. Sharma and M.G. Sardesai, Poona, 1941.
63. M.C. Joshi, 'Navigational Terms in the *Nāmaliṅganuśāsana*', in S.R. Rao ed., *Marine Archaeology*, Goa, 1991, p. 19 says that *potavaṇik* is a voyaging merchant. But the term *potavaṇik* which is the same as *vaṇikpota* may be better translated as a merchant vessel; the term *Yānapātra* stands better for a passenger ship.
64. Joshi, 'Navigational Terms', considers *aritra* to be a rudder, but the actual

meaning of *aritra* is oar. The use of rudder in early Indian visual representations of sea-going vessels is moreover a rarity; ships are generally found to have been fitted with a steering oar.

65. Joshi, 'Navigational Terms', suggests that *karṇadhāra* should be the same as the sail operator, implying thereby that early Indian vessels had sails fitted to them. But except the famous painting of a ship at Ajanta, the sail is rarely shown in the depiction of an early Indian seal. The widespread and regular use of sail on Indian sea-going vessels is not beyond doubt. Moreover the commentary on the *Amarakośa* clearly states that one who holds the steering oar is the *karṇadhāra* (*karṇamaritraṁ dhāryatīti karṇadhāraḥ*). Ordinary sailors (*karmakara*, literally meaning workers) were distinguished from the *niryāmaka/niyāmaka* (i.e. navigator). The latter appears to have been a member of a *śreṇi*-like body, as will be evident from the reference to a leader (*jeṭṭhaka*) of the *niyyamakas* (Jātaka, IV: 137).
66. *SI*, vol. I, p. 497.
67. *SI*, vol. I, p. 497, fn. 4.
68. S.R. Das, *Rajbadidanga 1962, Excavation Report*, Calcutta, 1968; S.R. Das, *Archaeological Discoveries from Murshidabad*, Calcutta, 1971.
69. Ray, 'Seafaring in the Bay of Bengal'.
70. Schlingloff, *Ajanta Paintings*, p. 200.
71. Schlingloff, *Ajanta Paintings*, p. 200.
72. Pliny, *Naturalis Historia*, speaks of the development of the sea routes between India and the West in four stages. Each succeeding stage provided shorter and safer journey to the voyager; the most developed route by the increasingly better utilization of the s.w. monsoon wind facilitated a ship's voyage from the Red Sea port of Ocelis to the Malabar coast in less than forty days.
73. Ptolemy, *Geographike Huphegesis*, VII.1.15.
74. Fa-hsien, *Fo kuo chi*, tr., H.A Giles, *The Travels of Fahsien*, Cambridge, 1923, Chap. XXXVII, p. 65.
75. J. Takakusu, tr., *A Record of the Buddhist Religion as Practised in India and the Malay Archipelago*, Oxford, 1896.
76. J. Deloche, 'Geographical Considerations in the Localisation of Ancient Seaports in India', *IESHR*, vol. XX, 1983, pp. 439-48.
77. *Periplus*, sec. 63.
78. Ptolemy, *Geographike Huphegesis*, VII.1.81.
79. Mukherjee, 'Kharoshṭī and Kharoshṭī-Brāhmī Inscriptions', p. 24.
80. For a general introduction to the site of Chandraketugarh see D.K. Chakrabarti, 'Chandraketugarh', in Ghosh, ed., *Encyclopaedia*, vol. II, pp. 95-6. For further notices of excavations carried out at Chandraketugarh from 1956-7 to 1967-8 vide the relevant volumes of *IAR*.
81. Ptolemy, *Geographike Huphegesis*, VII. 1; Pliny, *Naturalis Historia*, Book VI.

82. Paresh Chandra Dasgupta, 'Some Early Indian Literary References to Tāmralipta', *Modern Review*, 1953, pp. 31-4.
84. Dasgupta, 'Literary References to Tāmralipta'.
85. See in the context Asok Datta, 'A Report on the Field Survey in the Midnapur Coast', Section III of the unpublished report to the CSIR/EMR-II on the first year's work on the Indigenous Traditions of Navigation in the Bengal Coast (edited by B.N. Mukherjee and Ranabir Chakravarti). Gautam Sengupta, 'Archaeology of Coastal Bengal', in Himanshu Prabha Ray and Jean-François Salles, eds., *Tradition and Archaeology: Early Maritime Contacts in the Indian Ocean*, New Delhi, 1996, pp. 113-28, also impresses upon the cluster of sites around Tamluk and points to the homogeneity of the material culture thereof.
86. *SI*, vol. II, pp. 36-40.
87. The significance of these terms from the point of view of navigation and in the context of the description of the riverine port of Devaparvata is discussed by Chakravarti, 'Vaṅgasāgara-saṁbhāṇḍariyaka', included in this volume as Chapter 7. *SI*, vol. I, pp. 363-77; *SI*, vol. I, p. 340.
88. Bose, *Social and Rural Economy*, vol. II.
89. B.N. Mukherjee, 'Kharoshṭī Inscriptions from Chunar (UP)', *JAS*, vol. XXXII, 1990, pp. 103-8.
90. Mukherjee, *External Trade*, p. 34.
91. *Periplus*, sec. 64.
92. Watters, *Yuan Chwang*, pp. 194-204.
93. Watters, *Yuan Chwang*, p. 201. Hsüan Tsang's description closely corresponds to the Jaina account which describes Tāmalitti, i.e. Tāmralipta as a *doṇamukha (droṇamukha)*, i.e. where land and sea routes converged. See in this context J.C. Jain, *Life in Ancient India as Depicted in the Jaina Canonical Texts and Commentaries*, New Delhi, 1974.
94. *EI*, vol. II, pp. 343-7.
95. *SI*, vol. I, pp. 234 and 235; Jain, *Life in Ancient India* cites an interesting passage from the *Uttarādhyāyana Sūtra* (21.2) which speaks of a journey by a merchant named Palita from Campā to Pithuḍa (cf. Pityndra of Ptolemy) by a *poya* (i.e. *pota* or sea-going vessel). This voyage from Campā (near Bhagalpur) to Pithuṇḍa, between the deltas of the Mahanadi and the Krishna, must have been made through some ports in the Gangetic delta and then along the eastern seaboard.
96. Vimala Begley, 'Arikamedu Reconsidered', *American Journal of Archaeology*, vol. LXXXVII, 1983, pp. 461-81. For the significance of the widespread distribution of this ware from Sri Lanka to Chandraketugarh along the entire length of the eastern seaboard see Vimala Begley, 'From Iron Age to Early Historical in South Indian Archaeology', in Jerome Jacobson, ed., *Studies in the Archaeology of India and Pakistan*, New Delhi, 1986, pp. 297-316; Vimala Begley, 'Ceramic Evidence of pre-Periplus Trade

on the Indian Coast', in Begley and de Puma, eds., *Rome and India*, pp. 157-96; Himanshu Prabha Ray, 'Early Trade in the Bay of Bengal', *IHR*, vol. XVI, 1987-88, pp. 79-89.

97. Mukherjee, 'Kharoshṭī and Kharoshṭī-Brāhmī Inscriptions', pp. 34 and 73.
98. See in this context the itineraries of Fa-hsien (Giles, *The Travels of Fahsien*, Chap. XXXVII) and Itsing (Takakusu, *A Record of the Buddhist Religion*, pp. 75ff).
99. Watters, *Yuan Chwang*, p. 200. The possibilities of contacts between ancient Gangetic delta and South-East Asia is further strengthened by the regular use of Kharoṣṭī in the legend of coins of Dvārāvatī, an area mentioned by Hsüan Tsang. B.N. Mukherjee, 'The Coinage of Dvārāvatī in South-East Asia and the Kharoṣṭī-Brāhmī Script', in Debala Mitra, ed., *Explorations in the Art and Archaeology of South Asia: Essays Dedicated to N.G. Majumdar*, Calcutta, 1996, pp. 527-34.
100. Mukherjee, *Economic Factors*, appendix.
101. See note no. 94 for the decline of Tāmralipta.
102. B.N. Mukherjee, 'Commerce and Money in the Central and Western Sectors of Eastern India', *IMB*, vol. XVI, 1982, pp. 65-83.

CHAPTER 7

Vaṅgasāgara-saṁbhāṇḍāriyaka: A Riverine Trade Centre of Early Medieval Bengal

The ongoing and increasingly intense interactions between experts of earth and social sciences have in recent years left a definite mark on historical researches. Historians have been showing keen interests in the study of human settlements vis-a-vis the existing environmental, socio-economic and political conditions of past ages. There is little doubt that these interrelating factors do give shapes to human habitats which are among subjects of major concern of historians. Such trends in historiography appear to have encouraged historians of early India to take a close look at different types of settlements and their functional importance. It is only natural that the predominantly agrarian set-up of Indian society would generally favour a sustained research in rural settlements (both at micro and macro levels).[1] Despite the definite thrust on understanding rural settlements and society during the early period of Indian history, historians, however, are not disinclined to the study of non-rural spaces. In fact, the study of the processes of the emergence, spread and decay of early Indian urban centres over the last three decades has been one of the most significant facets of historical researches on ancient India.[2]

The major problem of taking up such a subject for an in-depth research is of course the paucity of evidence which plagues historians of early India, particularly those interested in socio-economic history. It is true that a judicious combination of archaeological and epigraphic data has often led to our better understanding of the nature of both rural and non-rural settlements of early India. The wealth of literary/textual information on different categories of settlements cannot of course be lost sight of. But these often tend to present a stereotyped and/or idealized picture which may have some relevance to the historian as and when they are corroborated and supplemented by epigraphic sources and archaeological remains known from explorations and excavations.

Among non-rural settlements the study of urban areas and commercial centres seem to enjoy historians' preference. But sustained studies of early Indian port-towns are not frequently carried out. The recent spurt of publications on the Indian Ocean studies is expected to give a definite boost to the researches on ancient ports—whether located near or on the coast or situated in the interior on the banks of rivers.[3]

II

These preliminaries may now be followed by our particular attention to a non-rural settlement of the early medieval Bengal. It must, however, be made clear at the outset that there was no 'Bengal' in pre-AD 1200 days. The undivided British province of Bengal embraced areas now substantially included within West Bengal and Bangladesh. Early Bengal may be taken here—for the sake of convenience—to denote roughly the same area. But in pre-AD 1200 period the area in question had within it four major geographical units with their distinctive ethos. These were: (i) Puṇḍravardhana (originally denoting northern part of Bengal, i.e. Rajshahi-Bogra-Dinajpur areas of Bangladesh and part of northern sector of West Bengal, but subsequently covering—in addition to the above mentioned zone—large areas to the east of the Bhagirathi up to Chittagong and Sylhet); (ii) Rāḍha (roughly denoting areas to the west of the Bhagirathi, i.e. present districts of Birbhum, Bankura, Burdwan, Hooghly, Howrah and Midnapur in West Bengal); (iii) Vaṅga (embracing Dhaka-Faridpur-Vikrampur, Barishal and Buckerganj areas in Bangladesh;[4] and (iv) Samaṭata-Harikela[5] (the territory to the east of the river Meghna, i.e. Noakhali, Comilla, Chittagong and adjacent areas in Bangladesh).[6] There was neither any uniform nor unilinear socio-economic development in these four units which were never unified under a single paramount political power in the pre-AD 1200 times.[7] The early medieval period did witness the rise of the Pālas and then the Senas as the most formidable powers over this area,[8] but they did not rule over the entire area of early Bengal. Among political powers of early medieval Bengal which made their presence felt in the history of this region, mention must be made of the Devas and Candras.[9] The Candra rulers would figure prominently in our present discussion. They came into political limelight in and around the beginning of the tenth century AD in eastern part of Bengal. Their earliest stronghold seems to have been in Harikela, but gradually their power grew to gain mastery over Samataṭa, Vaṅga and also Śrīhaṭṭa by the second quarter of the tenth century AD.[10]

The most reliable source of information for early medieval Bengal, including the territory under the Candras, is epigraphic. Most of the inscriptions record transfer of plots of land and/or transfer of revenue in favour of individual Brāhmaṇas and religious institutions by the issue of copper-plate charters. The present paper particularly focuses on one such copper plate, viz., the Madanpur copper plate charter of Śrīcandra, the most important ruler of the Candra dynasty, who is known to have had a long reign of nearly half a century (*c.* AD 925-75). The plate was first edited and partly translated by R.G. Basak[11] and was later commented upon by D.C. Sircar.[12] The plate was issued, according to Basak, in the forty-fourth year of Śrīcandra's reign, i.e. AD 969, while Sircar dated it to the forty-sixth regnal year, i.e. AD 971.

The main purport of the plate is to record the gift of a plot of land by Śrīcandra to a Brāhmaṇa named Śukradeva whose genealogy is also given in the text. The proclamation was issued from the victorious camp (*jayaskandhāvāra*) at Vikramapura. The donated plot measured, according to Basak, 8 *droṇas*; a revised reading by Sircar shows that actually 8 *droṇas* and 8 *gaṇḍas* of land were transferred to the donee.[13]

The area where the donated plot was situated gives us some interesting clues about the settlement. Land was donated to Śukradeva at a place called Vaṅgasāgara-saṁbhāṇḍariyaka in Yolāmaṇḍala (*maṇḍala*, an administrative unit smaller than a province) included within Puṇḍra-vardhanabhukti.[14] The administrative unit Yolāmaṇḍala also figures in the Dhulla copper plate of Śrīcandra.[15] N.K. Bhattasali places Yolāmaṇḍala to the north of the river Dhaleswari in the Manikganj subdivision of the Dhaka district.[16] Ancient Yolāmaṇḍala seems to have covered areas around modern Sabhar (about 24 km to the north-west of Dhaka) which has yielded many significant archaeological objects, including the present Madanpur copper plate under discussion.

The rather unusual toponym Vaṅgasāgara-saṁbhāṇḍāriyaka calls for a close scrutiny. Neither Basak nor Sircar offers any translation or explanation of such a queer place-name. The location of donated plots (recorded in copper plates) generally lies in rural areas, minute details of which appear in the record along with precise information regarding relevant administrative divisions and units. The Madanpur copper plate merely refers to the name of the *bhukti* and the immediately lower administrative unit, *maṇḍala* (literally, circle), without at all mentioning any name of a village. This may give one the impression that Vaṅgasāgara-saṁbhāṇḍāriyaka was not situated in a rural space. Moreover, no information regarding detailed boundary demarcations of the donated plot and adjacent rural areas figures in our record, though this is a very common feature of early medieval land grants. This further strengthens our inference that Vaṅgasāgara-saṁbhāṇḍāriyaka was a non-rural settlement.

The term *saṁbhāṇḍariyaka* may stand for a place where items (*bhāṇḍāra*) could be appropriately (*samyak*) stored.[17] Such storage of items may logically be associated with commercial activities at a given centre of exchange. This leads to a further inference that an exchange centre such as the one under consideration could also have offered warehousing facilities (*saṁbhāṇḍāra*). The *saṁbhāṇḍāriyaka*, as a non-rural centre of commerce, may correspond to *puṭabhedana*, literally meaning a place where lids (of merchandise) were broken (by merchants for sale).[18] A *puṭabhedana*, like the *saṁbhāṇḍariyaka*, seems also to have provided arrangements for the storage of 'sealed' items of trade, 'seals' having been stamped on consignments to attest their quality, purity and weight. Both *puṭabhedana* and *saṁbhāṇḍariyaka*, therefore, may have had similar functions as a particular type of trade centre which offered facilities of warehousing of commodities.

The other component of the place-name, Vaṅgasāgara may now be examined. It should denote the sea (*sāgara*) of Vaṅga. While Vaṅga generally covers the central part of deltaic Bengal (i.e. Dhaka-Vikrampur-Faridpur), it also occasionally included in it areas near the coast, known in ancient times variously as Vaṅgāla (Vaṅga + āla) and Anuttaravaṅga (southern Vaṅga).[19] Ancient and early medieval Vaṅga thus extended up to Barishal-Buckerganj areas of the present Bangladesh. Vaṅgasāgara may, therefore, indicate the early medieval name of the eastern sector of the Indian Ocean. This is possibly the earliest base of an indigenous name wherefrom later terms like the Bay of Bengal and Vaṅgopasāgara (in Bengali) were derived.

The history of maritime affairs in and associated with the Bay of Bengal has to be appreciated in the broader background of activities in the vast maritime space known as the Indian Ocean. The expression 'Indian Ocean' is based on the Latin expression '*mari Indicum*' used for the first time by Pliny in his *Naturalis Historia* (completed in or before AD 79).[20] His *mari Indicum* or the Indian Ocean apparently has a narrower connotation than that of the homonymous maritime space in modern times.[21] Pliny seems to have placed his *mari Indicum* to the south of Indian peninsula. In fact, Classical authors were better conversant with the Erythraean Sea by which a considerable part of the western Indian Ocean was denoted. The eastern segment of the Indian

Ocean was vague to the Classical authors. Ptolemy (*c.* AD 150) refers to the Gangetic Gulf[22] for the first time and this has usually been identified with the present Bay of Bengal. Sanskrit sources generally use two terms to differentiate between the Arabian Sea and the Bay of Bengal; these two are *paścima* (western) and *pūrva* (eastern) *jaladhi* (sea). Interestingly enough, some epigraphic records, datable to the second half of the sixth century AD, and discovered from Vaṅga[23] (i.e. Dhaka-Vikrampura-Faridpur region), speaks of *prāksamudra*. The expression has been interpreted to mean the eastern sea.[24] This is of course the same as the Bay of Bengal which was definitely known to the inhabitants of Vaṅga in the latter part of the sixth century AD. The Madanpur copper plate shows that the eastern sea or the Bay of Bengal was called Vaṅgasāgara in the third quarter of the tenth century AD.

The practice of naming the Bay of Bengal or parts thereof after a regional unit of early Bengal (i.e. Vaṅga) appears to have resembled the custom of naming the Bay of Bengal (or parts thereof) as Bahr Harkand (or Harkal) in Arab accounts.[25] The anonymous Persian text on geography *Hudud al Alam* (AD 982) uses this term to denote the Bay of Bengal which was one of the seas of India, according to the Arab writers.[26] The name Harkand or Harkal is derived from Harikela, a territory contiguous to Samataṭa, and identified with the modern Noakhali, Comilla, Chittagong and adjacent areas in Bangladesh. That Harikela was an important commercial zone since the late seventh century AD is clear from the Chinese evidence.[27] But its rise to prominence in the international maritime trade of the Indian Ocean in general and the Bay of Bengal in particular began from the ninth century onwards. Its major port Samandar (located at or near modern Chittagong) attracted considerable attention of Arab writers (and obviously merchants also).[28] The unmistakable evidence of the commercial activities in this area is furnished by the continuous minting of high quality silver coinage from seventh to the thirteenth centuries. The integration of this area into the larger maritime long-distance trade networks in the Indian Ocean can further be demonstrated by the discovery of a gold coin of the Abbasid Caliphate Abu Ahmad Ab dallah al Mustasim Billa (AD 1242-53) from Mainamati.[29] All these may drive home the suggestion that both Vaṅgasāgara and Bahr Harkand denoted more or less the same maritime space, the importance of which in seaborne trade can hardly be lost sight of.

One may remember that the Candras had their primary stronghold in Harikela.[30] This provided the platform wherefrom the Candras began to spread their authority over Vaṅga, Vaṅgāla and Śrīhaṭṭa, due principally to the aggressive designs of Śrīcandra.[31] This firmly established the Candras as the most formidable power in Vaṅga during the tenth-eleventh centuries. Significantly enough, the lexicographer Hemacandra of the eleventh century equated Harikela with Vaṅga.[32] If these two territorial names apparently became coterminous, it would be logical to suggest that Bahr Harkand and Vaṅgasāgara were virtually inter-changeable terms to denote the same maritime space, i.e. the Bay.of Bengal.

The compound expression Vaṅgasāgara-saṁbhāṇḍāriyaka may, therefore, speak of an exchange centre associated with the trade in the Bay of Bengal *(Vaṅgasāgara)*.[33] We may now take a close look at the officers present at Vaṅgasāgara-saṁbhāṇḍāriyaka at the time of the grant of land to Śukradeva. While most of the names of officers are commonly seen in many epigraphic records of early medieval Bengal, three names seem to be rather unusual. They are *nauvāṭaka*, *arddhanauvāṭaka* and *gocchakapati*. The term *nauvāṭaka* occasionally occurs in some records in the sense of a fleet of boats, the context being descriptions of movements of victorious fleets along certain rivers.[34] But the Madanpur copper plate of Śrīcandra furnishes the solitary evidence of the use of the term in the sense of a royal officer. 'In the context of our plate,' suggests Basak, 'the word *nauvāṭaka* may, therefore, refer to the Head of the royal navy.'[35] It would, however, be difficult to prove that the Candras ever maintained a regular navy. Seen from this angle, *nauvāṭaka* could have been an officer entrusted with the affairs of the mercantile marine. The expression *ardhanauvāṭaka*, also unique in the Bengal inscriptions, therefore stands for an officer of the same department, but junior to the *nauvāṭaka*.[36] The presence of the officer looking after the mercantile marine, along with his subordinate, at Vaṅgasāgara-saṁbhāṇḍāriyaka further highlights the commercial significance of the non-rural settlement. Now to the term *gocchakapati*. Basak equates it with Sanskrit *goṣṭhakapati*, i.e. the administrative head in charge of pasture lands and cowherds.[37] Without at all disputing Basak's interpretations, an alternative meaning may be ventured here. The term *goṣṭha/goṣṭhī* may also be taken to mean an association, a professional group or body. In this sense it has a close correspondence to terms like *śreṇī*, *gaṇa*, *pūga*, *saṅgha*, denoting a guild-like association of persons following a common craft or trade. *Goṣṭhakapati*, therefore, may signify an officer in charge of *goṣṭhīs* or guilds.[38] At a commercial centre such as Vaṅgasāgara-saṁbhāṇḍāriyaka the presence of an officer looking after *goṣṭhīs* or guilds is a distinctly likely possibility. The functions of these three officers, viz., *nauvāṭaka*, *ardhanauvāṭaka* and *gocchakapati* being oriented towards the non-rural sectors of the economy, they udnerline the material interests of the Candras in Vaṅgasāgara-saṁbhāṇḍāriyaka.[39]

III

The discussion so far may help understand the nature and possible functions of the area under review. But where was the area actually located? There is no direct evidence to suggest its location on or near the coast. On the other hand the record gives an impression that the donated plot was not far away from either the issuing centre (Vikramapura) or the findspot (close to Sabhar). The archaeological treasures of Sabhar have aroused interest of scholars over a long time. Lying at distance of 24 km to the north-west of Dhaka and on the bank of the river Bangshi, Sabhar has several mounds. The Kotbari mound has a large rectangular area (219.5 m x 167.6 m), enclosed by a mud wall the height of which was 7.6 m (as reported in 1921). That it was a flourishing Buddhist centre can clearly be seen in a number of Buddha images—inscribed as well as uninscribed (from the Rajasan mound)—a *stūpa* (near the bus-stand at Sabhar) and a *stūpa* complex of impressive size (from the Rajbari mound). Among other antiquities discovered from Sabhar, mention may be made of six post-Gupta gold coins and two inscriptions (from Harish Chandra Rajar Bari), a silver Harikela coin and a gold coin, datable to the eighth century.[40] The location of the site on the bank of river having connections with distant areas has naturally encouraged archaeologists to suggest that Sabhar was a riverine port in older times. It still commands a respectable commercial traffic in timber, rice, pulses and maintains linkages with Barishal, Sylhet and Rajshahi.[41] The importance of this rich site can hardly be overemphasized, particularly in view of its location on the bank of a river. Long ago, N.K. Bhattasali guessed that the present name Sabhar could have been derived from Sanskrit *sambhāra* which means wealth, collection of items, etc.[42] Such a name would aptly fit a riverine archaeological site with definite commercial significance. The discovery of the Madanpur copper plate of Śrīcandra from the Sabhar area may therefore strongly suggest that a *saṁbhāṇḍāriyaka* (a trade centre with warehousing facilities) could very well have existed at Sabhar in the early medieval times. Vaṅgasāgara-saṁbhāṇḍariyaka thus would closely correspond to present-day Sabhar and also appears to have been a riverine port under the Candras.

The suggested identification of Vaṅgasāgara-saṁbhāṇḍāriyaka with present-day Sabhar near Dhaka may raise another question: how is one to explain the possible connections of this *saṁbhāṇḍāriyaka* at Saṁbhāra or Sabhar with Vaṅgasāgara or Bay of Bengal which was at some distance from the said riverine port? The problem may be tackled by going back to the conditions in Vaṅga in the second half of the sixth century AD. It was during this time that Vaṅga emerged as an independent political entity under three rulers, Dharmāditya, Samācāradeva and Gopacandra.[43] The politico-administrative and socio-economic history of Vaṅga during the latter half of the sixth century AD is known from several copper plates issued by these kings. Land transactions were recorded in the Vārakamaṇḍala-viṣaya (*viṣaya* = district; the area embracing parts of Goalando subdivision and Kotalipara region in the Gopalganj subdivision of the Faridpur district), following the customs or practices prevalent in the territory up to the sea (*prāk-samudra-maryyādā*).[44] The expression *prāk-samudra* has also been taken to mean the eastern sea (i.e. the Bay of Bengal).[45] Whichever interpretation of *prāk-samudra* is accepted, it cannot but denote the Bay of Bengal. This unmistakably shows that the Vaṅga country, though not situated in a littoral tract, had an intimate association with the eastern sea. Ancient Vaṅga had in it another significant administrative centre named Navyāvakāśikā, where as important an officer as the *mahā-pratīhāroparika* (*mahāpratīhāra* = chief of palace guards and *uparika* = local governor), named Nāgadeva was stationed.[46] Navyāvakāśikā literally means a new opening or channel (*navya* = new and *avakāśa* = opening, canal).[47] The relevance of such a new opening in a territory designated '*prāk-samudra*' can be properly appreciated if we logically surmise that such 'new openings' (or canals) led to new access to the sea. Changes in river courses leading to new channels in the delta are quite common in this area. Such channels—old or new—were mostly navigable and must have facilitated riverine communications between Vaṅga and littoral areas in the Bengal coast. Ancient people and rulers of Vaṅga must have been well aware of the economic significance of the riverine connections of Vaṅga, oriented to the sea. That ancient Vaṅga (and also Samataṭa) was very rich in inland riverine communication network will clearly be illustrated by the frequent epigraphic references to *nau-bandhakas/nau-daṇḍakas* (parking stations for boats and vessels plying in rivers).[48] Even more interesting is the information about a *nāvātā-kṣeṇī*, figuring in a record from ancient Vaṅga. This term seems to have denoted a ship/boat building harbour (*nau* = boat/vessel/ships, *ātā* = door-frame; *kṣenī* from *kṣayaṇa* = harbour).[49] Information regarding *nau-vāṭakas* and *nāvātā-kṣenī* invariably occurs in the final portions of grants where boundary demarcations of the donated area are specified. Seen from this angle, boat-parking stations and boat/ship building harbours of ancient Vaṅga were prominent enough to have been regularly considered as important landmarks in the rural space. The commercial significance of riverine communication networks in ancient Vaṅga, cannot, therefore, be overemphasized. The awareness of the rulers of Vaṅga in that direction can clearly be appreciated in the appointment of an officer, *vyāpāra-kāraṇḍya* in Vārakamaṇḍala-vishaya during the reign of Dharmāditya.[50] He appears to have been an officer, according to Pargiter, 'who has to regulate trade'.[51] All these may help us understand why an administrative unit had to be set up at Navyāvakāśikā in the same *vishaya*. In this context the earlier suggestion of Bhattasali that Navyāvakāśikā was the same as Sabhar itself,[52] assumes special significance. The commercial significance of this area may, therefore, be pushed back to the latter half of the sixth century AD.

The area of Vaṅga continued to maintain connections with the Bay of Bengal and the littoral areas of Bangladesh in early medieval times through its many rivers. This must have resulted in the coining of the name Nāvya to denote a part of Vaṅga, as seen in the Calcutta Sahitya Parishad copper plate of the thirteenth century (*Pauṇḍravardhana-bhuktyantaḥpatī-Vaṅge nāvye*).[53] The same record speaks of the village of Vinayatilaka (in Nāvya) which had the sea (i.e. the Bay of Bengal) as its eastern boundary (*nāvye Vinayatilakagrāme pūrvve samudrasīmā*) and a channel as its southern limit (*dakshiṇe praṇullībhūḥ sīmā*).[54] The term *nāvya* was used definitely to highlight the navigability of water courses (rivers, new channels, canals, etc.), up to the sea. If B.C. Sen's reading of the Rampal copper plate of Śrīcandra is accepted, then the existence of Nāvyamaṇḍala, an administrative unit, in Vaṅga has to be recognized. B.C. Sen locates it in Barishal-Buckerganj area and it had the main stream of the Meghna as its eastern limit.[55] The navigability of rivers of ancient and early medieval Vaṅga may be appreciated in view of Sabhar's riverine communications with Barishal also in recent times.

IV

The issues discussed earlier would underline the importance of riverine commercial networks in early Vaṅga which had connections with the littoral areas. This explains the significance of the archaeological site at

Sabhar which seems to have functioned as an inland riverine port—first as Navyāvakāśikā and then as *Vaṅgasāgara-saṁbhāndāriyaka*—of ancient and early medieval Vaṅga. Trade at this centre and its riverine linkages with the Bengal coast were largely responsible for its being considered as an administrative centre under early rulers of Vaṅga and also the Candras. Around the sixth century AD it emerged as a riverine port, while in the third quarter of the tenth century it had a *saṁbhāṇḍāriyaka*, i.e. it probably offered storing/warehousing facilities.

But what happened at Sabhar between the sixth and tenth centuries remains in the dark. Precisely during this time, epigraphic evidence suggests that Devaparvata, situated in Samataṭa-Harikela region (i.e. roughly to the east of the Meghna) emerged as another riverine port of prominence. It has been identified with Mainamati-Lalmai in Comilla, Bangladesh. The earliest epigraphic description of Devaparvata figures in the Kailan copper plate of Śrīdharaṇarāta (*c.* AD 665-75). Devaparvata was encircled by the river Kṣīrodā (i.e. modern Khira or Khirnai), both banks of which were decorated by boats and in which elephants bathed. Devaparvata is further described as *sarvatobhadra*, meaning either it was approachable from all four sides (by river?) or it had gates on all four sides (*Atha mattamātaṅga-śata-sukha-vigāhyamāna-vividha-tīrthayā naubhir = aparimitābhir = upārachitakulayā parikṣitād = abhi-matanimnagāminyā Kṣīrodayā sarvvatobhadrakād = Devaparvvatāt.*[56]) This unmistakably shows Devaparvata to be a riverine port in Samataṭa in the second half of the seventh century AD. Devaparvata was also the principal political centre of the Rāta rulers. Apart from being a riverine port and a political centre, Devaparvata was situated in an area which had a distinct orientation to riverine communications. Towards the end of the record three boat parking-stations (*naudaṇḍakas*) appear. The eastern boundary of the donated plot had *villa-bhaṅga* (cf. the Bengali word *bil*, moss covered with water) which was associated with *niṣkrāntaka-praviṣṭaka* (facilities of entry and exit of vessels?). Terms like *nauprithvī*, *nau-sthira-vegā*, etc., are used to denote boundary marks.[57] The exact meaning of these unusual words is difficult to ascertain. But that these were intimately associated with the plying of boats in the inland riverine network is beyond doubt.

Devaparvata once again figures in the Asiatic Society copper plate of Bhavadeva Abhinavamṛgāṅka (*c.* AD 765-80), a ruler belonging to the Deva dynasty of Samataṭa.[58] Devaparvata's association with the river Kṣīrodā appears in this record too. An interesting point is that the epigraphic account of Devaparvata here is more elaborate and grand—

though doubtless stereotyped—than the one found in the Kailan copper plate inscription composed nearly a century ago. In the eighth century Devaparvata is explicitly stated to have been the *jayaskandhāvāra* (literally, victorious camp) which in the then phraseology was often coterminous with the royal capital or at least a major political centre.[59] The more elaborate account and the epithet *jayaskandhāvāra* of Devaparvata in the eighth century point to the enhancement of the status of Devaparvata both as a riverine trade centre and a political centre. The Devas as the local power of Samataṭa did not fail to appreciate the significance of this riverine port.

The last known epigraphic evidence of Devaparvata is furnished by the Paschimbhag copper plate of Śrīcandra (*c.* AD 925-75), dated in his fifth regnal year (i.e. *c.* AD 930).[60] Once again the recurrent feature of the account of Devaparvata is its location on the Kṣīrodā (*Kṣīrodām = anu Devaparvata = iti śrīmat = tad = etat puraṁ*), on which plied many boats. That Lālambīvana (same as the Lalmai) was searched by hundreds of boatmen (*Lālambivanam = atra nāvika-śatair = anviṣṭa*) is also mentioned by this record. This further underlines the navigability of Kṣīrodā and the role of Devaparvata as a riverine port. But significantly enough, the record was issued by Śrīcandra not from Devaparvata, but from Vikramapura, the *jayaskandhāvāra*. In fact, the reference to Devaparvata figures in the context of Trailokyacandra's (father of Śrīcandra) conquest of Samataṭa country and his authority over the riverine port. Though Devaparvata is mentioned in Śrīcandra's record of *c.* AD 930, it has its proper relevance to the previous reign of his father.

The earlier mentioned survey indicates that Devaparvata was the most important riverine port in Samataṭa country from the second half of the seventh to the first quarter of the tenth century. The Samataṭa-Harikela country during this period provided the primary power-base to the Rātaṣ, Devas and early Candra rulers. The accession of Śrīcandra to the throne in *c.* AD 925 signalled a remarkable expansion and growth of the Candra political power. By the time of the composition of the Paschimbhag copper plate (i.e. *c.* AD 930) Śrīcandra's authority spanned over wide areas including Kāmarūpa, Śrīhaṭṭa and Vaṅga,[61] while retaining his control over Samataṭa-Harikela zone. In or before AD 930 Vikramapura became the new *jayaskandhāvāra* or seat of power of the Candras, indicating the shift of the stronghold of the Candra power from Samataṭa to the very heart of Vaṅga. This probably became necessary in order to ensure a better administrative integration of the expansive Candra domain. The reasonable assumption would be to view Vaṅga as a more important zone than Samataṭa-Harikela area in terms of the Candra polity and politics.

As Vaṅga began to emerge into limelight, a riverine port like Sabhar, situated not far away from Vikramapura, would gradually come into greater prominence. Correspondingly, the earlier riverine harbour at Devaparvata in the Samataṭa country seems to have been relegated to a less significant position. The commercial activities at the harbour of Devaparvata are to be situated, at least on epigraphic grounds, in a period of three centuries when nothing is heard about the riverine port at Sabhar, whether as Navyāvakāśikā or under the new name Vaṅgasāgara-saṁbbhāṇḍāriyaka. The renewed importance of the riverine port at Sabhar in the tenth century appears to have been due, at least partly, to the interests of the Candras in this area.

V

The site of Sabhar, therefore, twice came into limelight in four centuries as a riverine port, having linkages with the littoral areas of Vaṅga: first as Navyāvakāśikā in the sixth century and then as Vaṅgasāgara-saṁbhāṇḍāriyaka in the tenth century. A common pattern in the history of this harbour is that on both occasions its commercial significance was followed by and/or associated with its being a local administrative centre also. Unlike Devaparvata, this riverine port never enjoyed the status of being a *jayaskandhāvāra*.

When the inland riverine port at Sabhar first came to our notice in the second half of the sixth century AD, the most famous port in Bengal, if not of the whole of north-eastern India, was Tāmralipta (in district Midnapur). Tāmralipta was in a flourishing condition for a further century or slightly more. The last known reference to this harbour figures in an eighth century record.[62] The gradual decay of this leading port must have adversely affected Bengal's seaborne trade and also the conditions of inland riverine ports like Navyāvakāśikā at Sabhar. The effect of the decline of this port of international connections seems to have been overcome with the rise of a major harbour at Samandar, located near present Chittagong in Bangladesh, from the ninth century onwards.[63] Samandar often appears in the accounts of medieval Arab writers as a major harbour. Thus the centre of maritime trade of Bengal seems to have shifted in the early medieval period from Daṇḍabhukti area to Samataṭa-Harikela. The rise of an international harbour in Samataṭa-Harikela would have certainly proved advantageous for an inland riverine port like Vaṅgasāgara-sambhāṇḍāriyaka.

Studies in the maritime history and maritime trade generally tend to highlight leading ports with far-flung international network where overland, coastal and overseas routes converged. Priority is given to such celebrated ports of early India like Barygaza, Muziris, Cambay, Quilon, Nāgapaṭṭanam, Kāverīpaṭṭinam, Tāmralipta and Samandar, by maritime historians of early and medieval India. The role of a harbour of international stature cannot adequately be appreciated merely in terms of its littorals and the immediate maritime space. The importance of a port is largely shaped, among other factors, by its hinterland and foreland.[64] The situation of a harbour vis-a-vis its hinterland and foreland can hardly be judged merely by being an 'at sea' historian. The conditions inland are inseparably linked with the affairs in the littorals. It was Fernand Braudel who made us conscious about the unity between the land and the sea by his magisterial study of the Mediterranean Sea. The history of the Mediterranean, wrote Braudel, 'can no more be separated from that of the lands surrounding it than the clay can be separated from the hands of the potter who shapes it'.[65]

Such a perspective may help us appreciate more meaningfully the role of inland riverine harbours of early Bengal, like Vaṅgasāgara-saṁbhāṇḍāriyaka. They would often remain in the background, overshadowed by international harbours either in an estuary or on a roadstead. But inland riverine ports hold the very lifeline of supplies to and from larger ports. The existence of a large port would invariably suggest the existence also of a series of secondary harbours around it or somewhere away, but having definite linkages with the greater port. These smaller inland ports like Navyāvakāśikā or later Vaṅgasāgara-saṁbhāṇḍāriyaka were generally rooted firmly in their respective rural spaces and hence could have held the key to the long-distance overseas trade in daily necessities, including crops.

An attempt has been made here to situate the riverine port at Vaṅgasāgara-saṁbhāṇḍāriyaka in the overall background of trade in the eastern sector of the Indian Ocean in the early medieval times. The focus on non-rural spaces often falls on celebrated urban areas, and tends to ignore the smaller ones. 'But it would be mistake,' as Braudel puts it, 'to count the sun-cities—Venice, Florence, Nuremberg, Lyons, Amsterdam, London, Delhi, Nanking, Osaka. Towns from hierarchies everywhere, but the tip of the pyramid does not tell us everything, important though it may be.'[66] If the historian of the Indian Ocean does not wish to be at bay, the importance of such inland riverine ports as the one that stood at Sabhar has to be weighed in.

NOTES

1. B.D. Chattopadhyaya, *Aspects of Rural Settlements and Rural Society in Early Medieval India*, Calcutta, 1990.
2. There are larger number of informative, analytical and highly sophisticated studies of the Harappan cities which belong to the first urbanization in India. For an updated overview on Harappan urbanism, see Allchin and Allchin, *Rise of Civilization*. The second urbanization came into the scene in the Ganga valley around 600 BC. See Ghosh, *The City*; Sharma, *Urban Decay*, situates the decline of urban centres in the feudal social formation in India in the early medieval times. B.D. Chattopadhyaya, 'Urban Centres in Early Medieval India: An Overview', in Romila Thapar and Sabyasachi Bhattacharyya, eds., *Situating Indian History for S. Gopal*, New Delhi, 1987, pp. 8-33 suggests 'third urbanization' in the early medieval period.
3. For trade in the Indian Ocean the following books are particularly helpful and significant: Das Gupta and Pearson, eds., *India and the Indian Ocean*; Chandra, ed., *The Indian Ocean*, Chaudhuri, *Trade and Civilization*; Chaudhuri, *Asia before Europe*. The thrust of the historians of the Indian Ocean is clearly on the post-1500 phase. For a study of port towns, though not with an in-depth analysis of ancient harbours of India, see Broeze, ed., *Brides of the Sea*.
4. The earliest connotation of Vaṅga denotes an area covering modern districts of 24-Parganas (both North and South), Hooghly, Howrah and Midnapore during the first three or four centuries of the Christian era. This earliest connotation of Vaṅga has been suggested by B.N. Mukherjee, 'Kharoshṭī and Kharoshṭī-Brāhmī Inscriptions'.
5. B.N. Mukherjee, 'The Original Territory of Harikela', *Bangladesh Lalitkala*, vol. I, 1975, pp. 115-19.
6. For an exhaustive treatment of these four units see Bhattacharyya, *Historical Geography*.
7. Barrie M. Morrison, *Political Centres and Cultural Regions in Early Bengal*, Jaipur, 1980 (rpt.) highlights the distinct ethos, political, socio-economic and cultural, of four major sub-regions in early Bengal.
8. D.C. Sircar, *Pal-Sen Yuger Vamsanucharit* (in Bengali), Calcutta, 1982. Political history of the Pālas has to be considerably revised with the discovery of the Jagajjibanpur copper plate of the time of the Pāla ruler, Mahendrapāla, son and successor of Devapāla.
9. Sircar, *Vamsanucharit*.
10. This is clearly proved by the Paschimbhag copper plate of year 5 (i.e. AD 930) of Śrīcandra (AD 925-75). See D.C. Sircar, *Epigraphic Discoveries in East Pakistan*, Calcutta, 1973, pp. 19-40 and 63-9.
11. R.G. Basak, 'Madanpur Plate of Śrīcandra, year 44', *EI*, vol. XXVIII, 1949, pp. 57-8.

12. D.C. Sircar, 'Madanpur Plate of Śrīcandra, year 46', *EI*, vol. XXVIII, 1949, pp. 337-9.
13. Sircar, 'Madanpur Plate', p. 339.
14. Basak, 'Madanpur Plate', p. 57. *Śrīcandrade [vaṅkuśa*]ī śrī-Pauṇḍra-bhu*kty= antaḥpāti-Yolāmaṇḍale Vaṅgasāgara-saṁbhāṇḍāriyake.*
15. N.G. Majumdar, *Inscriptions of Bengal*, vol. III, Rajshahi, 1929, pp. 165-6.
16. *EI*, vol. XXVIII, p. 55; N.K. Bhattasali is referred to by Basak.
17. I am grateful to B.N. Mukherjee and Sukumari Bhattacharji for kindly endorsing this interpretation of mine of the expression *Vaṅgasāgara-saṁbhāṇḍariyaka.*
18. Specimens of plaster jar-plugs used to seal jars have been found from excavations at Leukos Limen, an early historic port on the Red Sea. See Sidebotham, 'Ports of the Red Sea', particularly pp. 31 and 32, Figs. 2.16 and 2.19. An early *puṭabhedana* was Pāṭaligāma, which later became the Magadhan capital Pāṭaliputra. Pāṭaligāma, situated at the confluence of three rivers, the Ganga, the Son and the Gandak, is described in the *Mahāparinivvāṇa-suttanta.* The Buddha is said to have prophesied the future greatness of this non-rural centre. This *puṭabhedana*, like our *saṁbhāṇḍariyaka*, was also an inland riverine port. Mercantile activities at a *puṭabhedana* are even more clearly hinted at in the *Arthaśāstra* by the use of the term *paṇyapūṭabhedana. KAS*, II.3.3; also see Ghosh, *The City*, pp. 45-6; Kosambi, *The Culture and Civilization*, p. 130. Somadevasūri's *Nītivākyāmṛitam*, modelled on the *Arthaśāstra*, shows its awareness of the economic importance of a *paṇyapūṭabhedinī* in the tenth century. Somadevasūri, in his other work, *Yaśastilakachampū* equates *paṇya-pūṭabhedinī* with *peṇṭhā/piṇṭhā* (occasionally suffixed with *sthāna*). A more elaborate treatment is available in 'The Peṇṭhā as a Centre of Trade in the Deccan *c.* AD 600-1300', included in this volume as Chap. 10.
19. Bhattacharyya, *Historical Geography*, p. 56.
20. Pliny, *Naturalis Historia*, VI.XXI.56. The text reads: '*Indorumque gens incipit, non Eoo tantum mari adiacens verum et meridiano quod Indicum appellavimus*' (VI.XXI.56). I am deeply indebted to B.N. Mukherjee for kindly drawing my attention to this passage. The significance of Pliny's statement on the naming of the Indian Ocean has been discussed by B.N. Mukherjee in a Bengali article published in the fortnightly *Desh*, 5 December 1992, pp. 23-9. This being the earliest use of the term, Indian Ocean, it would now be difficult to agree with M.N. Pearson that the term was derived from the early medieval Arabic expression *al bahr al Hind* (Pearson, 'The State of the Subject', in Das Gupta and Pearson, eds., *India and the Indian Ocean*, pp. 9-10.
21. Pliny's *mari Indicum* appears to have been located south of the Indian peninsula. The present map of the Indian Ocean, published by the National Atlas and Thematic Mapping Organization, places this maritime space up

to the Cape of Good Hope in the west, to Antarctica in the south and includes the Red Sea, the Persian Gulf, the Arabian Sea and the Bay of Bengal, but leaves out the Java and the China Seas.

22. Ptolemy, *Geographike Huphegesis*, VII. 1.16 quoted in B.N. Mukherjee, op. cit., *Desh* (see note 20).
23. *SI*, vol. I, pp. 363-77 and 530-1.
24. Ramaranjan Mukherjee and Sachindra Kumar Maity, *A Corpus of Bengal Inscription*, Calcutta, 1967, p. 77.
25. The earliest use of this term is found in the *Akhbar Al-Sin Wa'l-Hind*, by Sulayaman Al-Tajir et al., compiled in AD 851. Maqbul Ahmad, tr., *Arabic Classical Accounts*, pp. 34 and 38.
26. *Hudud al Alam*, pp. 52 and 179.
27. In the first half of the seventh century Hsüan Tsang visited San-mo-ta-ta (Samataṭa), an area contiguous with Harikela. Samataṭa was known at that time to have contacts with several areas in South-East Asia. During the last quarter of the seventh century I-tsing reported about the voyage to Ho-lai-ka-lo (i.e. Harikela) from Sri Lanka. See B.N. Mukherjee, 'Commerce and Money'.
28. The earliest reference to Samandar figures in the *Al-Masalito Wa'l-Manalik* by Ibn Khurdadhbih; Maqbul Ahmad, *Arabic Classical Accounts*, p. 5; Mukherjee, 'Commerce and Money'; Arab chroniclers leave little room for doubt that Samandar maintained long-distance maritime contacts with Serendib (Sri Lanka), Kanja (Kāñcīpuram), and Uranshin (Orissa). Al Idrisi explicitly states that Samandar was situated on a *Khawr* or inlet/creek. S.M.H. Nainar, *The Knowledge of India as Possessed by Arab Geographers down to the Fourteenth Century* AD *with Special Reference to Southern India*, Madras, 1942, p. 89. Such a location must have facilitated anchoring at, entry into and exit from Samandar.
29. Mukherjee, 'Commerce and Money'.
30. Trailokyacandra (*c.* AD 900-25), an early ruler of the Candra dynasty, is described as 'the support of Fortune goddesses the umbrella of which was the royal insignia of the king of Harikela' (*Ādhāro Harikela-rāja-kakuda-cchatraṁitānām Śrīyam*), Majumdar, *Inscriptions of Bengal*, pp. 4 and 7.
31. Sircar, *Vamsanucharit*, pp. 106-8.
32. Majumdar, ed., *History of Bengal*, p. 15, fn. 9.
33. For a general account of the Bay of Bengal see Das Gupta, *Vangopasagara* and A. Toussaint, *History of the Indian Ocean*, London, 1968.
34. Basak, 'Madanpur Plate', pp. 55-6.
35. Basak, 'Madanpur Plate', pp. 55-6.
36. Basak, 'Madanpur Plate', p. 56.
37. Basak, 'Madanpur Plate', p. 55.
38. The *Lekhapaddhati* in and around the thirteenth century enlists thirty-two *karaṇas* or administrative departments, one of them being *śreṇī-karaṇa*,

i.e. the department concerning (in other words, supervising over) guilds. Officers of this *karaṇa* may have functioned in a way similar to the *gocchakapati* or *goṣhakapati*.

39. See, Mukherjee, 'Commerce and Money' for information regarding crafts and commerce during this period.
40. For a general overview of the archaeological discoveries at Sabhar see Dilip K. Chakrabarti, *Ancient Bangladesh: A Study of the Archaeological Sources*, Delhi, 1992, pp. 138-41.
41. Chakrabarti, *Ancient Bangladesh*, p. 138.
42. Nalini Kanta Bhattasali, 'The Ghughrahati Copper Plate Inscription of Samāchāradeva', *EI*, vol. XVIII, 1925-6, pp. 74-86.
43. D.C. Sircar, *Palpurva Yuger Vamsanucharit*, Calcutta, 1982.
44. *SI*, vol. I, pp. 363-7. In recent years the early subdivisions have been elevated to districts in Bangladesh.
45. See note no. 23.
46. *SI*, vol. I, pp. 367-8. D.C. Sircar suggests that Nāgadeva was first a Mahāpratīhāra and then an Uparika.
47. *SI*, vol. I, p. 367, fn. 10, also p. 370.
48. *SI*, vol. I, p. 369, fn. 8. *SI*, vol. I, p. 366. *SI*, vol. I, p. 344. The Faridpur copper plate of Dharmāditya, regnal year 3 speaks of *trighaṭṭikā*, 'a locality having three *ghāṭs* (landing places)', which could have been used as parking stations for boats. The Gunaighar copper plate of Vainyagupta (AD 507) mentions *nauyoga* denoting similar parking stations for boats and *naukhāta* or navigable ditch.
49. *SI*, vol. I, pp. 366-7.
50. *SI*, vol. I, p. 368.
51. *SI*, vol. I, p. 368. fn. 1.
52. The rulers of Vaṅga in the sixth century appear to have been aware of the commercial importance of Navyāvakaśikā and hence placed important officers there to look after trade. The most impressive list of officers of this time is found in the Mallasarul copper plate of Gopacandra, year 33. See note 42 for Bhattasali's identification of Navyāvakāśikā with Sabhar. *SI*, vol. I, pp. 372-7. Chakrabarti, *Ancient Bangladesh*, p. 141, states on the basis of Mustafizur Rahman's excavations at Sabhar that 'although the earliest date of occupation at the site is uncertain there is no reason why it cannot be put in the 6th or 5th century AD.' This chronology has a close correspondence with the rule of independent Vaṅga kings in the sixth century AD when Navyāvakāśikā came to prominence.
53. Majumdar, *Inscriptions of Bengal*, p. 146, line 42.
54. Majumdar, *Inscriptions of Bengal*, p. 146, line 47.
55. Majumdar, *Inscriptions of Bengal*, p. 5, reads the name of the *maṇḍala* as Nānya. But B.C. Sen, *Some Historical Aspects of the Inscriptions of Bengal*, Calcutta, 1942, p. 144, gives the alternative reading Nāvyamaṇḍala.

56. *SI*, vol. II, pp. 36-40, particularly lines 2-3.
57. *SI*, vol. II, pp. 38-9, particularly lines 29-31 and 36-8; latter lines mention some *naudaṇḍakas*.
58. *SI*, vol. II, pp. 744-50, lines 29-42.
59. Sircar, *Epigraphical Discoveries*, states that Devaparvata as a *jaya-skandhāvāra* served as the capital of Devas and Candras, if not of the Rātas also.
60. Sircar, ibid., for the text and commentary of the Paschimbhag C.P.
61. See note 10.
62. The last known definite epigraphic reference to Tāmralipta is found in the Dudhpani Inscription, palaeographically assignable to the eighth century AD. *EI*, vol. II, pp. 343-7.
63. In the present state of our knowledge of the economic history of the early medieval Bengal, it would be difficult to agree with R.S. Sharma and his followers on the possibility of a sharp decline in trade and particularly long-distance trade in north India, including Bengal (Sharma, *Indian Feudalism*). An irrefutable evidence of the brisk trade in Samataṭa-Harikela area can be seen in the continuous minting of high quality silver coins of this zone, prevalent from the seventh to the thirteenth centuries. See B.N. Mukherjee, 'The Place of Harikela Coinage in the Art and Archaeology of Bangladesh', *Journal of the Varendra Research Museum*, vol. VII, 1981-2, pp. 57-68. It is true that the Pāla-Sena domains did not witness any coinage issued by the rulers of Pāla and Sena families. The absence of a regular currency does not necessarily suggest a slump in trade, as other media of exchange (like cowrie-shell and dust currencies) played no mean a role in commercial transactions. For a detailed examination see Deyell, *Living Without Silver*; Mukherjee, *Media of Exchange*. Among the products of early medieval Bengal (both staple and luxury items), mention may be made of rice, sugar cane, swords and the famous textile products. As these commodities figure often in Arab chronicles, they must have attracted attention of the Arabs because of their quality and/or quantity.
64. The importance of the hinterland and foreland vis-a-vis a port town is discussed by Broeze, ed., *The Brides of the Sea*. Arab chroniclers inform us that Qamaruni aloe wood, in great demand in the West, was brought from Qamarun (= Kāmarūpa) to the port of Samandar by river. Similarly the fourteenth-century traveller Ibn Battuta undertook a riverine journey upstream from Sudkawan (Chittagong) to Habang (Habiganj). Mukherjee, 'Commerce and Money'.
65. Braudel, *The Mediterranean*, vol. I, p. 17.
66. Braudel, *The Structures of Everyday Life*, pp. 482-3.

CHAPTER 8

Seafaring in the Bengal Coast: The Early Medieval Scenario

INTRODUCTION

Sustained researches by historians, particularly since the 1950s, have effectively established the fact that pre-modern India had in it the elements of and capacities to change (along, of course, with the forces of continuity). Such changes are sought to be located not merely in the sphere of dynastic upheavals—which were numerous—but also in socio-economic, administrative and cultural conditions. This has led to the identification of several stages or phases in the history of early India (up to *c.* AD 1300). It will therefore not be a satisfactory exercise to treat the history of early India up to *c.* AD 1300 as a monolithic and undifferentiated chronological entity. Recent historiography of early India indicates that a distinct phase can be traced from *c.* AD 600 to 1300. This phase is variously termed as late ancient, post-Gupta, proto-medieval and early medieval, the last one being used more frequently than the others. In the political sphere it ushered in the rise of regional and local powers on an all-India basis. Cultural life during this period is also marked by regional developments in languages and literature, religious cults and sects and art and architecture.[1] Bengal too during the early middle ages witnessed a definite regional ethos taking shape in various factes of life. A palpable feature of the regional ethos of Bengal was its rise as a regional power during the period under review. Major parts of West Bengal and Bangladesh, together with Bihar was dominated by the two formidable powers, the Pālas and the Senas (*c.* AD 750-1200). As we have pointed out in the previous discussion on seafaring in the Bengal coast during the ancient phase (i.e. up to *c.* AD sixth century), there was no paramount political power over the whole of early Bengal. Independent ruling houses like the Candras and the Devas flourished in the eastern and south-eastern parts of Bengal alongside the two more formidable powers just stated. Though none of these powers were coastal in character and had little orientation to the adjacent maritime space (i.e. the Bay of Bengal), the rise of regional/local powers in different parts of Bengal did leave some mark on the coast of Bengal and the affairs of the Bay of Bengal.[2]

The very aim and objectives of the present essay are related to the fact that the Bay of Bengal was an integral part of the Indian Ocean, and a proper appreciation of the situation in the Bay of Bengal during the period under review can best be attempted in the overall affairs of the Indian Ocean. The primacy of the Indian Ocean in the maritime affairs of the world during the last two millennia has been well established. This maritime space became a major theatre of international maritime activity for the first time during the early centuries of the Christian era. The gradual decline of the commerce between the Roman empire and India around the third century AD may have led to some adverse economic situations. But the rise of the Sasanids in Iran till the end of the seventh century witnessed the distinct interest of this ruling house in the Persian Gulf and the western Indian Ocean. The Sasanid interests matched the simultaneuous interests of the Eastern Roman empire in the same maritime space.[3]

A profound change surface after the seventh century in the form of the spectacular rise of Islam in West Asia. This new faith with a distinct thrust on commerce and urbanism largely inspired the Arabs to dominate vast areas of Asia, north and east Africa and also some parts of Europe politically and also to play a very major role in the maritime commerce of the Indian Ocean zone for the ensuing eight or nine centuries. Sea-borne commerce was intimately linked to what is called 'the leapfrogging of Islamic preachers along maritime Asia'. Long-distance trade across the Indian Ocean had the following termini: in the west, Siraf and Basra in the Persian Gulf region and al Fustat and Aden in the Red Sea area (especially since the middle of the tenth century with the rise of the Fatimid Caliphate in Egypt); and the eastern termini were the ports in maritime South-East Asia and China. As the movements within this expansive maritime zone were largely guided by the more or less predictable alterations of the south-west and north-east monsoon winds and as the two seaboards of Indian subcontinent occupied a central position vis-a-vis the termini of the Indian Ocean network, Indian ports assumed the role of an indispensable commercial and geographical intermediary between the 'western' and 'eastern' ends of this network. Since the tenth century the principal destination of ships in the eastern sector was of course the Chinese coast, though China's attitude and policy to the sea were neither consistent nor continuous. It oscillated between complete 'closed door' policy and vigorous encouragement to foreign traders and brisk participation. As China did not belong, at least geographically, to the Indian Ocean world, her links with South and West Asia had to be maintained via South-East Asia. Śrīvijaya (around modern Palembang in the south-eastern part of Sumatra) rose to great prominence as a commercial intermediary between South and East Asia.[4] It is in this context that we seek to situate the maritime traditions of Bengal in the Bay of Bengal during the early medieval times.

SOURCES AND METHOD OF STUDY

The present enquiry follows the pattern and principle of study already set out in the previuos chapter on the maritime situation in the Bengal coast during the ancient times. Attempts will be made here to emphasize upon the unity between land and the sea. In other words, we cannot appreciate the seafaring activities of the region exclusively on the basis of the Bengal coast alone and is immediatly adjacent maritime space, i.e. the Bay of Bengal. The sea, the coast and the interior are sought to be integrated in this survey.

The evidence available and presented for this study, however, differs from that cited for the maritime activites in Bengal during the ancient phase. Field archaeological remains from explored and excavated sites are definitely less than those available for the period prior to AD 600. There are so far no discoveries of the remains of an early medieval vessel from this area, and the representation of a water craft in the visual art of early medieval Bengal is a rarity. Our understanding of water crafts and shipping has, therefore, to be developed from an all-India perspective. The relative lack of field archaeological evidence seems to have been somewhat offset by the profusion of epigraphic data (mostly copper plate landgrants).[5] Though inscriptions rarely furnish any direct information regarding the sea and human activities therein, the marginal evidence occasionally gleaned from these record stands in good stead for our present study. Indigenous literary texts, both theoretical treatises and creative literature, offer some evidence which range from general to specific for the Bengal coast.[6] As Arab merchants and seafarers made their presence felt at almost all the littoral areas of the Indian Ocean, their accounts provide vital clues to our understanding of the maritime scenario in the Bay of Bengal. The descriptions of the Arabic texts range from fantastic tales (e.g. *Kitab Ajaib ul Hind* by Buzurg ibn Shahriyar,

c. AD 953)[7] to geographical treatises (e.g. *Hudud al Alam* by an anonymous author, AD 982)[8] and travellogues (e.g. the *Rihala* of ibn Battuta).[9] The Chinese evidence, though less voluminous than the Arabic and Persian sources, presents important information in the form of official reports (like the *Chu fan Chi* by Chau-ju Kua, an officer supervising foreign trade under the Sung dynasty, AD 1225).[10] There is only one European account, namely the one left behind by the celebrated Venetian traveller, Marco Polo (late thirteenth century).[11]

It is neither desirable nor possible to study the Bengal littorals in isolation. Their importance in the overall context of the Indian Ocean is to be judged by comparing them with other coastal segments on both the seaboards of the Indian subcontinet.

The Maritime Space

The first attempt at naming this vast ocean after India was made in the second half of the AD first century by Pliny who designated it as *mari Indicum* (i.e. the sea of India).[12] A new term was coined by Muslim authors, viz., *al bahr al Hind*: the sea or the ocean of India. This ocean, according to them, had several segments. One of these was *bahr Harkand* or *bahr Harkal*, figuring as early as the middle of the ninth century in the *Akhbar al-Sin wal'Hind*, generally attributed to Sulaiman.[13] The term appears with remarkable frequency in all subsequent Arabic and Persian accounts. The name 'Harkand' or 'Harkal' is derived from Harikela, one of the well known subdivisions of early Bengal, embracing the present-day areas of Chittagong, Noakhali and Comilla in Bangladesh (an area to the east of the Meghna river).[14] As this *bahr* (or sea) is mentioned after *bahr Larvi* (Arabian Sea, the term Larvi being derived from Lāṭa, denoting southern Gujarat), as separated from Salaht (the Malacca Straits) and includes in it islands like Serendib (Sri Lanka) and Lajabajus (Andaman and Nicober islands), *bahr Harkal* cannot but stand for the present Bay of Bengal. Thus, the practice of naming the eastern sector of the Indian Ocean after a subdivision of Bengal can be traced back to the early middle ages. A perusal of the Arabic accounts also gives an impression that their authors had a better awareness of the Bay of Bengal than the Classical writers whose descriptions were often vague. One may logically perceive a more intimate connection of the eastern segment of the Indian Ocean with overseas Asian trade during the period of our study. The labelling of this sector after Harikela in a non-indigenous tradition would highlight that coastal Bengal and especially the littoral areas of Harikela had a significant role to play in the Indian Ocean affairs. The regularity of the mention of *bahr Harkal* from the tenth century onwards is also a clear index of the growth of maritime movements in the Bay of Bengal.

Significantly enough, an inscription of the Candra ruler Śrīcandra (found near Dhaka), dated AD 971, explicitly refers to *Vaṅgasāgara.*[15] The term should denote the sea (*sāgara*) of Vaṅga. Vaṅga generally meant the central part of deltaic Bengal (i.e. the Dhaka-Vikrampur-Faridpur regions, Bangladesh); it also included in it the adjacent coastal areas, variously called Vaṅgāla (Vaṅga+āla) and Anuttaravaṅga (southern Vaṅga).[16] Early medieval Vaṅga thus extended up to the Barishal-Buckerganj areas of Bangladesh. The Candra kings initially ruled from Harikela, but subsequently extended their power over a larger tract including Vaṅga with their capital at Vikrampura. The political expansion of the Candra rule may explain why Vaṅga was equated with Harikela (*Vaṅgāstu Harikelīya*) in the eleventh century. The term 'Vaṅgasāgara' thus stands for the present Bay of Bengal and is certainly the indigenous base from where the Bengali designation 'Vangopasgara' was derived. It may not be difficult to understand that *bahr Harkal* and *Vaṅgasāgara* corresponded to the same maritime space, i.e. the Bay of Bengal.[17]

Before the fifteenth century the Chinese presence in the Bay of Bengal was at best occasional. The Chinese accounts consequently provide us with only a vague reference to Bay of Bengal. The term '*Hsi yang*' (or *Hsi hai*) refers, from the Chinese point of view, to the western ocean. This must have meant Indian Ocean including the Bay of Bengal. One of the segments of the *Hsi yang* was *Hsi-lan hai*, literally the sea of Ceylon or Sri Lanka.[18] It would be logical to identify the *Hsi-lan hai* with *bahr Harkal* of the Arabic texts and *Vaṅgasāgara* in an inscription from Bengal, all referring to the Bay of Bengal.

PORTS IN THE BENGAL COAST

The premier port on the Bengal coast up to the end of the seventh century was certainly Tāmralipta or Tāmralipti (Tamluk, Medinipur district), with Gange and /or Chandraketugarh [24-Parganas district (North)] as the second port for coastal and overseas voyages from Bengal. In other words, the main outlet of the Bengal coast to the Bay of Bengal lay in the ancient subdivision of Rāḍha and Vaṅga. There is no further mention of Tāmralipta as a port in epigraphic records after the Dudhpani inscription, palaeographically assigned to the eighth century. The heydays of Tāmralipta as the principal port of not only Bengal but also of the entire land-locked Ganga valley were over by the eighth century. The main cause of its decline has been atributed to hydrography. By the tenth century, 'the channel on which Tamluk was situated and which afforded the facilities for navigation was silted up'.[19] In this connection one has to note that as early as the seventh century Samataṭa region emerged with considerable potential to offer facilities for long-distance maritime contacts. It is, however, not possible to evaluate at the present state of our knowledge whether the gradual emergence of Samataṭa to commercial prominence contributed to the fading away of Tāmralipta in the Rāḍha region.

There has been a convergence of opinions from diverse strands of historians that the decline of Tāmralipta in and around the eighth century spelt a doom for Bengal's flourishing long-distance maritime trade for several centuries. On the other hand, the frequent occurrences of the bahr Harkal in Arabic accounts, which recognizes the importance of the Bay of Bengal in the Indian Ocean network, urges us to re-examine this dominant historiographical standpoint.

The Arab accounts often mention a port named Samandar in the country of 'Dhm' (pronounced as Dhaum, probably referring to the kingdom of the famous Pāla king Dharmapāla). A perusal of the country of Dhm vis-a-vis the kingdoms of Balhara (the Rāṣṭrakūṭa realm in the Deccan) and Juzr (the Gurjara-Pratihāra kingdom with their capital at Kanauj) strongly suggests that the Arabic authors meant by the name Dhm the Pāla kingdom in Bengal. The name of the port Samandar appears to have been named after *samudra* or sea, thereby implying that it was located probably on or the near the coastal regions in Bengal. Al Idrisi (1162),[20] basing himself on the accounts of ibn Khurdadbeh (*c.* AD 882),[21] informs us that an island visited by various types of merchants lay close to Samandar. This is usually identified with the Sandwip island. Samandar, located close to Sandwip island, should logically be identified with a port in or near modern Chittagong. Both ibn Khurdadbeh and al Idrisi speak very highly of Samandar as a port. Moreover, al Idrisi states that Samandar was situated on a *khawar* or a creek-like formation.[22] This could have been particularly conducive to the ingress and egress of vessels in an estuarine area. What we would like to underline here is the distinct possibility of the rise of a major port in and around present Chittagong roughly from the ninth century onwards.

Ibn Battuta during his visit to Bengal in 1334 arrived at a major port on the Bengal coast, named Sudkawan. The description of Sudkawan that it was very close to the great sea and that ibn Battuta undertook a northerly journey from Sudkawan by a boat along the Blue river (generally identified with the Meghna) would strongly suggest that Sudkawan was located near Chittagong.[23] Sudkawan, also called Sattigaon, was previously sought to have been identified with Saptagram in the Hooghly district, West Bengal. Saptagram, a major port of medieval Bengal, was however located on the banks of the river Saraswati and definitely not located close to the Bay of Bengal. Samandar and Sudkawan may have been the same port in and around Chittagong in what was the Samataṭa-Harikela region of early Bengal. The regular mention of Samandar in Arabic and Persian texts as a major port leaves little room for doubt about the flourishing maritime trade on the Bengal coast.

Arabic texts speak of Samandar's seaborne contacts with Uranshin (Orissa coast), Kanja (Conjeeveram in the northern part of the Coromandel coast) and Serendib (Sri Lanka).[24] Such a network is implied by ibn Battuta who having planned to come to Bengal from the Maldives hired a vessel and reached Sudkawan via Serendib and Ma'abar (Coromandel coast).[25] This highlights the maritime linkages between a port in south-eastern Bengal and Maldives in the western sector of the Indian Ocean. On his return trip ibn Battuta sailed from Sunurkawan (Sonargaon, 24 km from Dhaka) for Jawa (Java) in a Chinese junk.[26] The Bengal coast was thus also incorporated into the overseas network with maritime South-East Asia, in addition to its trade with the Maldives. His journey by a Chinese junk is a further pointer to the connections between the Bengal coast and Chinese harbours via the Malacca Straits and South-East Asia.[27] The extensive maritime linkages of the port in south-eastern coast of Bengal were further buttressed by an impressive hinterland. The hinterland embraced Kamarūpa, Arakan and extensive areas in the Ganga valley. It is therefore in the fitness of things that the Portuguese would hail Chittagong as the 'porto grande' (premier port) in the sixteenth century. The centuries from the ninth to the fourteenth century witnessed the impressive rise of Samandar/Sudkawan (somewhere close to Chittagong) as the principal outlet of the Bengal coast to the sea. Chittagong certainly reached its zenith during the fifteenth and sixteenth centuries, as will be amply borne out by as many as four visits of Chinese official voyages to this port between 1404 to 1433 and the eloquent praise of this port by the Portuguese.[28] The important point to note is that from the ninth century onwards the major seaborne outlet of the Bengal coast shifted from the western (Rāḍha-Vaṅga) sector to the south-eastern (Samataṭa-Harikela) zone with far reaching consequences.

Samandar/Sudkawan of course stole the limelight as the premier port in the Bengal coast. But Samandar did not stand in isolation, but seems to have been linked up with other harbours in the Bengal littorals. These ports, certainly less illustrious than Samandar, were mostly riverine in character and played an important role in the inland riverine communication in coastal Bengal. These riverine harbours provided the vital linkages of the deltaic hinterland with the major port(s) on the coast. A few words on these riverine ports in early medieval Bengal will be in order.

In this context mention may be made of Devaparvata, located in or about Mainamati in Comilla, Bangladesh. One may recall here that Devaparvata figures as a port on the river Kṣīroda (modern day Khirnai) as early as in the second half of the seventh century (see our discussions on Devaparvata on the basis of the Kailan copper plate of Śrīdharaṇa Rāta). Devaparvata once again figures prominently as a riverine port in a copper plate of Bhavadeva Abhinavamṛgāṅka (*c.* 765-80), a Deva ruler of Samataṭa.[29] In fact a comparison of the description of Devaparvata in the seventh century record with that in the subsequent eighth century copper plate amply demonstrates that the riverine port probably became more important in the eighth century. In the second half of the eighth century Devaparvata, in addition to being a port town, became a *jayaskandhāvāra* (literally, a victorious military camp; but actually meaning a politico-administrative headquarter) of the Deva rulers of Samataṭa. The last known mention of Devaparvata is found in the Paschimbhag copper plate (AD 930) of Śrīcandra (*c.* AD 925-75), the greatest ruler of the Candra dyansty of eastern Bengal.[30] The recurrent feature of the description of Devaparvata is its location on the banks of the river Ksīrodā on which plied many boats (*Kṣīrodamanu Devaparvata iti śrīmattadedadpuram*). That Lālambīvana (i.e. present-day Lalmai, close to Mainamati) was searched by hundreds of sailors for medicinal herbs (*Lālambīvanamatra nāvikaśatairanviṣya*) further speaks of Devaparvata as a riverine port. It is also evident that the river Kṣīrodā remained navigable at least from the seventh to the tenth century. But the tenth century copper plate of Śrīcandra was, however, not issued from Devaparvata, but from Vikramapura (near Dhaka, Bangladesh), the new *jayaskandhāvāra* of the Candras. As Devaparvata no longer remained the political centre of the Candras since the early part of the tenth century, the importance of this riverine port seems to have lessened.

Another inscription of Śrīcandra, dated in AD 971, was found from Sabhar, near Dhaka. It informs us of a place named Vaṅgasāgara-saṁbhaṇḍāriyaka. Its association with Vaṅgasāgara or the Bay of Bengal is unmistakable. The term *saṁbhaṇḍāriyaka* may stand for a place where items could be stored (*bhāṇḍāra*) appropriately (*samyak*) enough. The relevance of storage activities can best be appreciated in terms of a centre of exchange. One may logically infer that an exchange centre would be called a *saṁbhaṇḍāriyaka* as it offered suitable storage or warehousing facilities. The compound expression, Vaṅgasāgara-saṁbhaṇḍāriyaka, must have then referred to a trade centre with warehousing facilites, related to the trade in Vaṅgasāgara. Now to a brief discussion on the possible location of this *saṁbhaṇḍāriyaka*. The inscription does not suggest that it was located on or near the seacoast. On the other hand it gives an impression that the site lay close to the issuing centre of this record, i.e. Vikramapura, and also the findspot of the record, i.e. Sabhar. The name Sabhar is possibly derived from Sanskrit *sambhāra*, meaning a collection or storage of commercial commodities. Sabhar is also a very well known archaeological site. We would like to identify Vaṅgasāgara-saṁbhaṇḍāriyaka with Sabhar which bears certain features of a riverine port.[31]

Turning our attention to the western sector of Bengal we do not come across a major port like Samandar. The Bhagirathi nevertheless must have remained a principal artery of movements along the Ganga delta. This is perceived in the frequent descriptions of fleets of vessels—often engaged in some victorious campaigns (*nauvāṭa, nauvāṭaka*)— in several inscriptions of the period. Though such accounts are stereotypical, they cannot but impress upon us the navigability of the Bhagirathi. Al Biruni (*c.* 1030) enlightens us on the regular riverine movements from Vāraṇasī to Gaṅgāsāgara, 'where the Ganges flows into the sea' via Pāṭaliputra, Mungiri (Monghyr) and Janpa (i.e. Campā, near Bhagalpur).[32] In 1192 a local ruler of the South 24-Parganas district, named Śrīmaḍḍommana-pāla is known to have relinquished his life close to what is known as Gaṅgāsāgara.[33] This strongly corroborates al Biruni's statement on the riverine accessibility of this part of the Ganga delta. A close perusal of the description of Ḍommanapāla's *svīya-muktikṣetra* (i.e. his final journey to the banks of the Ganga with the hope of dying there and thereby attaining salvation) shows that near Gaṅgāsāgara stood a place called Dvārahāṭaka. The suffix *hāṭaka* is possibly the same as *haṭṭaka*, i.e. a rural market centre. Seen in this light, Dvārahāṭaka appears to have been an exchange centre situated near the *dvāra* or gate of what may have been the confluence of the Ganga with the Bay of Bengal. In all likelihood a rural level market place, accessible by riverine routes, existed around the sacred centre of Gaṅgāsāgara. This suggestion gains ground when one takes into account the regular references to *khāṭikās* or channels of the Ganga in the Sena inscriptions which therefore point to the geographical realities typical in the southernmost sector of the Ganga delta. One can hardly lose sight of the large number of stone sculptures, bronze icons, architectural fragments, brick temples, structural mounds, tanks, embankments in what is the present-day South 24-Parganas district.[34] There is an unmistakable evidence of regular settlements in Sunderban areas during the early medieval times, in sharp contrast to the thick forest tracts in the same area since the early modern times.

Maritime activities in the Bengal littorals must have been conducted at large harbours with long-distance network. But relatively smaller centres, such as inland riverine ports—Devaparvata, Vaṅgasāgara-saṁbhaṇḍāriyaka and Dvārahāṭaka—played the vital role of feeder ports to the more celebrated *velākulas* (ports). They also provided the significant linkages—through riverine routes—between the littorals and the interior.

SHIPS, BOATS AND SHIPPING

Any inquiry into the ships and shipping on the Bengal coast during the early middle ages is repeatedly thwarted by the absence of the archaeological remains of ancient ships and boats. There is also no reliable visual representation of ships, vessels, etc., in the early medieval sculptures of Bengal, the like of which we had for the pre-AD 700 days. What is presented below is a sketchy mention of movements of different types of vessels along the Bengal coast and in the eastern sector of the Indian Ocean. The acute insufficiency of information relevant to the Bengal coast per se forces us to occasionally present general data on all-India nature on ships and shipping.

The famous writer of Sanskrit prose, Daṇḍin refers in his *Daśa-kumāracarita* (*c.* AD seventh century) to vessels like *vahitra* and *pravahana* in the context of the port of Tāmralipta.[35] Both *vahitra* and *pravahana* were sea-going vessels; mention about them also comes in inscriptions from the west coast. It has been suggested on the basis of early medieval inscriptions from the south Konkan coast that *vahitra* and *pravahana* were two distinct types of ships. While the former appears to have been used for overseas voyages (*dvīpāntara*), the latter was probably a coaster.[36] Significantly enough, Daṇḍin associates the *vahitra* in and around Tāmralipta with the Yavanas. As the Yavanas were most likely to have been non-indigenous people, their *vahitras* could have been logically seen as vessels fit for long-distance overseas voyages.

Early medieval inscriptions from Bengal are replete with references to *nau*. A *nau* may mean any water craft ranging from a riverine craft to a large sea-going vessel. The term *nau* is a blanket one without the necessary specificities of a particular type of water craft.

The prominence given to the port of Samandar in the Arabic accounts suggests the familiarity of Arab merchants with the port. This in its turn would further imply the movements of Arab vessels in the Bay of Bengal and on the Bengal coast. It is distinctly likely that the Arab dhows made their presence felt as mercantile marine over the greater parts of the Indian Ocean, including the Bay of Bengal. It would be then logical to infer that Arab dhows regularly visited a major port like Samandar on the Bengal coast.[37]

The Bengal coast could have become familiar with the sight of Chinese junks since the fourteenth century. Ibn Battuta boarded a junk for his return journey from the Bengal coast to Jawa (Sumatra). Ma Huan's celebrated accounts of the seven voyages of the Ming admiral Cheng ho leave little room for doubt that the Chinese fleet visited Sattigaon (i.e. Chittagong) no less than four times during the period from 1404 to 1433.[38] It is reasonable to assume the regular presence of Chinese junks in and around the port of Chittagong during the first four decades of the fourteenth century. The memory of the visits of Chinese vessels to the Bengal coast is probably retained in the occasional references to the *jaṅgadiṅgā*, manned by sailors of yellow skin (*pītanāvika*), in the medieval Bengali texts.[39] Ports on the Bengal littorals must have witnessed larger number of Arab dhows than Chinese junks. In spite of the stupendous success of the Ming ships in sailing across the greater parts of the Indian Ocean from 1404 to 1433, there was a sudden cessation of Chinese maritime presence after 1433.

Thus our knowledge about sailing crafts, both indigenous and foreign, in the Bengal coast during the period under review is meagre. But certain broader points on the general features of the traditional Indian vessels may be discussed here. Indian and Arab sea-going vessels appeared to have shared a common character: The wooden planks (*phalaka*) of the vessel were never nailed, but stitched or sewn with coconut coir (*rajju*). That is why the traditional Indian ship is described as being without iron (*nilloham*).[40] The most preferred material for manufacturing the wooden ship was teak. The teak was not only considered the most suitable and durable material for building a ship in Indian texts, the Arab accounts speak eloquently of the excellence of Indian teak, especially that from Konkan and Malabar. Indian teak and coconut coir regularly figure as exports of India to West Asia.[41] Arab accounts rarely failed to take note of the plantation of coconut and availability of cordage on both the seaboards of India and also in the Maldives and the Nicobar (Lanjabalus/Lajabalus) islands.[42] The regular reference to *nārikela* or coconut as a product of Bengal is seen in early medieval inscriptions, especially in those coming from deltaic and/or coastal Bengal.

Prior to the arrival of steam ships traditional vessels must have depended both on manual and wind power. *Nāvikas* or sailors do not appear to be entirely unknown in early medieval Bengal inscriptions. These records are generally available from south-eastern part of Bengal (the Samataṭa-Harikela region). *Nāvika* Dyota is explicitly mentioned in the Bhatera C.P. of Govindakeśavadeva of the thirteenth century.[43] The term *nāvika* certainly denotes an ordinary sailor. That they were the principal workforce on board the ship is evident from the expression *nāvikakarmakara* (often misspelt as *norikakarmakara*). The term *nāvikakarmakara* frequently appears in early medieval inscriptions from the Gujarat and the Konkan littorals, though not in contemporary Bengal epigraphs. Ordinary sailors are called *al askar* in the famous Arabic treatise on navigation by ibn Majid (*c.* fifteenth century).[44] The *nāvikanāyaka*, mentioned in the *Daśakumāracarita* of Daṇḍin, denotes the leader of the mariners.[45] He could have been the same as the captain of the ship. The Arabic term *nakhuda* (*nau* = ship/vessel, *khuda* = lord; literally the lord of the ship) occasionally denotes the captain of a ship. Buzurg ibn Shariyar, whose famous tales of seafaring sometimes speak of voyages in the bahr Harkal (Bay of Bengal), is called a *nakhuda* in the sense of the captain of a ship. The term *nakhuda* more commonly stood for a shipowning merchant, corresponding to and synonymous with *nauvittaka* (literally, one whose wealth is derived from ships) in early medieval Indian sources. It must be clearly stated here that *nauvittakas* and *nakhudas* are seen largely on the west coast of India and do not figure in the early medieval sources pertaining to Bengal.[46] Early medieval indigenous sources underline that the captain of a ship must have been an expert in the art of shipping (*naupracāravidyā*) and a master in bringing ship into the harbour (*āharaṇa*) and also in taking it out of the port (*apaharaṇa*).[47] Ibn Majid attaches immense importance to the *muallim* or the navigator in the sailing and proper management of the ship. He views the *muallim* as the person in overall charge of the ship with a number of subordinates under his direct command; even the passengers of the ship, according to Majid, had to obey his authority during the voyage.[48]

The sailors appear to have been largely employed for using the oars (*aritra/kenipāta*). Epigraphic accounts of royal fleet powered by oars occasionally appear in the eulogies of rulers of early medieval Bengal, in the context of riverine journeys along the Ganga.[49] The helmsman (*karṇadhāra*) certainly had a greater responsibility than an ordinary sailor, as he was entrusted with the proper steering of the sailing vessel. An important member of the crew, at least on Arab dhows, was the *didban* who had a seat atop a high pole erected next to the mast.[50] His main function was to be on the constant look out into the sea and pass on any important information to the *muallim*.

An understanding of early Indian shipping technique is closely related to the use of sails. The historian of the Indian Ocean maritime trade faces the problem that while early medieval texts describe sails (*sītapaṭa/sītapaṭṭa*; Prakrit *siyāvaḍa*) on ships, there is practically no visual representation of a sail in the depiction of a ship in early medieval sculptures. Representations of Arab and Chinese vessels in paintings are, on other hand, associated respectively with lateen and mat sails.

A basic technique to keep the ship afloat in the water is to fill up the hold of the ship appropriately with bulk items. While items of daily necessities and staples were the best form of bulk cargo, victuals and other provisions for sailors and passengers must also have served the purpose of bulk. Ibn Battuta's accounts have some bearing here. In his descriptions of the Maldives and its exchangeable items ibn Battuta brings to light the importance of cowries of Maldives. Maldivian cowries were in great demand over widespread areas including Bengal. Bengal imported cowries from the Maldives in exchange of the rice of Bengal. As a staple rice must have been shipped to the Maldives in bulk as a suitable cargo for the ballast. 'The people of Bengal', according to ibn Battuta, 'use them (i.e. cowries) instead of sand (as ballast) in their ships'.[51] His travellogue gives us an image of the use of three types of bulk items to fill the hold of the ship: cowries, rice and sand. Thus the cowry shell, in addition to its primary function as a medium of exchange, acted as a ballast in ships during overseas voyages.[52]

EXCHANGEABLE PRODUCTS

A quick survey of exchangeable items of trade may be made here. The issuance of landgrants during the early middle ages paved the way for agrarian expansion especially in the hitherto uncultivated, fallow and forest tracts. Early medieval sources are replete with the mentions of Bengal's diversified agricultural output, both cereals and cash crops. Our discussions in section IV underline the importance of the rice of Bengal as an exportable commodity in bulk which was well integrated to the long-distance overseas trade network from the Bengal coast. Puṇḍravardhana, i.e. the Dinajpur-Rajshahi-Bogra region, became so well known for the profuse production of sugarcane that very term *Pauṇḍra* (a product from Puṇḍra) signified the sugarcane from north Bengal. The thirteenth century Chinese officer Chau ju Kua was well aware of the cultivation of cotton (tou-lo) in Pong-kielo (i.e. Vaṅgāla).[53] Early medieval Bengal was specially noted for its superb textile products, as seen in the works of Chau ju Kua, Marco Polo and Arab authors.[54] The notice of these writers to the textiles of Bengal must have been drawn by the excellent quality and /or large quantity of these products, particularly in view of the fact that many of them never actually visited Bengal. Textiles had been, however, Bengal's major exportable item from the early centuries of the Christian era onwards. Arab authors also spoke highly of the swords from eastern Bihar which was under the occupation of the Pāla rulers (*c.* AD 750-1173).[55] Another prized product, appearing in the Arabic texts, was the aloes wood exported through the port of Samandar/Sudkawan. The aloes wood is however noted in the Arab accounts as a product of Qamarun or Kāmarūpa, i.e. the Brahmaputra valley. The Qamaruni aloes wood, according to ibn Battuta, was brought to the port of Sudkawan by floating the logs of wood down the Blue river, identified with the Meghna. The aloes wood of north-eastern India, rated by the Arab authors as second only to the aloes wood from Multan, reached the Arab world via Sudkawan which received the product in the form of transit trade with the north-eastern part of India. Another exotic commodity much sought after in the Arab world was the rhinoceros horns, a product evidently from the north-eastern India, far away from the Bengal coast. Like the aloes wood the rhinoceros horn also reached the Bengal coast for export to the Arab world in the form of transit trade between the Bengal littorals and the north-eastern region.[56] There is little doubt that there was an impressive range of exports from the Bengal coast, ranging from bulk and staple items like rice to exotic and luxury products like fine textiles, aloes wood and rhinoceros horns.

Of the items of imports mention must be made of the cowry-shells from the Maldives, a commodity certainly brought into Bengal in bulk. It is very likely that precious metals like silver was probably imported from Arakan and Pegu in Myanmar. Exotic spices and fragrances like sandalwood reached early medieval Bengal from south-east Asia which is noted for its close commercial cultural linkages with Bengal. One of the most important commodities imported into Bengal was the horse. The rise of the Pālas and the Senas as formidable regional powers in Eastern India certainly necessitated the building up of a strong cavalry. Bengal, however, was never famous for the availability of good quality war horses. War horses were mostly imported into Bengal from the north-west, a region traditionally associated with the availability of excellent horses from Central and West Asia. From the twelfth century onwards it seems that Bengal began to receive horses from the north-east also. That the Sena capital Lakhnauti (Lakṣmaṇāvatī) was daily supplied with 1,500 horses from a place called Karambattan in the north-eastern borderland of India is clearly evident from the *Tabaqat-i-Nasiri* by Minhajuddin. While Nudiah seems to have been familiar with the arrival of Arabic and Persian horses, Lakhnauti was noted for the availability of mountainous species from the north-east. These horses of hilly areas appear to have been branded as *kohi* type of horses, distinct from the Arab, Persian, *Tatatri* (From Tatar or Central Asian steppe lands) and *Baladasti* types, by ibn Battuta and Barani. Both ibn Battuta and Barani mentioned the *kohi* horses along with Arab, Persian and *Baladasti* types as war machines fit for recruitment in the cavalry of the Sultanate.[57] A perusal of the accounts of Minhaj, ibn Battuta and Barani on the mountainous horses strongly suggests that the *kohi* horse were probably the same as the *Tanghan* (*TNGHN*) horses. That the north-east emerged as the supply area of mountain horses to eastern India was also suggested by Marco Polo in the late thirteenth century. The celebrated Venetian traveller was aware of the availability of excellent and strong horses in Carajan. Carajan is identified with Yunnan and the Yunnanese town of Talifu. These horses were sent to India for sale.[58] According to Polo, Aniu also exported horses to India.[59] Determining the location of Aniu is not free from difficulty, but Digby has 'no doubt that it lay somewhere to the south of Carajan'.[60] Polo speaks of a westward route connecting Aniu with Caugigu which, in its turn, was linked with Bengala by an overland route. Horses from Yunnan could therefore reach Bengala through Pagan, which was connected with south-eastern Bangladesh and the Lushai and the Tripura hills. Following Polo, the overland journey from Carajan to Bengala could be completed between 45 to 55 days.[61] War horses were natural attractions for rulers. The Delhi Sultanate was no less eager than their contemporaries to procure war horses, whether by purchase or by pillage. The interests of the Sultanate to buy *bahri*, *Tatari* and *Shami* (Iraqi) horses are well documented. During the famous invasion of Malik Kafur, the general of Alauddin Khilji, in the Deccan and South India (1309-10), huge numbers of horses of various kinds were systematically captured and plundered from the stables of defeated rulers. Thus the ruler of Arangal or Warangal (i.e. the Kākatīya ruler Rudradeva in Andhra Pradesh) had to surrender 20,000 *kohi* and *bahri* horses to Alauddin's general.[62] This account demands a close scrutiny. It is not surprising that the Kākatīya cavalry would consist of a large number of *bahri* (Arabian and Persian horses brought to India by overseas voyages) horses, the best and costliest kind. But the mention of *kohi* horses in the stable of the Andhra king should be taken note of. The *kohi* is seen to have reached even the stable of the most formidable political power in the eastern Deccan during thirteenth-fourteenth centuries. In our opinion the *kohi* horse could have been brought to eastern Deccan through Bengal, an area which had already experienced its regular arrival from the north-east. Seen in this light, Bengal not merely received the regular supply of mountain horses, but also was involved in their transit trade to the eastern Deccan. In view of the known and well established chain of communication between Bengal and the eastern Deccan, it would be logical to infer Bengal's active role in the supply of north-eastern horses to Andhra (in addition to their demand and sale in Bengal itself).

Bengal and the trade in horses further figure in medieval Chinese evidence in the context of the celebrated voyages of Cheng Ho in the first half of the fifteenth century.[63] During his seven long-distance voyages spanning across the Indian Ocean, these official Chinese missions came to Bengal four times as parts or branches of the main Ming fleet, in 1412-14, 1415-16, 1420-1 and 1422-3. The vessels reached Chittagong, the premier port of early medieval and medieval Bengal up to the sixteenth century, from Semudera in maritime south-east Asia, having covered a distance of 1,952 km. The second leg of the journey was covered by a riverine trip from Chittagong to Sonargaon (distance 265 km) from where it finally reached Pandua in north Bengal. The Chinese missions were matched by no fewer than fourteen diplomatic missions from the Bengal Sultanate to China between 1404 and 1439. The commercial importance of these Chinese voyages is well established and studied in depth.[64] Of the impressive variety of articles imported by the Chinese from Bengal, attention may particularly be paid to the horse. The horse was the costliest ('1000 gold coins for one') of the twenty-five commodities exported from Bengal to China.[65] Haraprasad Ray informs us that Said Muhammad (= Sai-yi-ma-ha-mie or Sai-yi-de-ma-ha-ma in the Chinese texts), an envoy of the Bengal Sultanate, came to the Ming court and presented the Chinese emperor with 'thoroughbred horses in *Bengali* ships' (italics mine).[66] Ray further concludes after a painstaking study of the available Chinese documentation that 'the envoys of Bengal journeyed both ways in their own ships during these occasions, and not with Zeng He's (i.e. Cheng Ho) fleet'.[67] The Chinese evidence cannot but point to the overseas trade in horses from Bengal to China. Horses must have been transported overseas from the Bengal coast to China in what is called Ma Chuan (horse ships). Seven hundred of such ships with eight masts, outnumbering other categories of Chinese vessels, were employed.[68] All these are clear pointers to the interests of the Chinese court to procure horses. But perhaps more striking is the information regarding the export of horses in indigenous ships of Bengal. Whether medieval Bengal had ships built specifically to transport horses overseas cannot be ascertained at the present state of our knowledge. But the Chinese evidence, thanks to the researches of Ray, enlightens us on yet another aspect of trade in horses in medieval Bengal, viz., the role of Bengal in the maritime trade in horses. Ray, however, did not probe further into the problem of how Bengal could have engaged in the export of horses to China. Our preceding survey of Minhaj, Barani, Wassaf and Polo on the supply of north-eastern (*kohi*) horses to Bengal, in addition to the ones from the north-west, indicates that the steady supply of at least two varieties of war horses paved the way for the shipping of horses from Bengal to China in the early fifteenth century. Bengal's participation in the overseas shipping of horses to China, however, appears to have been of limited duration.[69]

In fine, the seaborne traffic in the Bengal coast involved transaction of both high value and luxury objects and daily necessity items. In view of the clear evidence of overseas shipping of rice and cowrie-shells, it is about the time that one questioned the long cherished notion that pre-modern Indian trade (especially long-distance trade) revolved only around high value, small quantity, luxury, portable and exotic commodities meant for elite consumers. The overseas contacts of the Bengal coast with the Arab world is demonstrated by the discovery of coins of Harun al Rashid (eighth century) and the Abbasid Caliph al Mustasim al Billah (twelfth century) from the excavated sites respectively of Paharpur and Mainamati. One has to note here the curious position that while the Pālas and Senas did not strike any coins, the Samataṭa-Harikela region experienced the uninterrupted minting and circulation of high quality silver coins (the sovereign authorities issuing these coins are unknown) for six centuries—from the seventh to the thirteenth centuries. B.N. Mukherjee's sustained research output amply demonstrates that these silver pieces corresponded to the well known Indian *purāṇa* or *dramma* standard of 57.6 grains. Coin terms like *purāṇa* and *dramma* do figure in the copper plates of the Pālas and the Senas. Mukherjee further observes that the Harikela silver coins after the tenth century became lighter in weight and broader in their flan with legends and motifs only on one side. The changes in the Harikela issues, according to him, had some conformity with the reformed Arab currency system. This would once again speak of intimate linkages between the Bengal coast and the trading world of the Arabs.[70] The lively scenario of trade in early medieval Bengal, including long-distance overseas trade from and to the Bengal littorals, does not uphold the image of a languishing trade and 'monetary anaemia', projected in the construction of Indian feudalism.[71] Our discusions also drive home the position that landgrants and minted currency system were not mutually incomaptible, but they could coexist in a given region. Mukherjee has also stressed on the possibilities of the easy convertibility of one silver coin of *purāṇa* or *dramma* variety with 1,280 cowries, a table figuring in the medieval Bengali arithmetics. He has also interpreted the term *cūrṇī*, appearing in inscriptions of the Senas, as dust of pure silver or gold. In other words, he perceives the introduction of a dust currency, of equal weight to the *purāṇa* (silver) standard and *suvarṇa* (gold) standard. The above discussions suggest a complex monetary scenario in early medieval Bengal. A three tier monetary system is suggested, consisting of the cowry shell (*kapardaka*) at the base, the minted metallic pieces at the top and the newly introduced dust currency in between the two.[72]

CONCLUSION

In the preceding pages an attempt has been made to depict the Bengal coast as an active zone in the Bay of Bengal and its gradual integration into the Indian Ocean maritime network during the seven centuries from

AD 600 to *c.* AD 1300. One of the few *āsamudrahimācala* (lying between the Himalayas and the sea) regions in India, Bengal in the early middle ages offers an excellent example of its maritime orientation during a phase when certain typical features of the Indian Ocean trade were taking their shape. Large number of navigable rivers—the Ganga and the Brahmaputra being the most important—provided easy and effective arteries of fluvial communications with the Bay of Bengal. Not merely the interior of Bengal, but the greater parts of the land-locked Ganga valley and north-eastern India were linked up with the delta and finally the Bay of Bengal by inland riverine movements.

The combined testimony of literary, epigraphic and other archaeological materials clearly attests to the flourishing agriculture and diversified crafts some of which were transported to distant market centres. An appreciable change in the material life can be seen in the gradual shift of the major maritime zone of Bengal from the Midnapur region to south-eastern Bangladesh during the early middle ages. The far-flung maritime commerce of Bengal touched the Orissan and Tamil ports and the harbours of Sri Lanka, maritime South-East Asia and the Maldives. How far early medieval Bengal had regular contacts with the Andaman and Nicobar islands cannot be assessed at the present state of our knowledge.

One has to situate Bengal's position in the overall context of India's role in the Indian Ocean trade in the early medieval times. Without in any way decrying the importance of this littoral, the Bengal coast may not have assumed a premier position like the Gujarat, Malabar and Coromandel coasts. Gujarat and Malabar were directly connected with the principal sea-lanes touching the eastern and western termini of the then Asian maritime commerce. Ibn Battuta noted in the early fourteenth century that Calicut was the meeting point—and by extension a transhipment point—of Arab dhows and Chinese junks. The Coromandel coast shone to great prominence during the heydays of the Coḷa rule which had a distinct orientation to the affairs in the Bay of Bengal and an eagerness to maintain intimate diplomatic and cultural contacts with South-East Asia and Sung China.[73] The Pāla, Sena and Candra rulers were not orientated to the sea to a similar manner. There was also no commercial organization in early medieval Bengal matching the vigour and network of Tamil mercantile groups (e.g. the 500 *svāmīs* of Ayyavole, the Nānādeśis and the Maṇigrāmam) which had close interactions with political authorities in Tamil and Telugu countries.[74] There was no king in Bengal like Coḷa Kulottuṅga (1070-1120) who enhanced the status of the port of Viśākhapaṭṭinam on the Andhra coast and did away with tolls and customs, obviously to encourage long-distance oceanic commerce. An *abhayaśāsana* (charter of security), like the one issued by Kākatīya Gaṇapati (1245) for assuring protection to maritime merchants from piracy at the port of Motuppali, is conspicuous by its absence in early medieval Bengal.[75] In other littorals of India one often gets the impression that ports on the coast were well integrated with their hinterland. This was largely possible because of the structure of trade which linked up rural market places (*haṭṭa*, *aḍḍa*, *santhe*, etc.), with major ports through a middle category centre of trade. These middle category trade centres proliferated and became prominent particularly in early middle ages. They are regularly encountered in Rajasthan, Gujarat, central India and the Doab under the name *maṇḍapikā*. The Deccan witnessed a similar centre in the shape of the *peṇṭhā/peṁṭa/ piṇṭhā* (modern peth). In the far south emerged the *nagarms* at supra-local *nāḍu* level and provided inter-*nāḍu* connections and linkages with *mānagarams* (large urban centres') and *paṭṭinams* (ports on or near the coast).[76] In more or less contemporary eastern India, including Bengal, one sees only *haṭṭas* in the interior and harbours in the littorals sans the vital linkages between the two through a *maṇḍapikā* or something analogous. This may explain why the Bengal coast, in spite of its immense potential, did not match the prominence and status of the ports of Malabar, Coromandel and Gujarat during the early medieval times.

NOTES

1. For an understanding of the possibilities of change in material life see Sharma, *Perspectives*; B.N.S. Yadava, *Society and Culture in North India during the Twelfth Century*, Allahabad, 1973; Chattopadhyaya, *The Making of Early Medieval India*.
2. An updated political history of early medieval Bengal is given by D.C. Sircar, *Pal-Sen Yuger Vamsanucarita* (in Bengali), Calcutta, 1982. The discovery of the existence of a new Pāla ruler, named Mahendrapāla, son and immediate successor of Devapāla, has led to a revision of the genealogy and chronology of the Pāla kings. See in this context, K.V. Ramesh and Subromaniya Ayyar, 'The Malda Museum Copper Plate of Pāla King Mahendrapāla', *EI*, XLI, pp. 6-29. Its importance has been discussed by Niharranjan Ray, B.D. Chattopadhyaya, Ranabir Chakravarti and V.R. Mani, *A Sourcebook of Indian Civilization*, Calcutta, 2000, pp. 622-4.
3. David Whitehouse and Andrew Williamson, 'Sasanian Maritime Trade', *Iran*, vol. XI, 1973, pp. 29-49.

4. Chaudhuri, *Trade and Civilisation*; Chaudhuri, *Asia before Europe*, Kenneth McPherson, *The Indian Ocean*, Delhi, 1993.
5. A recent list of early medieval Bengal inscriptions is available in Sircar, *Vamsanucarita*. This list requires an updating in view of the recent additions to our existing knowledge.
6. See the classified data in the Appendix to this chapter.
7. Buzurg ibn Shahriyar, *Kitab Ajaib ul Hind*, tr. G.S.P. Freeman-Grenville, London, 1980.
8. *Hudud al Alam*, ed. and tr. V. Minorsky, London, 1937.
9. Ibn Battuta, *The Rihala*, tr., H.A.R. Gibb, *The Travels of Ibn Battuta in Asia and Africa*, London, 1929.
10. Chau-ju Kua, *Chu fan Chi*, trs. F. Hirth and W.W. Rockhill, St. Petersburgh, 1911.
11. H. Yule and H. Cordier, trs., *Travels of Ser Marco Polo*, 2 vols., London, 1903.
12. This has been discussed by us in our preceding chapter on the 'Maritime Trade and Voyages in Ancient Bengal'.
13. Sulaiman's account is translated by S. Maqbul Ahmed, *Arabic Classical Accounts of India and China*, Shimla, 1989.
14. B.N. Mukherjee, 'The Original Territory of Harikela', *Bangladesh Lalitkala*, vol. I, 1975, pp. 115-19.
15. R.G. Basak, 'Madanpur Plate of Śrīcandra, year 44', *EI*, XXVIII, pp. 51-8. A revised reading of the date was given by D.C. Sircar, 'Madanpur Plate of Śrīcandra, year 46', *EI*, XXVIII, pp. 337-9.
16. A. Bhattacharyya, *Historical Geography*.
17. An exhaustive discussion on the term Vaṅgasāgara is made by Ranabir Chakravarti, 'Vaṅgasāgara and Other Related Terms: An Examination', in Asok Datta, ed., *History and Archaeology of Eastern India*, Delhi, 1999, pp. 254-64.
18. Ma Huan, *Ying-yai Sheng-lan*, tr. J.V.G. Mills, *The Overall Survey of the Ocean's Shores*, Oxford, p. 195; Haraprasad Ray, 'China and the "Western Ocean" in the Fifteenth Century', in Satish Chandra, ed., *The Indian Ocean: Explorations in History, Commerce and Politics*, pp. 128-34.
19. Radahakamal Mookerji, *The Changing Face of Bengal: A Study in Riverine Economy*: 185.
20. S. Maqbul Ahmed, tr., *India and the Neighbouring Territories*, Leiden, 1960.
21. For a translation of ibn Khurdadbeh's *Kitab al Masalik wa'l Mamalik*, see S. Maqbul Ahmed, *Arabic Classical Accounts*.
22. S.M.H. Nainar, *The Knowledge of India as Possessed by Arab Geographers down to the Fourteenth Century* AD *with Special Reference to Southern India*, Madras, 1942.
23. Ibn Battuta, *Travels*, p. 246.
24. Nainar, *Arab Geographers' Knowledge of Southern India*.
25. Ibn Battuta, *Travels*, p. 246.

26. Ibn Battuta, *Travels*, p. 271.
27. One of the best instances of Bengal's contacts with maritime South-East Asia during the early medieval times is seen in the request from the Śailendra ruler of Java to the Pāla emperor Devapāla (*c*. AD 805-40) to grant some land in favour of a Buddhist monastery at Nalanda; the request was upheld by Devapāla. These cultural contacts can hardly be divorced from the prevailing material interests of political powers in long-distance overseas connections which could have brought commercial advantages to Bengal. Merchants on distant journeys were often accompanied by religious preachers; merchants themselves were purveyors of culture. The celebrated Buddhist teacher Atīśa Dīpaṁkara is known to have undertaken a voyage to Suvarṇadvīpa (traditionally referring to maritime South-East Asia) for studying under the guidance of Candrakīrti. He went to Suvarṇadvīpa by a merchant vessel. On his return journey he sailed from Suvarṇadvīpa to Tāmradvīpa (Sri Lanka) and finally to the Bengal coast. From here he reached his final destination, Magadha. See, Majumdar, ed., *History of Bengal*, vol. I, p. 122.
28. Mukherjee, 'Commerce and Money'.
29. *SI*, vol. II, pp. 744-50.
30. D.C. Sircar, *Epigraphic Discoveries in East Pakistan*, Calcutta, 1973.
31. A more elaborate discussion on this riverine port is available in the chapter on 'Vaṅgasāgara-saṁbhāṇḍariyaka: A Riverine Port in Early Medieval Bengal', in this volume.
32. Al Biruni, *Kitabul Hind*, tr., E. Sahcau, *Albiruni's India*, London, 1910, p. 200.
33. The Rakshasakhadi copper plate of Śrīmaḍḍommanapāla was first edited by B.C. Sen, *IHQ*, vol. X, pp. 321ff; a revised reading was later offered by D.C. Sircar, *Indian Culture*, vol. I, pp. 379-82 and also *EI*, vol. XXX, pp. 42ff. Sircar's reading is followed here.
34. Gautam Sengupta, 'Archaeology of Coastal Bengal'.
35. Daṇḍin, *Daśakumāracarita*, tr. Arther W. Ryder, 1927, pp. 26, 148.
36. Chakravarti, 'Merchants of Konkan'; Ranabir Chakravarti, 'Coastal Trade and Voyages in Konkan: The Early Medieval Scenario', *IESHR*, vol. XXXV, 1998, pp. 97-123.
37. The Arabs never used the term dhow to denote their ships. Arabic words like *markab, jilab, burama, shafara* and *jahaj* refer to various types of ships, both coasters and those which sailed overseas. The general features of the dhow are described in G.F. Hourani, *Arab Seafaring in the Indian Ocean in the Ancient and Early Medieval Periods*, Beirut, 1951. Also see A. Lewis, 'Maritime Skills in the Indian Ocean 1368-1500', *JESHO*, vol. XVI, 1973, pp. 238-64; Ranabir Chakravarti, 'Ships, Seafarings and Ship-owners: India and the Indian Ocean (700-1500)', in David Parkin and Ruth Barnes, eds., *Ships and the Developments of Maritime Technology in the Indian Ocean*, London, 2002, pp. 28-61.

38. Ma Huan, *Ying-yai Sheng-ian*, tr. J.V.G. Mills.
39. I am thankful to Sri Rangan Kanti Jana for furnishing this information.
40. Lallanji Gopal, 'Indian Shipping in the Early Medieval Period', in Lokesh Chandra, et al., eds., *India's Contributions to World Thought and Culture*, Calcutta, 1970, pp. 108-22; especially p. 109.
41. The travel accounts of ibn Jubayr, an Andalusian, in 1183-4 (tr. R.J.C. Broadhurst, London, 1952) inform us, for instance, of the regular export of Indian teak and coconut coir to the Red Sea port of Aidhab.
42. Buzurg ibn Shahriyar, *Kitab Ajaib ul Hind*, tr. G.P.S. Freeman-Grenville, London, 1980, pp. 74-5 for an account of the Lajabalus islands. The Coḷas appear to have been aware of the importance of this area, as Mānakkāvaram (Nicobar islands) figures in the list of areas conquered during the famous Kaḍāram overseas campaign by Rājendra Coḷa in 1025.
43. *EI*, vol. XIX, pp. 277-86. In early medieval Bengal *nāvikas* probably belonged to the social group called the Mallas who were assigned a very low position in the *jāti* hierarchy. See Majumdar, ed., *A History of Bengal*, vol. I, pp. 573-4.
44. Ibn Majid, *Arab Navigation in the Indian Ocean before the Coming of the Portuguese*, tr. G.R. Tibbetts, London, 1971.
45. Daṇḍin, *Daśakaumāracarita*, p. 148.
46. Ranabir Chakravarti, 'Nakhudas and Nauvittakas: Ship-owning Merchants in the West Coast of India (*c.* AD 1000-1500)', *JESHO*, vol. XLIII, 2000, pp. 34-64.
47. Gopal, 'Indian Shipping in the Early Medieval Period', p. 148.
48. Ibn Majid, *Arab Navigation*, pp. 58-63.
49. The explicit reference to the use of *aritra* and *kenipāta* in boats plying in some mighty rivers in Samataṭa (Brahmaputra?) is seen in the Siyan inscription of Nayapāla; see D.C. Sircar, *Śilālekha Tamrasaśānādir Prasaṅga* (Bengali), 1982.
50. Hourani, *Arab Navigation.*
51. Ibn Battuta, *Travels*, p. 243.
52. J. Heiman, 'Small Exchange and Ballast: Cowry Trade and Usage as an Example of Indian Ocean Economic History', *South Asia*, vol. III, 1980, pp. 48-69.
53. Chau-ju Kua, *Chu fan Chi.*
54. Lallanji Gopal, 'Textiles in Ancient India', *JESHO*, vol. VII, 1964.
55. Niharranjan Ray, *Bangalir Itihas*, vol. I, Calcutta, 1980 (Bengali).
56. Mukherjee, 'Commerce and Money'.
57. Digby, *Warhorses and Elephants*; Ranabir Chakravarti, 'Horse Trade and Piracy at Tana (= Thana, Maharashtra, India): Gleanings from Marco Polo', *JESHO*, vol. XXXIII, 1991, pp. 159-82 emphasises on the classification of imported war horses, of which the *bahri* (seaborne) ones from Arabia and Fers were the costliest.
58. *Travels of Ser Marco Polo*, vol. II, p. 78.

59. *Travels of Ser Marco Polo*, vol. II, p. 119.
60. Digby, *Warhorses and Elephants*, p. 43.
61. *Travels of Ser Marco Polo*, vol. II, pp. 106-9 and 120.
62. Digby, *Warhorses and Elephants*, p. 48, quoting Amir Khusru.
63. Ma Huan.
64. Haraprasad Ray, *Trade and Diplomacy in India-China Relations,* Delhi, 1993.
65. Ray, *Trade and Diplomacy.*
66. Ray, *Trade and Diplomacy*, p. 69. cites the evidence of the Ming Taizong Shilu (*The Veritable Records of the Yongle Reign*), 1403-24, completed in 1430.
67. Ray, *Trade and Diplomacy*, p. 69.
68. Ray, *Trade and Diplomacy*, p. 26.
69. Ranabir Chakravarti, 'Early Medieval Bengal and Trade in Horses: A Note', *JESHO*, vol. XLII, 1999, pp. 194-211.
70. Mukherjee, *Media of Exchange.*
71. Sharma, *Urban Decay.*
72. Mukherjee, *Media of Exchange.*
73. R. Champakalakshmi, *Trade, Ideology and Urbanization*; also K.R. Hall, *Trade and Statecraft in the Age of the Colas*, Delhi, 1980.
74. Meera Abraham, *Two Medieval Merchant Guilds of South India*, Delhi, 1988.
75. For an exhaustive discussion on Viśākhapaṭṭinam and Moṭuppallī, see Ranabir Chakravarti, 'Rulers and Ports: Viśākhāpaṭṭinam and Moṭuppallī in Early Medieval Andhradeśa', in K.S. Mathew, ed., *Mariners, Merchants and Oceans*, New Delhi, 1995, pp. 52-77.
76. An overview of *maṇḍapikās, peṇṭhās* and *nagarams* is made by Ranabir Chakravarti, 'Between Cities and Villages: Linkages of Trade in India (*c*. AD 600-1300)', in Georg Berkemer, Tilman Frasch, Hermann Kulke and Jürgen Lütt, eds., *Explorations in the History of South Asia: Essays in Honour of Dietmar Rothermund*, New Delhi, 2001, pp. 99-120; see also our discussions on *maṇḍapikā* and *peṇṭhā* in two separate chapters in this volume.

APPENDIX

A Glossary of Terms Related to Ships/Vessels and Shipping: Gleanings from Early Medieval Texts

Early Indian literature, duly celebrated for its immensely rich diversity and profound depth, does not however offer a comprehensive and practical manual on shipping and shipbuilding technologies. Though India's importance in the affairs of the Indian Ocean is well driven home during the pre-1500 days, only faint glimpses of shipping and shipbuilding traditions are traced in the form of incidental notices, located mostly in non-technical literature. This appendix takes into consideration a survey of Sanskrit and Prakrit texts, assignable during the period *c.* AD 700-1300, to glean information on shipping and shipbuilding. This may help a better appreciation of the seafaring traditions in the Bengal coast during the early medieval times. Terms related to different categories of sailing crafts, to different component parts of the vessel and to sailors are presented here.

A. Categories of Ships/Boats/ Vessels

1. *Vāhana*—Vessel in general: *TM*, p. 105; *KSS*, Chap. 123, verses 109, 110.
2. *Pravahana*—Coastal craft: *DKC*, Chap. 4, p. 35; *KSS*, Chap. 18, verse 296, Chap. 101, verse 136.
3. *Vahitra*—Sea-going vessel: *DKC*, Chap. 6, pp. 155, 156.
4. *Yānapātra*—Sea-going vessel: *AK*, 13.490; *TM*, pp. 104, 106, 107, 113, 114, 116, 119; *AC*, 162.67-8.

(a) '*Tayā saha pratyāgacchanāmambutīrasyānatidūra . . . eva pravaha-nasya bhagnatayā . . .*'. *DKC*
(b) '*Āhantu niralamvano bhūjabhyāmitastataḥsyandamanāt kimapi kāṣṭhaṁ daivadattamurasopaśliṣya tāvadplosi yāvadapasara-dvasaraḥ sarvarīca sanva pratyūṣasyadasyat kimapi vahitra*'. *DKC*
(c) '*Yānapātraṁ ca gṛhītapracurasārabhāṇḍairbhūriśa*'. *TM*
(d) '*Ekenagṛhena dravīṇasaṁgṛharatnāni vāhanāni parijanāḥ*'. *TM*

The *Yuktikalpataru* of Bhoja (p. 228, verses 19-25) describes four categories of vessels on the basis of four types of woods with which they were constructed: Brāhmaṇa, Kṣatriya, Vaiśya, Śūdra. Another classification in the same text divides ships into two broad categories: ordinary or general (*sāmanya*) and special, i.e. sea-going (*viśeṣa*). *Sāmānyañca viśeṣaśca naukāyā lakṣmaṇadvayam.*

i. *Sāmanya* or ordinary type has the following subdivisions:

Type	Length (cubit)	Breadth (cubit)	Height (cubit)
kṣudra	16	4	4
madhyama	24	12	8
bhīma	40	20	20
capala	48	24	24
paṭala	64	32	32
bhaya	72	36	36
dīrgha	88	44	44
patrapuṭa	96	48	48
garbhara	112	56	56
manthara	120	60	60

ii. *Viśeṣa* (special, i.e. sea-going) types has two broad sub-types: *dīrgha* (long) and *unnata* (tall). *Dīrgha caivonnata ceti viśeṣe dvividha vida.*

Dīrgha sub-types

Type	Length (cubit)	Breadth (cubit)	Height (cubit)
dīrghika	32	4	3
taraṇī	48	6	4
lola	64	8	6
gatvara	80	10	8
gāminī	96	12	9
tarī	112	14	11
jaṅghāla	128	16	12
plāvinī	144	18	14
dhāriṇī	160	20	16
veginī	176	22	17

Unnata sub-types

ūrddhva	32	16	16
anūrddhva	48	24	24
svarṇamukhī	64	32	32
garbhinī	80	40	40
manthara	96	48	48

B. Different Parts of the Vessel

(a) *Phalaka*—plank: *DKC*, Chap. 4, p. 36; *TM*, pp. 109, 112. '. . . *jaladhaimagne pravahana nijadhatyā mayā saha phalakamekamavalmbya daivayogena kulamupeta*'. *DKC*

(b) *Kūpastambha/kūpadaṇḍa/guṇavṛkṣa*—Mast (Prakrit—*kuva-khamba*): *TM*, pp. 109, 112; *DKC*, Chap. 1, pp. 1, 2; *AK*, 13.491; *AC* 163. 77. '*Na vahayanti . . . yānapātreṣu pautikāḥ . . . kūpastambhakeṣu karṇadhāraḥ*'. *TM*

(c) *Sītapaṭa*—sail: *TM*, pp. 108, 109, 113, 114, 118, 119; *KM*, p. 67, *SK* IV, p. 202. '*Śaṅkhakuṇḍadhavala siyāvaḍa*'. *SK*

(d) *Rajju*—ropes: *TM*, pp. 118, 119. '*Mukulayat sitapaṭa rajju jalamagrat vistarīmatsyaeva vahati*'. *TM*

(e) *Sūtra*—ropes to tie sails(?): *TM*, p. 106. '*Āgatya ca mayā kṛtāṇi sarvānyapi susūtrāṇi yānapātrāṇi*'. *TM*

(f) *Mandira*—cabin: *YKT*, p. 228, verses 19-25. '*Sagṛhatrividha prokta sarvvamadhyāgramandira*'. *YKT*

(g) *Aritra/kenipāta*—oar: *AC*, 163.82; *AK*, 13.492; *AR*, 3.50. '*Aritraṁ koṭipatraṁ syatpuliṁdo maṅga ucyate*'.

(h) *Sekapātram*—vessel for bailing out excess water: *AK*, 13.493. '*kāṣṭhakuddālaḥsekapātraṁtu secanam*'. *AK*

(i) *Nāṅgara/nāṅgaraśilā*—Anchor/anchor stone: *TM*, pp. 114, 109; *SK* VI, p. 37. '*Tao sama gamanārambheṇa osario siyāvaḍo jiviyas viya vimukka nāṅgaraśilā nijjamaehi*'. *SK*

C. Crew

(a) *Niyāmaka*—captain: *AC*, 162.70; *AK*, 13.491.

(b) *Nāvika/ nāvikakarmakara*—sailor *AK*, 13.491. '*Samyātrikāḥ potavaṇik-karṇadhārstu nāvikāḥ*'. *AK*

CHAPTER 9

Trade at *Maṇḍapikās* in Early Medieval North India

One of the distinctive aspects of researches in early Indian socio-economic history over the last two and a half decades is the growing recognition of the fact that the society and economy of early India had in them the elements of and capacity to change. Different stages in early Indian economy have been discerned.[1] One of these stages, the early medieval (*c.* AD 600-1200), has received considerable attention of historians who highlight the distinct socio-economic ethos of that phase. Sharp breaks in the economic life of the early medieval from that of the early historical are shown within the framework of a new socio-economic formation, Indian feudalism.[2] The broad developments in early medieval economy are suggested to be (i) growth of individual ownership of land at the cost of royal and communal ownership, (ii) subjection of peasantry through subinfeudation, eviction and imposition of non-customary taxes and forced labour, (iii) conversion of income from trade and crafts into benefices, and finally (iv) the existence of a self-sufficient economy buttressed by lesser use of coins and comparative absence of trade.[3] It is, therefore, not surprising to find many historians concentrating on the agrarian economy of the early medieval period and only marginally on the non-agrarian sector of the economy. Recent years have witnessed a significant development in the economic historiography in that the general picture of a sharp economic decline in early medieval India has somewhat changed. Some historians are examining the non-agrarian sector of early medieval economy and important data and conclusions are now available on crafts, commerce and urbanism.[4]

It is in this context of growing interest in the commerce and urbanism of early medieval India that the present study of *maṇḍapikā* as an exchange centre is attempted here.[5] Several terms are known to have denoted various types of non-rural settlements of early historical times, for example, *pura*, *purī*, *nagara*, *pattana*, *puṭabhedana*, *sthānīya* and *nigama*.[6] Significantly the term *maṇḍapikā* does not figure in this list, but begins to appear in early medieval sources. The term in question literally stands for a pillared and covered hall or a pavilion.[7] It also denotes an exchange centre and survives in the modern word *maṇḍī* which means a wholesale market. Though *maṇḍapikā* emerges as an economic institution in the early medieval period, the earliest reference to it may go back to the third century AD. The Hirahadagalli inscription of Śivaskandavarman speaks of a *māṇḍavika*, that is an officer in charge of *maṇḍapikā*.[8]

In the early medieval period *maṇḍapikā* figures frequently in epigraphic records as an exchange centre and also as a centre of collection of levies, commercial tolls and duties. The importance of *maṇḍapikā* as a toll-collecting centre is clearly borne out by the expression *śulkamaṇḍapikā*, that is *maṇḍapikā* where *śulka* or tolls/customs were levied. *Maṇḍapikās* are mentioned in the context of imposition of cesses on various types of commodities (by rulers and/or merchants/mercantile communities) in favour of religious institutions. Important information, though hardly adequate, can be gleaned from these records on various aspects of commerce.

The present study is based on thirteen epigraphic records and the textual evidence of the *Lekhapaddhati* and inscriptions scattered over different areas of north India like Kangra, Gwalior, Bharatpur, Jabalpur, Nadol, Jalore, Kathiawad and Gujarat, with apparent concentration in Rajasthan and Gujarat. These inscriptions range in date from eighth to the twelfth centuries AD. The other source, the *Lekhapaddhati*, belonging to the thirteenth/fourteenth centuries, contains recommendation relating to the imposition of commercial cesses on *maṇḍapikās* and also to the attitude of administrators to merchants coming to *maṇḍapikās*.[9] Some *maṇḍapikās* appear to have been situated at major urban centres like Sīyaḍoṇi, Bilhari and Anhilwada where they are described as *pattanamaṇḍapikās*, that is *maṇḍapikās* at *pattanas* or large urban centres. They are obviously distinguished from exchange centres simply termed as *maṇḍapikās*, the latter being a smaller trade centre than the *pattanamaṇḍapikās*. The difference between a large and an ordinary *maṇḍapikā* is also recognized in the *Lekhapaddhati* under the expression *mahāmaṇḍapikā*.[10]

II

Actual transactions at *maṇḍapikās* may now be examined in the light of epigraphic records. In the Kangra valley of Himachal Pradesh a temple of Śiva Vaidyanātha was built by two brothers named Manyuka and

Āhuka belonging to a merchant family. The Baijnath-*praśasti* (no. 2; eighth/ninth centuries) informs us that the two brothers donated an oil-mill (*tailotpīḍanayantra*) to the same deity, obviously for providing lamps to the temple. The deity was further favoured by a gift of six *drammas* per day out of the collection at the *maṇḍapikā* of Kīragrāma (ancient name of Kangra).[11] The commercial character of Kīragrāma is evident from the presence of a family of merchants and imposition of levy at the *maṇḍapikā*. The daily collection of cess at the *maṇḍapikā* indicates that Kīragrāma had a regular market and not a periodic fair. This exchange centre, however, seems to have been located in a rural area, as it is given the epithet *grāma*. The presence of an oil-mill may suggest cultivation of oil-seeds in the rural areas adjacent to the *maṇḍapikā*.

From the *maṇḍapikā* in a rural surrounding in the Kangra valley, one may turn one's focus to a full-fledged urban commercial centre, viz., Sīyaḍoṇi near Gwalior. The site is explicitly designated as a *pattana-maṇḍapikā* in the Sīyaḍoṇi stone inscription.[12] Sīyaḍoṇi had several streets (*rathyās*), market centres (*haṭṭas*), professional quarters (*vīthīs*) and settlements of various groups (e.g. distillers or *kallapālas*, braziers or *kāṃsakāras*, oilmen or *tailikas*). Sīyaḍoṇi's significance as an exchange and manufacturing centre can hardly be doubted. Another factor that led to the prominence of Sīyaḍoṇi as an urban centre was its important position as an administrative centre under the imperial Pratihāras. Four rulers are mentioned in the span of sixty years (AD 907-68) in the context of gift of cesses at the *maṇḍapikā*.[13]

The *maṇḍapikā* at Sīyaḍoṇi is mentioned at least on five occasions in the context of donation of cesses to different deities. The most prominent figure at this commercial centre was the salt merchant (*nemakavaṇija*) Nāgaka whose father Caṇḍuka was also a dealer in salt. In AD 907, Mahāsāmantādhipati Undabhaṭa endowed in favour of Viṣṇubhaṭṭāraka, established by Caṇḍuka, a daily sum of 5 *drammas* out of the collection at the *maṇḍapikā*.[14] Five years later (AD 912) the salt merchant Nāgaka paid 1350 *drammas* to the markets (*haṭṭas*) of all distillers (*samastakallapālānām*) and the distillers agreed to pay every month ½ *vigrahatuṅgīyadramma* to god Viṣṇu on each cask of liquor.[15] This arrangement was made at the *maṇḍapikā* with the approval of the board of five (*pañcakula*). It appears that the merchant probably paid some dues on behalf of distillers at the liquor market and the latter, in return, consented to impose voluntary cesses on the sale of their product. Another merchant Vikrama built the temple of Bhāilasvāmīdeva to which all merchants (*samastamahājana*) unanimously decided to pay

$^1/_3$ of a *dramma* every month (AD 943-VS 1005).[16] Next, several oilmillers made a voluntary donation to Cakrasvāmīdeva to pay every month a *pālikā* of oil from each oilmill (*ghāṇakaghāṇakam prati tailapalikā pradatta*).[17] This act of patronage was made in AD 950. Towards the end of the record a statement is made of daily payment of ½ *kākiṇī*, but nothing more can be known since the lines are badly broken.[18]

The record leaves little room for doubt that the *maṇḍapikā* at Sīyaḍoṇi combined brisk commercial and manufacturing activities. Several items of daily necessities like salt and oil were sold here. The presence of many merchants, including one named Vikrama, should also be taken into account. The unanimous decision of *mahājanas* to make voluntary donation of cesses may suggest some kind of professional organization among merchants. That the oilmillers and distillers at the *maṇḍapikā* were organized under a guild may be inferred from the names of representatives of respective groups.[19] Several *pañcakulas* (board of five members) also figure at the *pattanamaṇḍapikā*, viz., those of Lodhuaka, Sihapa and Purandara, etc. These *pañcakulas* acknowledged the authority of the Pratihāra rulers and approved of different donations of cesses to deities. Members of the *pañcakulas*, therefore, appear to have been entrusted with management of revenue collection and administration at the *maṇḍapikā*. References to several *pañcakulas* in connection with different mercantile and professional groups may indicate that members of those *pañcakulas* probably represented their respective economic groups. It is not certain whether each of these *pañcakulas* functioned at different *maṇḍapikās* within the spatial limits of one *pattana* or several *pañcakulas* performed their activities at a single *maṇḍapikā* of the exchange centre. Though the second possibility looks more likely, the chance of the existence of several *maṇḍapikās* at one particular *pattana* cannot be entirely ruled out.

Two *maṇḍapikās* figure in the Bayana inscription from Bharatpur, dated AD 955. They were located at Śrīpatha and Vusāvaṭa probably situated near Bharatpur.[20] The local queen donated to a Viṣṇu temple three *drammas* at the *maṇḍapikā* of Śrīpathā and one *dramma* per horse at the market of Vusāvaṭa. Both these exchange centres are smaller in size and less important than Sīyaḍoṇi. But at least the one at Vusāvaṭa was a centre of horse trade; thus this centre had trade in a luxury and costly item.[21]

A *maṇḍapikā* of definitely larger size was situated in Bilhari, near Jabalpur. The Bilhari stone inscription (dated 975) speaks of transfer of various cesses in favour of Nohaleśvara.[22] The existence of the *pattana*-

maṇḍapikā here points to its location in an expansive urban space. Remarkable varieties of commodities were brought for transaction and levied at the *maṇḍapikā* of the city. The record enlists salt, betel nuts, black pepper, dried ginger and various other merchandise including vegetables, eggplants, grass and liquor. Apart from cesses levied on these items, taxes were also realized from oil mills, shops (*vīthī*) and fishermen (*dhīrmara*). While one *ṣoḍaśikā* coin was charged on the sale of each *khaṇḍikā* (amount uncertain) of salt, the same amount was taken every month from every oil mill. On various agricultural products the rate was fixed at one *paura* coin per load on *bhāraka* (of unspecified weight/size). Each shop had to pay one *kaparda* (cowry shell), and the same cess was imposed on green vegetables (*śākavārttākaṃ*). From dealers in liquors (*rasavaṇija*) and grass and fishermen only a small amount was levied (*yatkiñcit*). At the *maṇḍapikā* horses and elephants were also sold. On the sale of each elephant a cess of four *paura* coins was fixed, while on that of each horse, two *paura* coins. The interesting point is that the levy on the sale of horses was less than that on elephants, though the former, being not easily available in India, had to be usually imported at a very high cost. Another cess of one *paura* was fixed for a couple of *yugas* each day.[23] The term '*yuga*' means a document. In the context of levy of commercial cess, this may mean 'a voucher authorizing the owner to exhibit his articles in the market place for one day'.[24]

This account highlights the impressive range of commodities brought for transactions at Bilhari. On the one hand there are various types of essential commodities like crops, fish, grass, salt, liquor and oil. On the other hand luxury items like elephant, horse and pepper are also exchanged. The reference to *vīthīs* or shops is a clear pointer to the fact that the present *maṇḍapikā* was not only a centre of wholesale trade, but also of a retail trade. Some of the commodities particularly crops could have arrived at the *maṇḍapikā* from a hinterland not far from the trade centre. But betel nuts (*pūga*) and pepper (*marīca*) must have been supplied to Jabalpur area from the peninsular part of the subcontinent. Distant trade contacts can be assumed from the availability of horses which are not usually bred in Madhya Pradesh and had probably to be imported from north and north-west. The elephant, however, could have been brought from the forest areas of Madhya Pradesh. The custom of issuing license/certificates against the payment of some fees indicates the presence of administrative authorities there supervising transactions.

The geographical focus now shifts to Rajasthan. An inscription from Shergadh (AD 1017) records the daily gift of ¾ *tolā* of ghee out of the *maṇḍapikā* tax (*ādāyāt*). The endowment was made as a religious donation by three merchants, viz., Narasiṁha, Govṛṣa and Thirāditya. The commercial character of the *maṇḍapikā* is borne out by its association with three merchants.[25]

If we club together the evidence of three records from Nadole in Rajasthan (AD 1114,[26] AD 1155,[27] and AD 1161[28]), the gradual emergence of Nāḍḍula *maṇḍapikā* as an important exchange centre may be appreciated. The first record speaks of collection of six *drammas* at the Naḍḍulīya *maṇḍapikā*. A daily collection of one *rūpaka* from the same *maṇḍapikā* figures in the second record, once again pointing to the existence of regular market (and not a periodic fair) at Nadole. The revenue-bearing potential of commerce in this area is amply illustrated by the expression *Śrīnāḍḍula talapāḍa śulkamaṇḍapikā*. The *maṇḍapikā* is not only officially recognized as a toll-taking centre, but was situated in *talapāḍa* area. The last expression, according to D.C. Sircar, stands for lands fully assessed for revenue.[29] Further, five *drammas* out of the total collection at the *śulkamaṇḍapikā* were stipulated for providing incense and oil to the local temple. B.D. Chattopadhyaya's excellent study clearly establishes that, originally a village (*Naḍḍulagrāma*) at the centre of 12 villages, Nadole blossomed into a *pura* (urban centre), a *maṇḍapikā* (exchange centre) and ultimately a seat of power of the Cāhamāna ruling lineage. A strong agrarian base, the location of Nadole at a nodal point and establishment of a political centre—all combined to effect a change in the nature and character of this settlement.[30]

Another *śulkamaṇḍapikā* was situated at Nanana in Rajasthan.[31] Four *drammas* were to be paid monthly therefrom in favour of a deity.

The last record gives an account of the *śulkamaṇḍapikā* at Salakhanapurī in Gujarat (twelfth century).[32] Among dutiable items meant for exchange are *mañjiṣṭhā*, *paṭṭasūtra*, *pravālaka*, *karpūra*, *kastūrī*, *hiṅgu*, *kumkuma*, *aguru*, *mālapatra*, *jaiphala*, *jaivotra*, *kāpaḍa*, *marīca* and *kharjjura*. Great diversity in the range of commodities is unmistakable from a study of this record. It includes cash crops, finished textiles, yarn, spices, fragrants, fruits and gems. Cash crops and some agro-based products dominate this list. Some spices, particularly pepper, were brought to Gujarat from peninsular India. At this *maṇḍapikā* one finds juxtaposition of essential commodities and luxury items.

Items for transaction were brought to the exchange centre from areas of production, either from a nearby area or distant countries. The Mangrol inscription of AD 1114 from Kathiawad informs us that at the *śulkamaṇḍapikā* of Maṅgalapura (Mangrol) commodities were brought on oxen (*balīvarda*), asses (*rāsabha*) and camels (*uṣṭra*). The last animal was utilized in transportation of goods especially in the context of western India.

The revenue bearing aspect of commerce at a *maṇḍapikā* could have hardly escaped the notice of rulers. The revenue management problem from the point of view of the ruler is discussed in the *Lekhapaddhati*. The emphasis here is, however, on long-distance external trade and traders. Some *maṇḍapikās* in Gujarat must have participated in the brisk external trade. The proximity of the sea, the rise of several important ports and the settlement of Arab merchants in Gujarat should be taken into account.[33]

The *Lekhapaddhati* enlists several important revenue officers apparently connected with revenue collection (*dāna*) at *maṇḍapikā*. They are *māṇḍavī* (officer-in-charge of *maṇḍapikā*), *pathakīyas* (those collecting record cess), *uparihiṇḍīyas* (tax inspectors). These officers are to collect taxes from foreign merchants (*vacchivittas*) for importing and exporting (*āgamanigamādanam*) according to prevalent laws and customs. A small present or bonus (*vikarapadāni*), obviously in excess of usual taxes, may be taken from them, but according to conventional practices. The officers are cautioned not to tease or disturb foreign merchants by asking for higher cesses (*kimapyadhikaṃdānam*) as the fiscal extortion may lead to slump of taxes on foreign trade. This obviously means that excessive taxes forced foreign merchants to avoid troubled markets, thereby adversely affecting collection of commercial revenue. The foreign merchants and the caravan trader (*vinjara*/banjārā) are to be received well and honourably (*mānapuraḥsara*).

This account may illustrate the government's concern for framing a commercial policy which would not be detrimental to foreign trade. This text also recognizes and, in fact, legalizes up to a certain extent, corrupt practices like bribery and excess presentation of commodities, to the mutual advantage of both merchants and administrators. In some of our records tolls and customs were raised and donated by existing political authorities. On the other hand, individual merchants or mercantile groups are also found to have made voluntary donation of cess (in cash and kind) to some religious persons and institutions. At Sīyaḍoṇi, Nāgāka, the salt merchant, the entire *mahājana* community and several oil-millers voluntarily raised cesses on three separate occasions. Important urban elite groups, principally composed of merchants, are found to have been occasionally engaged in revenue collection at *maṇḍapikās*, parallel to government machinery. The *pañcakulas* consisting of representatives of merchants and artisans, approved of such imposition of cesses by non-governmental agencies. Participation in revenue administration through *pañcakulas* may have improved upon the status of some merchants. At Sīyaḍoṇi, one Purandara built a temple and was a member of a *pañcakula* also. Purandara is likely to have enhanced his prestige by participating in administration and also by providing patronage to temple building. At Sīyaḍoṇi, several *nemakavaṇija* or salt merchants were present who often followed their profession hereditarily. Once in the Sīyaḍoṇi record, a salt merchant is described as belonging to the *nemakajāti*. Heredity of occupation, economic well-being, act of patronage to religious and art activities may have contributed to the exclusiveness and social compactness of salt merchants to such an extent that they attained the status of a *jāti*.

The early medieval period, particularly from AD 600 to 1000 is suggested to have experienced a sharp economic decline in commercial and urban economy.[34] There was a definite and unmistakable spurt in the growth of urban centres and markets in the post-AD 1000 north India. The aforesaid survey of spatial distribution of *maṇḍapikās* may show significant emergence of exchange centres even prior to AD 1000. The data also strongly go against the theory of decline in trade.

The most significant point here is that a large number of essential commodities were transacted at the *maṇḍapikā*. The bulk of daily necessities consisted of various types of edible and cash crops. The importance of *maṇḍapikās* as centres of grain trade cannot be overlooked. Some of the crops appear to have been brought to the *maṇḍapikā*, from distant areas, indicating their commercial demand over extensive areas. Early Indian trade is often thought to have consisted of high value, small quantity, luxury, portable items. This line of argument must be revised in view of the growth of grain trade and trade in essential commodities. The development of grain trade in early medieval times can be explained in terms of the availability of exchangeable amount of surplus product. It may not be out of place to point out that creation of settlements through land grants in early medieval times was instrumental in the expansion of cultivation in backward areas. To this should be added the arrival of a new technological device for irrigation, *arghaṭṭa/ghaṭīyantra*. The rise of local level exchange centres over widespread territories facilitated transactions in grains. The local exchange centres were also often political centres of regional ruling lineages.

Early medieval trade, according to R.S. Sharma, languished because of, among other things, donation/transfer of commercial cesses,[35] the like of which we have encountered so frequently in our study of *maṇḍapikās*. Voluntary donations of levies on commodities by merchants/artisans and revenue transfers by political authorities/ administrative officers, however, may be seen as acts of patronage, the material basis of which was rooted in the gains derived from trade. This brings us to an altogether different theoretical proposition. Roberto S. Lopez, in the context of medieval Europe, found religious buildings as good economic indicators. Fernand Braudel uses this theory with approval and sees in the interruption of building of churches in exchange centres of Bologna (1223), Sienna (1265), Santa Maria del Fiore (1302), 'a sure sign of economic crisis'.[36] Viewed from this angle, regular patronage to construction and maintenance of temples out of the revenues collected at *maṇḍapikās* may be indicative of the commercial prosperity of *maṇḍapikās* and not otherwise.

Though originating as early as the third century AD, the *maṇḍapikā* appears to have been a product of the early medieval socio-economic milieu. With the exception of Sīyaḍoṇi, Bilhari and Anahilvada *pattanamaṇḍapikās*, which were located at fully developed urban commercial centres, *maṇḍapikās* at other sites were essentially local level exchange centres. These were often closely related to their adjacent rural hinterland. In the commercial structure and hierarchy of exchange centres the *maṇḍapikā* may be assigned a position intermediate between small, dispersed rural markets of periodic nature (*haṭṭa/haṭṭikā*) and developed urban centres (*pattanas*) involved in inter-regional and intra-regional trade. It is almost irresistible to check the temptation of invoking another European example: the Halls/Halles of late medieval Europe. The Hall/Halle had wide-ranging connotations from a 'simple covered market to the mighty building and complicated organization of the Halles which were from a very early date the belly of Paris'.[37] The present picture is far from clear in the case of early medieval India and even the idea of a rough parallelism between *maṇḍapikās* and Halls will not appear readymade. But enquiries about early medieval *maṇḍapikās* may be directed on similar lines, notwithstanding the paucity of data. In discussions of trade, markets and urban centres our attention is too often concentrated on large, celebrated cities, the 'sun-cities' of Braudel. 'But it would be a mistake only to count the sun-cities. Towns form hierarchies everywhere but the tip of the pyramid does not tell us everything, important though it may be.'[38] It sounds ambitious, if not precocious, to think in terms of Braudel's megascopic view of history, his breathtaking range and depth. But the challenge is worth attempting.

NOTES

1. R.S. Sharma and D.N. Jha, 'The Economic History of India up to AD 1200: Trends and Prospects', *JESHO*, vol. XVII, 1974, pp. 48-80. Sharma, *Perspectives*, particularly Chaps. IX and X.
2. Sharma, *Indian Feudalism*.
3. Sharma, *Indian Feudalism*, p. 109.
4. The most significant critique of the 'de-urbanization' theory is provided by B.D. Chattopadhyaya in his studies in early medieval commerce and urbanization. Chattopadhyaya, 'Trade and Urban Centres'; idem, 'Urban Centres in Early Medieval India'; idem, 'Markets and Merchants in Early Medieval Rajasthan', *Social Science Probings*, no. 2, 1985. These essays are incorporated in Chattopadhyaya, *The Making of Early Medieval India*. R.S. Sharma suggests growth of urban centres and commerce from AD 1000 onwards. Chattopadhyaya, on the other hand, cites important evidence of the development of commerce and urban centres before AD 1000, and labels the rise of urban centres in early medieval phase as the 'third urbanization'. Another important article in this connection is that of B.P. Majumdar, 'Industries and Internal Trade in Early Medieval North India', *Journal of the Bihar Research Society*, vols. LXV-LXVI, 1979-80, pp. 230-56.
5. The present study is largely inspired by B.D. Chattopadhyay's essays. He was extremely kind to give me typescripts of two of his last mentioned articles.
6. Ghosh, *The City*, p. 45.
7. Monier-Williams, *Sanskrit-English Dictionary*, p. 775.
8. *SI*, vol. I, p. 461.
9. *Lekhapaddhati*, ed., C.D. Dalal and G.K. Shrigondekar, Baroda, 1925, discusses *maṇḍapikā* in a section entitled *Dānamaṁḍapikāpatravidhi*.
10. *Lekhapaddhati*, p. 14.
11. *EI*, vol. I, Inscription no. 16, pp. 112-18; *maṇḍapikotpattiddhanadatta-ṣṣatpratyahaṁdramma*.
12. *EI*, vol. I, Inscription no. 21, pp. 162-79.
13. Chattopadhyay, 'Trade and Urban Centres' gives an exhaustive and detailed analysis of the growth of the urban centre at Sīyaḍoṇi.
14. For the Sīyaḍoṇi inscription see *EI*, vol. I, Inscription no. 21, p. 173, lines 5-6.
15. *EI*, vol. I, Inscription no. 21, p. 173, lines 18-19.
16. *EI*, vol. I, Inscription no. 21, p. 173, lines 28-9.
17. *EI*, vol. I, Inscription no. 21, p. 173, lines 30-1.
18. *EI*, vol. I, Inscription no. 21, p. 173, lines 45.
19. *EI*, vol. I, Inscription no. 21, p. 173, lines 19 and 31.
20. *EI*, vol. XXII, Inscription no. 20, pp. 120ff.
21. As the cess on the sale of horses is not categorically imposed on a daily

basis, Vusāvaṭa appears to have had a periodic fair of horses. Similar horse fairs (*ghoṭakayātrā*) were arranged in early medieval times at Pṛthudaka (Pehoa) (*EI*, vol. I, Inscription no. 23, pp. 184-90). Animal and cattle markets were known also as Kambalīhaṭṭa (Kaman stone inscription, *EI*, vol. XXIV, no. 45, pp. 329-36).

22. *CII*, vol. IV, pt. I, Inscription no. 45, p. 215, 223.
23. *CII*, vol. IV, pt. I, Inscription no. 45, p. 215, 1.31: *dinamanu ca yugayuge ca paurastu*.
24. *CII*, vol. IV, pt. I, p. 223, note 6.
25. *EI*, vol. IV, pt. I, p. 223, note 6.
26. Dasaratha Sharma, *Early Chauhan Dynasties*, New Delhi, 1959, pp. 181-2.
27. *IA*, vol. XII, pp. 202ff.
28. *EI*, vol. IX, pp. 63ff.
29. Sircar, *Epigraphical Glossary*, p. 333.
30. Chattopadhyaya, 'Merchants and Markets'.
31. Sharma, *Early Chauhan*, pp. 181-82.
32. *IA*, vol. VI, pp. 202ff.
33. For the settlement of Arab merchants in Gujarat in the thirteenth/fourteenth centuries and even earlier, S.C. Misra, *Muslim Communities in Gujarat*, Bombay, 1964.
34. Sharma has modified his views to some extent. While the early medieval period was previously considered by him as one of sharp economic decline, he has recently given due importance to the expansion of agriculture, proliferation of metal based (particularly iron) industries and growth of trade. One is surprised that Simon Digby virtually repeats R.S. Sharma's arguments without taking into account recent developments. Sharma, *Indian Feudalism*. R.S. Sharma, 'How Feudal Was Indian Feudalism', *Social Scientist*, no. 129, 1984, pp. 16-41. Simon Digby, 'Economic Conditions before 1200', in Tapan Raychaudhuri and Irfan Habib, eds., *Cambridge Economic History of India*, vol. I, New Delhi, 1984, pp. 45-8.
35. Sharma, *Indian Feudalism*.
36. Lopez's view is discussed by Fernand Braudel, *The Wheels of Commerce*, London, 1982, p. 35.
37. Braudel, *Wheels of Commerce*, pp. 33-6.
38. Braudel, *The Structures of Everyday Life*, pp. 482-3.

APPENDIX

Spatial Distribution of Maṇḍapikās (Epigraphic Records)

S. No.	*Source and Date*	*Area*	*Donation/content of record*	*Donor*
1	*2*	*3*	*4*	*5*
1.	Hirahadagalli C.P. of Pallava Śivaskandavarman; middle of the fourth century AD	Bellary, dt. Karnataka	Presence of various revenue officers including *māṇḍavika*	Śivaskandavarman
2.	Baijnath-*praśasti* (no. 2) eighth/ninth century	Kangra, Himachal Pradesh	To Vaidyanātha 6 *drammas* of money out of the daily collection at the *maṇḍapikā*; names of three hereditary merchants Siddha, Manyuka and Āhuka.	Rājanaka Lakṣmaṇacandra
3.	Siyadoṇi Stone Inscription tenth century (various dates)	Gwalior area Central India	At the *pattanamaṇḍapikā*	
	a. AD 907		Daily payment of a quarter of *pañciyak-dramma* to god Viṣṇubhaṭṭāraka established by salt merchant Caṇḍūka	Mahāsāmantā-dhipati Undabhata. Vassal of Pratihāra Devapāla
	b. AD 912		At the *pattanamaṇḍa pikā*. Payment of 1350 *ādivarāha-dramma* probably on behalf of distillers who in their turn agree to donate	Salt merchant Nāgāka and several distillers

1	2	3	4	5
			½ *vigrahatuṅgīya-dramma* on the sale of a cask of liquor per month in favour of Viṣṇubhaṭṭāraka	
	c. AD 948		Entire *mahājana* (trading) community to the god Bhāilasvāmī, established by merchant Vikrama monthly gift of 1/3 of a *dramma* at the *pattanamaṇḍapikā*; unanimous decision by *samasta mahājanas*; *pañcakula* present	
	d. AD 951		To the god Viṣṇubhaṭṭāraka established by salt merchant Caṇḍuka, cess from per oil-mill	Oilmen Keśava, Durgāditya Kesutaka, Ujoneka Tundia, etc.
4.	Bayana Inscription of Citralekhā, AD 955	Bharatpur, Rajasthan	To Viṣṇu, 3 *drammas* from the *maṇḍapikā* at Śrīpathā and at Vusāvaṭa 1 *dramma* per horse	Local queen
5.	Bilhari Stone Inscription of Yuvarājadeva II AD 975	Damoh Jabalpur area, MP	To a maṭha, donation of cess collected at *pattanamaṇḍapikā* on salt, oilmill, betel, fruits, pepper, dried ginger, shops, green vegetables, liquor grass, fisherman, elephants and horses	Yuvarājadeva II

1	*2*	*3*	*4*	*5*
6.	Shergarh Inscription AD 1017	Near Kota, Rajasthan	Daily gift of one *karṣā* (¾ of *tolā*) of ghee out of *maṇḍapikā* income to Bhaṭṭāraka Nāgraka	Three merchants, Narasiṃha, Govṛṣa and Thirāditya
7.	Mangrol Inscription AD 1114	Kathiawad	Information about transportation of commodities to the *śulkamaṇḍapikā* at Mangalapura by oxen, asses and camels	
8.	Nadole Grant, AD 1400	Rajasthan	Payment of 6 *drammas* out of Naḍḍula-*maṇḍapikā*	Local political authority
9.	Nadole Grant of Pratapasiṃha, AD 1155	Rajasthan	Payment of 1 *rūpaka* per day from the *maṇḍapikā*	Feudatory ruler
10.	Nanana Grant of Alhanadeva AD 1159	Rajasthan	4 *drammas* per month from *sulkamaṇḍapikā*	Alhanadeva
11.	Nadole Grant of Alhanadeva AD 1161	Rajasthan	Monthly payment of 5 *drammas* at the *Naḍḍulatalapadaśulka maṇḍapikā*	Alhanadeva
12.	Grant from Salakhanapuri, twelfth century AD	Gujarat	Mention of *śulka maṇḍapikā* cess on various commodities: *manjiṣṭhā*, *pattasūtra*, *pravālaka karpūra*, *kastūrī*, *hiṅgu*, *kumkuma*, *agura*, *mālapatra*, *jaiphala*, *jaivatri*, *kāpaḍa*, *malike*, *marīca*, *kharjuraka*	

CHAPTER 10

The *Penṭhā* as a Centre of Trade in the Deccan *c.* AD 600-1300

The discussions in the preceding chapter on *maṇḍapikās* in early medieval north India are now followed by a survey of linkages of trade in the Deccan during the period *c.* AD 600-1300. As the following pages would show, the *penṭhā* (with its varying forms and spellings) emerged in the Deccan as a locality level centre of both trade and administration and assumed considerable prominence in the socio-economic and political history of the Deccan. But before we delve into the enquiries into the *penṭhā* some other preliminary issues may be addressed here. The period from *c.* AD 600 to 1300 witnessed significant changes in political, socio-economic and cultural (including creative activities in literature and art) conditions. The changes are considered so significant that the centuries preceding *c.* AD 600 are portrayed as having witnessed a different kind of formation(s). There are considerable divergence of scholarly opinions on the perceptions of these changes and the causes and impacts these changes brought about. This is indicated by the various labels by which the seven centuries are designated in different genres of historical researches. The particular chronological segment is variously called post-Gupta, late ancient, late classical, early medieval and proto-medieval. The changes are sought to be located in the emergence and crystallization of regional features and tendencies in dispersed areas of the subcontinent. The rise of many regional powers and the endemic hostilities among them caught the imaginations of scholars presenting conventional accounts of dynastic history which is featured by the absence of a paramount political power either in north India, or the Deccan or the far south. In the conventional historiography little emphasis is placed on the issue whether these centuries were associated with appreciable changes in socio-economic and cultural situations. The other genre of historical research—best represented by Marxist historiography—highlights and explains the processes of fragmentation and parcellization of sovereignty which is linked up with the rise of *sāmantas* (vassals), languishing trade, marginal use of coins and widespread urban decay. In other words, this position situates significant changes outside dynastic shifts; the perceptions of a large number of Marxist historians in this context may be appreciated by what could be termed as 'decline syndrome'. Departures from these two dominant historiographical standpoints have also been attempted by some scholars designated as the 'non-aligned' historians. The last mentioned ones seek to explain the changes during these crucial seven centuries, neither by the yardstick of the oscillation between centralization and decentralization of polity, nor by the logic of a crisis or decline. The crystallization of regional features, in the estimation of the third group of scholars, was an outcome of local level formations, a development from within, rather than the breakdown of an earlier socio-economic and political order. An epicentric position is ruled out by these scholars for the appreciation of these local and regional formations.[1]

Local level formations appear to have been generated by an unprecedented expansion of agriculture from AD 600 to 1300 mainly with the practice of creating *agrahāras* (*agrahāramatisṛṣṭam*), i.e. the grant of land to a brāhmaṇa or brāhmaṇas or to religious establishments (Brahmanical temples and *maṭhas*, Buddhist *vihāras* and Jaina monasteries) by the issuance of copper plate charters under the instruction of the local and/or the apex politico-administrative authority. With this practice of granting land mostly in non-arable tracts were inseparably associated the penetration of the complex *jāti-varṇa* system into the relatively less differentiated tribal society and the gradual absorption of tribal deities within the Brahmanical *bhakti* cults. These developments from within are suggested to have ushered in monarchical system into areas hitherto experiencing pre-state polities; these were also conducive to the emergence of local and supra-local centres of trade. The spread of agriculture, the formation of local and regional polities and the development of local level exchange centres resulted in the emergence of urban centres in disparate regions of the subcontinent.[2] The significant point is that in the aforesaid scenario the village is not seen as an isolated or as undifferentiated type;[3] on the other hand, the image of trade and urban development certainly suggests the existence of different types and categories of non-rural settlements.

The above historiographical overview now may take us to the examination of a crucial issue of trade in the light of the possibilities of local level formations during the AD 600-1300 phase. A major problem of the understanding of early Indian trade lies in the indiscriminate use of a blanket term like 'trader' or 'merchant' to denote any type of purveyors of commodities. Both textual and epigraphic accounts, on the other hand, show a clear awareness of the authors of these texts of the different levels and types of merchants, e.g. *vaidehaka/vaṇik* (a petty trader), *banjara* (itinerant merchant or pedlar), *sārthavāha* (caravan trader), *śreṣṭhī* (a very rich merchant, also an investor of wealth in commerce), *rājaśreṣṭhī* (royal merchant), *nauvittaka* (ship-owning merchant), etc. That these terms referred to specific types of traders is unmistakable.[4] Similarly, the much-used generic expression 'trade centre' tends to blur the distinctiveness of diverse types of centres of exchange that existed during the period under review. Another steady notion is to describe an impressive urban area where trade thrived and to trace villages (adjacent to and distant from the urban centre) which served as the rural hinterland of a city. This simple two-tier arrangement rarely accommodates the scope of looking for the existence of intermediate areas or centres providing the vital linkages between urban settlements and their rural surroundings. The present essay is an attempt to address this problem.

It focuses largely on three types of exchange centres known as *maṇḍapikā*, *peṭha/peṇṭhā* (variously called *piṇṭhā* and *peṁta*) and *nagaram*. The three terms occur in literature (both normative and creative) and inscriptions alike respectively in the contexts of north India, the Deccan and the far south. No less significant is the fact that these terms are seldom encountered in sources prior to sixth century AD.[5] The regular appearance of these terms to denote centres of commerce in sources datable to the period of review urges us to situate them in the context of the seven centuries under discussion. It should be pointed out that the evidence at our disposal is not only very sketchy, but also not even directly related to trade. The inscriptions are mostly land grant records offering glimpses of commercial activities almost in the form of incidental notices; they often speak of transfer of revenue (including levies on commodities) to deities and temples. Literary texts either lay down certain socio-religious and political norms which may or may not relate to existing practices, or may offer stereotyped images of trade and traders. Moreover, it is nearly impossible to come across any quantifiable data on trade, traders and centres of trade from these sources which provide us with what Udovitch calls 'qualitative' information.[6]

The debates among historians concerning the nature, causes and impacts of changes occurring during the seven centuries are so intense that the period is considered as a 'much maligned monster' of Indian historiography.[7] It is difficult to miss the trend that enquiries into the seven centuries are mostly oriented to the north Indian situation and to some extent to the far south. But the assessment of the changing scenario in the Deccan, Dakṣiṇāpatha of Indian sources, appear to have been somewhat left out. The area lying between the Narmada and the Krishna rivers and stretching from the west to the east coast has not been given due weightage even in two excellent and updated survey of the state and economy from fourth to the thirteenth centuries. This is a desideratum which urges us to take a close look at the linkages of trade in the Deccan from *c.* AD 600-1300. This brings us to an examination of the *peṇṭhā* or *peṭha* in the socio-economic and political situation of the Deccan.

II

In the Deccan, embracing the modern states of Maharashtra, Karnataka, Andhra Pradesh and the southern part of Madhya Pradesh, can be seen numerous centres of supra-local trade with name-endings like *peṭh*, *peṭṭa*, *peṭṭai*, etc. The beginning of the use of these words can be pushed back to even prior to AD 600, as the following pages would show. It is interesting to note that the term *peṭha* in the sense of a centre of supra-village administration figured as early as 529 and 533 in two copper plates from the Bundelkhand region in central India.[8] Both the grants refer to the rule of the Uccakalpas of central India, who must have previously been subordiante vassals under the imperial Guptas, but became virtually independent in the third quarter of the sixth century when the Gupta empire was about to become a thing of the past.[9] The two records belong respectively to the reigns of Saṁkṣobha and Śarvanātha.

These two copper plates inform us about grants of land in favour of goddess Piṣṭapurikā. In GE 209 (AD 529-30), Mahārāja Saṁkṣobha made a grant of the village named Opāni within Maṇināgapeṭha in Ḍābhala in favour of goddess Piṣṭapurikā. To the same goddess was again granted two more villages after four years in AD 533-4 (GE 214) by the new Uccakalpa ruler Mahārāja Śarvanātha. The donated villages were Vyāghrapallikā and Kācārapallikā, both being included within Maṇināgapeṭha. That the said *peṭha* as an administrative tier stood above a cluster of individual villages cannot be doubted. Maṇināgapeṭha, in its turn, formed a part of the eighteen forest chiefdoms within the kingdom of Ḍābhala (*aṣṭādaśāṭavirājyābhyantara Ḍābhalarājyāntargata*).[10]

Besides being explicitly stated as a forest tract, the name of one village at least, i.e. Vyāghrapallikā cannot but suggest a further association with a forest. According to B.D. Chattopadhyaya, the two apparently synonymous and interchangeable terms like *grāma* and *pallī*—both generally taken to mean rural settlements—should be better interpreted respectively as regular sedentary agrarian villages and tribal hamlets or settlements. Maṇināgapeṭha in that case could have included within it agricultural tracts and tribal settlements located within a substantial forest area. An indication of this may also be seen in the name Pulindabhaṭa who was in charge of the worship of goddess Piṣṭapurikā. Pulinda being the name of a well known tribe (since at least the time of Aśoka), the existence of tribal population in and around Maṇināgapeṭha and the villages included within it can be reasonably inferred. Such grants of land in forest tracts must have resulted in the subsequent expansion of agriculture and the spurt of rural settlements. As an administrative tier above individual villages, Maṇināgapeṭhà was a witness to the presence of several high ranking functionaries, e.g. the *amātya* (minister or important royal officer), the *sandhivigrahika* (the officer-in-charge of war and peace), the *dūtaka* (royal envoy or messenger) and *lekhaka* (scribe) at the time of the making of the grants of land. This may signify the gradual penetration of the complex state society in this area. The *peṭha* in central India thus provided linkages between individual villages and the upper tiers of administration. The area in question also saw the non-agrarian economic activities of craftsmen (*kārus*) and merchants (*vaṇik*), mentioned in an inscription of AD 512. Changes of far-reaching consequences in the local society in Ḍābhala area appear to have been taking place from the beginning of the AD sixth century onwards. Maṇināgapeṭha, initially a part of a forest tract, gradually became well settled with rural agricultural units and combined administrative functions with those of a crafts and trade centre. The multiplicity of functions at this *peṭha* must have marked it out from an ordinary village, although Maṇināgapeṭha had not acquired any urban feature in the first half of the sixth century.

In the second half of the sixth century, the locality level administrative system in the Maitraka kingdom of Valabhī in Kathiawad seems to have been also conversant with the *peṭha* as a supra-local level of administration. In AD 571-2 (GE 252) Dharasena II of the Maitraka dynasty donated the village of Vaṭagrāma, located in Dīpanakapeṭha within Bilvakhātasthalī. The land grant in question thus refers to the donated village in terms of its linkages with upper tiers of administration like *peṭha*, and *sthalī*.[11] Another Valabhī grant would indicate that the *peṭha* and the *sthalī* were both included within the *viṣaya* or the district which was certainly a larger administrative unit than both *peṭha* and *sthalī*.[12] The *peṭha* as an administrative unit above villages is encountered both in central and western parts of India. Chronologically speaking the *peṭha* appears in central Indian records earlier than the western Indian grants, though it will be difficult to conclude whether the system was first introduced to central India and subsequently was also adapted by the Maitrakas of western India for locality level administration. In the case of western India the *peṭha* stood above the village but below a new and higher administrative tier, namely the *sthalī*. Placed above individual villages, the *peṭha* was conducive to providing linkages between villages in the interior and the upper tiers of administrative hierarchy.

It is true that the *peṭha* makes its earliest appearance not in the Deccan but in central and western India. The *peṭha* as an administrative unit is not encountered before the sixth century, implying thereby that significant, albeit slow, changes in the social, economic and political organizations at the locality level were in the offing around that time. The so far earliest known occurrence of *peṭha* in the context of the Deccan is seen in a grant from the Satara district, Maharashtra, issued during the reign of an early Rāṣṭrakūṭa king Abhimanyu (not belonging to the famous Rāṣṭrakūṭa house of Malkhed).[13] According to this charter, palaeographically assignable to the seventh century, Abhimanyu was residing at Mānapura, probably his capital—named after his great-grandfather. He granted the village of Uṇḍikavāṭikā belonging to the *peṭha* of Paṅgāraka in favour Dakshiṇa-Śiva, by pouring water into the hands of the ascetic Jaṭābhāra (*Tena Mānapuramadhyāsanenālaṅkurvvata . . . peṭha-Paṅgārakīya Dakṣiṇa-Śivasya Uṇḍikavāṭikā nāma grāmako Jaṭābhāra-pravrajitasya udaka-pūrvvako dattaḥ*).[14] At the time of this grant a high ranking officer, named Jayasiṁha and in charge of Harivatsakoṭṭa, was also present (*Harivatsakoṭṭanigraha Jayasiṁha-samakṣam*). Here once again we encounter the *peṭha* as an administrative unit standing above an individual village. It would be logical to assume that like the Maṇināgapeṭha in the sixth century Ḍāhala area, this *peṭha* in the Deccan too embraced within it a few villages. That the *peṭha* was linked with higher tiers of administration is well driven home by the officer-in-charge of a *koṭṭa* or a fortified settlement. The *koṭṭa* was certainly not a village, but probably signified a non-rural politico-military centre.

III

That the *peṭha* was a centre of commerce, besides an administrative unit between individual villages and a district, is amply demonstrated by a graphic description of trade at a *peṇṭhā* in the *Yaśastilakacampu* of Somadevasuri. Before delving into the literary images of the *peṇṭhā*, a few words about the text itself will be in order. The *Yaśastilakacampu* is a prose romance often drawing upon Jaina morals and teachings. It would be futile to seek historical actualities in this genre of literature. Moreover, many tales of this text are set in north India. Yet they often have an important bearing on the Deccan. Somadevasuri explicitly states himself to be a contemporary of Kṛṣṇa III (939-67), the last great ruler of the Rāṣṭrakūṭa empire, the most formidable regional power in the Deccan from the middle of the eighth to the late tenth century AD (*c.* 754-974). His remarkable awareness of political situation in the Deccan is best illustrated by his explicit statement that the text was composed in AD 959 when the victorious Rāṣṭrakūṭa ruler was residing not in his capital Mānyakheṭa but in Meḍupattyam or Melpadi in the North Arcot district within the Coḷa realm. His first-hand knowledge of the conditions in the Deccan is also seen in the excellent pen-picture of a cow-shed (*go-śālā*) in Karahāṭaka or present Karhad (Satara district, Maharashtra). All these endow this work of Somadevasuri with a Deccanese flavour.[15]

The account of a *peṇṭhā* (probably hyper-Sanskritized form of *peṭha*) is found in a tale which goes to demonstrate the disastrous outcome of theft (*steyaphala*). The story is set in the famous city of Prayāga; but it is perhaps not necessarily related to the Ganga valley situation. We have already clarified why Somadeva and his works are to be associated with the Deccan. The narrative centres around a cunning brāhmaṇa minister named Śrībhuti who established the *peṇṭhāsthāna*. The *peṇṭhā* was divided into many well laid out chambers (*vibhaktānekāpavara-karacanāśālinī*); it had also large storage areas for merchandise (*mahābhāṇḍavāhinī*) and was provided with drinking places (*prapā*), feeding houses (*sattra*), assembly hall with seats (*sabhāsanātha*) and streets or shops (*vīthi*). Merchants from different directions and quarters flocked at the *peṇṭhā* (*nānādigdeśopasarpanayujāṁ vaṇijām*). Covering an area of a couple of miles (*gorutpramāṇa*) the *peṇṭhā* was marked by ditches (*kulyāḥ*), rampart (*vapra*), fortification (*prākāra*) and a moat (*parikhā*). The description highlights the impressive size of a trade centre where excellent items were stored in boxes which were watched over by adequate number of guards (*bhāṇḍanārambhodbhaṭabharīrapeṭaka-pakṣarakṣāsāram*). The most important point to establish the character of this *peṇṭhā* as a centre of trade is its epithet *puṭabhedinī.*[16] The term *puṭabhedana* or *puṭabhedinī* literally denotes a place where lids of boxes (of merchandise) were broken (i.e. opened). It would therefore refer to a stockade with warehousing or storage facility,[17] a point which is highlighted in the account of the *peṇṭhāsthāna* in the *Yaśastilakacampu.* Śrībhuti, according to this text, let out spaces to merchants for storage, display and sale of their commodities and established the system of collecting tolls, shares and rent at a moderate rate (*praśāntaśulka-bhāgahāravyavahāramacikarat*).

A similar type of trade centre, but with a slightly different designation *piṇṭhā*, figures in another work of Somadevasuri. Somadevasuri is credited with composing a theoretical treatise on polity, named *Nītivākyāmṛtam*, which closely follows the model of the *Arthaśāstra*, albeit in an abridged form. In this text Somadevasuri explains *piṇṭhā* as a *paṇyapuṭabhedinī*, which is obviously the same as *puṭabhedana*. Here one can easily discern that Somadeva was rooted to the *Arthaśāstra* tradition. By preferring the term *paṇyapuṭabhedana* to *puṭabhedana*, found in the pre-Mauryan Pāli canonical text, *Mahāparinivvāṇasuttanata*, Kauṭilya probably tried to underline particularly the commercial character of the *puṭabhedana*. Somadevasuri too describes the *peṇṭhā/piṇṭhā* as *paṇyapuṭabhedinī*. The *piṇṭhā* is further considered by Somadevasuri as a trade centre which generates tolls and customs (*śulkasthāna*). The *peṇṭhā* or *piṇṭhā* of Somadevasuri, more or less the same as a *peṭha*, thus combines trade and administrative functions. The *Nītivākyamṛtam* lays down that the *piṇṭhā*, if judiciously and righteously maintained, would be a wish-fulfilling cow for the ruler (*nyāyena rakṣitā puṭabhedinī piṇṭhā rajñāṁ kāmadhenu*).[18] This, in other words, points to the considerable revenue-bearing potential of this trade centre and that is why Somadevasuri highlights its importance to the ruler. A major difference between the accounts of the two texts of Somadevasuri lies in that the *peṇṭhā* in the *Yaśastilakacampu* was owned by the minister himself, while in the *Nītivākyāmṛtam* it is viewed as being under the jurisdiction of the king.

The possibilities of commercial transactions at the *peṇṭhā/piṇṭhā* are therefore beyond any doubt. By placing it in the category of *puṭabhedana*, the author clearly underlines the regularity of trade there; the literary image of trade is far from that of periodic nature.[19] It is quite different from weekly rural market places and seasonal fairs. Somadevasuri, however, does not call it a city or town (*nagara/pura*). In fact, his recommendation on *piṇṭhā* in the *Nītivākyāmṛtam* figures in the *Janapadasamuddeśa* (concerning countryside) section and not in the *Durgasamuddeśa* (concerning fortified urban settlement) section. Śrībhuti, the cunning minister in the *Yaśastilakacampu*, is said to have driven away from his newly established *peṇṭhā* jesters, wrestlers, dice-players and other kinds of entertainers. Once again one may underline Somadeva's drawing from the Kauṭliyan dictum on the creation of a new settlement. According to the *Arthaśāstra*, the ruler should not allow any kind of entertainers in the newly created settlement as they are branded as a distraction from and detrimental to wealth-producing activities (*karmavighna*) of the new settlers. This does not, however, mean that an attempt is made here to fall back on the *Arthaśāstra* to trace the origin of the *peṭha/peṇṭhā*. What is underlined here is the conscious borrowing of some ideas of the *Arthaśāstra* by a tenth century Deccanese litterateur in his descriptions of a *peṁṭhā/piṇṭhā*. It is difficult to agree with both K.K. Handiqui and V.K. Jain that the *peṇṭhā* of Somadevasuri denoted a fair. Somadevasuri's perceptions of *peṇṭhā/peṭha* are strongly related to the regularity of commerce there. The fair is principally featured by its periodic and /or seasonal-festival character as a market place, an image which is not conveyed by the *Yaśastila-campu*. By enumerating the fortification (*prākāra*), rampart (*vapra*) and moat (*parikhā*) as components of the market place of the *peṇṭhā*, Somadevasuri in fact renders it with a near urban look. Somadevasuri keeps us in the dark about the nature of commodities brought to the *peṇṭhā* for transactions. The commentary on the *Nītivākyāmṛtam*, though later in date, enlists *kuṁkuma*, *hiṅgu* (asafoetida) and textiles (*vastra*) as goods, the containers of which were unsealed at the *peṇṭhā-puṭabhedinī* (*paṇyānāṁ vaṇigjanānāṁ kuṁkuma-hiṅguvastrādinī krayānakāni teṣām puṭaḥ sthānāni bhindyate yasyāṁ sā puṭabhedinī*). The impression conveyed is that exchangeable agricultural products in bulk and other daily necessities were mostly brought at the *peṇṭhā*. The *peṇṭhā/peṭha*, standing above individual villages as a supra-local centre for trade and administration, could have acted as a nodal point among surrounding and neighbouring villages.

It is difficult to present an unbroken chain of references to *peṇṭhās* in the sources of the Deccan after the tenth century. However, in the inscriptions of the Kākatīyas of Warangal, the most formidable regional power in the Eastern Deccan during the thirteenth and fourteenth centuries, we come across *peṁṭas*, which are certainly the same as the *peṇṭhā* and *piṇṭhā* of Somadevasuri. Inscriptions speak of different types of trade centres like *aḍḍa*, *santhe* and *peṁṭa*. These terms and their relation vis-a-vis the *peṁṭa/peṇṭhā* require a careful scrutiny. The word *aḍḍa* is the same as *haṭṭa* in Sanskrit, generally denoting a village-level market centre. Such a market place in rural areas usually took place on a particular day or days of a week. The term *santhe* stands for a fair, which could have been organized during a particular season or on the occasion of some festivities. It closely corresponds to what is called *yātrā*[20] in north Indian sources. The trade at *santhe* could also be earmarked for a certain day of the week; that is why, terms like a Wednesday-fair (Budhavāra-santhe), Saturday-fair (Śaṇivāra-santhe) are commonly come across in inscriptions of the Deccan from *c.* AD 1000 onwards. The point to take note of is that our sources clearly distinguished *santhes* and *aḍḍas* from *peṁṭas* (i.e. *peṇṭhā* or *peṭha*).[21] The principal distinctiveness of the *peṁṭa/peṇṭhā* lies in their being a centre of regular and daily transactions, vis-a-vis the periodic nature of exchanges taking place in *santhes* and *aḍḍas*. Moreover, while references to *aḍḍas* are mostly associated with individual villages, the *peṁṭa* is generally located at a nodal point of a supra-local character.

This helps us appreciate the description of a *peṁṭa*, according to a Kākatīya record, being located in a very large village. Such a village in all likelihood was little different from Naḍḍula in Rajasthan which, because of its being a node among twelve surrounding villages, transformed from a village to a *maṇḍapikā*. The *peṁṭa* in the Kākatīya records yielded *peṁṭasuṅka*. *Suṅka* is the same as *śulka* or tolls and customs. We may recall that Somadevasuri was fully aware of a *peṇṭhā* being a *puṭabhedana* and a *śulkasthāna* as well. Such *peṁṭasuṅkas* were often collected by *mānyagaṁḍaru* or tax farmers. These general comments on *peṁṭas* in Kākatīya inscriptions help us take a close look at two specific instances.

During the time of Gaṇapati (1199-1261), the most powerful ruler of this family, a few *peṁṭas* were located in Warangal. The Warangal fort inscription of Gaṇapati (1249) speaks of three such *peṁṭas*. Āku-*peṁṭa* was noted for the presence of the Sasirbaru group of merchants who dealt in betel leaves, coconuts, mangoes and tamarind. The second one was known as Nuvula-*peṁṭa* and there the Sasirbaru group of merchants and the Svadeśī-Paradeśī group of traders are said to have participated in the transactions of wheat, paddy, gram, millet and edible oil. Trade in salt took place at the third one, Uppu-*peṁṭa* (*uppu*=salt). The inscription conveys the message that the *peṁṭas* were marked by transactions in bulk commodities and daily necessities, including agricultural products.

About six decades later, another *peṁṭa* figures in the Koccherlakota inscription of AD 1310. In this *peṁṭa* there were thatched sheds (*pāṁkas*) where merchants could keep their merchandise temporarily against the payment of a rent in cash (1 *gadyanaka*). Commodities stored in *pāṁkas* could be displayed at the time of transactions at the market yard; this required the merchant to pay another *gadyanaka* coin. In other words, the Kākatīya administration levied separate charges for letting out spaces in the storage area and also for the market-yard where items were taken from sheds. Further, there were also shops (*aṁgāḍis*) where the presence of the Bacchus and Kommati merchant groups have been noted. A levy, called *aṁgāḍi-mudrā-suṁka*, was imposed for registering articles which were to be taken into *aṁgāḍis* or shops, probably from the thatched storage spaces (*pāṁkas*).[22] One cannot fail to note the close correspondence between the tenth century textual account of a *peṇṭhā* and the epigraphic images of the *peṁṭa* in the Kākatīya realm. The features of the *peṇṭhā* in the narratives of Somadevasuri seem to have matured in the twelfth and thirteenth centuries.

IV

The far south, located to the south of the river Krishna, seems to offer another regional type of locality level trade centres. Neither the *maṇḍapikā* nor the *peṇṭhā* appears in the inscriptions of the Pallavas and the Coḷas (especially those of the Coḷas, the most formidable regional power in the far south from *c.* 985 to 1150).[23] The far south presents a scenario of inland commerce in which a new centre, *nagaram*—rarely appearing before the eighth century—gains considerable prominence. Our understanding of the *nagaram* as a locality level centre is enriched by the in-depth empirical research of Hall.[24] The wealth of data from profuse number of Coḷa inscriptions is effectively utilized by Hall to argue his case. He has enlisted as many as 93 *nagarams*, widely distributed over different parts of the extensive Coḷa realm. The *nagaram* of the far south is not the same as the Sanskrit *nagara* or city. Instead, the *nagaram*, in his estimation, is both an administrative centre and at the same time the commercial centre of a *nāḍu*. Drawing largely from the quantifiable epigraphic data presented by Subbarayalu and also the theoretical perspectives of a segmented polity, formulated by Burton Stein, Hall views the *nāḍu* as an autonomous locality level unit.[25] The *nāḍu* stands above and incorporates several villages. Thus the *nāḍu* is perceived as an agglomeration of several villages. The role of the *nāḍu* in the integration of the agrarian order in the Coḷa realm, which like other regions of India also experienced expansion of sedentary agricultural settlements, is particularly stressed by Stein who argues for a brāhmaṇa-peasant voluntary alliance that consolidated the organization of *nāḍu*.

The *nagaram* is clearly distinguished in the Coḷa records from a *brahmadeya* (villages granted to brāhmaṇas) and an *ur* (a village with non-brāhmaṇa residents). *Nāḍus* with their *naṭṭar* assemblies are considered the real foci of the Coḷa political organization. The autonomy of the *nāḍu* became so pronounced and effective that it could, according to Stein, check the penetration of the Coḷa monarchy into the locality level. Firmly entrenched in the idea of the autonomy of the *nāḍu*, Hall further incorporates the model of Skinner to understand the hierarchy of market places in south India. This has led him to consider the *nagaram* as the administrative centre and also the commercial centre of the *nāḍu*. The principal point of interest here is the image of the *nagaram* as a supra-village level market centre.

The *nagaram* as a market place appears to have within its space a bazaar (*kaḍai*), permanent shops (*aṁgāḍi*) and even stables and stalls for elephants and horses. The members of the *nagaram* assembly were entrusted with the collection of levies from shops (*aṁgāḍikuli/ aṁgāḍippaṭṭam*) and bazaars (*kaḍaippaṭṭam*). An inscription from Tanjavur, the very core area of the Coḷas, informs that local *nagaram* assembly levied taxes on flowers, dry crops, areca nuts, betel leaves, saffron, ginger, sugar cane, salt and goldsmith's produce sold at the *nagaram*. Like the *maṇḍapikās* and *peṇṭhās*, the *nagaram* in south India is also noted for the impressive range and commodities transacted at this supra-local trade centre. Information is available in the Coḷa inscriptions about the inspection of commodities entering the *nagaram's* market place, supervision by clerks (*karaṇam*), regulation of weights and measures and fine imposed on adulteration. Strongly clinging to the notion of the autonomy of both the *nāḍu* and the *nagaram*, Hall argues that the *nagaram* had an effective organization of merchants and precluded the easy penetration of non-local and itinerant merchants into the market place of the *nagaram*. He, therefore, postulates a *nāḍu-nagaram* collaboration with a view to exercising control over their locality and hindering the access of itinerant and foreign traders into rural areas included within the *nāḍu*.

There are other dimensions of the *nagaram* as a supra-local centre of trade. Besides the intra-*nāḍu* exchanges, Hall upholds the possibilities also of the inter-*nāḍu* trade. The interlinkages among different *nagarams* in different *nāḍus*, as proposed by Hall, could pave the way for the horizontal spread of trade. Above the *nagarams* were placed ports (*paṭṭinam/paṭṭanam*), located in or near the seacoast and larger market places at extensive urban centres (*erivīrapaṭṭinam/ mānagaram*). These ports and urban market places occupied the highest tier in the hierarchy of markets in the far south under the Coḷas. The exchange centres in individual villages can be conveniently placed in the basic and lowest tier of this structure. The *nagaram*, according to Hall, thus performed the crucial role of the intermediate stage between the rural markets deep in the interior villages and the celebrated urban markets and ports at the top. At the *nagaram* converged agricultural produce and bulk items from the adjacent rural hinterland; the *nagaram* also helped the supply of local produces and manufactured items to ports and more important (as well as larger) urban markets. From these larger markets precious commodities like gold and goods and services could have reached the middle tier of the *nagaram*, which would help some of those commodities reach the smallest and farthest exchange centres in villages in the interior. The *nagaram*, according to Hall, serves a series of local villages by providing them with a vital linkage with the upper levels of a market hierarchy. The role of the *nagaram* as a middle-tier centre of trade, offering commercial linkages between distant rural hinterlands and large urban markets and ports, is highlighted to such a degree by Hall that he strongly argues for the existence of one *nagaram* per *nāḍu* in the Coḷa kingdom.[26]

The insistence of Hall on the 1:1 ratio of the *nāḍu* vis-a-vis the *nagaram* in the Coḷa realm, however, has been sharply criticized. It has been rightly pointed out that Subbarayalu's study reveals the existence of 112 *nāḍus* (excluding 114 *nāḍuvil-nāḍus*, which would give a total of 226) in Coḷamaṇḍalam itself, the very core area of the Coḷa kingdom. The present districts of Tiruchirappalli, Pudukoṭṭai and Tanjavur embracing Coḷamaṇḍalam area, have yielded for Hall 9, 6 and 24 epigraphic references to *nagarams* respectively. Thus the total number of *nagarams*, in Hall's counting, is a mere 39 against the recorded existence of 112 *nāḍus* (if not 226) in Coḷamaṇḍalam. If the assumed ratio of 1:1 for the *nāḍu* and its *nagaram* does not hold water even in the very core area of the Coḷa state, doubts have been raised about its applicability in the intermediate areas like Toṇḍaimaṇḍalam and Pāṇḍimaṇḍalam and peripheral zones like Koṅgumaṇḍalam in the Coḷa realm.[27] In fact the formulation of the segmented nature of the Coḷa polity, the pivotal feature of which is the 'autonomous' *nāḍu*, has been effectively debated on empirical and conceptual grounds.[28] The important role of the non-local and itinerant merchants in the development of local and supra-local trade in the far south has been ably highlighted in recent literature.[29] That would once again raise some reservations about Hall's portrayal of the *nagaram* as an effective check against the infiltration of non-local merchants in the *nāḍu*-level trade. In spite of several limitations in the perspectives, methods and conclusions of Hall, his presentation of rich epigraphic material on trade in the Coḷa time has certainly established *nagarams* as centres of supra-local trade, as vantage nodes providing opportunities of intra-*nāḍu* and inter-*nāḍu* trade and as middle-tier centres of exchange linking rural market places with *mānagarams*, *erivīrapaṭṭinam* and *paṭṭinams*.

The foregoing pages attempt to examine the possibilities and the nature of the linkages of trade, spanning over seven centuries. The *maṇḍapikā*, the *peṇṭhā/peṭha* and the *nagaram* as nodes of commerce have distinct regional features. This is seen in their respective zones of spatial distributions. It is true that the *nagaram* as a middle category centre of exchange did not continue to figure prominently in sources after the fifteenth century. In fact the term *peṭh*, which is still commonly seen as a name-ending to many inland trade centres in the Deccan, is also encountered in the Tamil area. The *peṇṭhā* (=*peṭh*) assumes the form of *veṇṭha* in several inscriptions of the Vijayanagar empire.[30] A Vijayanagar inscription of fifteenth century speaks of a *saṁte-peṭe,*[31] showing that the centre of exchange was a combination of a *saṁte* (fair) and *peṭha* (regular market). In other words, the term may suggest the gradual transformation of a *santhe* into a *peṭha*; or it might also suggest that the centre was in the stage of transition from *santhe* to *peṭe*. Another Vijayanagar inscription of 1554 from Holalkere taluq in Karnataka records the restoration of an old *peṭha*. Narasiṁhaiya of the customs or *suṅka* (probably an officer in charge of the collection of *suṅka)* took note of the *peṭha* in Bagur-sime being in ruins; he made a petition to Viṭhana-nāyaka, the administrator of the locality, who 'directed to have the *peṭhe* rebuilt, giving it another name of Kṛṣṇapura after Era-Kṛṣṇāppā-Nāyakkya and populate it. Those who settle here will be free of all taxes for one year from the time they come; after that they will not only be included in the family agreement, but if they had taken possession, we and the subjects will give up our claim'.[32]

The process continues even in the late eighteenth century Coromandel.

A recent study enlightens us how new *peṭhas* like Nyenda Petta (160 km from Chennai, receiving cotton from the hinterland and then sending the same to ports in the Nellore district), Lalapet (96 km from Chennai) and more significantly Wallajahpet (109 km from Chennai) came into prominence. Nyenda Petta was an important receiving centre of cotton grown 400 km north-west of Chennai. The cotton was then sent from Nyenda Petta to the ports lying between Armagaon and Carera ports in the Nellore district; the cotton was meant largely for the market in Bengal. Lalapet too was a *peṭha* known for having linkages with the rural areas producing cotton yarns. The price cotton yarns fetched at Lalapet ranged from 1,20,000 to 1,50,000 *pagodas* annually. Cotton yarns brought to Lalapet then reached all the weaving centres in the northern Coromandel coast. Once again the image of the *peṭha* as an intermeditae trade centre between villages and the coastal areas is highlighted here. Founded by Rayoji, minister of Nawab Muhammad Ali Walajah, Wallajahpet was an outstanding trade centre. One of the busiest of marts, Wallajahpet had eighteen *peṭṭas* or squares which had convenient shops surrounding a small temple at the centre of this commercial town. It was initially exempted by Rayoji from taxes to induce merchants of neighbouring *peṭhas* to flock at Wallajahpet. Wallajahpeth was especially famous in the eighteenth century for bulk trade in grains and cotton with Madras, Mysore and ceded districts. It is not surprising why Buchanan was so impressed with its commerce. All these *peṭhas* were instrumental in providing the crucial linkages between the Coromandel coast and its hinterland.[33] A more or less similar pattern is also discernible in the continuous spread, development and proliferation of *maṇḍis* in north India during the early modern times, especially the eighteenth century. North India also witnessed the emergence of *qasbas* to prominence as commercial suburbs of large urban centres.[34]

One may venture here to suggest that the centuries after 1300 probably mark the phase of maturity and consolidation of the middle category centres of trade both in north India and the trans-Vindhyan India, where the beginnings of the process are located around AD 600. The *maṇḍapikā*, the *penṭhā* and the *nagaram* were certainly rooted to their respective regions and endowed with regional features. Their emergence cannot be explained in terms of a crisis in 'early medieval' society, economy and polity. On the other hand, their significance is to be appreciated in terms of local formations. All such centres were largely facilitated by the remarkable expansion of agriculture, the resultant availability of exchangeable grains and cash crops and the emergence of local and regional powers which could exploit their local-level resource bases. Another common feature of these centres can be seen in the transactions in daily necessities and agricultural products. In spite of their pronounced regional features, the *maṇḍapikā*, the *peṇṭhā* and the *nagaram* appear to have shared certain common traits spanning across regions and centuries. They were mostly situated at important nodes where breaking the bulk was possible; this is especially conveyed by the epithet *puṭabhedana* or *paṇyapuṭabhedinī* associated with *peṇṭhāsthāna* in Somadevasuri's works. Some of these supra-local centres also assumed urban features. In the study of urbanization of pre-modern India scholarly attention is perhaps excessively focused on very large cities, premier ports towns and politico-administrative headquarters—which Braudel labelled as 'Sun cities'. He also underlined the fact that urban centres often form hierarchies and the tip of the urban pyramid, however significant, does not always throw light on other tiers of the urban hierarchy.[35] It is to address this issue that the present exercise has been made.

NOTES

1. Differing and divergent perceptions of the period *c.* AD 600-1300 have resulted in debates which have indeed enriched Indian historiography. Burton Stein considered these debates as among the 'stunning developments' of Indian historiography. See Burton Stein, 'A Decade of Historical Efflorescence', in *South Asia Research*, vol. X, no. 2. Niharranjan Ray, 'Medieval Factors in Indian History', General President's Address, in *PIHC*, Patiala session, 1967, locates significant changes and the beginnings of regional features in Indian society and cultural life from *c.* AD fourth century onwards. The Marxist perspectives of these centuries revolve around the concept of Indian feudalism. Kosambi, *Introduction*; Sharma, *Indian Feudalism*; Yadava, *Society and Culture in North India*; D.N. Jha, ed., *Feudal Social Formations in Early India.* For a critique of the 'decline syndrome' in the historiography of Indian feudalism see Chattopadhyaya, *The Making of Early Medieval India* (Chattopadhyaya has elaborated on the 'decline syndrome' in a recently delivered, but yet unpublished, lecture in the Department of History, University of Calcutta). Also see R. Champakalakshmi, 'State and Economy in South India: 400-1300'; and B.D. Chattopadhyaya, 'State and Economy in North India: Fourth to Twelfth Century', in Thapar, ed., *Recent Perspectives of Early Indian History*, Bombay, 1995, pp. 266-308. The discussions on the formation of local and regional powers in different parts of India as an outcome of 'integrative polity' are available in Hermann Kulke, ed., *The State in India 1000-1700*, New Delhi, 1994. A recent statement has also been made by Ranabir Chakravarti, 'Politics and Society in India (AD 300-1000)',

in K. Satchidananda Murty, ed., *Life, Thought and Culture in India (AD 300-1000)*, vol. II, pt. 1, pp. 58-171. A large number of historians designate this period as 'early medieval', suggesting thereby that this phase is to be located between the 'early historical' or 'ancient' and the 'medieval' phases of Indian history. Romila Thapar, 'The Tyranny of Labels', in *Social Scientist*, vol. XXIV, Sept.-Oct. 1996, analyses the problems of the naming of different chronological segments. Kesavan Veluthat, 'Into the Medieval and Out of It', Presidential Address, *PIHC*, sec. II, Bangalore session, 1995 strongly argues against clinging to the European tripartite division of historical studies (ancient, medieval and modern) in the context of the study of non-European (including Indian) history.

2. See Chattopadhyaya, *The Making of Early Medieval India*; also idem, 'The State and Economy in North India'. D.C. Sircar, *Indian Epigraphy*, New Delhi, 1965 provides lengthy discussions on the creation of revenue-free settlements of different types.
3. B.D. Chattopadhyaya, *Aspects of Rural Settlements and Rural Society*; the much cherished notion that Indian villages were self-sufficient and closed and hence bereft of changes and linkages is strongly questioned nowadays.
4. Chakravarti, 'Merchants of Konkan'; idem, 'Merchants and Other Donors at Ancient Bandhogarh', included in this volume.
5. An overview of the situation prior to AD sixth century is presented by Ranabir Chakravarti, ed., *Trade in Early India*, especially the Introduction.
6. A.L. Udovitch, 'Commercial Techniques in the Medieval Islam', in D.S. Richard, ed., *Islam and the Trade of Asia*, Pennsylvania, 1970, pp. 37-62.
7. Chattopadhyaya, *The Making of Early Medieval India*, uses this expression to characterize the debates on early medieval India, borrowing the term from Partha Mitter's book, *Much Maligned Monsters*.
8. J.F. Fleet, *CII*, vol. III, pp. 115ff for the inscription of 529 and pp. 135-9 for the inscription of 533.
9. This will be evident from the use of the Gupta era (beginning from *c.* AD 319-20) in the two copper plates.
10. This area of central India, acting almost like a corridor between the Ganga and the Narmada valleys and the Vindhyan region, has been well known for the existence of forest tracts. Aśoka was well aware of the Āṭavikas who were actually cautioned by the Maurya emperor in his Rock Edict XIII. See R.G. Basak, *Asokan Edicts*, Calcutta, 1959. The Āṭavikarājas were reduced to servitude by Samudragupta (*paricarakīkṛtasarvāṭavikarāja*), probably sometime after his uprooting the north Indian rulers and before his famous Dakṣiṇāpatha campaign (Fleet, *CII*, vol. III).
11. *IA*, vol. XV, pp. 187-8.
12. *IA*, vol. VI, p. 12.
13. Abhimanyu's ancestors are mentioned in the record, viz. (i) Mānaṅka, the ornament of the Rāṣṭrakūṭas (*aneka-guṇa-gaṇālaṁkṛta-yaśasāṁ*

Rāṣṭrakuṭānāṁ tilaka-bhūto Mānaṇka itirāja)—as the great grandfather, (ii) Devarāja—grandfather, and (iii) Bhaviṣya—father. The genealogy clearly differentiates him from the line of the Rāṣṭrakūṭa kings of Mānykheṭa.

14. *EI*, vol. VIII, pp. 163-6. Paṅgāra is identified with Pagara, 4 miles from Panchmarhi, Satara district, Maharashtra.
15. Sivadatta and Parab, eds., *Yaśastilakacampu*. The Rāṣṭrakūṭa ruler's presence in the Toṇḍaimaṇḍalam area of the Coḷa kingdom is explained by Kṛṣṇa III's major military success against the Coḷa king Parāntaka I (907-55) in the battle of Takkolam in AD 949. See G. Yazdani, ed., *Early History of the Deccan*, vol. I, London, 1960 especially the chapter on the Rāṣṭrakūṭas by A.S. Altekar.
16. The description of the *peṇṭhāsthāna* is found in the *Yaśastilakacampu*, Book VII, sec. 27.
17. Chakravarti, 'The Puṭabhedana as a Centre of Trade in Early India', in this volume.
18. Sastri, ed. and tr., *Nītivākyāmṛtam*, see verse 19.21.
19. Handiqui, *Yaśastilaka and Indian Culture*, pp. 119-20; Jain, *Trade and Traders* maintains that the *peṇṭhā* was a fair or an exchange centre of periodic/seasonal nature. This is a position difficult to accept in the light of our analysis of the *Yaśastilakacampu*.
20. See note 11.
21. A. Appadurai, *Economic Conditions in Southern India 1000-1500*, vol. I, Madras 1936; G.R. Kuppuswamy, *Economic Conditions in Karnataka AD 973-1336*, Dharwar, 1975.
22. The references to *peṁṭas* and *peṁṭasuṅkas* in Kākatīya inscriptions are mainly drawn from Parabrahma Sastry, *The Kākatīyas of Warangal*, pp. 449ff. Parabrahma Sastry, however, does not offer any substantial analysis of the epigraphic data on *peṁṭas*, as his principal interest lies in presenting a conventional dynastic narrative.
23. For a general overview of the political organization and economic conditions in the Coḷa empire, see Nilakanta Sastri, *The Coḷas*.
24. K.R. Hall, *Trade and Statecraft in the Age of the Coḷas*. Our foregoing study of the *nagarams* in the Coḷa inscriptions is largely based on Hall.
25. Y. Subbarayalu, *The Political Geography of the Coḷa Country*, Madras, 1973; Burton Stein, *Peasant State and Society in Medieval South India*, New Delhi, 1980. Stein based himself heavily on the study of the numerical distribution of *nāḍus* made by Subbarayalu. Stein attempts to provide an alternative to the conventional historiography of the Coḷa state which is considered to have combined two dissimilar systems, the centralized, almost Byzantine, monarchy of the Coḷas and the local-self bodies at the rural and locality levels. Sein and his followers consider the *nāḍus* as the peasant macro region and the real foci of the Coḷa state, which was not marked by political integration. The Coḷa ruler's effective political control is assumed to have been limited only to the core area of the Coḷas who had little

bureaucratic organization, neither a standing army nor a sound resource base. Borrowing from the African model of the Alur society (A. Southall, *The Alur Society*, Cambridge, 1956), Stein proposed that the Coḷa state consisted of a loose assemblage of segments. Coḷa political control would fade, according to him, as one went from the core area of the Coḷa state to the intermediate and peripheral areas. The Coḷa polity is therefore seen by him as a segmented polity, opposed to a centralized state system.

26. Hall, *Trade and Statecraft*, is influenced in his formulation of the hierarchical structure of the market centres in the Coḷa kingdom by G. William Skinner, *Marketing and Social Structure in Rural China*.
27. B.D. Chattopadhyaya's review of Hall's *Trade and Statecraft*, in *IHR*, vol. X, 1984, pp. 186-9.
28. Kulke, ed., *The State in India*, Editor's Introduction and the Annotated Bibliography; B.D. Chattopadhyaya, 'Political Processes and Structures of Polity in Early Medieval India: Problems of Perspective', Presidential Address, *PIHC*, sec. I, Burdwan session, 1983, incorporated also in Kulke, ed., *The State in India*; R. Champakalakshmi, 'Peasant State and Society in Medieval South India: A Review Article', *IESHR*, vol. XVIII, 1981, pp. 411-26; Hermann Kulke, 'Fragmentation and Segmentation versus Integration? Reflections on the Concepts of Indian Feudalism and Segmentary State in Indian History', *SH*, vol. 4, 1982, pp. 237-63; R.S. Sharma, 'The Segmentary State and the Indian Experience', *IHR*, vol. XVI, 1990, pp. 80-108; Kesavan Veluthat, *The Political Structure of Early Medieval South India*, Delhi, 1993.
29. Meera Abraham, *Two Medieval Merchant Guilds of South India*, New Delhi 1988; R. Champakalakshmi, *Trade, Ideology and Urbanization in South India*.
30. The term *veṇtha* occurs in two inscriptions from Harihar, respectively of AD 1354 (*Journal of the Bombay Branch of the Royal Asiatic Society*, vol. XII, p. 347) and AD 1538 (*IA*, vol. IV, p. 331).
31. *Annual Report of Indian Epigraphy, 1918-19*, Inscription no. 223 of 1918.
32. *EC*, vol. XI, Holalkere Taluq, pp. 131-2; Inscription no. 112.
33. Bhaswati Bhattacharyya, 'The Hinterland and the Coast: The Pattern of Interaction in Coromandel in the Late Eighteenth Century', in Rudrangshu Mukherjee and Lakshmi Subramanyan, eds., *Politics and Trade in the Indian Ocean World: Essays in Honour of Ashin Das Gupta*, New Delhi, 1998, pp. 19-51.
34. B.R. Grover, 'An Integrated Pattern of Commercial Life in Rural Society of North India during the Late Seventeenth and Early Eighteenth Centuries', in Sanjay Subrahmanyam, ed., *Money and Market in India 1100-1700*, New Delhi, 1990, pp. 219-55.
35. Braudel, *The Structures of Everyday Life*, pp. 482-3.

CHAPTER 11

Nakhuda Nuruddin Firuz at Somanātha: AD 1264

Our previous discussions on maritime trade and voyages in ancient and early medieval Bengal attempt at situating the affairs of the Bay of Bengal in the broader background of the Indian Ocean commercial network. This essay once again is related to maritime trade, but takes the reader to western India, to the celebrated cultural centre, Somanātha, in Kathiawad in the western littoral of India. If one looks at the major issues addressed by historians of early Indian trade and maritime commerce, they generally revolve around commodities of exports and imports, routes of communications, monetary situations and ports and marts. But merchants and more specifically maritime merchants, who were the real participants in such transactions, are often conspicuous by their absence in the historiography of early Indian trade. The merchant in early India, especially the maritime merchant, is often a faceless figure, as he is rarely accorded a high ritual status in the traditional *śāstras* and only occasionally a central figure in a biographical tale (e.g. the *Jagaḍucarita*). More often than not the merchant is branded as a open thief (*prakāśya taskara*) by the law giver; yet the law book, on the contrary, considers commerce as the abode of the goddess of fortune (*vāṇijye vasate lakṣmī*). Our understanding of early Indian merchants is further dimmed by the frequent use of a blanket term like 'merchant' or 'trader' to denote all men engaged in trade. Early Indian sources, on the other hand, appear to have made clear distinctions among different categories of merchants, ranging from petty dealers (*vaidehaka/vaṇik*), pedlars (*banjaras*), caravan traders (*sārthavāhas*) and very rich merchants (*śresṭhīs*).[1] These preliminaries may help us appreciate the activities and position of a distinct type of merchants who appear in the commercial scenario of India around AD 1000 under the category *nauvittaka* in Indian sources and as *nakhuda/nakhoda* in Arabic and Persian accounts and business letters of medieval Jewish traders. While the term *nauvittaka* can be explained as one whose wealth (*vitta*) lies in his (possessing) ships or *nau*,[2] the word *nakhuda* denotes the lord (*khuda*) of the ship/vessel (*nau*). The term *nakhuda* also appears as *nawakhidh*. Both the terms would mean ship-owning merchants. As we have said before, the regular presence of *nakhudas* and *nauvittakas* is clearly indicated in the western littorals of India. Similar ship-owners must have been there in the eastern littoral too, but as yet they are not revealed to us from early sources.

The western seaboard of India has three major segments: (a) the Kathiawad-Gujarat coast, (b) the Konkan coast and (c) the Malabar coast. The first half of the second millennium is known for a remarkable spurt of both long-distance and coastal voyages in the western seaboard of India.[3] The Arabic, Persian and Chinese texts and the accounts of Marco Polo enlighten us on the importance of the west coast of India, dotted with numerous ports of varying importance, which became particularly integrated to the maritime network of the western Indian Ocean. The linkages of the western seaboard of India with the Red Sea and the Persian Gulf areas are unmistakable in these documentation. It is true that these sources were not commercial documents and often suffer from stereotypical and repetitive descriptions of the ports and harbours of the west coast of India. In many cases the authors of such accounts never actually visited the coast and wrote on the basis of earlier accounts, experience of sailors and merchants and the existing geographical knowledge of India in the Arab world. The Jewish business letters, on the other hand, speak of actual transactions in which Jewish merchants of the category of 'India traders' (an expression coined by S.D. Goitein) participated. These Jewish merchants maintained a brisk trading network from Alexandria, al-Fustat (Old Cairo) to Aden at the mouth of the Red Sea and finally the Malabar coast in India. The recipient of the largest number of such business letters in India was Abraham Yishu. Hailing originally from al-Mahdiya (Tunisia), Abraham Yishu spent some time in al Fustat before he came to al Manjrur (i.e. Maṅgalapura, present Mangalore) and stayed at this important port town from 1132 to 1149. The correspondences of Abraham Yishu are replete with references to various types of shipments and it is in this context that *nakhudas* loom large in the *genizah* papers. In the *genizah* documents concerning 'India traders' the ship-owning merchant is invariably called *nakhuda*, but this term never occurs in the context of shipping in the Mediterranean. The Sanskrit term *nauvittaka* has close correspondence to the Perso-Arabic word, *nakhuda*. In fact the terms *nakhuda* and *nauvittaka* occur only in the context of the coastal society in the western seaboard of India. This does not mean that there were no ships and ship-owners outside the western seaboard and beyond the chronological segment of our present study. But the use of the terms *nakhuda* and *nauvittaka* is limited to the western seaboard of India. Both the terms, began to surface from AD 1000 onwards, implying thereby that they made their presence felt in the coastal society along the western seaboard of India as the second millennium entered its latter half. This, in its turn, would suggest greater integration of the west coast of India into the growing maritime trade network in the western Indian Ocean. The term *nakhuda* or *nakhoda* in recent times is used in the sense of the captain of a ship, rather than the owner of the vessel. It must be pointed out here that the term was undoubtedly used during the period of our study in the sense of a ship-owning merchant, and almost never in the sense of a captain or navigator of the vessel. The *nakhuda* in our sources is clearly differentiated from the *rubban* and the *muallim*.[4]

Of the three coastal segments in the western littorals, the Gujarat coast—including the coastal tracts of the Kathiawad peninsula—is of outstanding importance. Famous for its agricultural prosperity, Gujarat was noted for cotton plantation and indigo production which immensely contributed to its flourishing textile industries. Gujarat seems to have witnessed considerable growth in the production of oil-seed which was intimately associated with remarkable proliferation of oil-mills (*ghānakas*) particularly since AD 1000. The agricultural prosperity of Gujarat at the turn of the first millennium is attributed to the expansion of agriculture and better irrigation facilities around AD 1000.[5] To this has to be added the importance of the arrival of the Cālukya rulers whose rule of nearly three centuries contributed to the rise of Gujarat as a leading regional power in western India.[6] The long political presence of the Cālukyas not only resulted in the political integration of the greater parts of Gujarat, but paved the way for linkages between the coastal tracts and the extensive interior with a number of important overland routes too. These routes were used by troops, itinerant merchants and pilgrims alike. The stage was set for the spurt of urban centres in Gujarat from AD 900 onwards. It would be difficult to miss the importance of trade in the non-agrarian sector of the regional economy of Gujarat. Besides the overland routes of communication, Gujarat's coastline has been for long associated with a number of famous ports from remote antiquity. Southern Gujarat and the Kathiawad peninsula are endowed with suitable coastlines which are washed by the Arabian Sea, the Gulf of Cambay and the Gulf of Cutch which are dotted with a number of estuarine ports. Mention may be made of the Harappan port of Lothal[7] on the Mahi, the early historical port of Barygaza (Bhṛgukaccha of Indian traditon) on the mouth of the Narmada,[8] Stambhatīrtha/Stambhapura of Indian sources (Khambayat/Kanbaya in the Arabic and Persian accounts) or Cambay on the Sabarmati from *c.* 900 to the sixteenth century[9] and finally Surat on the Tapi (Tapti) during the seventeenth and eighteenth centuries.[10] This certainly impresses upon the remarkable continuity of Gujarat's seaborne commerce from the Harappan times to the first half of the eighteenth century. The other significant point about pre-modern ports of Gujarat is not merely their extensive hinterland, but their impressive foreland too. The sixteenth century account of Tome Pires did not fail to note that Cambay's two commercial arms reached out to Aden in the Red Sea and Malacca in the Malay peninsula.[11] In the flourishing conditions of these celebrated ports of Gujarat, however, there was a positive role of a number of relatively smaller and less prominent harbours which acted as feeder ports to their more salient counterparts. In the thirteenth century when Cambay stole the limelight among the Gujarati ports, there were two other ports in the Kathiawad littorals, viz., al-Dyyb (i.e. Diu of the sixteenth century when it looms large under the Portuguese in the affairs of the Indian Ocean)[12] and Somanātha. Our present essay focuses particularly on the last mentioned port.

It can hardly be denied that the historiography of India is more conversant with the sacred character of Somanātha, a celebrated centre of Śaiva pilgrimage, than with its role as a seaport. Variously called Somanāthapaṭṭana, Someśvarapaṭṭana and Devapaṭṭana in inscriptions and texts referring to it,[13] Somanātha was celebrated for its famous Śaiva temple in which was enshrined the Śiva lingam. The suffix *paṭṭana* is a clear indicator of its character as a port. Somanātha's prominence also lies in its being the primary symbol of the widespread looting, pillage and raids that played havoc in north and western India during the invasions of Sultan Mahmud of Ghazna (997-1026).[14] Al Biruni, the celebrated Arab scholar, was one of the early writers to have been aware of Somanātha's role as a port and also of the devastation Somanātha suffered in 1025 as a result of the Ghazanavid raid.

II

Al Biruni, apart from describing the plunder and desecration of the Śaiva temple of Somanātha, also gives his explanation of the prominence Somnath enjoyed. 'The reason why in particular Somnath has become so famous is that it was the harbour for seafaring people, and station for those who went to and fro between Sufala in the country of Zanz and China.'[15] The famous Śaiva pilgrimage in coastal Kathiawad was therefore well known for reasons other than being a sacred centre to a foreign scholar, as perceptive and observant as Al Biruni. The position of Somanātha as a harbour close to the coast is also portrayed in a late thirteenth century inscription. According to the Cintra *praśasti* (1287),[16] Somanāthapaṭṭana was situated at the confluence of the river Sarasvatī and the Arabian Sea (*Saravatīsāgarasamprayogavibhūṣita*). Al Biruni, however, is possibly the only author who spoke of such a widespread network of the maritime trade of Somanātha. Unsupported by other sources, it is difficult to take Al Biruni's statement at its face value at this moment. Al Biruni, also offers an unfavourable comment on the situation around the port of Somanātha which, according to his account, was much troubled by pirates of the Kathiawad coast. It is not impossible that piracy in Kathiawad coast precluded the fulfilment of the potentials of the port of Somanātha. The Ghaznavid raids also could have posed serious threats to the prosperity of the port.

Yet, the ferocity and fury of the Ghaznavid invasion did not finish off the importance of Somanātha. This is indicated not by documents from Somanātha but evidence coming from elsewhere. Somanātha as a celebrated Śaiva pilgrimage continued to figure regularly in royal inscriptions from the Deccan. The Kadamba ruler of Goa, Ṣaṣṭhadeva in an inscription of 1038 (i.e. only twelve years since the devastation of Somanātha by Mahmud) enlists the sacred centres he visited. Among these figure the names of Sthānaka (Thana, Thana district, Maharashtra) and Someśvara.[17] The journey to Thana and Someśvara was certainly undertaken by a coastal voyage, and that is why Ṣaṣṭhadeva was eulogized as one proficient in crossing the sea (*ambhonidhipāraga*). One encounters here an account of a long coastal voyage from Goa to Somanātha in the Kathiawad coast via Thana in the north Konkan coast. A similar voyage, but with a more elaborate narrative, appears in an inscription of 1125, issued during the reign of Cālukya Vikramāditya VI and his vassal Kadamba Jayakeśī. Jayakeśī's ancestor Caṭṭāyadeva, eulogized in the inscription as the Lord of the Ocean, set on a voyage from Gove (Goa) to Saurashtra in his own ships; his principal intention being the visit to the temple of Somanātha. Caṭṭāyadeva was further praised for having lowered the price of root camphor (*karpūra*) as it was favourite of the deity of Somanātha.[18] This account, spread over four verses, once again informs us about the coastal connections between Somanātha in Kathiawad and Goa in Konkan. The description of royal voyages between Goa and Somanātha seems to have been a regular facet of the court poetry in the Kadamba records of eleventh and twelfth centuries. We may here refer to an interesting variation to this theme. Another inscription of the Kadambas describing a royal voyage from Candrapura (a port to south of Goa and the same as Sindabur in Arab chronicles) to Somanātha narrates that King Guhalladeva started from Candrapura. But he suffered a shipwreck near Gopākapaṭṭana or Goa where he was rescued by Āliya of Tajiya descent (*tajiyavaṁśajaḥ āsit . . . Ālīyamākhyāya*). The name Āliya is surely a Sankritized form of the Arabic name Ali, while *tajiya* stands for a Tajik or Arab. Moreover, Āliya is given the epithet *nauvittakādhimāna*, i.e. a *nauvittaka* or a ship-owning merchant. The rescuing act by an Arab ship-owning merchant probably resulted in Āliya's grandson Saḍhaṇa being appointed as the vassal of Goa under the Kadambas as a reward. Saḍhana, a pious Muslim and belonging to the family of ship-owners, is further credited with establishing a *mijigiti* or a *masjid*, i.e. a mosque. The mosque was to be maintained by tolls and other dues collected at the port of Goa which was visited by vessels from Gurjjara (Gujarat), Saurashtra (Kathiawad peninsula), Lāṭa (southern Gujarat) and Konkan, etc.[19] The emergent image is the participatory role of the port of Somanātha in the coastal network in the western littoral spanning from Kathiawad to Malabar. The authors of these Kadamba inscriptions and their patrons leave a clear impression that even after the desecration and plunder of Somanātha by the Ghaznavid raid, the sacred centre and the port of Somanātha did not die down. One can read into these poetic descriptions the resilience of Somanātha since the second half of the eleventh century. The seaborne network of Somanātha in the eleventh and twelfth centuries is largely along the west coast, as far south as Goa, but not perhaps extending overseas into the western Indian Ocean as Al Biruni thought. Maybe the Ghaznavid raids and the corsairs' activities around Somanātha thwarted the potential of Somanātha as an impressive seaport in the eleventh century.

The second half of the thirteenth century, which is our principal focus here, suggests a changed scenario regarding Somanātha. Almost at the turn of the thirteenth century, the celebrated Venetian traveller Marco Polo commented that Somanātha was not only a place of great trade, but also that its inhabitants were not corsairs and lived by 'trade and industry as honest people ought'.[20] Somanātha could have been less troubled by pirates in the thirteenth century, possibly as a result of the effective rule of the Cālukyas of Gujarat since mid-eleventh century.

The *Prabandhacintāmaṇi* tells us about the concern of the Cavaḍa ruler Yogarāja at the rampant piracy at Somanātha. The Cālukya rule seems to have integrated the coastal areas of Somanātha with the hinterland in the interior by establishing a number of overland routes. Thus Cālukya Siddharāja is credited with building a road between capital Anahilapura (Patan, Gujarat) and Somanātha, connecting on its way Munjapura, Jhinjuvada, Viramgam, Wadhwan, Saela, Gondal, Jetpur, Vanthali. The celebrated Kashmiri author, Bilhana (the composer of *Vikramāṅka-devacarita*) travelled from Mathurā to Somanātha through Kānyakubja, Prayāga, Vārāṇasī, Dhārā and Anahilapura. If this account speaks of Somanātha's contacts, mostly pilgrimage-oriented, with north and central India, Bilhana's final destination to the Western Cālukya court in Karnataka impresses on Somanātha's overland connections with the Deccan too. As a premier sacred centre, Somanātha also yielded religious taxes to the ruling Cālukya dynasty in the twelfth and thirteenth centuries, if the *Prabandhacintāmaṇi's* testimony is accepted.[21]

III

The stage now seems ready for a more concentrated study of Somanātha in 1264 on the basis of a remarkable bilingual inscription in Sanskrit and Arabic. It speaks of the visit of Nakhuda/Nauvittaka Nuruddin Firuz to Somanātha in 1264. Both the versions have the same purport, i.e. recording the religious munificence by Nuruddin Firuz. Interestingly enough, the Sanskrit version is longer and more elaborate, while the Arabic one is shorter and synoptic. Though the donation is made by a Muslim the more exhaustive details of the patronage are offered in Sanskrit, possibly with a view to acquainting the local people of Somanātha with the contents of the record. The inscription carries four systems of reckonings: VS 1320, Valabhisaṁvat 945, Siṁhasaṁvat 151 and the twenty-seventh day of the month of Ramadan, AH 662—all corresponding to AD 1264 (the Sanskrit inscription was composed on 25 May, while the Arabic version was prepared on 23 July). The Sanskrit record was originally edited by Hultzsch and later an improved reading was prepared by D.C. Sircar; for our present discussion preference is for Sircar's readings.[22] The Arabic version was edited and translated by Z.A. Desai.[23] An unusual inscription, it offers very rich details of commerce, communities and cultural situation in this port city. The principal purport of the two versions is to inform the construction of a *masjid* or *mijigiti* by Nuruddin at Somanātha. For a better understanding of the situation at Somanātha the evidence of the bilingual inscription will be supplemented with another inscription of 1287, better known as the Cintra *praśasti*,[24] also throwing much light on Somanātha. In 1264 Somanātha was included within the realm of Cālukya ruler Vāghela Arjunadeva and in 1287 the ruler was Sarāṅgadeva. The point to note is that the visit of Nuruddin Firuz and his patronage for the *mijigiti* at Somanātha took place when Gujarat was very much under the control of the Hindu rulers.

The central figure of our narrative is Nuruddin Firuz, who appears in the Sanskrit version as Noradīna Piroja. We can immediately recall here the prevalent practice of Sanskritizing Muslim Arabic names in inscriptions from coastal western India. Nuruddin Firuz, according to both the versions of the 1264 inscription, was a ship-owning merchant (a *nauvittaka* in Sanskrit and *nakhuda* in Arabic) who came to Somanātha (Sumnat in Arabic) from the famous port of Hormuz at the opening of the Persian Gulf (*Hormujavelākula*; *velākula* = harbour/port) on some business (*kāryavaśāt*). Noradīna Piroja, the *nākhu* (obviously an abbreviation of the term *nakhuda*), was the son (*sūta*) of *nau* (an abbreviated form of Sanskrit *nauvittaka*) Ābubrāhima (i.e. Abu Ibrahim in Arabic), the *khojā* (= Arabic *khwaja*). The very epithet *khojā* or *khwaja* speaks of Abu Ibrahim as a very wealthy merchant. The terms *nauvittaka* and *nakhuda* used as epithets respectively of Noradīna and his father cannot but show them as ship-owners; in other words, Nuruddin Firuz was a hereditary ship-owning merchant. The eloquent introduction to Nuruddin in the Arabic version demands our attention: He was the 'great and respected chief (*sadr*), prince among ship-owners (*sultan-al-nawakhidh*) and king of kings of merchants (*malik ul-tujjar*)'. Two points should be underlined at this juncture: first, the two terms *nauvittaka* and *nakhuda* were used almost as synonyms in the coastal society of Somanātha, as the two terms were used as epithets of both Nuruddin and his father. The second point of note is the use of abbreviations of the two words, *nauvittaka* and *nakhuda*, respectively as *nau* and *nākhu*. This instance of using abbreviations of a Sanskrit and an Arabic/Persian word in an official Cālukya inscription strongly suggests the regular currency of the two interchangeable terms in coastal Gujarat to denote ship-owners. This in its turn would speak of the presence of ship-owners in and around different ports along the western coast of India.[25]

Although the exact purpose of Nakhuda Nuruddin Firuz's visit to Somanātha has not been specified in either of the versions, it is only likely that a ship-owning merchant of his stature travelled from Hormuz to Somanātha for some commercial venture. A few words on Hormuz, the centre of Nuruddin's trading activities, may not be out of place here. Noted as Harmozeia, Ormus and Ormuz in the Kirman province of Iran in the Classical accounts of the voyage of Nearchus, Hormuz began to figure as a port at the opening of the Persian Gulf from the Sasanid times. But its rise to prominence in the seaborne network of the Indian Ocean really became noticeable only from the late tenth century. The anonymous author of the *Hudud al Alam* (982) recognized its importance. Marco Polo, the celebrated Venetian traveller, came to Hormuz not once but twice, in 1272 and then two decades later in 1293. The other landmark in the glory of Hormuz was the visit there by the famous traveller ibn Battuta in early fourteenth century. It was also one of the prized ports of call during the great voyages of the Chinese admiral Cheng ho or Zeng he (1404-33). If Aden was the gateway into the Red Sea, Hormuz commanded a similar position in the Persian Gulf. The premier port in the Persian Gulf was Siraf up to the end of the tenth century; the decline of Siraf and the nearly simultaneous rise of the Red Sea as the major sealane in the western Indian Ocean seem to have reduced the importance of the Persian Gulf.[26] The rise of Hormuz as the leading port in the Persian Gulf once again shifted the focus to the Gulf; the importance of Hormuz was already noted in 1225 by Chau-ju Kua, the Chinese officer-in-charge of foreign trade.[27] The growing importance of Hormuz did not also fail to touch the Indian ports on the western littorals. While Arabic and Persian accounts occasionally refer to voyages between Hormuz and Kulam Mali or Quilon in Malabar and Kanbaya or Cambay the premier port in Guajart,[28] the inscription of 1264 amply bears it out that the shipping network of Hormuz brought Somanātha in its orbit too. Does it suggest that Somanātha's importance as a port on the Kathiawad coast enhanced to a considerable extent in the second half of the thirteenth century? In fact, the growing contacts between Hormuz and Stambhatīrtha or Cambay, the principal port in Gujarat began to figure in a few thirteenth and fourteenth century literary texts, namely the biographies (*caritas*) of celebrated Gujarati merchants like Vastupāla and Jagaḍu. Hormuz in these biographies figures as Ārdrapura and is generally mentioned as a *velākula* or a harbour. The regularity of Gujarat-Hormuz commercial contacts is further illustrated in this genre of literature by the mention of ships of Hormuz (*Hormujīvāhana*) visiting Gujarati ports.[29] These discussions thus help situate the visit of Nakhuda Nuruddin Firuz to Somanātha in 1264; at least, it is clear that a voyage by a Hormuzi *nakhuda* to a port in Kathiawad in the thirteenth century was neither accidental nor exceptional.

IV

A close study of the Arabic and Sanskrit versions of the 1264 inscriptions in fact strongly suggests Nuruddin's considerable familiarity with both Somanātha and the local elites—including merchants—thereof. It is a familiarity which is unlikely to have sprouted by a single or first encounter with the port-town. What we would like to stress here is that Nuruddin's acquaintance and ties with Somanātha and its leading men could have developed through his several visits to the port town, before 1264 and if not, also since. At Sumnat or Somanātha Nakhuda Nuruddin Firuz caused to make a *masjid* (in Arabic) and *mijigiti* (in Sanskrit). The *mijigiti* is clearly described as a sacred place and it faced the east (*pūrvābhimukhamijigitidharmasthāna*). The religious structure was constructed on a plot of land which was purchased by Firuz for that specific purpose. The said plot of land stood in Sikottari-mahājanapallī outside the city of Somanātha (*Somanāthadevanagaravāhye*), probably at the outskirts of the city. It is likely that Firuz purchased the plot of land for the *masjid* purposely outside the limits of the sacred Śaiva centre. On the other hand, the *mahājanapallī* itself was attached to the property of the temple of Somanātha (*Śrīsomanāthadevadroṇī-pratibaddha*). It is remarkable that the plot for the construction of a mosque was made available to a *nakhuda* from the land originally held by a premier Hindu temple. Both the versions of the inscription enlist the names of a number of leading men of Somanātha who formally witnessed (*pratyavekṣa*) the purchase and the ultimate endowment of the plot by Nuruddin. That these witnesses were eminent persons of the city will be amply demonstrated by the honorifics like *bṛhatpuruṣa* and *ṭhakkura* attached to their names. They were: Śripalugīdeva (Ar. Bailakdev), Someśvaradeva (Ar. Somesardev), Rāmadeva (Ar. Ramdev), Bhīmasiṁha (Ar. Bhimsih) and Śrī Chāḍa (Ar. Jada Rawat, son of Nānasiṁha/Nansih). Of these, as we shall see later, Chāḍa was the most prominent among them and probably himself a merchant. The *mahājanapallī* where stood Nuruddin's *mijigiti* could have been a quarter for merchants, as the term *mahājana* in contemporary Guajarati inscriptions and particularly in the inscription of 1287 meant a merchant. Among the leading local Hindus the most eminent, at least to Nuruddin, was Chāḍa. Apparently he was perhaps most instrumental and helpful in procuring the land of the mosque for Nuruddin. That is why the Sanskrit version describes Nuruddin and Chāḍa as *dharmabāndhava* or righteous friends,[30] though the friends obviously did not share a common religious belief. In view of the fact that the two persons belonged to two differrent religious faiths, their friendship rested on their righteousness (*dharma*). This is a striking illustration of the spirit of cooperation, tolerance and amity between a Muslim *nakhuda* and a local Hindu elite whose friendship cut across their personal religious faiths. The transfer and endowment of the landed property in favour of the mosque were approved and endorsed by the town council of Somanātha. This town council is called *pañcakula* in the inscription of 1264, indicating that it probably consisted of five members. The most significant point here is that the head of the *pañcakula* body in 1264 was the great Śaiva Pāśupata priest and erudite scholar Vīrabhadra (*pāśupatācārya mahāpaṇḍita mahattara dharmamūrtti gaṇḍa śrī para*: the term *para* is an abbreviation of *purohita*). The other important member of the *pañcakula* was *pārīksika* (coin examiner) Mahattara Śrī Abhayasiṁha. The *pañcakula* of the port town thus accommodated at once a famous Śaiva Pāśupata priest and a merchant, the latter possibly as a representative of the mercantile community. No hindrance to the endowment for the mosque was caused by the *pañcakula*. What is called *pañcakula* in the inscription of 1264 is possibly the same as the local-self body at Somanātha, called *caturjātaka* in the inscription of 1287. Like the *pañcakula* the *caturjātaka* was also headed in 1287 by a Śaiva Pāśupatācāryya, named Tripurāntaka. The unmistakable point is the congenial atmosphere in the cultural life of the port town which accommodated religious heterogeneity in the form of a mosque (or mosques) in a primarily Śaiva centre.

A perusal of the inscription of 1264, however, suggests that Nuruddin did not settle down in Somanātha. As he was not a permanent resident of Somanātha it is only logical that several arrangements were made for the maintenance and provisions of the *mijigiti* on a long-term basis. We would like to take a close look at these provisions which, Nurudddin wished, would be maintained perpetually. Nurudddin made adequate arrangements for observing every year two special Muslim religious festivals, namely Barātiśabī and Khatamarātri. What cannot escape our attention is the mention of these two Muslim festivals only in the Sanskrit version, while the Arabic text is completely silent on the annual holding of these two Muslim festivities. Barātiśabī is the Sanskritized name of the well known Muslim festival, Sab-e-Barat; Khatamarātri is the sacred occasion when the entire Quran is recited in a single night. The Sanskrit version brands both Sab-e-Barat and Khatamarātri as special religious festivities (*viśeṣapūjamahotsava*). This is probably the earliest mention of the two Muslim religious festivals in a Sanskrit inscription, implying thereby considerable acquaintance of the local community, or at least the author of the Sanskrit text, with some of the Muslim festivals. The two festivals are further specifically associated with Muslim ship-owning merchants (*nauvittakānāṁ samācareṇa*); it is logical that Nuruddin, being himself a ship-owner, would wish the observance of these festivals in the *mijigiti* he patronized and constructed. One may also logically infer the presence of a number of Muslim ship-owners in Somanātha, since the term *nauvittaka* is used here in plural (*nauvittkānām*). Early Indian sources rarely offer insights into the religious rites and observances of maritime merchants; and that is why, the Sanskrit version of the Veraval inscription is of exceptional importance. It should also be taken into consideration that Muslim ship-owners here were given the epithet *nauvittakas*, instead of the more customary *nakhuda*. This would once again demonstrate that the coastal society of Somanātha perceived little professional differentiation between a Muslim *nakhuda* and a Hindu *nauvittaka*. From the festivals in the mosque, we can now turn our attention to religious personages associated with it. They are *muazzin* (literally crier, entrusted with giving the call of prayer/namaj to devotees), *khatiba* (*khatib* or the reader of the *khutba*) and *imam* (religious leader organizing and directing the prayer).

Nuruddin left behind instructions for the due observance of the two *viśeṣapūjāmahotsava*—Barātiśabī and Khatamarātri, the proper maintenance of the religious personages and the annual whitewashing and necessary repair of the *mijigiti* (*prativarṣam coha-cūrṇabhagnaviśīrṇa-saṁskāraṇāya*). Nuruddin must have pooled considerable resources for the *dharmasthāna* for defraying these expenses. The discussion on the provision and resources of the *mijigiti* follows soon. But before that, the phraseology describing arrangements for repairs, etc., of the religious structure should be taken up. In numerous grants to Brahmanical, Buddhist and Jaina religious establishments it was more or less customary to refer to the provisions of annual and necessary repair to the religious structure (cf. *khaṇḍa-phuṭṭa-pratisaṁskāra-karaṇāya*). The provisions for repairs and whitewashing of the *mijigiti* were described in the Sanskrit text with a remarkably similar phraseology as one finds in the case of land grants to other religious shrines. The inscription gives us the image that the *mijigiti* in Somanātha was viewed as another *dharmasthāna* like many other religious shrines and establishments abounding in Somanātha. The Sanskrit version does not give any hint of religious animosity towards the *mijigiti* which seems to have been accommodated within the religio-cultural sphere of the Śaiva sacred centre.

Now to the resources that Nuruddin left behind for the proper maintenance of the mosque. Fortuantely for us some indications of these provisions have been recorded in the inscriptions under study. Apart from buying the land in Sikottarī-mahājanapallī for constructing the mosque, Nuruddin also purchased some other landed properties in favour of the *mijigiti*. He purchased a *palladikā* or a freehold,[31] originally belonging to the temple of Bakuleśvara. The inscription furnishes in this context a few striking information. Two priests were largely instrumental in this transaction of landed property for the mosque. They were two *purohitas* (*purohita* being abbreviated as *para*), respectively Śrī Tripurāntaka and Para Śrī Ratneśvara. The former was the *sthānapati* or the chief priest of Navaghaneśvara temple/*maṭha* and the latter the priest of Vināyakabhaṭṭāraka temple. How and why two priests of two different temples became involved in the sale of a plot belonging to a third temple, is unknown to us. They could have acted as the chief advisors or liaison in the transaction. No less important is the information about the location of this *palladikā*. While the plot of the mosque was located in Sikottarī-mahājanapallī outside the city of Somanātha, the newly acquired *palladikā* stood within the city limits of Somanātha (*Śrīsomanāthadevanagaramadhye*). Besides, Nuruddin purchased another freehold facing north (*uttarābhimukha palladikā*), an oilmill (*ghānaka*) and held the right to have a share of the oil produced therein. The oilmill and its yield were certainly required for lighting lamps, etc., in the mosque. The Sanskrit text further enlists the names of local men from whom these items were bought. They are: Nirmālya, Lūnasīha, son of Sohana, Kilhanadeva, son of Ṭhakkura Soḍḍhala and Āśādhara. The list ends with Chāḍa, already figuring as Nuruddin's very intimate friend. From Chāḍa the *nakhuda* purchased two shops or market places (*haṭṭadvayam*). The sale proceeds of the shops/market places are likely to have gone to the mosque, obviously to enrich the resources of the *mijigiti*. It is also clear that Chāḍa owned, among other things, shops. In other words, he was possibly a wealthy merchant, in addition to being a *ṭhakkura* and *rawat*. The inscription leaves a strong impression that Nuruddin's mosque, although situated outside the town, was not dissociated from the socio-cultural life of Somanātha and in fact, closely integrated to the urban space of the Śaiva pilgrimage.

V

The construction of and patronage to a mosque by a Hormuji *nākhuda* in 1264 have to be appreciated in the existing socio-cultural and political milieu of Somanātha in the second half of the thirteenth century. The Sanskrit version of the inscription does not portray any image of crisis in the socio-cultural life in the Śaiva sacred centre; neither does it offer any indication that there was an element of forced construction of a mosque by Muslims in this holy city of the Hindus. In 1264 there were temples of Navaghaneśvara, Ratneśvara and Bakuleśvara in Somanātha, besides, of course, the most important Somanātha temple itself. That it was a flourishing centre of trade with *mahājanapallī* and *haṭṭas* is unmistakable. The presence of an oilmill (most probably there were several such) should also be taken into consideration.

The discussion in this vein may be carried a bit further, even risking some digression from the main focus of the paper, i.e. a *masjid* of a *nakhuda* in a Śaiva centre. More elaborate probes into the social and cultural life of Somanātha are possible on the basis of an inscription dated 1287. Composed twenty-three years after the bilingual Veraval inscription the Cintra *praśasti*, now in Portugal, highlights the activities of a Śaiva priest, Tripurāntaka. One recalls that Tripurāntaka had already figured in the 1264 record as the *sthānapati* of the Bakuleśvara temple. After nearly a quarter of a century he emerged a key cultural figure in Somanātha. He appears in the record of 1287 as an outstanding religious personality of the Lākulīśa sect of the Śaivas. His importance can be appreciated in terms of the description of his credentials as a disciple of Vālmīkirāśi who in his turn was the disciple of Kārttikarāśi. His religious lineage thus being established, the record highlights his pilgrimages to distant sacred centres (*tīrthakṣetra*) like Kedāra, Prāyaga, Śrīparvata, banks of the Narmadā, Godāvarī, Trymabaka (Trimbak near Nasik), Rāmeśvara and Devapaṭṭana (Somanātha). He not only settled down in Somanātha and was considered as a leading religious figure there, in 1287 he was also a member of the *caturjataka* or the town council of Somanātha. The main purport of the 1287 inscription is to record the religious munificence of this Lākulīśa priest. He built five Śiva temples, five images and a two pillared gateway (*toraṇa*). The immense importance he commanded in Somanātha will be driven home by the fact that the Śaiva images enshrined in the five temples were named Tripurāntakeśvara, the deity being clearly named after its founder Tripurāntaka himself.

An excellent pen picture of Somanātha as a port and a cultural centre is available in the inscription of 1287. The list of commodities, mentioned in the context of donations to the five temples built by Tripurāntaka, is quite impressive in their range and diversities. On the one hand, there are references to staples like husked rice (*coṣa*), pulses (*mudga*), oil (*taila*), betel nuts and betel leaves, and on the other, more precious and prestige goods like sandalwood, soft cloth (*yugāśca komalāḥ*) and incense (*guggula*) also figure. Of the more expensive items, sandalwood and incense are unlikely to have been local products and were probably brought to Somanātha from distant areas. That Somanātha was a flourishing market centre in the second half of the thirteenth century is well driven home by the mention of merchants or *mahājanas*. The *mahājanas*, according to the record of 1287, agreed to assign the sum of one *dramma* per shop to the temples. In fact, the shops are clearly described as excellent, indicating thereby the flourishing state of retail trade in the sacred centre. The *caturjātaka* or the city council of Somanātha issued an edict (*śāsana*) to arrange for the payment of one *dramma* to the temple of Paśupāla by the *maṇḍapikā*. Our previous discussions on the *maṇḍapikā* clearly establish its commercial character in north India. There are also several instances of *maṇḍapikās* yielding *śulka* or tolls and customs (*śulkamaṇḍapikā*) in north India, especially in many areas in Rajasthan and Gujarat since AD 1000. It has been argued that the *maṇḍapikā* as a centre of trade occupied a position intermediate between markets of large urban centres and rural-level weekly or periodic market places (*haṭṭa/haṭṭikā*).[32] The thriving non-agrarian economic activities at the port-town of Somanātha are well brought out in the inscriptions of both 1264 and 1287. It is only to be expected that Somanātha was also well acquainted with various professional groups and craftsmen. Thus in the inscription of 1287 is stated the presence of the professional body of gardeners (*mālākāra*) and stone mason (*śilpin*), the former being instructed to supply lotus flowers daily to one of the temples built by Tripurāntaka. What we have tried to highlight by digressing a little into the conditions of Somanātha in 1287 is that Somanātha experienced considerable diversity in its functions. It was not merely a celebrated Śaiva pilgrimage centre; its role as a port and a trade centre with linkages with the interior can hardly be lost sight of.

VI

In the light of the earlier discussions we would like to revert to the situation in 1264. Gujarat and Kathiwad were under the rule of the Cālukya dynasty when Nurudddin had the bilingual inscription engraved to record the event of the construction of a *mijigiti* at a Śaiva centre under Hindu rule. Vāghela Arjunadeva was the Cālukya ruler. What light does the inscription throw on the attitude of the politico-administrative authority towards the patronage and donation by Firuz? This becomes a valid enquiry in the light of the amiable relation between the *nakhuda* and local elites—including leading businessmen and religious personalities—of Somanātha. That prominent people were present as witnesses to the endowment of the land to the mosque has already been discussed. The purchase of the plot of land by Firuz and its final endowment to the mosque were clearly approved by the local town council (*pañcakula*), headed by a famous Śaiva Pāśupata priest and erudite scholar. The *pañcakula* certainly accommodated representatives of the religious community and the mercantile groups alike. The *pañcakula* had no objection that the grant of land and all other arrangements for the mosque were declared as everlasting as the sun and the moon (*ācandrārkasthāyī*), i.e. it recognized the grant as a religious donation for perpetuity. The land and other properties were handed over to the mosque preceded by the ritual of sprinkling water (*evametadudakenapradattam*). The most striking feature in this recording of the endowment is that almost identical phraseology is generally used when a similar endowment is made over to a Brahmanical, Buddhist and Jaina institution(s) or religious personalitiy (or personlities). The local *pañcakula* at Somanātha thus did not visualize any difference between the act of patronage to Brahmanical, Buddhist and Jaina establishments and that to a *masjid* and therefore did not consider it relevant to devise a separate phraseology to record the endowment to the *mijigiti*. The *mijigiti* at Somanātha was certainly another additional religiuos structure and institution in a city strewn with shrines, but was not perceived as an 'other', antagonistic to the belief systems of the majority. The endorsement of the *pañcakula* was duly approved of by Rāṇaka Māladeva, the provincial authority of Kathiawad and finally by the apex political authority, Cālukya king Arjunadeva. The upper tiers of the politico-administrative authority shared a similar attitude of welcoming and approving of the construction of a mosque by a Hormuji *nakhuda* at Somanātha.

VII

There is little doubt that Nuruddin was a pious and devout Muslim. In the Arabic version of the record he expressed his desire that Sumnat (Somanātha) would in future be an Islamic city. This is, however, absent in the Sanskrit version. We are also not sure whether this was expressly the desire of Nuruddin or of the composer of the Arabic version. Apart from the wish about the future of Sumnat, the *nakhuda* also laid down certain instructions regarding the resources of the *mijigiti*. In case there was some savings of resources after meeting all expenditure of the *masjid*, that should be sent every year to *dharmasthāna* Maṣā-Madīnā (*yatkiñcit śeṣadravyamudgīrati tatsarvaṁdravyaṁ Maṣā-Madīnā dharmasthāne prasthāpanīyam*). Maṣā-Madīnā *dharmasthāna* is none other than Mecca and Madina, the holiest of holy pilgrimages of Muslims. No other and earlier Sanskrit texts/documents have designated Mecca and Madina so clearly as the premier sacred centres of Islam. We would like to underline the significance of the term *dharmasthāna*. The *mijigiti* at Somanātha is called a *dharmasthāna*, so also are Mecca and Madina. One may logically argue that there was a conscious attempt to project the *mijigiti* as a true representation of Mecca and Madina as *dharmasthānas* of Islam. In Nuruddin's wish to send savings to Mecca and Madina one can also read some measures to keep proper accounts of the endowment, though this is not explicitly stated. Whether or not any wealth was actually transferred from the Somanātha *masjid* to Mecca, the Muslim community in Somanātha must have maintained its linkages with Mecca during the annual *hajj* pilgrimage. As Somanātha itself was a port in the western Indian Ocean, it could easily have been a point of embarkation of pious Muslims bound for the Red Sea port of Jidda or Aidhab. There are in fact several Arabic epitaphs of thirteenth and fourteenth centuries, discoverd from various parts of coastal Gujarat, which record the demises of wealthy Islamic merchants and ship-owners like Nuruddin. All these merchants and *nakhudas* are almost invariably hailed as the supporters of pious *hajj* pilgrims.[33] There are fascinating accounts of the *hajj* pilgrimages, including the one left behind by the Andalusian traveller Ibn Jubayr (1184). The accounts of Jubayr leave little room for doubt that the *hajj* brought enough opportunities of long-distance trade and voyages.[34] The very existence of the Red Sea ports of Jidda and Aidhab depended on the movement of 'pious passengers', as Pearson puts it.[35] The owners of *jilabah* or typical Red Sea vessels really thrived on this annual crossing of the Red Sea. These ports not only received ships carrying pilgrims, but also cargoes. While there were many luxury goods being brought for transcation during the holy season, two bulk and staple items from India, according to Jubayr, reached the Red Sea ports via Aden during *hajj*. These are pepper and teak, the latter being an indispensable raw material for building Arab

of the Indian Ocean and merchants thereof as bridges among diverse communities cannot be brushed aside. And in this story the role and attitude of both the ship-owning merchant from Hormuz and his Indian counterpart beckon a message that is fit to be remembered.[36]

NOTES

1. Different types of merchants have been discussed by Ranabir Chakravarti, 'Merchants of Konkan'. Chakravarti, 'Merchants and Other Donors at Bandhogarh'.
2. Cf. the term *govittaka* is used as an epithet of a *seṭṭhi* to denote that he became wealthy by having (i.e. by dealing in) cattle. See Ivo Fiser, 'The Problem of the Seṭṭhi in the Buddhist Jātakas', *Archiv Orientalni*, vol. XXII, 1954, pp. 238-66; this is also included in Chakravarti, ed., *Trade in Early India.*
3. Chaudhuri, *Trade and Civilization.*
4. Goitein, *Letters*, shows that the term *nakhuda* in the sense of a ship-owner was not used in the Mediterranean world. For an understanding of the *rubban* and the *muallim* see the manual of ibn Majid (tr. G.A.R. Tibbetts, *Arab Navigation in the Indian Ocean before the Coming of the Portuguese*, London, 1971). Ibn Majid, the most celebrated of the *muallims* in the Indian Ocean maritime trade network during the fifteenth century, always considered the *muallim* to be far superior to a *rubban*. The *rubban* is viewed by Majid with some contempt as a petty pilot/navigator of coastal crafts in the Red Sea sector. Buzurg ibn Shahriyar, the famous captain and author of the *Kitab Ajaib ul Hind* (*c.* AD 955, tr. G.S.P. Freeman-Grenville, *The Book of Wonders of India*, London, 1981) is a rare and rather early instance where the captain was given the epithet *nakhuda.*
5. Jain, *Trade and Traders.*
6. A.K. Majumdar, *The Calukyas of Gujarat*, Bombay, 1956.
7. S.R. Rao, *Lothal and the Indus Civilization*, New Delhi, 1973. Rao's identification of a large structure with a dry dock has not been unanimously accepted. See the critique by Jean Deloche, 'Geographical Considerations in the Localisation of Ancient Sea-Ports'.

7. The image of brisk trade at Barygaza in the early centuries of the Christian era is available in the *Periplus*, secs. 43-6 and 49. Barygaza figures prominently also in the Buddhist Jātakas under the name Bharugaccha or Bharuyaccha; see in this context Bose, *Social and Rural Economy*, vol. II.
8. The gradual rise of Cambay as the premier port of Gujarat at the turn of the millennium is discussed by Jain, *Trade and Traders*, also see Lallanji Gopal, *Economic Life of Northern India c.* AD *700-1200*, Varanasi, 1965; S. Arasaratnam and Aniruddha Ray, *Masulipatnam and Cambay: A History of Two Port Towns 1500-1800*, New Delhi, 1994.

9. For a masterly treatment of Surat see Ashin Das Gupta, *Indian Merchants and the Decline of Surat 1700-1750*, Weisbaden, 1979; also idem, *Merchants of Maritime India 1500-1800*, London, 1994 (relevant essays).
10. A. Cortesao, tr., *The Suma Oriental of Tome Pires*, London, 1944.
11. Both the Arabic name al-Dyyb and the Portuguese name Diu are based on the Sanskrit name *dvīpa*. S.D. Goitein, 'Specimens of Correspondence of Jewish Merchants in the Twelfth Century', *JESHO*, vol. XXI, 1980, pp. 43-66 informs us of a coastal voyage from Malabar to al Dyyb from where the ship went to Aden. The fifteenth century navigational manual of ibn Majid (*Arab Navigation in the Indian Ocean*) also refers to this port.
12. These names of Somanātha are mentioned in two inscriptions dated AD 1264 and 1287; both the inscriptions are exhaustively used for our present study.
13. The devastations of the Ghaznavid raid are portrayed in some early Arabic accounts. See, Henri Elliot and James Dowson, *The History of India as Told by Its Own Historians*, vols. I, II and III, Aligarh, 1953, relevant sections. Henri Elliot seems to have had a preference for the citation of the orthodox point of view of the *ulemas*; as a result of such selection of sources the image of Muslims as raiders and destroyers of Indian religion was highlighted by Elliot and Dowson. Andre Wink, *al Hind*, vol. II, New York, 1998 has presented a recent study of Arabic accounts of the devastation of Somanātha by Ghaznavid invasion.
14. E. Sachau, tr., *Alberuni's India*, vol. II, Chap. 58, p. 105.
15. G. Buhler, 'The Cintra Praśasti of the Reign of Sāraṅgadeva', *EI*, vol. I, pp. 271-87.
16. G.M. Moraes, *The Kadambakula*, Bombay, 1931, pp. 387-93.
17. L.D. Barnett, 'Inscriptions at Narendra', *EI*, vol. 13, p. 302.
18. Moraes, *The Kadamba Kula*: pp. 394-400, also pp. 265-71. Ranabir Chakravarti, 'Coastal Trade and Voyages in Konkan: The Early Medieval Scenario', *IESHR*, vol. XXXV, 1998, pp. 97-123, presents an exhaustive study of the coastal network. The Konkan coast, particularly its northern segment, became well known for the settlements of a number of Tājiya (= Tajik or Arabic) merchants since early tenth century. This is not only mentioned by Arab authors like al Masudi, but also names of Muslim merchants in their Sanskritized forms (e.g. Allīya = Ali, Mahumata/ Madhumati = Muhammad, Sahriyārahāra = Shahriyar, etc.) appear in a few Sanskrit copper plates from the north Konkan port of Sanjan (= Sindan of the Arab authors). An analysis of the combined evidence of Arab accounts and Indian inscriptions clearly demonstrates that the Rāṣṭrakūṭas very much favoured the settlement of Arab merchants in the north Konkan coast. The Śilāhāras, originally a vassal power under the Rāṣṭrakūṭas and subsequently an independent power of the Konkan coast, continued this favourable political attitude to Muslim settlers in the Konkan littorals. See, Ranabir

Chakravarti, 'Monarchs, Merchants and a Maṭha in Northern Konkan (*c.* AD 900-1053)', *IESHR*, vol. XXVII, 1990, pp. 189-208. B.D. Chattopadhyaya, *Representing the Other? Sanskrit Sources and Muslims*, New Delhi, 1998, opines that the term *tājiya* or *tājjika* denoting a Muslim last appeared in a Sanskrit inscription in the Sanjan record of Rāṣṭrakūṭa Kṛṣṇa II. The Kadamba inscription of Jayakeśī points to the continuity of this term to refer to an Arabic Muslim in eleventh century Goa. The Kadamba inscription mentioning Ṣaḍhana's munificence for a mosque is an early instance of the construction of a *mijigiti* in an Indian harbour. A later and more celebrated example of similar construction of mosque is discussed later in this paper.

19. *Travels of Ser Marco Polo*, tr. H. Yule and H. Cordier, vol. II, 1903, pp. 398-9.
20. Jain, *Trade and Traders*, has elaborately discussed the possibilities of the improved network of trade in coastal Kathiwad, including in and around Somanātha.
21. E. Hultzsch, 'A Grant of Bāghela Arjunadeva, dated 1264 AD', *IA*, vol. XI, pp. 241-5; D.C. Sircar, *EI*, vol. XXXIV, pp. 141-50; also *SI*, vol. II, pp. 402-8.
22. *EI*, Arabic and Persian Supplement, 1961, pp. 11-15.
23. Buhler, 'Cintra Prasasti of the Reign of Sāṁgadeva'.
24. A recent assessment of the activities of ship-owning merchants, Indian, Arabic and Jewish in the western littorals of India and also in the western sector of the Indian Ocean has been made by Ranabir Chakravarti, 'Nakhudas and Nauvittakas: Ship-owning Merchants in the West Coast of India (c. AD1000-1500)', *JESHO*, vol. XLIII, 2000, pp. 34-64.
25. For an overview of Hormuz, see R. Stube, 'Hormuz', in *The Encyclopaedia of Islam*, vol. II, Leiden, 1916.
26. *Chu fan Chi* by Chau-ju Kua, F. Hirth and W.W. Rockhill, St. Petersburgh, 1911.
27. G.F. Hourani, *Arab Navigation*; Chaudhuri, *Trade and Civilization*; idem, *Asia before Europe*.
28. B. Sandesara, *The Literary Circle of Mahāmātya Vastupāla*, Bombay, 1953; G. Buhler, ed., *Jagaḍūcarita of Sarvānanda*, Wien, 1892. The *Jagaḍūcarita* narrates the tale of the voyage of the ship of merchant millionaire Jagaḍu to Ārdrapura or Hormuz. One may note here the attempt at Sanskritizing an Arabic toponym. The *Lekhapaddhati* (p. 27) mentions the arrival of vessels from Hormuz to Ghogha (Ghoghā *velākula*), bringing horses to the Gujarati harbour.
29. Sircar, *Indian Epigraphical Glossary*, p. 92 renders two meanings of this term: (a) 'one whose only friend is his religious faith' and (b) 'a person who has become the friend of another on an oath in the name of his religious faith'. B.N. Mukherjee suggests that the term *dharmabāndhava* could be

compared with the word *kalyāṇamitra*, regularly occurring in Buddhist texts.

30. This English rendering of the technical term is made on the basis of D.C. Sircar, *EI*, vol. XXXIV and idem, *Epigraphical Glossary*, p. 228.
31. See our previous chapter, 'Trade at *Maṇḍapikās* in Early Medieval North India'; the importance of the *maṇḍapikā* as a middle tier centre of trade between a rural market and a larger urban trade centre has been recently assessed in the broader context of the pattern of trade in the subcontinent during the period from 600-1300. See, Chakravarti, 'Between Cities and Villages: Linkages of Trade in India (*c.* AD 600-1300)', in Georg Berkemer, Tilman Frasch, Hermann Kulke and Jürgen Lütt, eds., *Explorations in the History of South Asia: Essays in Honour of Dietmar Rothermund*, New Delhi, 2001, pp. 99-120.
32. These epitaphs were edited by Z.A. Desai, 'Inscriptions from the Prince of Wales Museum, Bombay', *EI, Arabic and Persian Supplement:* 1957-8, pp. 12-13; idem, 'Arabic Inscriptions of the Rajput Period from Gujarat', *EI, Arabic and Persian Supplement*, 1962-3, pp. 17-24; idem, 'Inscriptions of the Gujarat Sultans', Inscription no. XIX, *EI, Arabic and Persian Supplement*, 1963, pp. 32-4. Their significance as epigraphic data on the ship-owners is discussed by Chakravarti, see note 24.
33. R.J.C. Broadhurst, tr., *Travels of Ibn Jubayr*, pp. 62-5.
34. M.N. Pearson, *The Pious Passengers: The Hajj in Earlier Times*, London, 1994.
35. The situation may be compared with the religious patronage of Jagaḍū, the famous Gujarati merchant and the hero of the *Jagaḍūcarita* of Sarvānanda (see note 28). Chiefly celebrated for his munificence to the Jaina community, he is also lauded for constructing a *masiti* or a *masjid* for the Shimālī or the Ismaili community (canto VI, *śloka* 64).

CHAPTER 12

Information, Exchange and Administration: Case Studies from Early India

Globalisation and information technology, from the closing years of the twentieth century, have almost become mantras in our way of life. Their impact has brought about significant changes in institutional structures and social life especially in developing countries, also labelled as the Third World, like India. One obvious outcome has been the worldwide recognition of India as an IT giant, driving a firm perception that IT and communication developments could well be the all-purpose key to ameliorating the age-old seclusion and the interminable poverty which perennially tag the image of India. The revolutions in the arena of IT and communications system indeed tend to transcend national, economic, political and cultural barriers and are capable of transforming a traditional society, an expression which is widely used to encapsulate the essence of the ways of life in pre-modern India. The image of India as immutable and changeless over millennia, as a giant in slumber, was carefully constructed as a category contrastive to the vibrant, dynamic, innovative and hence, progressive and civilising Occident to which it stood in binary opposition. Considerable and sustained scholarly input over the last half a century has forced a rethinking and rejection of this stereotype. It is now well understood that identifiable variations, changes and discontinuities have marked India's society, economy, culture and polity not only in different phases of her history but also in lively regional variations. The emergent image of plurality, contrary to a homogenised portrayal of Indian society, also suggests the operation of a complex process of accommodation and interlocking of these pluralities on an overarching subcontinental level.[1] Seen from this angle, one may not rule out the possibilities of gathering and dissemination of information in pre-modern times. Major advances in historical research—both at empirical and conceptual levels—have also dispelled the long cherished notions of the insularity and isolation of India during the pre-modern period. While this essay by no means even hints at the possibility of the anticipation of modern IT and communication technologies by Indians in remote times, it, however, underlines that the significance of information and communication in the matters of statecraft and exchange-related activities was given due recognition. This theme will be elaborated and worked out, in the context of early India (up to AD 1300), in two major facets of material life: administration and trade. The essay certainly does not aim at presenting a comprehensive survey of the information and communication during the early period of Indian history; it intends to take up a few relevant case studies and also attempts to highlight the mutual compatibility in the conduits of information and communication.

II

A case in point may be seen in the making of the first large-scale empire in Indian history, namely the Maurya empire (*c.* 324–187 BC). This power has been widely studied from the point of view of state formation, the question of its supposed unitary character, or otherwise, and the extent of the state's control over economic life. As the Maurya empire embraced a nearly pan-Indian territory, accommodating within it different economies, societies and diverse ethnic groups, integration of the empire would logically require gathering and dissemination of information among the three distinct zones of the empire: the metropolitan state, the core areas and the peripheral zone.[2] An in-depth enquiry into the *Arthaśāstra*, the classical accounts, and Aśoka's edicts may reveal the information and communication networks during the Maurya rule. It is not merely the geographical distribution of Aśoka's edicts which demonstrate the wide expanse of the Maurya empire, but Aśoka himself informs us that his realm (designated by him as *vijita, rāja-viṣaya, Jambudvipa and pṛthvī*) was vast (*mahalaka*).[3] That Aśoka caused engraving of his edicts all over his realm for disseminating his administrative promulgation and his ideas and principles of Dhamma is well-known; what is significant is his acknowledgement of the possibilities of various versions of his promulgations in different parts of the empire. This is clearly betrayed by his own statement that there were extended (*vistata*), abridged (*saṁkhita*) and medium-sized (*majhima*) versions of his edicts (*dhammalipis*).[4] If this implies that the text of his promulgations could be adapted according to local/regional requirements by his officers, it also suggests that there were central drafts of the edicts, emanating from the apex political centre of the empire at Pāṭaliputra to dispersed parts of the realm. While this speaks of the presence of a super-ordinate political authority at the centre, on the other hand, there is a clear impression of the absence of a monolithic and unitary state system which could function by accommodating some of the local/regional factors or situations. A complex polity such as this could be practicable if there were at least some opportunities of access to, and distribution of, information through established channels of communication. In one such edict, for instance, the royal decree addressed the Mauryan crown prince (*Āryaputra*) stationed at Suvarṇagiri, the southern provincial headquarters of the empire, though the actual administrative instructions were meant for officials at the town of Isila.[5] A logical reading would be to suggest a distinct chain of command between the apex political centre and an administrative area in a peripheral zone. The very preparation of his edicts in Aramaic and Greek, found in Afghanistan and Taxila, indicates translation, transliteration of certain terms and summaries of existing Prakrit edicts. While enlisting the virtues to be practised by people to uphold Dhamma, the Kandahar Greek edict, clearly based on the REs XII and XIII, enjoins the subjects to mind or have in mind 'firm devotion to the interests of the ruler' (*ta tou sumpheronta basileos noi*).[6] Aśoka's demand for complete allegiance of his subjects to the ruler is expressed here in no uncertain terms by a translation of the Prakrit term *diḍhabhatitā* into Greek; this once again implies the circulation of the messages of the emperor from the metropolitan area to the northwestern borderland of the subcontinent. The simultaneous use of Greek and Aramaic in the northwestern borderland of the subcontinent and Prakrit over the rest of the Maurya realm (including the Dravidian speaking zone) upholds the principle of multi-linguality for the dissemination of royal messages and decrees among diverse ethnic, socio-economic and religious groups. It has been observed that the sites for engraving Asokan edicts were well chosen, since these were engraved at places or points which were easily visible or which acted as points of convergence of people from various areas. The choice of such sites for erecting Asokan pillars or engraving of his edicts was thus deliberate with a view to communicating the imperial message to the subjects.[7] That the emperor was intent upon establishing linkages and communication when he himself was on tour is also borne out by several edicts. In one such edict from Pangurariya, Aśoka sends his message to *Kumāra* Sāmba, a provincial governor of royal blood, during his pilgrimage to Upanitha vihāra when he was away from the capital for 256 nights.[8] This careful recording of the duration of his absence from the capital cannot but suggest that the channels of communication and information with the emperor on tour were systematically kept alive. On another occasion, the emperor chose to send his instructions straight to officers of the relatively subordinate rank (*Mahāmātra* and the *Lājavacanika*) stationed at Tosāli and Samāpā in Orissa by bypassing the *Kumāra* or provincial governor in Kalinga, though there was indeed one such *Kumāra* at Tosāli, the provincial seat of administration in Kalinga.[9] One gets an unmistakable impression of the possibilities of movements of people and officials alike both within and beyond the empire. This is demonstrated by the visit of the Seleukidian ambassador, Megasthenes, from Arachosia (Kandahar) to the Maurya capital Pāṭaliputra, obviously by an overland journey. Megasthenes and Eratosthenes, the latter a junior contemporary of Aśoka, inform us about a royal road of the Maurya times linking Pāṭaliputra with Susa. The Classical authors further speak of a class of Mauryan officers, *Agronomoi*, who looked after, among other things, the maintenance of the royal road that was provided by markers of distance and direction.[10] An incontrovertible confirmation of the Classical accounts is available in the two Aramaic edicts of Aśoka from Laghman in Afghanistan. The two edicts are unique in the range of Aśokan edicts in that these two expressly refer to a royal road (*karapathi*) and give details of distance and directions of several destinations.[11] These are actually road-registers, a forerunner of mileposts, and offer combined glimpses of the infrastructure of communications and information regarding communication network from a place that was, significantly enough, almost at the gateway of the sub-continent. Such a royal highway seems to have been instrumental in the reaching out of the messages of Dhamma to five Yavana rulers of West Asia. It was also possible for a scribe, Cāpaḍa by name and conversant with Kharoṣṭi script in use in the north-west, to be present in the Deccan, which was certainly not in a Kharoṣṭi using zone. Once again it points to the movements of people across vast distances in the Maurya empire.

The Maurya capital, Pāṭaliputra, it is likely, was connected with different parts of the empire. A particular group of city officials (*Astynomoi*), according to the Greek accounts, were in charge of the care of foreigners. Another such group of *Astynomoi* officers kept records of births and deaths not only for the sake of noting demographic information but also for revenue purposes. A close parallel to this system of gathering information about population is offered by the *Arthaśāstra.*[12] The *Samāharttā*, the officer in charge of revenue collection and also entrusted with municipal/urban administration, is enjoined by Kauṭilya to be aware of families, the number of males and females and the young and old therein, their professions, livelihood and income and expenditure in urban areas (*kulānāṁca strīpuruṣānāṁ bālavṛddhakarmacaritra-jivyāvyayaparimāna vidyāt*).[13] The Kauṭilyan penchant for access to and control over information for strengthening royal power is best illustrated by his recommendation for an efficient espionage/secret service (*gūḍhapuruṣa*).[14] The Greek accounts also enlighten us on the regular use of spies/overseers/inspectors (*episcopoi/iphor*) in the Maurya realm which seems to have developed a secret service for the first time as an integral part of the administration.[15] The most elaborate and systematic discussion on this subject is offered by Kauṭilya. He broadly divides secret agents into two categories, *sañcara* (roving) and *saṁstha* (stationary)—further subdivided into ten groups—who were under the jurisdiction of the *Samāharttā*, the head of the secret service. There seems to have been some method of routing the information gathered; the data collected by the *sañcara* were to be first sent through the stationary spies who then would pass them on to the head of the secret service. Kauṭilya, who rarely takes anything for granted, opines that a piece of information gathered by a secret agent would be accepted and accessed only when the same is corroborated by three other sources of information. The thrust is not merely on collection of information but on the confirmation of its reliability too. Among the most important functions of the spies was to be vigilant about and collect information on, the activities of the highest officers of the realm, including the *mantrī, purohita, yuvarāja* and *senāpati*. But most significantly, the *Samāharttā* or the head of the secret service was himself under the scanner of the secret agents who, therefore, held allegiance only to the king. Kauṭilya also recommends the employment of the *gūḍhapuruṣa* for gathering information regarding public opinion about the ruler. The spy should not only find out the attitude of the public about a ruler, but also try to mould peoples' opinion in favour of the ruler and also to identify/track down the disgruntled and dangerous elements (*kaṇṭaka* or thorn) from the point of view of the state authority.[16] Kauṭilya rarely hides his open distrust and suspicion of employees in the finance department and enlists 41 types of malpractices of these officers who must be closely watched over by the secret agents. Though Kauṭilya was indeed aware of the importance of employing spies in another kingdom, his spies seem to have played a greater role in gathering information on the internal situation within a realm.

The principal purpose of recruiting spies is to ensure the elimination of suspect elements to the ultimate political benefit of the ruler. The importance of secret agents in the management of the state is duly recognised in the later normative treatises. Spies are considered to be the eyes of the ruler (*caracakṣusā mahīpati*). The *Kamandakīya Nītisāra* makes a distinction between envoys (*dūta*) on open assignments and those employed for gathering secret information (*cara*).[17]

The *dūta* looms large in official records approving grant of revenue-free plots of land to religious donees. This practice began in and around first/second century AD, especially in the Deccan and proliferated immensely in the period subsequent to AD 400 to assume a nearly pan-Indian character. At least once in the second century Deccan, a copy of the deed of land grant favouring a Buddhist monastery was kept at the local administrative office.[18] One may logically infer that the requirement of keeping proper records and copies of land grant documents was felt almost from the very inception of this institution.

Land grants of the Gupta and post-Gupta times repeatedly refer to the *dūta* who carried the official message of the transfer of revenue-free landed property to the donee(s) from the apex political authority, stationed at the premier politico-administrative centre, to the actual place of property transfer. This logically implies a system of dissemination of official information and at once, the physical carrying of the information by a *dūtaka*, who is likely to have followed an established route of contact.[19] On many occasions a high-ranking officer, *sandhivigrahika*, acted as a messenger of such royal orders. When the Pāla king Mahendrapāla (ninth century) granted some land in favour of a Buddhist monastery in north Bengal, the official messenger of the order was Śūrapāla, the younger brother of the ruler himself.[20] The relation between the two brothers is compared with that between Rāma and Lakṣmaṇa, implying thereby the ability and reliability of the messenger in carrying the royal order to the actual area of property transfer with utmost care and loyalty. One also comes across many such land grants where the king formally wishes the well-being of his subjects and seeks their approval to the royal order of granting land (*matamastu-bhavatām*). There are also instances when the ruler straightaway notifies his subjects about the property transfer (*vijñāpitam, ādiśayati*).[21]

III

Communication and information system was an indispensable aspect of state affairs and exchange-related activities as well. Trade being seen as action at distance[22] could not exist without some form of conduits and channels of communication through which would be carried both merchandise and information regarding transactions of goods at marketplaces. Significantly enough the term *vārttā* in Sanskrit stands for both information and the science of occupations, the latter meaning being derived from *vṛtti* or profession. *Vārttāśāstra*, according to Kauṭilya, includes agriculture (*kṛṣi*), cattle-keeping (*paśupālya*) and trade (*vāṇijya*). Both the merchant and the animal breeder are generally more mobile than the sedentary agriculturists. The professions of the merchant and the animal-breeder cannot be dissociated from linkages and communications within some circuits. The animal-breeders, often nomadic and semi-nomadic communities, not only move to places along with their stock of animals, but they also participate in exchange of items outside formal and more complex commercial operations.

Recent studies of early Indian economy bring to focus the importance of trade, both within the subcontinent and beyond, in the making of the history of India. Without at all questioning the predominantly agrarian material milieu of the pre-modern times, it is also evident that trade was a major ingredient of economic and social life of early India, though within the overarching agrarian economy. Not only does Kauṭilya include *vāṇijya* within *vārttā*, the Buddhist texts consider commerce as one of the excellent professions (*ukkaṭṭhakamma*) to be practised by persons having an excellent pedigree (*ukkaṭṭhakula*). The discussions on early Indian trade generally revolve around exchangeable products, merchants and mercantile organisations, medium of exchange and trade routes.[23] The last mentioned aspect demands a close scrutiny. It is now beyond any doubt that there were both overland and water routes (*sthalapatha* and *vāripatha* of Kauṭilya) connecting different parts of the subcontinent and also connecting South Asia with Southeast, East, West and Central Asia and the eastern Mediterranean regions. Two major regions of the subcontinent, Uttarāpatha and Dakṣiṇāpatha, must have been so named after two major trade routes respectively linking north India and the Deccan. A very familiar and frequent image of the *sārthavāha* type of merchant (the caravan trader) in the Buddhist texts is their journey from *puvvanta* (eastern frontier) to *aparānta* (western limit).

The study of routes of communication often presents an unchanging scenario. The routes of communication also had their own dynamics often shaped by commercial interests and/or political situations. The linking of South Asia with the Silk Road in Central and West Asia was largely an outcome of the expansion of the Kuṣāṇa power in the early centuries of the Christian era. The overland route connecting Taxila and Charsadda with Bactra, the Kuṣāṇa capital in Afghanistan, holds a crucial clue in this regard.[24] Archaeological researches by the Pak–German scholars have brought to light antiquities in the Karakorum highway. These demonstrate the convergence of Sogdian, Chinese and Bactrian merchants along with Kharoṣṭi using north-westerners at places like Gilgit, Chilas, Hunza, Thalpan Bridge, etc.[25] Epigraphic and pictorial data leave a telling mark on the emergence of a new route from Central Asia to South Asia through Kashmir, a shorter route than the usual Bactra, Kabul, Peshwar, Taxila network; but the shorter one was also extremely hazardous. This may correspond to the Chi-pin or Kashmir route figuring in the Chinese annals of the Han dynasty. These routes were regularly traversed by merchants of various types and religious preachers alike. It was not unusual for Buddhist monks to undertake distant journeys from Kalyan to Dalverjin Tepe in Central Asia, as inscribed gold tablets of these monks inform us.[26] One has to take note that both the merchant and Buddhist monks were regularly itinerant, often traversing the same routes. It is also likely that during the four months of the rainy season both would find a convenient sojourn in the numerous cave shelters, especially in the northern and western Deccan. The three important passes in the Sahyadri range, namely Thalghat, Bhorghat and Nanghat are noted for access to these cave shelters where monks and merchants converged. Not far away from these sites of cave shelters were located a number of craft-guilds and Buddhist monasteries. The linkages among the routes, the guilds and the cave shelters are unmistakable in the context of the western Deccan. It has been cogently argued that the cave shelters were also instrumental in providing commercial information to merchants because these were the places of congregation.[27]

No less spectacular was the development of the sea-route to India from the West, now better understood in the light of Pliny's *Naturalis Historia* and some archaeological artefacts. Pliny speaks of the increasing improvement of the sea-route to India from the Red Sea ports in four stages, each succeeding stage ensuring a shorter and safer crossing than the preceding one. The most developed maritime network could bring Greek and Roman ships from the Red Sea port of Myos Hormos and/or Berenike to Muziris in Malabar in forty days, if not even in twenty days, by utilising the south-western monsoon wind.[28] A mid-second century AD loan contract document on papyrus throws new light on the communication system between the west coast of India and the Red Sea. Muziris received commodities even from the Gangetic delta, evidently brought to south India by a coastal voyage along the east coast. Then, items were loaded on to the vessel lying at anchor at Muziris. The Greek vessel, Hermapollon, sailed from Muziris to either Berenike or Myos Hormos; from there goods were carried on camels to Coptos where these were loaded on the riverine boats on the Nile. The Nile boats finally carried the commodities to Alexandria, the premier port in the Nile Delta.[29] The important point to note here is the linkage and the mutual interdependence of the coastal, overseas, overland and fluvial routes of communication. This integration of diverse routes considerably contributed to the growth of trade between the Roman empire and India.

The same holds good for other premier ports of India. Bhṛgukachha or Barygaza on the mouth of the Narmada stole the limelight as the premier port of western India in the first four centuries AD. Barygaza was served by an extensive hinterland up to the Ganga–Yamuna doab region which was well connected with Gujarat by a network of overland routes through Rajasthan and Malwa. The port of Tāmralipta in the Ganga delta acted as the outlet for the landlocked Ganga valley that maintained its linkage with Tamralipta through overland and fluvial routes. In the early fourteenth century, Ibn Battuta explained the remarkable rise of Calicut as a great port in Malabar as there converged both Chinese junks and Arab sea-going vessels. The trans-shipment facilities available at Calicut partly accounts for its immense prosperity in the Indian Ocean network since the fourteenth century.[30]

The premier figures in these ports and other market places must have been diverse types of merchants. Merchants are, however, only dimly known from our sources. A regular image of the merchant in available literature is his undertaking long-distance journeys, obviously for commercial gains. The merchant's movements must have been shaped by some information about the situation of the market, the relative demand for—or lack of it—some specific commodities, the speed and safety of journeys, and the possibilities of profit or the dread of a financial loss. Some images of these aspects of trade are occasionally offered by sources though these do not necessarily point to actual situations or tangible mercantile speculation. The *Kuvalayamālā* of the eighth century presents a lively image of a *vaṇik-meli* at the well-known port of Śūrpāraka. The term *vaṇik-meli* does not stand for a professional organisation of merchants, but refers to a meeting point for traders. At this *vaṇik-meli* merchants would exchange their experiences and impressions of distant markets with particular emphasis on the demand for certain types of commodities, largely luxury items. Merchants also described the dangers of travel and communications and presented accounts of the profits they enjoyed.[31] There is no further corroborative evidence to back up this account of the *vaṇik-meli*, though it is highly likely that such exchanges of information did take place among a group of assembled merchants. The element of boasting and exaggerations about trading ventures by merchants is possibly a part of the baggage of the merchants' tales of their experience. The voice of a successful merchant can be heard in the following extract from a Malayalam text: the context is the merchant's bragging to his subordinates or relatively junior/ordinary merchants at a market place, named Kandiyur:

> If I sell a *jonakakuttira* in the Cola country I will immediately get 2000 *anayaccu* in cash. For my elephant I will get eight thousand. . . . If I go to Kollam or Kollapuram I can sell quickly all the good *karpuram*. I can get as much as I want from the ships at Valayapattanam. I found in the Pandyan fort a lot of silk.[32]

Even discounting for some exaggeration, the text nevertheless, highlights that the merchant had valuable understanding about prices of certain exotic and precious commodities including horses as war machines.[33] That he was willing to communicate his impressions of commerce in these commodities with his subordinates is also evident here.

But the most eloquent and dependable testimony comes from the letters of Jewish merchants of the eleventh and twelfth centuries who were interested in reaching the west coast of India, especially the Kanara and the Malabar littorals. These business letters are unique sources of Indian Ocean trade network and are a mine of information on the actual transactions of merchants. The Jewish merchants generally had their principal moorings in Egypt, especially Fustat (Old Cairo), and even further west, al Mahdiyya (Tunisia). Their eagerness to travel up to India led to their labelling as *Musafir ul Hind* (travellers to India), christened by Goitein as 'India Traders'.[34] The Red Sea ports like Qus and Aydhab were their major business centres; Aden in Yemen was indeed, their most important commercial hub in the Red Sea. At Fustat and Aden there were representatives of Jewish merchants who kept uninterrupted correspondence with the travelling merchants and also looked after their business interests. Many merchants stayed for long periods in port towns of the west coast of India. In Malabar there lived a Jewish merchant of Tunisian origin, Abraham b. Yiju from 1132 to 1149, whose correspondence has come to light.[35] These letters describe not only the activities of Jewish merchants, but their interactions with a large number of Muslim merchants of Egypt, the Red Sea region, and Aden, as well as several Indian merchants. A particular type of merchant, the ship-owner (*nakhuda*)[36] occupies a prominent position in these letters, as the trade network is largely oriented to the Indian Ocean and ports integrated to this maritime network. Apart from extremely important insights on commodities, prices and routes, these letters contain what may be termed as commercial intelligence. Sharing or passing on business information in the commercial circuit is an integral aspect of this correspondence.

The names of merchants, figuring in the correspondence, reveal information about their bases of operation and the commodities they dealt in. Thus, the name Joseph al Adani al Mamswai reveals that this particular merchant was a native of Aden but residing in Mamsa in Morocco, obviously for commercial ventures. The Representative of Jewish Merchants at Fustat abu Zikri Kohen had a suffix, Sijilmasi, signifying that he originally hailed from Sijilmasa in southern Morocco. Similarly, the name Hiba al Hamwi conveyed the message of his connection with Hama in Syria. Ahmad b. Nili, a prominent seafaring merchant frequenting western Indian littorals, was so named as he was engaged in the dealing of *nil* or indigo. The name Fofali, borne by an Indian ship-owner of the twelfth century, suggests he was a dealer in betel nuts.[37]

One of the most prominent of the Jewish merchants at Fustat was Ibn 'Awkal (eleventh century), a stationary merchant who employed a large number of subordinate agents spread as far west as Tunisia. His business correspondence throws light on the system of the exchange of commercial information regarding as many as 83 products, including a few Indian commodities. Among the Indian commodities was the Sindani indigo which was exported from the Indian port of Sindan or Sanjan, located to the north of the Dahanu taluk of the Thana district, Maharashtra. The correspondence provides crucial information about the quality of Sindani indigo *vis-à-vis* the Amtani (from Palestine) and the Kirmani (from southwestern Iran) varieties of indigo and the different prices they fetched. The business correspondence of Ibn 'Awkal unravels before us the transportation of Indian indigo to al Fustat in Egypt and the farther afield, up to al Mahdiya or present Tunisia.[38] These correspondences were integral to the operations of Ibn 'Awkal who, as a sedentary merchant seated in al Fustat, maintained contacts, sent out instructions and received feedback from his itinerant agents over distant areas through written communications.

Correspondence between merchants also speak of formal communications when a partnership among them was established. Undertaking long-distance journeys and voyages, volatility of the market, immense costs of investments, enormous risk factor involved, unknown political circumstances in faraway lands and uncertainties of profit—all these challenges were often countered by formally entering into a partnership in which merchants meticulously laid down terms and conditions of their mutual investments and risks and the sharing of future profit. There are several instances where such information was passed on to other business compatriots in formal letters with a view to keeping merchants abreast of the developments of activities and engagements among certain traders for a specific venture. What is remarkable and striking is the occasional combination of the communication of a very informal nature among merchants along with the information on partnership. In this, Abraham Udovitch finds an amalgam of formalism and informalism in the commercial network and communication among Jewish 'India traders'.[39] A letter of the twelfth century offers a telling tale in this context: Amram b. Joseph, a noted merchant of Alexandria, writes to the learned banker Nahray b. Nissim at Fustat. Amram's sister's husband, Abul Faraj, sent from India a sizeable amount of camphor to Aden through Hasan b. Bundar. Abul Faraj also sent to Isaac b. Bundar, a very prominent merchant of Aden, a large consignment of Indian products like lac, fine textiles and spikenard with the express instruction to forward these commodities, distributed in eight shares, to merchants in al Fustat. It was, indeed, a complex business operation with at least two middlemen involved in forwarding the cargoes from Aden to al Fustat. No less complex was the circuit of information in currency among interested businessmen spread over a vast zone from India to Egypt. These exchanges of information were indeed, formal in content and address. But there is another layer of information of a more personal nature, of a concern growing out of an intimate relation. Abul Faraj probably ran into rough weather in his business dealings and incurred the strong displeasure of his partners who sued Faraj in a court of law for business irregularities. The news reached his brother-in-law Amram whose sister was Faraj's wife. There was a frantic search for Faraj at various ports on the west coast of India and at a few Red Sea ports, though all these efforts were futile.[40] This was a personal burden for the family and those close to the family. This was what Amram wished to confide to the banker, Nahray b. Nissim to whom the formal aspects of the business contracts of Faraj and legal problems ensuing out of them were also revealed.

In a similar vein, Madmun b. Hasan, a very prominent Jewish merchant and the Representative of Jewish Merchants at Aden wrote to his close friend, Abraham b. Yishu in Malabar in 1120s. The image of personal ties and intimacy between the two merchants (including the mention of some items of gifts for ben Yishu from Aden) is juxtaposed with the highly significant information that Madmun had entered into a partnership with the local governor of Aden, Bilal b. Jarir, to launch a shipping business. The ship, drawing on the joint investment of Madmun and the local governor, plied between Aden and Malabar and Sri Lanka for well over two decades.[41] The very high cost of construction of a sea-going vessel and the attendant expenses of running a shipping network were evidently beyond the means even of a local governor and a business magnate and therefore, the pragmatic need for a formal partnership. The information of striking a professional accord with the governor was possibly passed on to impress upon Abraham Yishu that Madmun had access to corridors of power and certainly belonged to the elite society of Aden. Though the Jews in greater parts of West Asia and North Africa were under the Crescent and considered *dhimmis*, a formal business contract between a Muslim governor and a prominent Jewish merchant was not frowned upon. In 1141, Nahray b. Allan, a leading India trader, informed Arus, his uncle and father-in-law, of his repeated crossings of the Arabian Sea—voyaging from Aden to Malabar and back—as his business ventures in the Red Sea port and the Malabar coast proved successful. Along with his passing detailed business reports to Arus, Nahray b. Allan could not hide his frustration and anger for a frivolous junior merchant who was enjoying prostitutes' association at Lakhaba (close to Aden) and also the company of a wine-serving boy.[42] Once again, we are dished out here a fascinating combination of the simultaneous informal-formal, personal-impersonal information that was doing its round in the Malabar–Aden–Fustat business network.

Driven by the urge to gain profit, the merchant's itineraries to distant destinations inevitably intertwined with separation from family and the loved ones. Such a situation could indeed, take a heavy toll on the merchant and members of his family. A letter of *c.* 1204 superbly illustrates this.[43] An Indian trader from Fustat came to India via Aden, and plied regularly between India and Aden. He went to Malabar or the Coromandel coast; he was away from home and family for at least two years and uncertain about his homecoming. His wife must have been frustrated by this long absence and extremely displeased. Her letters to this merchant have not yet been found. But the reply given by the merchant in response to his wife's frustration and accusations very clearly indicates that the wife was even contemplating a divorce. The merchant writes:

> Now if this is your wish, I cannot blame you. For the waiting has been long. And, I do not know whether the Creator will grant relief immediately so that I can come home, or whether matters will take time, for I cannot come home with nothing. . . . Now, the matter is in your hand. If you wish separation from me, accept the bill of repudiation and you are free. But if this is not your decision and not your desire, do not lose these long years of waiting: perhaps, relief is at hand and you will regret at a time when regret will be of no avail.[44]

In this moving letter, the merchant also bared his heart to his wife by confessing that he was forced to consume lots of alcohol, 'but I conducted myself in an exemplary way'.[45] He clearly assured his wife that he did not keep slave girls or visit whore-houses during these years. The pangs of separation are so poignant when he states, 'All day long I have a lonely heart and am pained by our separation. I feel that pain while writing these lines.'[46]

The central theme of the correspondence of Jewish merchants was, of course, the accounts of their trading activities. These merchants constantly exchanged what may be called commercial intelligence through their letters. That disseminating and collecting these business information was a vital component of their ventures is demonstrated beyond any doubt by these letters. Exchanging information within a given circuit of merchants was no less important than transactional exchanges. A Jewish merchant in the twelfth century writes to his counterpart to report that there was huge demand for Indian iron of different sorts in Aden; actually there was no stock of iron left in Aden. Having thus informed about this market situation, he urges his counterpart in India to send as quickly as possible fresh supplies of iron. Similarly, messages were sent to Abraham Yishu in Mangalore from Aden to energise Indian banyans Sus Siti (Sesu Setti?) Kinbati and Ishaq—who were not so up and doing—to send fresh consignments of Indian iron to Aden by the earliest possible shipment. From Aden also arrived the business report that Indian products like pepper, iron, ginger, fine aloes wood, 'were selling well' in Aden.[47] The commercial information, circulated by and for merchants, also included the prices that certain commodities fetched. That Indian iron was selling at the price of 20 *dinars* per *bahar* (a weight equivalent to 300 pounds or about 150 kgs) at Aden is a typical case in point. The price of pepper, one of the most important Indian exports, figures repeatedly in the business correspondence. In the twelfth century its price ranged roughly from 30 to 35 *dinars* per sack. In 1198, according to a business letter, the price of Indian pepper at Aden soared to 52 *dinars* per sack, though it later came down to 47 *dinars*. A boom in the market forced the merchant to rush, as Nahray b. Allan reported to his uncle that he had made advanced booking for storage space in ships for Indian iron and pepper, as these were in great demand in Aden.[48]

As expected, these business correspondences are replete with sharing of information about profits and losses incurred by merchants, occasional but inevitable loss of lives and merchandise because of shipwreck, and various types of government dues to be paid by merchants at ports and different trade centres. Madmun wrote to ben Yishu in Mangalore in 1139 to report a misfortune. One of the two ships of an Indian ship-owner carrying iron and pepper sank close to Aden. As an outcome of this shipwreck, the entire cargo of pepper was completely lost, but iron was partly salvaged by employing a number of professional divers from the port of Aden. Madmun also did not miss to inform ben Yishu of the cost incurred in hiring divers and of the deduction of that sum from the profit accruable to ben Yishu.[49]

These business letters are also, perhaps most importantly, glowing examples of modes of communication fostering social cohesion. It is already pointed out that the Jewish India traders (*musafir ul Hind*) closely acted and interacted with merchants of different ethnic, religious and cultural affiliations, especially Arabic-speaking Muslim merchants and Indian merchants. There were inevitable instances of rivalry and competition among them, borne out by these letters. But there was seldom any case of intolerance of religious faiths of merchants towards any one group, whether in India or elsewhere in the western Indian Ocean. On the other hand, it hardly raised anyone's eyebrows when Abraham Yishu's 'Hindu' slave and business agent Bama was endearingly addressed as 'Brother Bama' by Madmun in a letter from Aden. In 1145, Judah b. Joseph ha Kohen, the Representative of Jewish merchants at Fustat, unfortunately was attacked by pirates somewhere close to present day Thana during his voyage to Broach (in southern Gujarat). The news of this unfortunate incident reached Mahruz b. Jacob, a prominent Jewish shipowner (*nakhuda*), then at Mangalore. He implored Joseph ha Kohen to immediately return to Mangalore by availing of the earliest possible ship plying along the coastal network. He also sent some cash to Joseph through an Indian 'Hindu' ship-owner, Tinbu by name. 'If my lord,' he continues,

> you need any gold, please take it on my account from the nakhoda Tinbu, for . . . between him and me there are bonds of inseparable friendship and brotherhood.[50]

The cooperation and amity among different merchants of various faiths amply demonstrate that their communications, indeed prompted by financial considerations, lowered cultural barriers and fostered inter-faith cohesion. Unlike the official records of the East India Companies of the Dutch, the French and the English, these letters are not business papers, offering loads of quantifiable data; but they light up the human face of participating merchants. The documentary genizah, besides uniquely informing about the world of Indian Ocean merchants, enlightens us on the sharing of information, business fortune or otherwise, emotions, cultural codes and values of these merchants at inter-personal, inter-group and intra-group levels, in a way that is seldom encountered in any other contemporary source.

NOTES AND REFERENCES

1. D.D. Kosambi, *An Introduction to the Study of Indian History*; Romila Thapar, *Early India from Origins to c. AD 1300*; R.S. Sharma, *Perspectives*; B.D. Chattopadhyaya, *Studying Early India.*
2. Romila Thapar, *The Mauryas Revisited.* The earlier view that the Mauryan state was a monolithic and unitary polity has undergone considerable modifications; the elements of centripetality in the Mauryan polity, however, are not doubted.
3. See *SI*, R.G. Basak, *Asokan Edicts*, for these terms figuring in Rock Edicts II, XIII and XIV and Minor Rock Edict I of Aśoka. The term *pṛthvī* occurs in the Nittur version of Minor Rock Edict I—see Sircar, *Asokan Studies*, p. 14.
4. *SI*, Rock Edict, XIV.
5. Ibid., p. 47; Minor Rock Edict I, Siddhapur, Jatinga-Rameshwar and Brahmagiri versions.
6. Mukherjee, *Studies in the Aramaic Edicts of Aśoka.*
7. H.C. Raychaudhuri, *Political History of Ancient India with a Commentary by B.N. Mukherjee*, pp. 617–40.
8. Sircar, *Asokan Studies*, pp. 94ff.

9. See the two Separate Rock Edicts of Aśoka from Dhauli and Jaugada (both in Orissa); Sircar, *SI*, pp. 40–6.
10. R.C. Majumdar, *The Classical Accounts of India.*
11. Mukherjee, *Aramaic Edicts*, pp. 9–22.
12. Majumdar, *The Classical Accounts*; G. Bongard Levin, *Mauryan India.*
13. Vide *KAS*, II, 36 (*Nāgarikapraṇidhi*).
14. *KAS*, I, 12.
15. Majumdar, *The Classical Accounts.* The Classical authors considered the spies as forming the sixth group in their seven-fold classification of Indian society.
16. U.N. Ghoshal, *A History of Indian Public Life*, vol. II, finds in this Kauṭilyan scheme a clever application of mob psychology by secret agents to create a favourable disposition to the ruler.
17. Kane, *History of Dharmasastra*, III.
18. Nasik inscription of Gautamīputra Sātakarṇi, yr. 24; Sircar, *Select Inscriptions*, p. 201.
19. The point has been excellently illustrated by Barrie M. Morrison with the mapping of the issuing centres of land grants and locations of property transfers in Bengal from the fifth to the thirteenth centuries in the light of inscriptions. See his *Political Centres and Cultural Regions in Early Bengal.*
20. Ray, Chattopadhyay, Chakravarti and Mani, *A Sourcebook of Indian Civilization*, pp. 621–4.
21. Sircar, *Indian Epigraphy.*
22. Colin Renfrew, 'Trade as Action at Distance', in *Ancient Trade and Civilization*, ed. J.A. Sablov and C.C. Lamberg-Karlovsky, 1975, pp. 3–59.
23. Ranabir Chakravarti ed., *Trade in Early India*; particularly the Introduction; idem., *Trade and Traders in Early Indian Society.*
24. There is a voluminous literature on the Silk Road trade and India's trade with the Roman world. Only a few recent and outstanding works are mentioned hereunder. M.G. Raschke, 'New Studies in the Roman Commerce with the East', *Aufstieg und Niedergang in der Romischer Welt*, vol. IX, Berlin, pp. 604–1361; Xin Ri Liu, *Ancient India and Ancient China AD 1–600*, 1986; A.G. Frank, 'The Centrality of Central Asia', *Studies in History*, vol. VIII, 1992, pp. 43–98; Irene M. Frank and David M. Brownstone, *The Silk Road: A History*, New York and Oxford, 1986; *Cambridge History of Iran*, vol. III (chapter on economic history); Garry K. Young, *Rome's Eastern Trade, International Commerce and Imperial Policy 31 BC–AD 305*, 2001; Richard Stoneman, *Palmyra and its Empire*, 1992; G.W. Bowersock, *Roman Arabia*, 1983; Vimala Begley and Richard Daniel de Puma, eds., *Rome and India*, 1992 (Ind. rpt); Marie-Françoise Boussac and J.F. Salles, eds., *Athens, Aden, Arikamedu*, 1995; F.de Romanis and Andre Tchernia, eds., *Crossings*, 1997; B.N. Mukherjee, *The Rise and*

Fall of the Kushāṇa Empire, 1989; R.N. Frye, 'The Rise of the Kushan Empire', in *History of Humanity*, vol. III, pp. 456–60.

25. Karl Jettmar, ed., *Antiquities from Northern Pakistan*, vol. I, 1989.
26. Mukherjee, *Rise and Fall of the Kushāṇa Empire.*
27. This was first pointed out by D.D. Kosambi, *Combined Methods in Indology and Other Essays*, edited with an Introduction by B.D. Chattopadhyaya, 2003 (especially the essay 'Dhenukakata', originally published in 1955); this was later elaborated by Himanshu Prabha Ray, *Monastery and Guild*, 1986.
28. Begley and De Puma, eds., *Rome and India*, especially L. Casson's essay therein; Pliny, *Naturalis Historia*, tr., H. Rackham, vol. VI, line 104, p. 26.
29. A superb translation of this document is made by L. Casson, 'New Lights on Maritime Loans: P. Vindob G 40822', in Chakravarti, ed., *Trade in Early India*, pp. 228–43 (originally published in *Zeitschrift fur Papyrologie und Epigraphik*, Band 84, 1990); also, Ranabir Chakravarti, 'On Board the Hermapollon: Transporting Gangetic Nard from Muziris', in Martin Brandtner and Shishir Kumar Panda (eds), *Interrogating History, Essays for Hermann Kulke*, 2006, pp. 146-64.
30. These points have been discussed by Chakravarti, ed., *Trade in Early India*.
31. A.N. Upadhyay, ed., *The Kuvalayamālā of Udyotanasuri*, 1969.
32. Damodara, *Unniyaticaritam*, tr. M.G.S. Narayanan, 1971; extract quoted in Ray, Chattopadhyaya, Chakravarti and Mani, *A Sourcebook of Indian Civilization*, pp. 457–8.
33. Contemporary South India was noted for the import of impressive number of Arabic/Persian war horses by sea-borne trade. That is why these were known as *bahri* or sea-borne horses in the Arabic and Persian texts. Particularly important in this connection are the accounts of Marco Polo, Ibn Battuta and Abdullah Wassaf. See, Simon Digby, *Warhorses and Elephants in the Delhi Sultanate*, 1971; also Ranabir Chakravarti, 'Horse Trade and Piracy at Tana (Thana, Maharashtra, India): Gleanings from Marco Polo', *JESHO*, vol. XXXIV, 1991, pp. 159–82. *Karpura* or camphor was brought to India from South-East Asia. Recent readings into an inscription from Baruch (Indonesia), dated AD 1088, recording the presence there of an important Tamil mercantile organisation, suggest that both China and Baruch were notable sources of camphor, consumed in India. See, N. Karashima, ed., *Ancient and Medieval Seafaring in the Indian Ocean: the Evidence of Inscriptions and Ceramic Sherds*, 2002.
34. The greatest and most celebrated scholar in this field is S.D. Goitein, *Letters*, 1973; S.D. Goitein, *A Mediterranean Society*, in 6 vols., 1967–96. A fantastic collection of letters of Jewish 'India Traders' (about 400 documents) was prepared by Goitein, but remains unpublished till date. I was given very kind permission to use the Goitein Geniza Laboratory, Dept. of the Near East, Princeton University, Princeton, USA; grateful thanks are recorded to Professors Mordechai Friedman, Abraham Udovitch and M.R. Cohen.

Roxani Margaritti, of Emory University (USA) was gracious enough to have presented me with her unpublished Ph.D. thesis ['Like the Place of Congregation on Judgement Day: Maritime Trade and Urban Civilization in Medieval Aden (*c.* 1083–1229)']. Without their immense help and cooperation, my studies of the 'India Trader' would have certainly been very limited. For an understanding of the importance of Fustat, see Abraham Udovitch, 'Fatimid Cairo: Crossroads of World Trade—From Spain to India', in Marianne Barrucand, ed. *L'Egypte Fatimide*, 1999, pp. 681–91.

35. Based on these letters, Amitav Ghosh created a masterly narrative of Abraham b. Yishu; see, *In an Antique Land*, 1990.
36. Ranabir Chakravarti, 'Nakhudas and Nauvittakas: Ship-owning Merchants on the West Coast of India (AD 1000–1500)', *JESHO*, vol. XLII, 2000, pp. 34–64; idem., 'Ships, Seafarings and Ship-owners: India and the Indian Ocean (*c.* AD 700-1500)', in David Parkin and Ruth Barnes (eds.), *Ships and the Development of Maritime Technology in the Indian Ocean*, 2002, pp. 28–61.
37. Joseph al Adani in *India Book* (Ch. IV, no. 32); Zikri Kohen in *Letters*, pp. 14, 181, 197, 199, 203; Hiba al Hamawi, *Letters*, p. 247; Ali b. Muhammad Nili in *Letters*, p. 190 and Fofali in *Letters*, p. 63.
38. Norman A. Stillman, 'The Eleventh Century Merchant House of Ibn 'Awkal', *JESHO*, vol. XVI, 1973, pp. 15–88; also Ranabir Chakravarti, 'The Export of Sindani Indigo from India to the 'West' in the Eleventh Century', *IHR*, vol. XVIII, 1996, pp. 18–30.
39. Abraham Udovitch, 'Formalism and Informalism in the Social and Economic Institutions of the Medieval Islamic World', in A. Banani and S. Vryonis, Jr., eds., *Individualism and Conformity in Classical Islam*, 1977, pp. 61–71.
40. *India Book*, Ch. II, no. 2, p. 45.
41. *Letters*, pp. 183 and 200.
42. *India Book*, Ch. V, no. 11, p. 243. Goitein suggests that the mention of the company of the wine serving boy possibly indicates the homosexual inclination of the merchant.
43. *Letters*, pp. 220–26.
44. *Letters*, p. 225.
45. *Letters*, p. 225
46. *Letters*, p. 225.
47. S.D. Goitein, 'From Aden to India: Specimens of Correspondence of India Traders in the Twelfth Century', in *Trade in Early India*, ed. Chakravarti, pp. 416–34 (originally published in *JESHO*, vol. XXIII, 1980). The name Sesu Setti was suggested by Ghosh, *In an Antique Land*.
48. 'Portrait of Medieval India Trader: Three Letters from the Cairo Geniza', *Bulletin of the School of Oriental and African Studies*, vol. XLVII, 1987, pp. 448–64.
49. *Letters*, pp. 185–92, especially p. 189.

50. *Letters*, pp. 62–5; also Ranabir Chakravarti, 'Coastal Trade and Voyages in Konkan: The Early Medieval Scenario', *Indian Economic and Social History Review*, vol. XXXV, 1998, pp. 97–124. How communication promotes social cohesion is brought out on a different context (the *varṇa-jāti* society and the non-*varṇa* society of traditional India) by R.S. Sharma, 'Communication and Social Cohesion', in *Perspectives*; also see Kunal Chakrabarti, 'Textual Authority and Oral Exposition: The Vrata Ritual as a Channel of Communication in Early Medieval Bengal', *Studies in History*, vol. X, 1994, pp. 217–91.

The correspondence among merchants, in the documentary geniza, also occasionally unravel disputes and quarrels among them. In other words, these letters do not offer merely images of amiable interactions among merchants, but lay bare mutual trading of charges against one another, something not entirely unexpected in the tough, competitive world of business. In several such correspondences of the eleventh century one Jewish merchant wrote about another Jewish merchant being liar, untrustworthy and unscruplous. One merchant was in fact labeled by another as a thief. These have come to light, thanks to the study of Moshe Gil, 'Jewish Merchants in the Light of Eleventh-Century Geniza Documents', *JESHO*, 46, 2003, pp. 273-319; especially pp. 305-14. It is however significant to note that, according to Gil, letters referring to disputes among merchants form

> only a small percentage—something like five percent of the letters, and a much smaller percentage of the number of transactions described in the letters. We may conclude that except for unusual cases involving anger, unfair competition, lack of trust, breach of agreement and the like, business generally ran smoothly and was characterized by fairness, based on both family ties and friendship. (p. 314)

CHAPTER 13

An Enchanting Seascape: Through Epigraphic Lens

In the understanding of Indian history the land question has for long been considered critically important. There has been an unbroken continuity over several millennia—especially during pre-modern times—in the overwhelming importance of agriculture in the economic life of the subcontinent. The making or unmaking of large territorial powers, the daily life, the belief systems and associated ritual practices in India cannot be delinked from the agrarian scenario. There is, however, another geographical reality: the subcontinent is washed on three sides by the sea. Its long coastlines jut out far into the Indian Ocean, the only embayed ocean on earth. That the subcontinent (along with Sri Lanka) stands at the centre of the Indian Ocean, which occupies about 20 per cent of the total maritime space on this planet, is an inescapable fact of geography. Both the littorals are dotted with numerous ports of varying importance, and connected with the vast continental space by overland and fluvial routes. A long-term view of history, say spanning over the last three millennia, certainly underlines how different sea-lanes of the Indian Ocean acted as bridges among diverse communities in South, South East and West Asia and in North and East Africa. Yet, the general perception of Indian history either shuts out the sea or marginalizes it. The sea begins to acquire significance only in the historiography of its colonial phase when India and the Indian Ocean were incorporated into the colonial and capitalist world economy. The huge archival materials of the Portuguese Estado da India, the French, the Dutch and the English East India Companies provide immense data, especially statistical information, to the historian for delving into the world of Indian Ocean maritime trade.[1]

The dominant perception has been that the 'age of discoveries', beginning in the late fifteenth century with the advent of the Portuguese, prepared the stage for the Indian Ocean to be reckoned as an oceanic space fit for the study of maritime history. Such a recognition stems from the idea that the Indian Ocean emerged for the first time as a vast zone of economic, naval and political activities from the early sixteenth century onwards. Seen from this angle, the principal agent of change in the Indian Ocean situation was the European presence in terms of its economic, technological, military and political superiority. The essence of K.M. Panikker's identification of the Vasco da Gama epoch lies in this logic. This Eurocentric view of the maritime history of the Indian Ocean has been effectively critiqued by many specialists, notably J.E. van Leur and Ashin Das Gupta.[2] One has to remember that Vasco da Gama had to take the guidance of an experienced Arab navigator (*muallim*) to reach Calicut, the premier port in fifteenth-sixteenth century Malabar, from Malindi in east Africa, since the Indian Ocean was a completely unknown maritime space for him. This maritime space was on the other hand frequented by a large number of East African, West Asian, South Asian, South East Asian and Chinese merchants, shippers, sailors and pilgrims.[3] There is an impressive body of literature on this subject. The manual of Ibn Majid, the greatest *muallim* in the fifteenth century Indian Ocean, is a case in point; he recorded in his manual of navigation a considerable volume of floating traditions of the seafaring in the Indian Ocean during and prior to the fifteenth century.[4] To this one can add the celebrated voyages of the Ming admiral, Zeng he (Cheng ho), across the Indian Ocean from 1404 to 1433.[5] What I would like to emphasize is that the Indian Ocean was not undiscovered before the arrival of the voyagers from the North Atlantic. The long history of seafaring in the Indian Ocean prior to the sixteenth century is recognized by Bouchon and Lombard.[6] A strong case has been made out in recent historiography for the study of trade and cultural networks in the Indian Ocean prior to the establishment of European hegemony. 'The economic impact of this trade was not incidental, as indeed also its imprint on various cultures and its linking of Roman, Arab, Indian and Chinese centres'.[7]

There has of late been a spate of publications on the commercial and cultural contacts between South Asia and the Roman empire from the late first century BC to third century AD. The 1980s saw two fresh translations of the *Periplus of the Erythraean Sea* by an anonymous seafarer, an indispensable source material for the study of commerce and contacts in the Indian Ocean in the days before the arrival of the European.[8] But South Asia's maritime history is no longer studied on the basis of textual accounts alone; archaeological artifacts have become indispensable for this enquiry.[9] Along with a proliferation of research on early trade history, there has been a major rethink on old orthodoxies. The notion that the west (in this case, the Roman empire) was the active agent of this history has been questioned, and the significance of the role of Indian traders in this commerce has been recognized.[10] Yet, the writings on maritime history for the period subsequent to AD 300 look marginal when compared to the plethora of publications on agrarian economy, land systems, peasant society, state formation, belief systems and ideologies. From the 1960s to the 1980s, Indian history-writing on early medieval (*c.* AD 500-1300) period focussed predominantly on the assumed fragmentation/segmentation of polity, and the processes of peasantization and agrarian expansion, the concern with the latter being often developed in opposition to the focus on commerce and cities. In fact, the unprecedented agrarian expansion was seen as a fallout of the widespread urban decay in India between AD 300 and 1200, a phase in which Indian feudalism was said to have developed. The most telling evidence in support of this formulation was culled from a vast number of inscriptions, mostly copper plates recording grants of revenue-free landed property to religious and secular donees. Historians of Indian feudalism cited the relative silence about merchants and cities in the inscriptions as evidence of the marginalization of trade, in particular sea-borne long distance trade during AD 500-1000. The emphasis on epigraphic data led to a persistent neglect of other types of data. Ships, sailors, merchants and pilgrims frequenting the Indian Ocean in the post-500 AD period became almost invisible in this historiography.[11]

II

These preliminary remarks help us appreciate the significance of the book presently under review.[12] An exploration of Indian seafaring cannot but take us to the peninsular part of the subcontinent, because of its proximity to the Indian Ocean. The western seaboard seems to have received more sustained and regular attention of scholars. The study of commerce through the western seaboard has had to depend on the impressions of various Arab, Persian, Chinese and European authors, datable from the mid-ninth to the fourteenth centuries, many of whom may not have themselves visited India. Inscriptional data of this period may also occasionally fill up some of the gaps in our understanding of this commerce. But these sources rarely tell us much about the merchants, the actual players in the game. Of late, there have been attempts to delve into the evidence of the Jewish Geniza documents which offer rare insights into the world of merchants, especially the Jewish 'India traders' (*musafir ul Hind*), merchants from the Islamic civilization and Indian merchants.[13] The history of the Deccan and South India—especially the Tamil country—has been, on the other hand, a subject of sustained debate, with studies looking at the nature of state polity, agrarian structure, urban experience and, to an extent, commerce.[14] One distinctive characteristic of trade in South India during the early medieval period is the presence of mercantile organizations often loosely labelled as 'guilds', the likes of which are virtually absent in contemporary north India. Known as the 500 Svāmis of Ayyavole, the Maṇigrāmam, the Nānādeśī, the Añjuvannam and suchlike, these bodies have prominently figured in a few works, but seldom with a focus on the Indian Ocean network that was burgeoning during this time.[15] Herein lies the significance of the present volume of essays edited by Noboru Karashima.

Consisting of twenty chapters and four appendices, the volume unravels the maritime linkages of the Tamil country with Sri Lanka, both mainland and maritime South East Asia and China during the period from the ninth to the fourteenth centuries. The bulk of the evidence comes in the form of inscriptions and Chinese ceramic sherds (the primary data has been placed in the appendices), many of which are recent findings. The availability of the original texts, the translation of many of these records, and the attempt at classifying the quantifiable epigraphic data (a hallmark of Karashima's researches) make this volume an invaluable sourcebook for south Indian maritime commerce.

The book is the outcome of an international research project entitled 'Medieval Commercial Activities in the Indian Ocean as Revealed from Inscriptions and Chinese Ceramic Sherds' under the aegis of Taisho University, Tokyo. Besides the obvious addition to our existing knowledge on this subject, the efforts of Karashima and his colleagues (especially Y. Subbarayalu) also raise a number of methodological issues. During the 1980s and 1990s, our knowledge of the history of South India from *c.* eighth to the sixteenth centuries (till the end of the Vijayanagar empire) was immensely deepened by a very large number of epigraphic records. The availability of a mass of inscriptions made possible statistical and quantitative studies, something rarely done for the ancient and early medieval times. Besides Karashima and Subbarayalu, several others including Burton Stein, George Spencer, K.R. Hall, R. Champakalakshmi and Vijaya Ramaswami arrived at a range of conclusions on the nature of state and society in South India during this period.

The principal thrust of these studies was on the analyses of state, agrarian society and the ideology of sectarian devotional (*bhakti*) cults. Hall, Meera Abraham, Ramaswami and Champakalakshmi explored the epigraphic data to understand the non-agrarian sector of the economy, viz., crafts, commerce and cities. These studies discussed inland trade but left out the trade of the Indian Ocean. For the study of long-distance trade, historians continued to prefer accounts of foreigners to epigraphic data, with almost a set belief that early medieval inscriptions primarily tell us about rural societies and the agrarian milieu.[16]

The present volume under Karashima's editorship provides a significant and welcome point of departure, away from this conventional approach to epigraphic materials. The focus is on merchants, their professional organizations and seafaring activities through the lens of as many as 314 inscriptions, out of which about 150 are related to one mercantile organization, the Ainūrruvar. This is a substantial advancement of our understanding of the Tamil mercantile organization, because Abraham's study of the Ainūrruvar and Maṇigrāmam was based on about 150 inscriptions. Karashima and Subbarayalu believe that the Ainūrruvar was in fact an overarching umbrella organization of merchants within which were included bodies like the Maṇigrāmam and Nānādesī. While the very term Nānādesī highlights the itinerant nature of the professions of its members, the Maṇigrāmam derived its name, as Kosambi rightly suggested, from Vaṇiggrāma (or a collection/body of merchants).[17] The Añjuvaṇṇam seems to have denoted a body of non-Indian merchants, discussion on which will be taken up later.

The Ainūrruvar, the umbrella organization of merchants, is the subject of close study in this volume. The Ainūrruvars are said to have originated from Ayyappolilpura or Aihole (Bijapur district, Karnataka), the seat of goddess Parameśvarī; they descended from three gods, Vāsudeva, Kandali and Mūlabhadra. They possessed 500 charters *(vīraśāsanam);* practised the dharma (code of conduct like honesty and braveness) of merchants *(bananju/valañjiyar)* and frequented 18 *paṭṭanas* and 32 *velāpuras* (ports, cf. the Sanskrit term *velākula,* meaning a port). Their close association with Ayyavole (Aihole) accounts for the common expression denoting these merchants: the '500 Svāmīs of Ayyavole'. Interestingly enough, a larger number of inscriptions mentioning these merchants come from Tamil Nadu (especially Thanjavur, Tiruchirappalli and Madurai districts) than from Karnataka. The earliest Tamil eulogy of the Ainūrruvar goes back to *c.* AD 950, while their regular presence in inscriptions from Karnataka is noticeable only from the eleventh century, with a clear spatial concentration in Dharwar, Bijapur and Mysore. Thus the Ainūrruvar merchants, though described as having originated from Aihole, made their presence felt in the eastern part of the Tamil country, and significantly close to the Coromandel coast. Herein lies the significance of the present study: it situates the Tamil merchant in the Indian Ocean network prior to the fifteenth century.

These merchants and their organizations figure in inscriptions in diverse contexts. Sometimes the inscriptions record a donation to a temple by a merchant belonging to the Ainūrruvar; on some other occasion a tank is named after the mercantile body, which is entrusted with its upkeep. The inscriptions record resolutions or agreements reached by the organization of merchants, and give us instances when the Ainūrruvar confered the status of *'erivīrapaṭṭinam'* on certain commercial centres where their merchants and guardsmen resided. They also tell us that the Ainūrruvar at times transferred the right to collect *paṭṭanappāguḍi* (cesses on diverse commodities, both staples and luxuries) to sacred centres, and pronounced punishments against non-Ainūrruvar merchants. One of the most startling features of these inscriptions, without parallel in contemporary North India, is the absence of any eulogy of a political authority. In other words, these inscriptions help us directly hear the voices of merchants of South India. The only other source that relates to merchants—including Indians—in the Indian Ocean network are the letters of Jewish merchants recovered from the Cairo Genizah.

Interestingly, many of these inscriptions of Tamil merchants are found in regions outside India, leaving little room for doubt on their regular presence in Sri Lanka, Myanmar, Thailand, Sumatra and China. Karashima, Subbarayalu, Pathmanathan, Shanmugam and Ramesh have either revisited readings of some of these inscriptions by earlier experts, or brought to light hitherto unknown evidence. A ninth century inscription from Takua pa in southern Thailand, edited earlier by Hultzsch, talks about the Maṇigrāmam, protecting a tank. A thirteenth century record from Pagan, Myanmar, first studied by Hultzsch, refers to a gift to a Viṣṇu temple by a Nānādesī merchant from Mahodayapuram in Mālaimaṇḍalam. It is a bit strange that there is no comment on the identification of Mahodayapuram with the great early port of Muziris (Muciripattanam of the Sangam texts) near Cranganore in Kerala. Whether Muziris still continued to be a port of some note in thirteenth century Malabar, or was a shadow of its past, or experienced a revival in the thirteenth century are points which Karashima has ignored. The inscription refers to a merchant of Malabar crossing the Bay of Bengal which must have been well connected with the Coromandel ports.

Karashima rightly includes in his study the Tamil inscription from Quanzhou in China of AD 1281 (originally edited by T.N. Subramaniam) which tells us about the installation of a Śiva image by Campanda Perumal with the permission of Ceccai Khan (Chinese emperor Kublai Khan). The temple itself is called Tirukkaniccuram, so named certainly after Kublai Khan, possibly because the very purpose of installing the deity was to 'pray for the health of the authority' (p. 16) Quanzhou was one of the leading ports in south China which must have witnessed the presence of Tamil merchants on so regular a basis that the need for a Śiva temple was felt. The nature of interactions between the Tamil merchants and their Chinese counterparts could have been probed further. Information from the Quanzhou inscription could have been supplemented with evidence on the China-Coromandel maritime network available in the Sung annals, the *Chu fan chi* of Chau ju Kua (*c*. 1225) and Marco Polo's travel accounts (late thirteenth century).[18] The Quanzhou inscription must be seen as part of a larger corpus of information on the network between the Middle Kingdom and Chu-lien which was definitely established since the time of Rājarāja Cola.

Karashima and his colleagues have brought to light two hitherto unknown Tamil inscriptions. The first, dated either to 1183 or 1283, is at the Nakhon Si Thammarat in Thailand, and records the gift of one Damana Senāpati to brāhmaṇas. The second inscription, possibly from the latter half of the thirteenth century, is at the Jakarta Museum. It records a charitable deed by one Senāpati Rakan Dīpaṅkara for the merit of the ruler, Peritu Śrī Mahārāja. It is a bilingual record with Tamil and Javanese sections, proof of regular communication between the users of the two languages.[19] No less significant is the name of the donor, Dīpaṅkara, implying his Buddhist leanings. Dīpaṅkara in Pali is equivalent to the Sanskrit *dvīpaṅkara*, literally a mariner who crosses the sea to reach islands (*dvīpas*), and actually, an epithet for the Buddha himself.

The re-reading of the inscription from Barus, Indonesia (1088) by Subbaryalu is an excellent scholarly contribution. Previously studied by K.A. Nilakantha Sastri, this inscription narrates the presence of the mercantile organization. The Five Hundred of the Thousand Directions, at the *velāpuram* (port) of Varochu (Barus), also known *as Mātaṅkari-vallava-teci-uyyakkoṇṭa-paṭṭinam*. The purpose of the inscription is to record some grants in cash to the *nakara-senāpati nāṭṭuceṭṭiyār* ('the captain of the town, the merchant of the locality'), *paṭinenbhūmi-teci-appar* ('the man of the merchants of the 18 countries) and *mavettu* (possibly 'guardsmen of the trade guild'). Subbarayalu suggests that

Barus or Varocu derived its importance from the availability of two types of camphor: from Barus (*Vārocu cūtan*) and China (*Cīna-cūtan*). Camphor was in great demand in India as a fragrance and as a necessary ingredient for burning a lamp and/or incense before a deity. The inscription highlights the transit trade in Chinese camphor (cf. the expression *cīnakarpūram* in the Motuppalli inscription of Gaṇapati as a dutiable item of trade in 1245)[20] through Barus. The next logical step is to assume the significance of maritime South East Asia as a link between China and the south eastern littorals of India.[21] The Barus epigraph also brings to light visits to Varocu by people having something to do with ships (*mārakkalam*), who are clearly differentiated from the *mārakkala-nāyan* (ship-captains) and *kevis/kevus* (oarsmen). Thanks to the insightful reading of the record by Subbarayalu, the image of the Tamil shippers and sailors in Indonesia is clearly visible. The present reviewer fully agrees with him that the men having something to do with ships should be taken to denote the ship-owners. This is the first time that the presence of a particular type of Tamil merchant, namely the ship-owner, is revealed by epigraphic evidence. Subbarayalu is also right when he traces in the expression 'the owners of *mārakkalam*' the possible root of the terms *maraikkayan* or *maraikkar*, denoting the seafaring merchants of South India since the sixteenth century.

Out of this record emerge a few more issues which, however, have not been addressed by Subbarayalu. The ship-owning merchants were well known in the western Indian Ocean and the western littorals of India—from Gujarat to Malabar. They figure in the Arabic and Persian accounts and the business letters of Jewish merchants as *nakhudas;* the term literally stands for the lord (*khuda*) of a ship (*nau*). This term corresponds to the Sanskrit word *nauvittaka* denoting an extremely rich merchant whose wealth (*vitta*) was derived from ships (*nau*). In other words, the *nauvittaka* was a ship-owner. So regular was the active presence of these ship-owners on the west coast that Sanskrit inscriptions frequently used two abbreviations, *nau* for the *nauvittaka* and *nākhu* for the *nakhuda;* at least on one occasion these two were used as interchangeable terms. Among the men who actually manned the ship the foremost was the captain, variously known in Sanskrit as *karṇadhāra, mahānāvika* and as an expert in *naupracāravidyā* (art of navigation). In the celebrated manual of Ibn Majid the figure of the *muallim* or the navigator looms large. The other sailors, obviously under the general command of the ship-captain or the navigator, were known as *nāvikakarmakara* in Sanskrit inscriptions from the west coast datable from AD 1000 to 1500, and as *al askar* in ibn Majid's text. The correspondence between the *mārakkala-nāyan* and the *mahānāvika is* unmistakable and the same can be said about the *kevi/kevu* and the *nāvikakarmakara/al askar.*[22] The significance of the Barus inscription is thus best appreciated when it is situated in the broader context of India's role in the Indian Ocean network. Subbaryalu's readings have established evidence for the expected but hitherto unproved presence of Indian ship-owning merchants, captains and sailors in maritime South East Asia.

The volume also enlightens us on the presence of Tamil merchants in neighbouring Sri Lanka. Chapters 4, 5 and 8 specifically address this issue in the light of epigraphic records from Viharehinna, Lankatilaka and Budumuttava. The readings into the Lankatilaka record, in conjunction with the thirteenth century Piranmalai inscription, deserve our special attention. The latter lists a very impressive range of commodities, from bulk agricultural products (salt, paddy, rice, areca nuts, iron) to precious and prestige goods (silk, sandal, camphor, oil of camphor, aloes wood and horses), thus presenting a clear image of the juxtaposition of staples and luxuries in India's maritime trade in the Indian Ocean. This is a point that needs to be emphasized, as the conventional historiography of early Indian maritime commerce generally relegates the transaction in bulk commodities to a marginal position and lays undue stress on the trade in exotic and precious goods that were portable and traded in small quantities. Of the luxury items mentioned in the Piranmalai record, several must have been of South East Asian origin (e.g., camphor, camphor oil and sandal), while the horse, absolutely indispensable for the cavalry, was shipped from the Persian Gulf, Oman and Hadramawat coasts and from Aden to Malabar and Sri Lanka. That is why these horses were described in Arabic and Persian accounts as *bahri or* sea-borne horses.[23]

Sri Lanka features repeatedly in Arabic and Persian texts as Serendib or Silandib, highlighting the role of the island in the maritime commerce of the western Indian Ocean. Malini Dias' contribution to the volume focuses on the relatively less known participation of Sri Lanka in the Bay of Bengal trade. She presents an overview of the trading links between Sri Lanka and Myanmar.

It goes to the credit of the editor and contributors that the epigraphic data are presented along with the evidence of Chinese ceramic sherds from several coastal sites in Tamil Nadu (Periyapattinam Kayal, Darasuram, Velur, Gangaikondacholapuram, Arikamedu) and Sri Lanka.

The importance of pottery for the study of ancient long-distance commerce in India has been established by the Arretine Ware, the Rouletted Ware and the Roman amphorae. The scholarly interest in the evidence of Chinese ceramics found in South Asia is a relatively recent trend. It provides material/visual proof of maritime links between the subcontinent and China, which is only partially revealed through textual and epigraphic documentation. Many of the finds of these ceramic sherds have been close to the coast, and help locate some of the port sites in Coromandel. The emergent picture is one of lively linkages between the Coromandel coast and China, which peaked during the famous voyages of the Ming admiral Zeng he in the early fifteenth century.

Among the ports discussed in the volume is Viśākhapaṭṭinam, located in the northern Andhra littorals. The essay on the Ainūrruvar speaks of this port, though not in detail. Karashima and Subbarayalu look at it as a coastal commercial centre with an active presence of the mercantile group Añjuvaṇṇam. Following Meera Abraham they have considered the Añjuvaṇṇam as a body of non-indigenous merchants, mainly Arabs. The famous Cochin copper plates of AD 1000 clearly show that Añjuvaṇṇam stood for a body of non-indigenous merchants, mostly of Jewish origin, with a chief named Joseph Rabban.[24] The Arab merchants are generally described in inscriptions from coastal Western India as *tājjikas* or *yavanas.* Inscriptions from early medieval Konkan clearly distinguish the *tājjika* from the *haṁjamāna* or *haṁyamāna.* The *haṁjamāna* are often seen to be the same as the Añjuvaṇṇam. Is it possible to see in the Añjuvaṇṇam of the Viśākhapaṭṭinam inscription the presence of Jewish merchants on the eastern sea board?

Even more important is the epigraphic evidence for the change in the name of Viśākhapaṭṭinam that first figures as a port in an inscription as early as 1068. Sometime between 1068 and 1090, the port was renamed Kulottuṅgacoḷapaṭṭinam, obviously after emperor Kulottuṅgacoḷa I (1070-1120). This is the solitary instance of renaming an existing port after a reigning Coḷa king. By attaching his name to this Andhra port, Kulottunga certainly enhanced its status, though it was far away from the Kaveri delta, the core area of the Coḷa kingdom. The renaming of the port seems to have coincided with Kulottunga's decision to withdraw tolls and customs *(sunga),* obviously to promote long-distance maritime trade.[25]

In highlighting the seafaring activities of the Tamil mercantile groups, the book explores the South East Asian context. Moving away from earlier notions of 'Indianization' of South East Asia and the development of Hindu colonies in the Far East, the authors explore the cultural exchanges and interactions between India and South East Asia, without however, obliterating the markers of Indian influences on the region. This probe into epigraphic materials effectively demonstrates that Tamil merchants undertook the voyages despite the many risks and dangers. These inscriptions also underline the fact that *sastric* injunctions against sea voyages were regularly ignored by Indian merchants, ship-owners and mariners. This being the central message of this excellent volume, I was surprised by the indefensible assertion of K.V. Ramesh:

> In spite of the fact that India has a long coastline on the east as well as west, Indians never displayed interest in seafaring activities and in building and plying their own ships, as can be inferred from the loud silence about the seas in Indian inscriptions, except in conventional contexts.[26]

The incongruity of Ramesh's perceptions about early Indian seafaring is self-evident. The statement contradicts all that is so painstakingly recovered from numerous inscriptions. It is in fact an indication that even a highly competent epigraphist like Ramesh can be completely off the mark as he looks merely at the text and misreads the context.

Reviewing a book such as this is a pleasure. When the very facticity of evidence is being repeatedly challenged nowadays, this volume underlines the primacy of source materials for the appreciation of the past. That inscriptions offer descriptive categories vis-a-vis the prescriptive categories in the Dharmaśāstras is tellingly displayed by the volume.[27] Karashima and his colleagues have opened new vistas for future studies. The only limitation of this volume is the lack of an overview that seeks to combine insights from epigraphic sources with other materials to portray the world of Indian merchants in the Indian Ocean network prior to AD 1500. The authors could also have attempted a fresh explanation of the Coḷa rulers' sustained interest for nearly 140 years in the affairs of the Bay of Bengal. Without being explicit, this volume seems to suggest that the Coḷa naval exercises in the Bay of Bengal were not prompted by what Spencer termed as plunder dynamics. A long range view of seafaring in the Indian Ocean prior to 1500 also indicates that merchants, in spite of forming compact professional organizations, were not political animals and seldom strove to capture political power. On the other hand, political powers of the pre-1500 days seem to have been aware of the revenue-bearing potential of maritime trade, but barring exceptions, did not consider the Indian Ocean as an arena for establishing their sovereignty. With the arrival of the North

Atlantic merchants and powers, there was a sea change in the Indian Ocean scenario.

NOTES

1. Ashin Das Gupta, one of the founding fathers of Indian Ocean studies, maintained that statistical data in official Company papers was not an all-purpose key to solving the historian's problems of understanding the sea and the people connected with it. See for example his collection of essays, *The World of the Indian Ocean Merchants 1500-1800*, New Delhi, 2001.
2. *Ibid.*, J.C. van Leur, *Indonesian Trade and Society*, The Hague, 1955. Van Leur's two principal points—that traditional Asian merchants were pedlars and that the traditional trade of Asia consisted merely of luxuries—have been strongly critiqued. His position that pre-modern Asian trade was changeless has also not gone unchallenged.
3. Hourani, *The Arab Seafaring*; Chaudhuri, *Trade and Civilisation*; ibid., *Asia before Europe.*
4. The English translation of this treatise is by G.R. Tibbetts, *Arab Navigation in the Indian Ocean before the Coming of the Portuguese,* London, 1971.
5. J.V.G. Mills (trn.), *Ying-yai-Sheng-lan* by Ma Huan.
6. Genevieve Bouchon and Denys Lombard, 'India and the Indian Ocean in the Fifteenth Century', in Ashin Das Gupta and M.N. Pearson, eds, *India and the Indian Ocean 1500-1800*, Calcutta, 1987.
7. Romila Thapar, 'Great Eastern Trade: Other Times, Other Places', Vasant J. Sheth Memorial Lecture, Mumbai, January 2002. Also see Romila Thapar, *Early India from Origin to AD 1300,* London, 2003; Chakravarti, ed., *Trade in Early India*; Champakalakshmi, *Trade, Ideology and Urbanization*; Ray and Salles, eds, *Tradition and Archaeology*; Himanshu Prabha Ray, ed., *The Archaeology of Seafaring*, 1999; J. Deloche, *Transport System and Communication in India Prior to Steam Locomotion*, vol. II, New Delhi, 1994.
8. G.W.B. Huntingford (trn.), *The Periplus of the Erythraean Sea*, 1980; Lionel Casson, ed. and trn., *The Periplus Maris Erythraei.*
9. See for example, Begley and de Puma, eds, *Rome and India*; Ray and Salles, eds, *Tradition and Archaeology.*
10. Such was the position of E.H. Warmington, *Commerce Between the Roman Empire and India,* and also Wheeler, *Rome Beyond the Imperial Frontiers.* Recent studies of the trade between India and the Roman empire negate such a notion. See for example, Romanis and Tchernia, eds, *Crossings*; Thapar, 'The Black Gold'; Lionel Casson, 'New Lights on Maritime Loans: P. Vindob G 40822', in Chakravarti, ed., *Trade in Early India*, pp. 228-43; Young, *Rome's Eastern Trade.*

11. Sharma, *Indian Feudalism*; Ibid., *The Urban Decay in India*; Yadava, *Society and Culture in Northern India*; Jha, ed., *The Feudal Order*, New Delhi, 2001.
12. Noboru Karashima, ed., *Ancient and Medieval Commercial Activities in the Indian Ocean: Testimony of Inscriptions and Ceramic-sherds*, Tokyo, 2002.
13. Goitien, *Letters*, 1973; Chakravarti, 'Coastal Trade and Voyages in Konkan'; Chakravarti, 'Trade and Later Indian Powers in the Indian Ocean (c. AD 400-1300)', in Alok Tripathy, ed., *Procedings of the International Conference on Marine Archaeology*, New Delhi, 2004, pp. 35-54.
14. Burton Stein, *Peasant State and Society in Medieval South India*, 1980; George W. Spencer, *The Politics of Expansion: The Cola Conquests of Sri Lanka and Srivijaya*, 1983; Hall, *Trade and Statecraft in the Age of the Colas*; J. Heitzman, *The Gifts of Power*, 1996; Hermann Kulke, ed., *The State in India 1000-1700*, 1995; Chattopadhyaya, *The Making of Early Medieval India*; Champakalakshmi, *Trade, Ideology and Urbanization*; Champakalakshmi, 'State and Economy in South India: AD 400-1300'; Vijaya Ramaswamy, *Textiles and Weavers in Medieval South India*, 1985. Also see *Studies in History*, 4, 2, 1982, specifically devoted to the study of the state in South India.
15. A. Appadurai, *Economic Condition in Southern India 1000-1500*, in two volumes. Nilakantha Sastri, *The Colas*; Abraham, *Two Medieval Merchant Guilds of South India*; Champakalakshmi, *Trade, Ideology and Urbanization*.
16. K.A. Nilakantha Sastri, *Foreign Notices of South India from Megasthenes to Ma Huan*, 1939. For a critique of fundamentalist approaches to early Indian history, see Chattopadhyaya, *Studying Early India*, Chap. 1.
17. D.D. Kosambi, 'Dhenukakta' in *Combined Method*.
18. Hirth and Rockhill (trn.), *Chu fan Chi of Chau ju Kua*; Yule and Cordier, *The Travels of Ser Marco Polo*.
19. This can be seen for example, in the Sanskrit-Arabic inscription from Somnath (1264) recording the construction of a mosque at Somnath by a ship-owning merchant from Hormuz, named Nuruddin Firuz. For discussions, see B.D. Chattopadhyaya, *Representing the Other?*; Ranabir Chakravarti, Chap. 11 in this book; Romila Thapar, *Somanatha, The Many Voices of a History*, New Delhi, 2004.
20. Ranabir Chakravarti, 'Rulers and Ports'.
21. K.R. Hall, *Trade and Statecraft*; Hermann Kulke, 'Rivalry and Competition in the Bay of Bengal in the Eleventh Century and its Bearing on Indian Ocean Studies', in Om Prakash and Denys Lombard, eds, *Commerce and Culture in the Bay of Bengal 1500-1800*, New Delhi, 1999, pp. 17-36.
22. Ranabir Chakravarti, 'Nakhudas and Nauvittakas', *JESHO*; Chakravarti, 'Ships, Seafaring and Ship-owners', in David Parkin and Ruth Barnes, eds, *Ships and the Development of Maritime Technology*.
23. Ranabir Chakravarti, 'Horse Trade and Piracy at Tana'.
24. For an English translation of the inscription, see Ray, Chattopadhyaya, Chakravarti and Mani, *A Sourcebook of Indian Civilization*, pp. 485-86.

25. Chakravarti, 'Rulers and Ports'.
26. K.V. Ramesh, 'Reconsidering Cultural Intercourse between India and Southeast Asia: An Epigraphical Report', in Karashima, ed., *Ancient and Medieval Commercial Activities*, p. 153.
27. The importance of inscriptions for offering descriptive category of data is illuminated in a recent study of the Kākātīya state in eastern Deccan (12th to early 14th Century). See Cynthia Talbot, *Pre Colonial India in Practice*, New York, 2001. She however has not dwelt adequately upon the importance of maritime commerce in the Kākātīya realm, although the well known Motuppalli inscription dishes out significant data. This inscription views that to seafaring merchants wealth was more important than life itself (*praṇebhyo'pi gariyasī*). It must also be recorded here that long ago D.C. Sircar in his numerous publications clearly recognized and underlined the significance of epigraphic documents for generating images and information often not conforming to normative treatises.

CHAPTER 14

Three Copper Plates of the Sixth Century CE

Glimpses of Socio-Economic and Cultural Life in Western India

Sanjeli Copper Plates of Toramāna

A few preliminaries may help us appreciate the three copper-plate charters of the Hūṇa ruler Toramāna, dated in his regnal year 3, 6 and 19. Found at Sanjeli (ancient Saṅgamapallikā) in the Zalod taluk of the Panchmahal district of Gujarat, the three copper plates were first edited and translated by R.N. Mehta and A.M. Thakkar (1978); the plates are now in the collection of the museum of the Maharaja Sayaji Rao University, Baroda (Vadodara). The plates were subsequently edited and translated once again by K.V. Ramesh (1986), who offered some new identifications of ancient place names and a few improvements on the first readings of the plates. But overall, there is not much contradiction between the studies by Mehta and Thakkar and the one by Ramesh.

Scholarly interest in these records has so far been limited to assigning nearly twenty years of reign to the Hūṇa King Toramāna, who had previously been thought to have ruled for about fifteen years (*c.* 500-15 CE) on the basis of the Eran stone boar inscription (regnal year 1) and the undated Kura inscription from the Salt Range area in present Pakistan.[1] The three copper plates taken together may throw interesting light on the economic, social and cultural conditions in Gujarat during the first two decades of the sixth century.

The Hūṇa occupation of parts of Gujarat is to be dated by the third year of Toramāna's reign; in other words, almost immediately after his rule is recorded in eastern Malwa in the Eran stone boar inscription of his subordinate Dhanyaviṣṇu in his regnal year 1.

The three inscriptions under review reveal the name of a family of subordinate rulers under Toramāna, namely Mātṛdāsa (I), his son, Bhūta, and Mātṛdāsa (II), son of Bhūta and grandson of Mātṛdāsa (I). Their subordinate position is clearly shown by their title '*mahārāja*', distinct from the superior titles, '*mahārājādhirāja*' and '*paramabhaṭṭāraka*' assumed by. Toramāna as the suzerain political authority.

The first copper plate, of the year 3, is a single sheet of copper measuring 36.5 cm × 19.6 cm × 3 mm, and weighing 1079 g. The second plate, dated in the year 6, weighs 2005 g and is also a single sheet of copper measuring 51 cm × 22 cm × 3 mm. The third plate, issued in the regnal year 19, weighs 635 g and measures 36.4 cm × 18.7 cm × 1.55 mm (Ramesh 1986).

The three hereditary and successive subordinates of Toramāna were in charge of the *viṣaya* or district of Śivabhāgapura, identifiable with the 'triangle formed by Bharukaccha, Khetaka and Malwa' (Mehta and Thakkar 1978:3). The administrative headquarters, Vadrapālī, is sought to be located by Mehta and Thakkar in Varunda in the Zalod taluk of Panchmahal district, Gujarat. Varunda is situated 13 km to the West of Sanjeli. Ramesh offers an alternative identification of Vadrapālī by locating it in Vadphali in the northwestern extremes of West Khandesh, *i.e.* about 50 km to the Southeast of Sankheda, identified by Ramesh (1986:180) with Saṅgaḍhyaka, figuring in the plate of the year 3.

It is only natural that rural areas included within this *viṣaya* would be referred to in the copper-plate charters recording a grant of landed property. These are Saṅgamapallikā (= Sanjeli, the find spot of the records, in Zalod taluk of Panchmahal district; regnal year 19), Tantiyaka (= Tisana-muvada, lying 4 km to the East of Sanjeli), Āmrilika (Amalia in Limkheda taluk, 8 km to the South of Sanjeli) and Anukikkavāṭaka (=Anaka, located 6 km to the North of Sanjeli).[2]

Agricultural activities in the rural areas within the *viṣaya* of Śivabhāgapura will be evident from the references to paddy (*dhānya*), molasses (*guḍa*) and cotton (*kārpāsa*). A further indication of the overall agrarian prosperity of the region may be seen in the account of the granting of a plot of arable land or *kṣetra* in the copper plate of the year 6. Interestingly enough, the plot is given the epithet *pañcavrihīpiṭaka-vāpakṣetra,* underlining the fertile nature of the soil *(vāpakṣetra*), which was surely conducive to paddy *(vrīhi)* cultivation. One may note here the similar occurrence of the term *vāpakṣetra* in the near-contemporary copper plates from eastern Bengal.[3] The word *piṭaka* or basket probably stands for a measurement of land of an unknown and unspecified quantity; it may logically denote an area of capacity of the seeds sown.[4] Little information is available on the system of measurement of land, save the term *guṇṭha,* which significantly is more associated with the system of land measurement in early medieval and medieval Orissa.

The other important point is the mention of the production of molasses or *guḍa* which must have been a by-product of the sugar cane plantation in the area concerned. The impression of the generation of cash crops in the *viṣaya* of Śivabhāgapura, in addition to a cereal like paddy, is left in the reference to the production of molasses and plantation of cotton *(kārpāsa)*. It is therefore hardly surprising to come across references to local-level irrigation projects such as a well (*kūpa*) and a tank (*taḍāga*) in the copper plates under discussion.

The non-agrarian sector of the local economy is also indicated in the three inscriptions. A goldsmith *(suvarṇakāra)* is explicitly mentioned in the inscription of the year 6. The cultivation of cotton may logically imply the existence of textile workers, for which Gujarat has been traditionally famous. Salt or *lavaṇa* figures in at least one record, suggesting thereby the likely presence of salt-makers, although salt could have been brought from elsewhere. Several references to making a provision of oil for the lighting of lamps at temples may also lead us to infer the presence of oilmillers, a trend particularly prominent in Gujarat since 1000 CE.

Trade and Traders

But the most significant data on economic life relate to trade and traders. It is rather unusual to come across numerous merchants and their merchandise in an early-sixth century epigraphic context. That is why the copper plate of the year 3 calls for a close scrutiny.

In *c.* 503 CE a number of merchants assembled at Vadrapālī, the administrative headquarters of Śivabhāgapuraviṣaya, to offer voluntary cesses on certain commodities in favour of the Vaiṣṇava deity, Jayasvāmī, whose temple was caused to have been constructed by the Queen Mother, Virāḍhyikā, *i.e.* the mother of Mahārāja Mātṛdāsa I. The list of traders consists of both local (*vāsṭavya*) merchants and non-local ones who came from elsewhere in all directions (*caturdiśābhyāgatakavaideśya*). Their names and the places they hailed from figure in the record in the context of their having agreed to pay voluntary cesses on certain commodities in favour of the deity.

They are:[5]

1. Gomika of Daśapura (Mandasore);
2. Pitṛyaśa Cirāyuṣa of Kānyakubja (Kanauj in the Ganga-Yamuna *doab);*
3. Gdusuyebhassam of Ujjaiyinī (Ujjain in western Malwa);
4. Droṇasoma Bhakkala of Varuṇodari;
5. Bhannitīya Dhruvabhakṣaṇa Agniśarmmā of Mahiṣhradaka;
6. Bhakkura of Pracakāśa (= Prakasa on the Tapi);
7. Rudradatta from Gaṇyatara;
8. Bharaṇa Bhaṭṭīśa Śarmā from Priyajñarayasa;
9. Kalayottikabhaṭṭi of Saṅgaḍhyaka;
10. Datta Gujjara of Rivasulavaṇijaka;
11. Bhaṭṭi Mahattara;
12. Svāmika Maheśvara Mallaka;
13. Koṭtadeva of Sadgama

These merchants met at the house (*gṛhavāstuveti)* of another merchant (*vāṇijaka*), Ṣaṣṭhī. The merchants, who are mentioned without any reference to their respective areas, may safely be assumed to have been local (*vāstavya*) traders at Vadrapālī. Ṣaṣṭhī's residence would certainly make him a local merchant at Vadrapālī, a point further strengthened by his making the gift of his own house (*svadīyagṛhavāstu)* in favour of a Viṣṇu temple *(paramadevatābhāgavatāyatana)*, the donation being recorded in the charter of the year 6 (*c*. 506 CE). The local merchants are also given the epithet *poṭṭalikā-puttrāḥ*. The term *poṭṭalikā* or *poṭalikā* stands for a packet or bundle. The suffix-*puttrāḥ* would probably denote a small packet or bundle. The local dealers at Vadrapālī therefore appear to have been petty traders engaged in small-scale retailing (Ramesh 1986:176).

The inscription certainly impresses upon the convergence of merchants from Daśapura, Kanauj and Ujjaiyinī and from various parts of Gujarat (see note 5) at Vadrapālī, which therefore can be viewed as a nodal point in the overland supra-local trade network. The name of the merchant, Gdusuyebhassam, hailing from Ujjaiyinī, strongly suggests that he was a non-Indian. No less significant is the name ending with *śarman* of at least two merchants, Bhannitiya Dhruvabhakṣaṇa Agniśarmā and Bharaṇa Bhaṭṭīśasarmā. The name ending with *śarman / śarmā* is typically that of a *brāhmaṇa* and should therefore speak of their participation in commerce, a profession normally not sanctioned by the Śāstric injunctions on the ideal functions of the *brāhmaṇa.*[6]

An even more significant point is that these merchants are categorically described as belonging to a *vaṇigrāma* or a professional body of merchants. The term *grāma* here does not connote a village, but stands for a collection or group of persons following a common profession. That the term *vaṇiggrāma* (variously spelt as *vāṇiyagrāma* and *vaṇigrāma)* denoted a professional body of merchants of different areas and dealing in different commodities was first driven home by D.D. Kosambi on the basis of a second-century BC donative record from Karle in Maharashtra[7] and the more elaborate and famous charter of Viṣṇuṣeṇa (= Maitraka Viṣṇubhaṭa) from western India), dated 592 CE.[8] Kosambi also rightly suggested that the *vaṇiggrāma* attained considerable prominence in early medieval South India under the name *maṇigrāmam.* The charter of Viṣṇuṣeṇa, of 592 CE, speaks of administrative arrangements, in 72 clauses, to ensure and facilitate the settlement of *vaṇiggrāma (ācāra-sthiti-patra)* at Lohāṭagrāma in Kathiawad. According to the charter of 592 CE, the local political authority hailed the arrival of *vaṇiggrāma* merchants from far and near, enlisted agricultural and crafts products on which were levied, cesses and allowed various fiscal immunities and facilities to these merchants with a view to induce them to settle down in Lohāṭagrāma.

The importance of the charter of the third regnal year of *Mahārājādhirāja* Toramāna is that it indicates the active role of the *vaṇiggrāma* mercantile organization in western India even prior to the famous record of 592 CE. In fact, the data in the inscription of *c.* 503 CE suggest the shape of things to come in the next nine decades in the history of trade and mercantile organizations of western India.[9] This charter of Toramāna further indicates that the *vaṇiggrāma* was an association of merchants belonging to the locality (*vāstavya*) and also hailing from distant areas (*caturdiśābhyāgatakavaideśya*).

Commodities Traded

From traders and their organization we may now focus on the commodities transacted. Transactions in molasses, grains, salt and cotton are explicitly stated. What demands our attention here is the image of trade in daily necessities, probably in bulk. The use of the words *bhāṇḍa* and *bhāraka,* respectively meaning 'bales' and 'weight', would strengthen the possibility of transaction of staples in bulk. Another term, *setinika/setinaka,* also figures in the context of levying self-imposed cesses by merchants on grain and salt. The term *setinika* is explained as a measure of weight equal to two handful.[10] Grains reached the exchange centre at Vadrapālī by cartloads, as the expression *dhānyaśakaṭa* would bear it out. The use of the donkey as a beast of burden for transporting bulk items is demonstrated by the expression *gardabha-bhāraka.* The frequent references to coin terms such as *rūpinaka* for a silver coin and *viṃśopaka / viṃśopanikī* (for a copper coin equal to 1/20th of the value of a silver coin) should be duly taken into consideration. These underline monetary transactions during trading activities at Vadrapālī. It may also point to the prevalence of imposing cesses on exchangeable commodities in cash along with levies in kind.

Vadrapālī, apart from being a nodal point in local and supra-local trade, was certainly an administrative centre too. As the administrative headquarters of Śivabhāgapuraviṣaya, it was the seat of power of *Mahārājas* Mātṛdāsa I, Bhūta and Mātṛdāsa II. Vadrapālī was expectedly the issuing centre of copper plate charters recording religious benefactions and grant of landed property. The presence of diverse administrative functionaries, ranging from the *kumārāmatya* and the *dūtaka* to an ordinary guard or *ārakṣika* at the time of grants of land, tallies with our understanding of Vadrapālī as a district level administrative centre which was also a nodal point in the overland trade network.

The Vaiṣṇava Context of the Grants

The three grants were made in favour of Vaiṣṇava temples. Thus the record of regnal year 3 granted cesses in favour of Jayasvāmī. Three years later land was granted in favour of the worship of Paramadevatā in the *bhagavatpādāyatana.* The term 'Paramadevatā' should logically stand for Viṣṇu, because the epithet *paramadaivata* since the fifth century CE denoted a devout Vaiṣṇava. It is likely that in an *āyatana* or temple the feet of Viṣṇu (*bhagavatpādāyatana*) were worshipped in the form of an image. Around 519 CE the third record informs us about a temple (*devakula*) of Nārāyaṇa.[11] The popularity of Vaiṣṇavism in Malwa and western India is known since the Gupta times and seems to have continued unabated during the Hūṇa occupation of the area. While the Eran inscription and the three records of Toramāna under review here certainly speak of the flourishing conditions of Vaiṣṇavism in western and central India, Toramāna's son and successor, Mihirakula, is known to have been a devout Śaiva. One is not sure whether Toramāna himself became a Vaiṣṇava, or his feudatories and local administrators, such as Dhanyaviṣṇu, Mātṛdāsa I, Bhūta and Mātṛdāsa II, were Vaiṣṇavas.

The three grants from Sanjeli cannot but give the impression that the Vaiṣṇava temples were situated close to Vadrapālī. If this is so, then Vadrapālī combined religio-cultural activities with administrative functions and commercial transactions. In this context special attention is to be paid to the temple of Paramadevatā mentioned in the grant of the year 6. Attached to this temple was a rest house where came devotees, disciples and the deserving (*bhaktacailādyapraguṇaḥ*). Moreover, the temple was provided with a centre for medical facilities offering therapy and medicinal diet (*bhaiṣajapathyabhojana*) to mendicants and male and female servants serving the temple and the devotees, disciples, etc. The Vaiṣṇava temple, in addition to being a place of worship, thus assumed features more complex than those of a mere shrine or a place of worship. Its role as an employer of male and female servants (*dāsa* and *dāsī*) is unmistakable. Buddhist monasteries in contemporary times were noted for their providing medical care to monks and the laity; but here an early-sixth century Vaiṣṇava temple in western India functioned more or less similarly.

CONCLUSION

The significance of the three grants is manifold. We have deliberately not touched upon its importance as source material for Hūṇa political control. It is quite evident that the Hūṇa occupation of Malwa, 'parts of Gujarat, central India and as far West as the Salt Range in Pakistan must have taken place mainly at the cost of the Gupta rulers. But the Huna rule was not associated with any profound break or crisis in the political, administrative and socio-economic situations existing in these areas in the previous century during the heydays of the Gupta empire.[12] Of special significance is the emergence of Vadrapālī as a politico-administrative centre, a nodal point in the trade network and a cultural centre noted for Vaiṣṇava leanings and medical facilities. No less important is the fact that in the voluntary gift of commercial cesses by merchants and / or by a traders' association to a Viṣṇu temple in the early sixth century may be seen a forerunner of such very regular transfers of commercial cesses in early medieval India.[13] It is for offering the images of these crucial linkages with processes seen in subsequent centuries that the three early-sixth century grants deserve our attention.

NOTES

1. For these two earlier inscriptions of Toramana and also the Gwalior inscription of Mihirakula, see Sircar 1965b. The political history of the Hūṇas is discussed by Biswas 1973. For an updated discussion on the chronology and political history of the Hūṇa rulers, see Raychaudhuri 1996.
2. Mehta and Thakkar 1978:24-8. While Ramesh agrees with Mehta and Thakkar about the location of ancient Saṅgamapallikā, he identifies Tantiyaka and Undura (mentioned in the plate of year 6) respectively with Tankhala, North of Vadphali and Undara, Lunawada taluk, Fanchmahals district (Ramesh and Tiwari 1986: 183).
3. These are the sixth-century Faridpur copper plates of Samācāradeva and Gopacandra. See Sircar. 1965b: 363-72; also Morrison 1970 for an analysis of the contents of these plates.
4. Compare the terms *droṇavāpa, āḍhavāpa* and *kulyavāpa* occurring frequently in twelve copper plate records of fifth and sixth-century Bengal as units of land measurements. See Basak 1919-20; also Sircar 1965b and 1966.
5. Mehta and Thakkar 1978:17-18. This particular plate has been cited and discussed also by Ray, Chattopadhyaya, Mani and Chakravarti 2000:615-16. Following Ramesh (1986:180), Mahiṣahrada may be identified with Mahisa, Nandiad taluk in Kaira district; Goṇḍatārā with Godhra, Godhra taluk in Panchmahals district; Rayasa with Raychchha, Chote-Udepur taluk in Baroda district; Kalottiya with Khilodi, East of Godhra; Rivusulavaṇijaka with Rasela, Nandod, taluk in Broach district.
6. Cārudatta, the hero of the famous drama *Mṛcchakaṭika* of Śūdraka, a text of the sixth century CE, was a *sārthavāha* or caravan trader, though born as a *brāhmaṇa*. This will be evident from his epithets *dvija* in Act 1 and *vipra* in Act 9 of the drama. According to the drama, his grandfather Vinayadatta and father Sāgaradatta were also merchants. The *Mṛcchakaṭika* therefore portrays Cārudatta as being of *brāhmaṇa* descent and following the profession of a merchant hereditarily. He is said to have dwelt in the

merchants' quarter in the city of Ujjaiyinī *(sa khalu sārthavāha-vinayadattasya naptā sāgaradattasya tanayah sugrhitanāmna ārya-cāntdailonāma Śreṣṭhicatvare prativasati).* See ed. Kale 1962:321. In 465-6 CE (Gupta era 166), during the reign of Skandagupta, two merchants of *kṣatriya* birth (*kṣatriyavaṇik*) recorded their donation and patronage to a Sun Temple at Indrapura (=Indore, Bulandshahr district, U.P); see the Indore copper plate of Skandagupta, Sircar 1965b:318-21.

7. Kosambi 1955:66. The inscription reads: This pillar is the gift of the traders' association at Dhenukāikaṭa (*dhenukākaṭa vāṇiya-gāmasa ṭhambho dānam*)'.
8. Kosambi 1959 (also included in Chakravarti 2001). Kosambi presents a sharp critique of D.C. Sircar's editing of the said charter of 592 CE (Sircar 1953-4:161-80).
9. It is strange that Ramesh (1986:178) chose to translate the term *vaṇiggrāma* as a 'mercantile village'! Both Sircar and Kosambi understood it in the appropriate sense of an organization of merchants, and not as a rural locality where merchants dwelt. He is evidently not aware of the previously known instances of *vaṇiggrāmas* in the inscriptions mentioned above. See notes 10 and 11. Ramesh, in spite of his competent editing and translation of this plate, thus missed a vital point.
10. Sircar 1966. Ramesh (1986:177) suggests that the term occurs in the Anjaneri copper plate of Pṛthvīcandra Bhogaśakti of the seventh century CE in the sense of a liquid measure. Following N.P. Chakrabarti, Ramesh considers that *setaka / setinika* was probably equivalent to 4 *pala*s or approximately 14 *tola.*
11. Ramesh (1986:185) rightly points out that this temple was caused to be constructed by Mahārāja Mātṛdāsa II in memory of his grandmother (*pitāmahī*) Virāḍhyikā, who figures in the copper plates of regnal years 3 and 6. It is implied therein that the corporeal remains of his departed grandmother (*pitāmahīkayikā*) found its station at the feet of Nārāyaṇa (*nārāyaṇapāda*).
12. The Hūṇas were defeated not only by Gupta emperors such as Skandagupta and Narasiṃhagupta Balāditya, but also by Iśānavarman Maukhari of Kanauj, Prabhākaravardhana of Sthāneśvara, and Yaśodharman of Kanauj. That the Hūṇa King Toramāna was defeated by the Aulikara King Prakāśadharman of Daśapura, *i.e.* of Mandasore, is clearly seen in the Risthal inscription, dated Malava era 572_r i.e. 515 CE (Ramesh and Tiwari 1983:101-2; see also Ray, Chattopadhyaya, Mani and Chakravarti 2000:617-18). The initial military success of Mihirakula over an extensive zone was obviously short-lived. In view of these military reversals the Hunas (both Toramāna and Mihirakula) suffered in India, it would be difficult to perceive that their inroads were among the primary causes of the decline of the Gupta empire.
13. Chattopadhyaya 1994; Abraham 1988; Champakalakshmi 1996.

REFERENCES

Primary Sources

Basak, R.G. 1919-20. 'The five Damodarpur copperplate inscriptions of the Gupta period'. *Epigraphia Indica* 15:113-45.

Mehta, R.N., and A.M. Thakkar 1978. *M.S. University Copper Plates of the Time of Toramana.* Vadodara (M.S. University Archaeology Series 14).

Ramesh, K.V. 1986. 'Three early charters from Sanjeli in Gujarat'. *Epigraphia Indica* 40:175-86.

Ramesh, K.V., and S.P. Tiwari 1983. 'The Risthal inscription of Aulikara Prakasadharman (Vikrama) year 572'. *Studies in Indian Epigraphy = Bhāratīya Purābhileka Patrikā; Journal of the Epigraphical Society of India* 10:96-103.

Ray, N. (gen. ed.), B.D. Chattopadhyay (ed.), V.R. Mani and R. Chakravarti (ass. eds) 2000. *A Sourcebook of Indian Civilization.* Calcutta [etc.].

Sircar, D.C. 1953-4. 'The charter of Vishnushena, samvat 649'. *Epigraphia Indica* 30:163-81.

——1965b. *Select Inscriptions Bearing on Indian History and Civilization.* Vol. 1, *From the Sixth Century* BC *to the Sixth Century* AD, 2nd rev. and enl. ed. (orig. pub. 1942). Calcutta.

Śūdraka. *Mṛcchakaṭika. The Mṛichchhakaṭika of Śūdraka.* Ed. with the commentary of Pṛithvidhara (enlarged where necessary), various readings, a literal English transl., notes and exhaustive introd. by M.R. Kale. 2nd ed. (orig. pub. 1924). Delhi [etc.], 1962.

Secondary Sources

Abraham, M. 1988. *Two Medieval Merchant Guilds of South India.* New Delhi. (South Asian Studies 18)

Biswas, A. 1973. *The Political History of the Hūṇas in India.* New Delhi.

Chakravarti, R. (ed.) 2001. *Trade in Early India.* New Delhi [etc.]. (Oxford in India Readings, Themes in Indian History).

Champakalakshmi, R. 1996. *Trade, Ideology and Urbanization: South India 300* BC *to* AD *1300.* New Delhi [etc.].

Chattopadhyaya, B. 1994. *The Making of Early, Medieval India.* Delhi [etc.].

Kosambi, D.D. 1955. Dhenukākaṭa. *Journal of the Asiatic Society of Bombay*, n.s. 30/2:50-71. .

——1959. 'Indian feudal trade charters'. *Journal of the Economic and Social History of the Orient* 2:281-93.

Majumdar, R.C. (gen. ed.) 1951. *The Vedic Age.* London. (The History and Culture of the Indian People 1)

Morrison, B.M. 1970. *Political Centers and Cultural Regions in Early Bengal.* Tuscon. (Association for Asian Studies, Monographs and Papers 25)

Nandi, R.N. 1984. 'Economic growth in rural feudal India'. Presidential address, Section I. *Proceedings of Indian History Congress* (Annamalai session), pp. 25-91.

Raychaudhuri, H.C. 1996. *Political History of Ancient India: From the Accession of Parikshit to the Extinction of the Gupta Dynasty*. 8th ed. (orig. pub. 1923). New Delhi.
Sharma, R.S. 1980. *Indian Feudalism: c. A.D. 300-1200*. 2nd ed. (orig. pub. 1965). New Delhi [etc.].
Sircar, D.C. 1965a. *Indian Epigraphy*. Delhi [etc.],
——1966. *Indian Epigraphical Glossary*. Delhi [etc.].

CHAPTER 15

Gujarat's Maritime Trade and Alternative Moneys (*c*.550-1300 CE)

Gujarat's pre-eminent position as a trading zone, whether by inland/overland, riverine, coastal and overseas network in South Asia has a long-range and sustained history. Pre-modern Gujarat was noted for its crops, including a few commercial crops; the presence of some important rivers which fertilize the land and also offer crucial conduits to the sea; its diverse craft products, especially its famed textiles and its ports, the last factor making Gujarat one of the most significant maritime zones in the protracted Indian Ocean history. In this premier commercial zone in western India it is impossible to miss how Gujarat's port commanded a sizeable hinterland, reaching Ujjayini in western Madhya Pradesh and northern Konkan and the Ganga-Yamuna doab through eastern Gujarat, Rajasthan and finally the Bayana-Bharatpur-Agra axis. A perusal of current historiography also highlights the impressive foreland of Gujarati ports reaching out to the Persian Gulf and the Red Sea areas. Like Bengal on the eastern flank of north India, Gujarat provided the outlet to the sea at the western end of the land-locked north Indian plains. This essay wishes to offer some insights into the maritime profile of Gujarat and the realm of money (or more precisely the various media of exchanges), the latter being integrally connected with the material milieu of the diverse maritime communities in western coastal India.

Gujarat, endowed with a long coastline from Kathiawad to Daman, is known for its maritime tradition and prospects as the Gujarat coast houses a number of ports, bustling with sustained activities of both indigenous and non-indigenous merchants. These were mostly estuarine ports, except Bhṛgukachchha/Bharugachchha/Barygaza which stood in the delta of the river Narmada. If modern Gujarat derives much economic benefit from Okha, it also enjoys a pride of place for a very long tradition of its orientation to the sea, especially the western Indian Ocean. In this coast were situated a few outstanding ports in different periods of its long history. The first important port in Gujarat was Lothal that flourished during the days of the Bronze age Harappan civilization *c*.2600-1800 BCE.[1] This was followed by the port of Bhṛgukachchha, celebrated in Buddhist and Jaina texts as Bharugachchha. It is identical with Barygaza, repeatedly figuring as the premier port in western India in Greek and Latin texts during the heydays of India's trade with the Roman empire, *c*. late 1st century BCE-300 CE.[2] Now known as Broach, Bhṛgukachchha/Barygaza faded out as the premier port of western India around seventh century. From around 1000 CE, another great port emerged to prominence in the Gujarat coast, namely Stambhatīrtha/Stambhapura, from which the name Khambayat/Khambat/Kanbaya was derived in the Arabic and Persian texts on geography and travel. This is the port of Cambay which was perhaps at its zenith during the sixteenth century.[3] Cambay was followed by Surat, the *Bandar-i-mubarak* of the Mughals, which was repeatedly visited by European ships, belonging to the Portuguese Estado da India and to the East India Companies of the Dutch, the English and the French.[4] The gradual decline of Surat at the turn of the nineteenth century paved the way for the rise of a new port in northern Konkan: the port of Bombay (modern Mumbai) as the premier port of western India of modern times.[5] With this for the first time in South Asian history a Konkan port overshadowed all other ports not only in western India, but also along the entire western sea-board.[6] This marks a significant shift, not merely in geographical terms—from the Gujarat coast to its adjoining coastal tract in Konkan; the rise of Bombay from the nineteenth century onwards signaled the emergence of a port located directly on the seafront. All other pre-modern ports in the subcontinent were located not exactly on the sea-front, but situated inland in the estuary or delta of a river. Thus, Lothal was on the Sabarmati, Barygaza in the Narmada delta, Cambay on the Mahi and Surat on the Tapi/Tapti.

As this essay largely focuses on the pre-1500 maritime scenario in the Indian Ocean with a particular orientation to the Gujarat coast and the ports thereof, we propose to take a close look here at the monetary scenario of about seven or eight centuries spanning from *c*. 550 to 1300 CE. The reasons for bringing money matters in the context of the maritime commerce of Gujarat during these centuries need to be addressed here. The historiography of the Indian Ocean has the maximum and obvious thrust on three centuries, 1500-1800 that witnessed the advent of north Atlantic powers and joint stock companies in the Indian Ocean impacting the Indian Ocean zone with far reaching changes. From the mid-nineteenth century onwards the Indian Ocean was incorporated in the capitalist world economy under the British colonial empire that claimed the Indian Ocean as a British lake. The massive statistical and quantifiable data in the official records of the Estado da India and of the East India Companies of the Dutch, the English and the French would logically attract the maximum attention of the historians of the Indian Ocean. Yet, Pearson has rightly reminded us that these centuries, however important and transformative, form a relatively tiny segment of the very long history of engagements of diverse communities in the Indian Ocean zone.[7] Recent advances in our knowledge firmly establish that the Indian Ocean was traversed regularly for centuries, if not millennia, prior to 1500 when the north Atlantic elements and factors began to penetrate into the Indian Ocean.[8]

One cannot lose sight of the scholarly recognition of the importance of the Indian Ocean during the first three centuries of the Common Era when this maritime space witnessed a remarkable boom in the maritime commerce with the eastern Mediterranean which was during those times under the control of the Roman Empire. The Eurocentric approaches to the Indian Ocean history paid some attention to this maritime trade in the Indian Ocean, but erroneously marked it as 'Indo-Roman' commerce which is perceived to have come to an end around mid-third century CE and certainly not going beyond 300 CE. The vibrant nature of South Asia's maritime trade with the Mediterranean is recovered by demonstrating the availability (among a variety of sources, including textual, epigraphic and field archaeological) of gold coins, issued by South Asian powers and also brought from the Roman world.[9] In sharp contrast to this, the gradual disappearance of the fine gold currency in South Asia from around 550 CE onwards and the circulation of debased gold currency, or the minting of gold coins of questionable intrinsic quality have been strongly argued as a sure signal of the steady slump of India's long-distance maritime trade. The perception of trade, especially maritime commerce, having been relegated to marginalia and near invisibility, is situated in the context of 'monetary anaemia', 'urban anaemia' which paved the way for a self-sufficient and enclosed rural material milieu during the 300-1200 CE phase.[10] While this influential formulation has generated considerable debates and counter-arguments, dishing out considerable data and conceptual categories to challenge the perceptions of languishing long-distance commerce and de-urbanization, the point that the relative paucity of coins of precious metals (especially in gold) has resurfaced regularly, thereby keeping the debates alive. This is the historiographical platform from which our ensuing arguments would stem.

Even at the risk of repeating a point already thrashed out by several experts previously, it needs to be underlined that while the presence of minted metallic pieces as a medium of exchange certainly points to the vitality of trade, the relative absence of coins may not automatically establish languishing trade or a slump in trade. A case in point will be the experience in the Deccan during the early centuries CE, when the Sātavāhana realm figured prominently in the history of long-distance maritime trade without having to strike gold currency; in fact the Satavahana rulers regularly used coins in baser metals of lead, potin and copper. This currency situation did not stand in the way of either the flourishing of ports in both the sea-boards of the Deccan, or in the significant presence of the area in the Greek and Latin textual sources which spoke in volumes on the importance of India from the point of view of the Roman empire.

The Greek and Latin texts on the trade between the Roman empire and South Asia regularly waxed eloquence on Barygaza or Bhṛgukachchha in the Gujarat sea-board as the premier port in western India.[11] Contrary to the common belief that Barygaza began to fade out with the gradual passing away of this maritime network, Bhṛgukachchha continues to figure prominently, along with another Gujarati port of Hastakavapra (an excavated coastal site identified with Astacapra of Ptolemy), in the Sanskrit-Brahmi inscriptions of Indic seafarers found from the island of Socotra in the Gulf of Aden (now in the Republic of Yemen). Thanks to this path-breaking epigraphic researches by Ingo Strauch and his comrades, the continuity of these two Gujarati ports well beyond the heydays of Roman trade with South Asia – at least up to fifth century CE – drives home the point that the Indian Ocean maritime trade did not primarily depend on external stimuli, particularly the Mediterranean and the European impetus.[12] The sustainability of Gujarat's maritime trade beyond 250 CE is impossible to deny and miss.

The above plea for revisiting and revising the commercial scenario in Gujarat gains further ground in the light of three early sixth century copperplates from Sanjeli, during the reign of the Hūṇa ruler Toramāna (*c*.500-520 CE). The most interesting scenario presented by these three copper plates is the presence of an organization of merchants (*vaniggrāma*) who came from and neighbouring aeas (*vastavya*) as well as from elsewhere (*vaidesya*) and who donated in cash and kind to a local Vaiṣṇava shrine. This Vaiṣṇava shrine also accommodated a hospital (*ārogyaśālā*). The three records, taken together, highlight two salient features of commerce: (a) the transactions in daily necessity products, including commercial crops and (b) regular mention of terms denoting a particular type of silver coins (*rūpyaka*) and its sub-multiples (e.g. *vimsopaka/vimsopanika*). These epigraphic references to the coin terms are in the context of the donations made by the merchants' body that decided to voluntarily impose upon themselves various cess on the commodities they dealt in at the exchange centre at Vadrapali. Along with the self-imposed cess in kind on some products, the merchants' body donated cess in cash in favour of the Vaishnava temple. This bears tell-tale marks of commercial transactions and the attendant circulation of money in Gujarat in early sixth century CE, offering little, if any, impression of a crisis in commerce and non-availability of coins in Gujarat.[13]

The same is more eloquently voiced in another inscription from Kathiawad, dated in 592 CE, issued during the time of Vishnushena, a Maitraka ruler of Valabhi. The organization of merchants (*vaniggrāma*) appears here in much greater details. Vishnushena issued a charter (consisting of 72 clauses, all related to merchants) to authorize a permanent settlement of the *vaniggrāma* at Lohatagrama. The categorical reference to the ingress and egress of sea-going vessels (*vahitra*) at Lohatagrama would demonstrate that Lohatagrama was a coastal site, if not a port, in Kathiawad. The maritime orientation of Lohatagrama is quite evident from the mention of voyaging crafts during the rainy season. No less significant is the regular and repeated occurrence of coin terms in the context of exemption from various types of dues imposed on artisans and exchangeable commodities (including cess on indigo-producing vats or *nīlaḍumphakas*). The list of exemptions from various types of levies is actually indicative of the revenue-bearing potentials of commerce, including sea-borne trade.[14]

It is true that one hears less about Bhṛgukachchha in these epigraphic sources than the mentions of this great port in the pre-300 CE texts (e.g. the Jātakas). But this cannot imply the waning fortune of the port. When Xuan Zang (travels in India from 629 to 645 CE) came to Po-lu-kie-che-to (Bharugachchha) he spoke about the commercial activities thereof, though he did not explicitly describe the thriving long-distance and coastal commerce at Bharugachchha.[15] He spoke about the commercial activities thereof, but his accounts did not leave an impression of the thriving long-distance and coastal commerce at Bharugachchha.[16] As Bharugachchha declined after seventh century, the port of Sanjan (in the northernmost part of Konkan, adjoining southern Gujarat or Lāṭa) acquired considerable prominence in the Arabic accounts datable from the mid-ninth to the eleventh centuries, in five inscriptions (from *c.*900 to about 1050 CE) and also in the recent excavation conducted there.[17] Sanjan in coastal Konkan and Lāṭa were controlled by the formidable Rāṣṭrakūṭa rulers of mainland Maharashtra and Karnataka.

The Rāṣṭrakūṭas, like their contemporary Pāla kings of Bihar and Bengal, did not issue metallic medium of exchange. This led to the influential perception of the decline of maritime and long-distance trade and of the 'monetary anaemia', symptomatic of the feudal formation. It needs to be emphasized that the minimal appearance of dynastic coinage for nearly four centuries in different parts of Indian subcontinent may not suggest a situation bereft of metallic currency. There are considerable data on the minting and circulation of non-dynastic coins during this period. A case in point is the payment of annual rent (*srotaka*) of 40 *drammas* (silver coins) by the authorities of a goddess temple at Sanjan to an adjacent shrine of Madhusūdana (Viṣṇu): this figures in the Chinchani grant of the time of Rāṣṭrakūṭa Kṛṣṇa II in early tenth century. The striking point is that the coins were manufactured by the money-merchant (*śreṣthī-sārtha*), Gambhuvaka; in other words, the *dramma* coins were non-dynastic silver currency. A recent study of 64 land-grants of the Śilāhāras of Kolhapur and coastal Konkan demonstrates that from around tenth century CE onwards annual revenue of a village began to be assessed in terms of cash payment. Even if it is accepted that the actual revenue was realized more in kind than in cash, the preference for stating the assessed revenue in cash is a palpable pointer to the increasing orientation to money economy even when agrarian revenue was assessed. As Konkan, like Gujarat, in western India began to experience unprecedented agrarian expansion, the possibility of growing exchangeable agrarian commodities cannot be ruled out. This is particularly borne out by the revenue-yielding potentials of orchards and plantations of coconut and arecanut in the Konkan coast. Wood (*kāṣtha*), apparently an inexpensive floral item, also began to yield commercial revenue expressed in minted metallic currency in the records from Konkan. The increasing instances of revenue demands on and the assessment of agrarian commodities, especially cash crops, paved the way for a greater familiarity with the money economy.

Without going into elaborate discussions here one would like to underline that Gujarat and Konkan gained considerable eminence in the maritime network in the western Indian Ocean, which had two important sea-lanes, viz., the Persian Gulf and the Red Sea. This is particularly highlighted in the Arabic and Persain texts on travel, geography and commerce. The distribution of different types of pottery across the western Indian Ocean too points to a lively maritime trade involving Gujarat where the outstanding port from 1000 CE onwards was Stambhapura/Stambhatīrtha/Kanbaya (modern Khambat or Cambay. Cambay had certainly eclipsed the erstwhile eminence of Bhṛgukachchha which seems to have continued as a feeder port of Cambay. The continuity of Bharuch/Broach as an important, but not the premier, port in Gujarat, is illustrated by some business letters of eleventh and twelfth centuries. These are the correspondence among the voyaging Jewish merchants who came from North Africa to Aden and from thence to the western sea-board of India. Along with the exchange of business information, e.g. entering into partnership, elaborate accounts of expenses, profit and loss for merchants, diverse commodities and mercahnts (including shipowners), these business letters documented court cases and legal disputes.[18] A particular document, involving a court case in Egypt in 1097 CE, offers interesting insights into money matters.

A court document issued at Fustat, Old Cairo, informs us a legal dispute between two Jewish India traders. The matter goes back to 1097-8 CE.[19] It speaks of the sale of storax in Dahlak (a port located in the southern tip of the Red Sea) for 40 Dahlak dinars, equivalent to 10 Egyptian dinars; then the remainder of the storax was taken to India by Joseph Lebdi. The remainder of storax was sold for 120 Nahrwara dirhems, worth about 8 Egyptian dinars. The storax is an aromatic resin procured in Asia Minor; from there it was sent to India through Alexandria, Cairo and Aden.[20] Before delving into the actual monetary transactions, it appears from the Gujarati sea-borne connections with the Red Sea ports like Dahlak and Aydhab that sometimes voyaging merchants reached these Red Sea ports without touching the great Yemeni port of Aden. Gujarat's maritime interactions with two Red Sea ports thus deserves our attention. The sale of a certain quantity of this storax for 120 Nahrwara dirhams, of a value lower than the Egyptian dinar, highlights the possibility that the final destination of this imported product in this case was Gujarat. Nahrwara or Anahilapaṭṭana being an inland city in Gujarat, the storax is likely to have reached a port in Gujarat coast and thence transported to Anahilapaṭṭana by an overland or riverine route. Such a Gujarati port could either be Kanbaya or Barus, though it cannot be ascertained. These Nahrwara dirhams probably refer to various types of silver *dramma* coins, figuring in contemporary inscriptions from Gujarat and the *Lekhapaddhati*.[21] That the Nahrwara dirhams, issued in Gujarat, had entered the currency zone of the Red Sea ports and also could be exchanged with and/or converted to Egyptian dinars, cannot but speak of the acceptance of some of the Gujarati currency in areas across the sea, a fact not otherwise known to us. How not only the Gujarat ports and commodities, but also the Gujarati silver currency played a significant role in the transaction network in the first half of the twelfth century looms large in this correspondence.

It is, however, difficult to agree that the period from *c*.600 to 1,000 CE, if not up to 1200, has not yielded enough specimens of precious metal coins, particularly in gold and silver.[22] Gold currency actually reappeared at the turn of the second millennium in the central Indian realm of the Kalachuris. Both the Kalachuri branches of Tripurī and Ratanpur struck gold coins.[23] Though all Kalachuri coins bear the name of a single ruler, Gāṅgeyadeva, the palaeography of the legend Gāṅgeyadeva ranges in date from eleventh to twelfth centuries. This clearly suggests that the successors of Gāṅgeyadeva too struck gold coins, but did not feel any urge to mint coins in their respective names. The point here is that striking coins was not considered to be an invariable and indispensable marker of sovereignty in India up to *c.*1200 CE. Several other dynasties of early mediaeval, north, central and western India did strike gold coins and also silver coins (*drammas*), though their number is not impressive. It is also true that in many cases the metallic currency were of doubtful intrinsic value; neither the metrology was always uniform. Interestingly enough, Ṭhakkara Pheru, the assay master of Sultan Alauddin Khilji of Delhi, strongly recommended minute examination of the weight standard and metallic purity at least three times before allowing a coin to enter the treasury of the Sultanate.

Similar caution has been voiced in the *Lekhapaddhati*, a text instructing the manners of writing model documents, which had a distinct bearing on Gujarat and western India. One has to take into account the wide circulation of the Indo-Sassanian silver currency in western India, including Gujarat; these are popularly known as *gadahiya* or *gadhaiya* coins.[24] The *Lekhapaddhati* considers the *gadahiya* coins as typically associated with Gujarat (*Gurjarabhūmi*). John Deyell's detailed analysis of early mediaeval coin hoards underline the regular circulation of metallic currency in north, western and central India. By citing the empirically rich analysis of the coin hoards Deyell demonstrated the 'fragility of the interpretative model'[25] of feudal economy, marked by 'monetary anaemia'.

As we have already argued before, even by conceding that metallic money was either insufficient or of questionable weight standard and metallic purity, this does not lead to a straightforward conclusion that trade, especially long-distance commerce, suffered a serious set back. Here looms large the role of non-minted media of exchange. One major alternative to minted metallic pieces was the cowry shell. Cowry shell was a perennial currency in eastern India (including Bengal, Bihar, Assam and Odisha) and many parts of northern India. It is difficult to subscribe to the erroneous view that cowry shells were meant only for small scale trading network and restrictive of long-distance trade. Good quality cowry shells were not native to India and not locally available. These reached the subcontinent from the Maldives in shiploads. The cowry shells were undoubtedly part and parcel of Indian Ocean long-distance commerce.[26] Unlike the eastern part of the subcontinent and the greater parts of the Ganga valley, Gujarat's thriving maritime trade did not integrate cowry shells as a medium of exchange. There were other alternatives to minted metallic pieces in Gujarat. This is lit up by the *Lekhapaddhati* which in the context of giving samples of model documents of mortgage, loan, sale deeds, etc., spoke of the regular use of the bill of exchange (*huṇḍika*). The term *huṇḍika* as a credit instrument functioned in close association with similar financial instruments acting in lieu of coined money. These are the *chirikā* and the *ādeśa*. The significant point to note here is that the *huṇḍika*, *chirikā* and *ādeśa* as instruments of credit and as alternate moneys were known in areas as far away as Kashmir. Both the *Rājataraṅgiṇī* of Kalhaṇa and the *Lokaprakāśa* of Kshemendra were well acquainted with these alternatives to metallic medium of exchanges. One has to remember in this context that coins were struck and in circulation in Kashmir. Thus, in Kashmir the importance of these alternative forms of money was clearly recognized while coins were in vogue in Kashnir. The point to note is the widespread prevalence of the bill of exchange from Kashmir to Gujarat. Though the *Rājataraṅgiṇī* is a text composed in mid-twelfth century, this local chronicle of Kashmir more or less accurately recorded events and situations in Kashmir from the eighth century onwards. It seems that the references to *huṇḍi/huṇḍika* in the *Rājataraṅgiṇī* were earlier than those in the *Lekhapaddhati*. One may reasonably infer that the practice of issuing *huṇḍi* started in Kashmir and then gradually spread as far as Gujarat. That the bill of exchange had entered the monetary scenario prior to the establishment of the Sultante may be safely assumed.

Kalhaṇa narrating the events during the reign of Partha (906-22 CE) lamented that: 'In this land the rulers of which had conquered Kanyakubja and other countries, the kings now maintained themselves by giving *huṇḍika* to Tantrins (landed aristocracy or kingmaker group)'. The Tantrins, along with the Ḍāmaras and the Ekangas, were land-holding intermediaries who became powerful enough to reduce the apex political authority to a puppet. The ruler had often to appease these intermediaries by giving them lavish amounts of money with which he virtually purchased his existence on the throne. Payment of such heavy sums required the issuance of *huṇḍika* or the bills of exchange. There are other passages in the *Rājataraṅgiṇī* describing the wretched plight of the ruler who could not pay the actual money due on his *huṇḍika* to the Tantrin as he was short of cash; the ruler had to run away for his act of defaulting.[27] Moreover the *Lokaprakāśa* of Kshemenedra, once again from Kashmir, spoke of *dīnāra huṇḍika* and *dhānya-huṇḍika*.[28] The former obviously denoted the bill of payment in *dīnāra* or gold coins, while the second term implied a bill of payment in terms of paddy which in this context functioned as some kind of money. In this case the term *dhānya-huṇḍikā* suggests the use of paddy (which must have been available in profusion) as a medium of exchange.

A close perusal of the *Lekhapaddhati* hints that the use of *huṇḍi* was quite widespread on Gujarat. The bill of payment (*huṇḍikā*) needed to be encashed in fifteen days from the issuance of the document. For the failure to transfer the money beyond the stipulated date the debtor had to pay, in excess of the stipulated amount, one (silver coin) per day. One specimen document in the *Lekhapaddhati*, supposed to be dated to 1231 CE, mentions about the *rāja-huṇḍikā* or royal bills of exchange. By this particular specimen of the bill of exchange a local administrator enjoins upon his subordinate functionaries to ensure the transfer of the sum of 300 *drammas* by *huṇḍika* in favour of a Paramāra ruler.[29] The accurate historicity of the Paramāra ruler and his receiving a sum through *huṇḍikā* is not the primary point here. What is of crucial significance is the acceptance of a piece of written document, promising the transfer of a quantum of money, as bill of payment. Thus the *huṇḍi* would emerge as an alternate mode of monetary transactions. There is little doubt that the system of *huṇḍi* not only provided an alternative instrument to actual minted metallic pieces, but also it was accepted as a legal tender in the prevalent practices of credit without which commercial transactions would have been impossible to operate. This would have assumed particular significance in a thriving zone of maritime commerce like Guajrat. One would like to join V.K. Jain's argument that the prevalence of *huṇḍikās* or bills of exchange in Gujarat 'could facilitate large-scale commercial without handling much of currency'.[30] The alternate money in the shape of *huṇḍikā* provided merchants an important option of not carrying coins of precious metals and/or bullion.

NOTES

1. S.R. Rao, *Excavations at Lothal*, New York: Asia Publishing House, 1973; Shereen Ratnagar, *Understanding Harappa: In the Greater Indus Civilization*, New Delhi: Tulika, 2006.
2. Marie-Francoise Boussac, Jean-Francois Salles and Jean-Baptiste Yon, eds., *Ports of the Ancient Indian Ocean*, New Delhi: Primus, 2016.

3. V.K. Jain, *Trade and Traders in Western India c. AD. 1000–1300*, New Delhi: Munshiram Manoharlal, 1989.
4. Ruby Maloni, *Surat: The Port of the Mughal Empire*, Mumbai: Himalaya Publishing House, 2003; M.N. Pearson, *The Indian Ocean*, New York: Oxford University Press, 2004.
5. Ashin Das Gupta, *Indian Merchants and the Decline of Surat 1750–1800*, Weisbaden: South Asian Institute, 1974; idem, *The World of Indian Ocean Maritime Merchants*, collected by Uma Das Gupta with an Introduction by Sanjay Subrahmanyam, New Delhi: Oxford University Press, 2001.
6. The Konkan coast, stretching from Daman in the north to Karwar Point in the south, is considered by Jean Deloche ('Geographical Consideration in the Localization of Ancient Sea-Ports of India', ed. Ranabir Chakravarti, *Trade in Early India*, New Delhi: Oxford University Press, 2001, pp. 312-26) as the coastal strip best suited in India for the natural sites for ports. However, the Konkan coast, sandwiched, as it were, between the Gujarat and the Malabar coastal tracts, did not flourish to the extent of its two other counterparts. See Ranabir Chakravarti, 'Merchants, Merchandise and Merchantmen in the Western Sea-board of India: A Maritime Profile (*c.* 500 BCE-1500 CE)', ed. Om Prakash, *The Trading World of the Indian Ocean 1500-1800*, New Delhi: Pearson, 2012, pp. 53-116.
7. Pearson, *The Indian Ocean.*
8. Boussac, Salles and Yon, *Ports of the Ancient Indian Ocean.*
9. Roberta Tomber, *Indo-Roman Trade, from Pots to Pepper*, London: Bloomsbury Publishing, 2008.
10. R.S. Sharma, *Indian Feudalism AD 300-1200*, New Delhi: McMillan, 1980 (2nd edn.); idem, *Urban Decay in India AD 300-1000*, New Delhi: Munshiram Manoharlal, 1987; D.N. Jha, ed., *The Feudal Order*, New Delhi: Manohar, 2000; B.D. Chattopadhyaya, *The Making of Early Medieval India*, New Delhi: Oxford University Press, 1994.
11. L. Casson, ed. and tran., *Periplus Maris Erythraei*, Princeton: Princeton Univeristy Press, 1989; E.L. Stevenson, tran., *Geographike Huphegisis of Claudiius Ptolemy*, New York: New York Public Library, 1932.
12. Ingo Strauch, *Foreign Sailors on Socotra*, Bremen: Hempen Verlag, 2012; Ranabir Chakravarti, 'Vibrant Thalassographies of the Indian Ocean: Beyond Nation States', *Studies in History* 31(20): 235-48.
13. These inscriptions were edited by K.V. Ramesh, *Epigraphia Indica*, XLI; for a study see Chakravarti, 'Three Copper Plates of the Sixth Century AD: Glimpses of Socio-economic and Cultural Life in Western Inda', ed. Ellen Raven, *South Asian Archaeology* 1999, Gronignen: Egbert Forsten, 2008, pp. 395-9, included in the present volume.
14. D.D. Kosambi, 'Indan Feudal Trade Cahrters', in idem, *Combined Methods of Indology and Other Writings*, collected with an Introduction by B.D. Chattopadhyaya, New Delhi: Oxford University Press, 2004.
15. Samuel Beal, trans., *Si-Yu-Ki of Hiuen Tsiang, Buddhist Records of the*

Western World, New Delhi: Asian Education, 2003, rpt., vol. II, pp. 253-60. It is interesting to note that the Chinese pilgrim reached Broach from Mo-ha-la-cha (Maharashtra, then under the rule of Chalukya Pulakesi II); he left Broach to reach Mo-la-po (Malava, possibly area around Ujjaiyini). The linkages of Broach with western Deccan and the Malwa plateau in the early seventh century closely corresponds with the account in the *Periplus*. The author of the *Periplus* observed that the hinterland of Barygaza stretched up to Paithan and Ter (Aurangabad dt, Maharashtra) and Ozene (Ujjaiyini).

16. Beal, *Travels*, pp. 259-60.
17. Suchandra Ghosh and Durbar Sharma, 'The Port of Sanjan/Sindan in Early Medieval India: A Study of Its Cosmopolitan Milieu', ed. Kenneth R. Hall, Rila Mukherjee and Suchandra Ghosh, *Subversive Sovereigns of the Sea*, Kolkata: Asiatic Society, 2017, pp. 67-88.
18. Ranabir Chakravarti, 'India Traders in the Early Medieval Times (1000-1300)', *Studies in People's History* II, 2015, pp. 27-40.
19. S.D. Goitein and Mordechai A. Friedman, *India Traders of the Middle Ages: Documents from the Cairo Geniza* ("*India Book*"), Leiden, Boston: E.J. Brill, 2008, p. 188.
20. Ibid., p. 171, fn. 20.
21. Jain, *Trade and Traders*; Pushpa Prasad, trans., *The Lekhapaddhati*, New Delhi: Tulika, 2001.
22. K.M. Shrimali, 'Money, Market and Feudalism', ed. R.S. Sharma and K.M Shrimali, *A Comprehensive History of India*, vol. IV.2, New Delhi: Manohar, 2008, pp. 729-60; Viswa Mohan Jha, 'Economic Condition: North India', ed. R.S. Sharma and K.M. Shrimali, *A Comprehensive History of India*, vol. IV.2, New Delhi: Manohar, 2008, pp. 261-310.
23. Susmita Basu Majumdar, 'Typological Studies and Typological Progression in Indian Numismatics—A Case Study of Early Medieval Kalachuri Coins of Ratanpur', *South Asian Archaeology 2010*, 2017, pp. 276-87.
24. B.N. Mukherjee, *Media of Exchange in Early Medieval North India*, New Delhi: Harman, 1992; Jain, *Trade and Traders*; L. Gopal, *Early Medieval Coin Types*, Varanasi: Benares Hindu University, 1966.
25. J.S. Deyell, *Living Without Silver, a Monetary History of Early Medieval North India*, New Delhi: Oxford University Press, 1990.
26. B.N. Mukherjee, 'Commerce and Money in the Central and Western Sectors of Eastern India (AD 750-1200)', *Indian Museum Bulletin*, vol. XVI, 1982, pp. 65-83; Susmita Basu Majumdar, 'Monetary History of Bengal: Issues and Non-issues', ed. D.N. Jha, *The Complex Heritage of Early India: Essays in Memory of R.S. Sharma*, New Delhi: Manohar, 2015, pp. 585-606.
27. M.A. Stein, tran., *Rajatarangini*, New Delhi: Motilal Banarsidass, 1974, rpt., vv. 266 and 302.
28. Lokaprakasa cited by Jain, *Trade and Traders*, pp. 200-1.
29. Ibid., p. 201.
30. Jain, *Trade and Traders*, p. 251.

Bibliography

Bibliography to the Third Edition Updated by Devdutta Kakati

PRIMARY SOURCES

I. General

de Barry, William Theodore, *Sources of Indian Tradition,* New York: Columbia University Press, 1958.

Ray, Niharranjan, B.D. Chattopadhyaya, V.R. Mani and Ranabir Chakravarti, *A Sourcebook of Indian Civilization,* Hyderabad: Orient Longman, 2000.

II. Archaeological Sources (including field archaeological, epigraphic and numismatic sources)

Barnett, L.D., 'Inscriptions at Narendra', *EI,* vol. XIII, 1915-16, pp. 298-316.

Basak, R.G., 'The Five Damodarpur Copper Pate Inscriptions of the Gupta Period', *EI*, vol. XV, 1919-20, pp. 113-45.

———, 'Madanpur Plate of Śrīcandra, year 44', *EI,* vol. XXVIII, 1949, pp. 57-8.

———, *Asokan Edicts,* Calcutta: Firma KL Mukhopadhyay, 1959.

Bhattasali, N.K., 'The Ghughrahati Copper Plate Inscription of Samāchāradeva', *EI,* vol. XVIII, 1925-6, pp. 74-86.

Buhler, G., 'Two Praśastis of Baijnath', *EI,* vol. 1, 1892, pp. 97-118.

———, 'Cintra Praśasti of the Reign of Sāraṅgadeva', *EI,* vol. I, 1892, pp. 271-87.

Burgess, James and Bhagawanlal Indraji, *Inscriptions from the Cave Temples of Western India,* Delhi: Indological Book House, 1976 (rpt.).

Chakrabarti, N.P., 'Brāhmī Inscriptions from Bandhogarh', *EI,* vol. XXXI, 1955, pp. 167-86.

Chanda, R.P., 'Some Unpublished Amaravati Inscriptions', *EI,* XV, 1919, pp. 257ff.

Chapekar, B.N., *Report on the Excavations at Ter, 1958,* Poona: Deccan College, 1969.

Codrington, O., 'On a Hoard of Coins Found at Broach', *Journal of the Bombay Branch of the Royal Asiatic Society*, XV, 1882-3, pp. 339-70.

Das, S.R., *Rajbadidanga 1962, Excavation Report,* Calcutta: Asiatic Society, 1968.

———, *Archaeological Discoveries from Murshidabad,* Calcutta: Asiatic Society, 1971.

Desai, Z.A., 'Inscriptions from the Prince of Wales Museum, Bombay', *EI, Arabic and Persian Supplement,* 1957-8, pp. 12-13.

———, 'Arabic Inscriptions of the Rajput Period from Gujarat', *EI, Arabic and Persian Supplement,* 1962-3, pp. 17-24.

———, 'Inscriptions of the Gujarat Sultans', *EI, Arabic and Persian Supplement,* 1963, pp. 32-4.

Fleet, J.F., *Corpus lnscriptionum Indicarum,* vol. III: *Inscriptions of the Imperial Guptas,* Calcutta: Superintendent of Govt. Printing, 1888.

Gaur, R.C., *Excavations at Atranjikhera,* New Delhi: Motilal Banarsidass, 1983.

Ghosh, A., 'Taxila (Sirkap) 1944-45', *AI,* vol. 4, 1948, pp. 66-78.

———, 'Rajagriha 1950', *AI,* vol. VII, 1951, pp. 66-78.

Ghosh, N.C., *Excavations at Satanikota 1977-78,* New Delhi: Archaeological Survey of India, 1986.

Gnoli, R., *Nepalese Inscriptions in the Gupta Characters,* Rome: IsMEO, 1956.

Hartel, H., *Excavations at Sonkh,* Berlin: D. Reimer, 1993.

Hultzsch, E., 'A Grant of Bāghela Arjunadeva, dated 1264 AD', *IA,* vol. XI, 1882, pp. 241-5.

———, 'Inscription of Abhimanyu', *EI,* vol. VIII, 1903, pp. 163-6.

Hussain, A.B.M., M. Harunur Rashid, Abdul Momin Chowdhury (eds.), *Mainamati, Devaprvata,* Dhaka: Asiatic Society of Bangladesh, 1997.

Karashima, Noboru (ed.), *Ancient and Medieval Commercial Activities in· the Indian Ocean: Testimony of Inscriptions and Cosmic-shreds,* Tokyo: Taisho University, 2002.

Kielhorn, F., 'Siyadoni Stone Inscription', *EI,* vol. I, 1892, pp. 162-79.

Krishnan, K.G., *Uttankita Vidyaranya Sanskrit Epigraph Series,* vol. II, Mysore: Uttankita Vidyaranya Trust, 1989.

Lal, B.B., 'Sisupalgarh 1948: An Early Historical Fort in Eastern India', *AI,* vol. V, 1949, pp. 37-9.

———, 'Excavations at Hastinapura and Other Explorations in the Upper Ganga and Sutlej Basins', *AI,* vol. XI, 1955, pp. 5-151.

Lal, B.B. and K.N. Dikshit, 'Sringaverapura: A Key Site for the Protohistory and Early History of the Central Ganga Valley', *Puratattva,* vol. X, 1978-9, pp. 1-8.

Lüders, H., 'A List of Brahmi Inscriptions up to AD 400 with the Exception of Those of Aśoka', being a supplement to *El,* vol. X, 1912.

———, *Mathurā Inscriptions,* ed. K.L. Janert, Gottingen, 1961.

Majumdar, N.G., *Inscriptions of Bengal,* vol. III, Rajshahi: Varendra Research Society, 1929.

Marshall, J., *Taxila, an Illustrated Account of Archaeological Excavations Carried out at Taxila under the Orders of the Government of India between the years 1913 and 1934,* Cambridge: Cambridge University Press, 1951.

Marshall, J. and J.Ph. Vogel, 'Excavations at Charsadda', *Annual Report of the Archaeological Survey of India 1902-3.* 1903, pp. 141-84.

Mehta, R.N. and A.M. Thakkar, *M.S. University Copper Plates of the Time of Toramana*, Vadodara: M.S. University, 1978.

Mirashi, V.V., *Corpus Inscriptionum Indicarum,* vol. IV, in two parts, *Inscriptions in the Kalachuri-Chedi Era,* Ootacamund: Archaeological Survey of India, 1955.

———, *Corpus Inscriptionum Indicarum,* vol. VI, *Inscriptions of the Śilāhāras,* New Delhi: Archaeological Survey of India, 1978.

Mukherjee, B.N., *Kushāṇa Coins in the Land of Five Rivers,* Calcutta: Indian Museum, 1979.

———, *Studies in the Aramaic Inscriptions of Aśoka,* Calcutta: Indian Museum, 1984.

———, 'Kharoṣṭī and Kharoṣṭī-Brāhmī Inscriptions from West Bengal, India', *IMB,* vol. XXV, 1990, pp. 1-80.

———, 'Kharoshti Inscriptions from Chunar (U.P.)', *JAS,* vol. XXXII, 1990, pp. 103-8.

Mukherjee, Ramaranjan and S.K. Maity, *A Corpus of Bengal Inscription,* Calcutta: Firma KL Mukhopadhyay, 1967.

Nagaswamy, R., 'Excavations at Korkai', *Damilica,* vol. I, 1970, pp. 50-4.

Narain, A.K. and T.N. Roy, *The Excavations at Rajghat, Varanasi,* Varanasi: Benares Hindu University, 1976.

Ramesh, K.V. and Subromania Aiyar, 'The Maida Museum Copper Plate of the Pāla King Mahendrapāla', *EI,* vol. XLI, 1983, pp. 6-29.

Ramesh, K.V. and S.P. Tiwari, 'The Rishtal Inscription of Aulikara Prakasadharman, (Vikrama) Year 572', *Studies in Indian Epigraphy, Bhāratīya Purābhilekha Patrikā, Journal of the Epigraphical Society of India* 10, 1983, pp. 96-103.

Ramesh, K.V., 'Three Early Charters from Sanjeli in Gujarat', *EI*, vol. XL, 1986, pp. 175-86.

Roy Chowdhury, Chittaranjan, *A Catalogue of Early Indian Coins in the Asutosh Museum, Calcutta,* Calcutta: University of Calcutta, 1962.

Sankalia, H.D., *From History to Prehistory at Nevasa,* Poona: Deccan College, 1960.

Sarkar, H. and B.N. Mishra, *Nagarjunakonda,* New Delhi: Archaeological Survey of India, 1972.

Sarkar, H. and S.P. Nainar, *Amarāvatī,* New Delhi: Archaeological Survey of India, 1973.

Sharma, G.R., *Excavations at Kauśāmbī 1957-59,* Allahabad: University of Allahabad, 1960.

———, *Excavations at Kauśāmbī 1949-50,* New Delhi: Archaeological Survey of India, 1969.

Sen, B.C. and D.P. Ghosh, 'A Dated Copper Plate Grant from Sundarban', *IHQ,* vol. 10, 1934, pp. 321-31.

Sinha; B.P. and Sitaram Roy, *Vaiśālī Excavations 1958-62,* Patna: Directorate of Archaeology and Museums, 1969.

Sinha, B.P. and L.A. Narain, *Pataliputra Excavation 1955-56,* Patna: Directorate of Archaeology and Museums, 1970.

Sircar, D.C., 'Sunderban Plate of Ḍommanapāla', *IC,* vol. I, 1934-5, pp. 679-82.

———, 'The Kailan Copper Plate Inscription of King Śrīdharana Rāta of Samataṭa', *IHQ,* vol. XXIII, 1947, pp. 221-41.

———, 'Madanpur Plate of Śrīcandra, year 46', *EI,* XXVIII, 1949, pp. 337-9.

———, 'Copper Plate Inscription of King Bhavadeva of Devaparvata', *JAS,* Letters, vol. XVII, 1951, pp. 83-94.

———, 'Rakshasakhali (Sunderban) Plates: Śaka 1118', *El,* vol. XXX, 1953, pp. 42-6.

———, 'The Charter of Vishṇuṣeṇa', *EI,* vol. XXX, 1953, pp. 163-81.

———, 'An Inscription from Veraval', *EI,* vol. XXXIV, 1957-8, pp. 141-50.

———, *Select Inscriptions Bearing on Indian History and Civilization,* in 2 vols.; vol. I, Calcutta: University of Calcutta, 1965; vol. II, New Delhi: Munshiram Manoharlal, 1983.

———, *Epigraphic Discoveries in East Pakistan,* Calcutta: Sanskrit College, 1973.

———, *Asokan Studies,* Calcutta: Indian Museum, 1979.

———, *Śilālekha Tamraśāsnādir Prasaṅga,* Calcutta: Sahityalok, 1982 (in Bangla).

Sinha, K.K., *Excavations at Śrāvastī 1959,* Varanasi: Benares Hindu University, 1969.

Wheeler, R.E.M., A. Ghosh and Krishna Deva, 'Arikamedu: An Indo-Roman Trading Station on the East Coast of India', *AI,* vol. II, 1946, pp. 17-124.

Wiese, Harald and Sadananda Das, *The Charter of Viṣṇuṣeṇa*, Halle: Martin Luther University, 2019.

III. Literary Sources: Indian Texts and Foreign Accounts

Abhidhānacintāmaṇi by Hemacandra, ed. with a commentary in Hindi by Nemaichandra Sastri and Haragovinda Sastri, Varanasi: Chowkhamba, 1964.

Abhidhānaratnamālā by Halayudha, ed. Krishnaji Govinda Ojha, Delhi, 1981.

The Acts of St. Thomas, tr. A.F.J. Klein, Leiden: E.J. Brill, 1962.

Aitareya Brāhmaṇa, ed. T. Aufrecht, Bonn, 1879; tr. A.B. Keith, *HOS,* vol. 25, 1920.

Ancient India as Described by Megasthenes and Arrian, tr. J.W. McCrindle, Calcutta: Chakrabarty and Chatterjee, 1921.

Aṅgavijjā, ed. Muni Punyavijayaji, Varanasi: Indological Book House, 1957.

Aṅguttaranikāya, ed. R. Morris and E. Hardf, in 5 vols., London: PTS, 1885-1900; tr. F.L. Woodward and E.M. Hare, *The Book of the Gradual Sayings,* in 5 vols., London: PTS, 1906-15.

Arab Navigation in the Indian Ocean before the Coming of the Portuguese by ibn Majid, tr. G.R. Tibbetts, London: Royal Asiatic Society of Great Britain and Ireland, 1971.

Arabic Classical Accounts of India and China, by Sulaiman and ibn Khordadbeh, tr. S. Maqbul Ahmed, Shimla: Indian Institute of Advanced Study, 1989.

Baudhāyana Dharmasūtra, tr. G. Biihler, *SBE,* vol. XIV, London, 1882.

Chufan Chi by Chau-ju Kua, tr. F. Hirth and W.W. Rockhill, St. Petersburgh: Imperial Academy of Sciences, 1911.

The Classical Accounts of India, ed. R.C. Majumdar, Calcutta: Firma KL Mukhopadhyay, 1960.

Daśakumāracarita by Daṇḍin, tr. Arthur W. Ryder, Chicago, 1927; also tr. Isabelle Onians, *What Ten Young Men Did,* New York University Press and JJC Foundation, 2005.

Dīgha Nikāya, ed. T.W. Rhys Davids and J.E. Carpenter, in 3 vols., London: PTS, 1890-1911; tr. T.W. Rhys Davids, in 3 vols., London: Sacred Books of the Buddhists, 1899-1926.

Foreign Notices of South India from Megasthenes to Ma Huan, compiled and edited by K.A. Nilakanta Sastri, Madras: University of Madras, 1939.

Fu kuo chi by Fa-hsien, tr. James Legge, *The Travels of Fahsien,* Delhi: Oriental Publishers, 1974 (rpt.).

Gathāsaptaśatī by Hāla, tr. R.G. Basak, Calcutta: Asiatic Society, 1970.

Geographike Huphegesis by Claudius Ptolemy, tr. E.L. Stevenson, New York: N.Y. Public Library, 1932.

Geographikon by Strabo, tr. H.L. Jones, London and Cambridge, Mass.: LCL, 1942 (rpt.).

The History of India as Told by Its Own Historians, tr. Henri Elliot and J.M. Dowson, ed. S.H. Hodivala with a Foreword by Mohammad Habib, vols. 1-3, Aligarh: S. Gupta, 1939.

Hudud al Alam, ed. and tr. V. Minorsky, London: Haklyut Society, 1937.

India and the Neighbouring Territories by al Idrisi, tr. S. Maqbul Ahmed, Leiden: E.J. Brill, 1960.

Jagaḍūcarita by Sarvānanda, ed. G. Bühler, Wien: Akademie der Wissenschaften, 1892.

The Jātakas, ed. V. Fausboll, in 6 vols., London, 1877-97; tr. E.B. Cowell, in 6 vols., Cambridge, 1895-1907.

Kāmasūtra by Vātsyayāna, ed. K.R. Aiyangar, Lahore, 1924.

Kathāsaritsāgara, tr. C.H. Tawney with notes by A.N. Penzer, London, 1924-8.

Kauṭilīya Arthaśāstra, ed. and tr. R.P. Kangle, in 3 parts, Bombay: University of Bombay, 1966-72.

Kitab Ajaib ul Hind by Buzurg ibn Shahriyar, tr. G.S.P. Freeman-Grenville, London: East West, 1980.

Kitabul Hind by Al Biruni, tr. E. Sachau *(Al Biruni's India),* London: Trunber, 1910.

Kuvalyamālā by Udyotanasuri, ed. A.N. Upadhyaye, Varanasi, 1969.

Lalitavistara, ed. P.L. Vaidya, Darbhanga: Chowkhamba Sanskrit Series, 1958.
Lekhapaddhati, ed. C.D. Dalal and G.K. Shrigondekar, Baroda: Central Library, 1925; *The Lekhapaddhati,* tr. Pushpa Prasad, New Delhi, Tulika, 2001.
The Literary Circle of Mahāmātya Vastupāla, ed. B. Sandesara, Bombay: Bharatiya Vidya Bhavan, 1953.
Manusaṁhitā with Medhātithi's Commentary, ed. Gangannath Jha, Bibliotheca Indica Series, Calcutta: Asiatic Society, 1932; tr. G. Bühler, *SBE,* vol. XXV, 1886.
Milindapañho, ed. V. Treckner, London: Royal Asiatic Society of Great Britain and Ireland, 1928; tr. C.A.F. Rhys Davids, Oxford: Clarendon Press, 1890.
Mṛcchakaṭika of Śūdraka, ed. and tr. with the commentary of Prithvidhara with an introduction, M.R. Karle, Delhi, 1962.
Nāmaliṅgānuśasana (also called *Amarakośa)* by Amarasiṁha, ed. H.D. Sharma and N.G. Sardesai, Poona: Oriental Book Agency, 1941.
Naturalis Historia by Pliny, tr. H. Rackham, London and Cambridge, Mass.: LCL, 1942.
Nītivākyāmṛtam by Somadevasuri, tr. Sushil Kumar Gupta, Calcutta: Modi Foundation, 1987.
Northern India According to Shui Ching Chu, tr. L. Peteche, Rome: IsMEO, 1950.
Periplus of the Erythrean Sea, tr. G.W.B. Huntingford, London: Haklyut Society, 1980; *Periplus Maris Erythrean,* ed. and tr. Lionel Casson, Princeton: Princeton University Press, 1989.
Rajatarangini, tr. M.A. Stein, New Delhi: Motilal Banarsidass, 1974 (rpt.).
Ṛgveda, tr. R.T.H. Griffith, Varanasi: Motilal Banarsidass, 1973 (Indian rpt.).
The Rihala by ibn Battuta, tr. H.A.R. Gibb *(The Travels of Ibn Battuta in Asia and Africa),* London: G. Routledge and Sons, 1929.
Samaraiccakahā, ed. Hermann Jacobi, Calcutta: The Asiatic Society, 1927.
Śatapatha Brāhmaiṇa, tr. J. Eggeling, *SBE,* vols. II, XXVI, XL, XLIII, XLIV, 1888-1900.
Suma Oriental by Tome Pires, tr. A. Cortesao, London: Haklyut Society, 1944.
Sumaṅgalavilāsinī by Buddhaghoṣa, ed. T.W. Rhys Davids and J.E. Carpenter, London: PTS, 1931.
Suttanipāta, ed. V. Fausboll. in 2 vols., London: PTS, 1885-94; tr. V. Fausboll, London, *SBE,* vol. X, 1924.
Ta-Tang hsi-ÿu Chi by Hsüan Tsang, tr. S. Beal, New Delhi: Motilal Banarsidass, 1983 (rpt.); T. Watters, *On Yuan Chwang's Travels,* New Delhi: Motilal Banarsidass, 1961.
Tilakamañjarī by Dhanapāla, ed. Pandit Bhavadatta Sastri, Bombay, 1903.
Travels of Ibn Jubayr, tr. R.J.C. Broadhurst, London: J. Cape, 1954.
Travels of Ser Marco Polo, tr. H. Yule and H. Cordier, in 2 vols., London: John Murray, 1903.
Yaśastilakacampu by Somadevasuri, ed. Sivadatta and K.P. Parab, Bombay: Nirnay Sagar Press, 1901-3.

Ying-yai-Sheng-lan by Ma Huan, tr. J.V.G. Mills, *The Overall Survey of the Ocean's Shores,* Oxford: Oxford University Press, 1970.

IV. Jewish Trade Letters.

Goitein, S.D., *Letters of Medieval Jewish Traders,* Princeton: Princeton University Press, 1973.

———, 'From Aden to India: Specimens of Correspondence of India Traders of the Twelfth Century', *JESHO,* vol. XXI, 1980, pp. 43-66.

———, 'Portrait of a Medieval India Trader: Three Letters from the Cairo Geniza', *Bulletin of the School of Oriental Studies,* vol. XLVII, 1987, pp. 448-64.

Goitein, S.D. and Mordechai A. Friedman, *India Traders of the Middle Ages: Documents from the Cairo Geniza* (*India Book*), Leiden, Boston: E.J. Brill, 2008.

Shaked Shaul, *Tentative Bibliography of Genizah Documents,* Paris: Mouton, 1964.

SECONDARY SOURCES.

Abraham, Meera, *Two Medieval Merchant Guilds of South India,* New Delhi: Manohar, 1988.

Agrawala, V.S., *India as Known to Pāṇini: A Study of the Cultural Material in the Ashṭādhyāyī,* Lucknow: University of Lucknow, 1953.

Aiyangar, S.K., *The Maṇimekhalai in its Historical Setting,* London: Luzac & Co., 1938.

Allchin, Bridget and F.R. Allchin, *The Rise of Civilization in India and Pakistan,* Cambridge: Cambridge University Press, 1982.

Allchin, F.R., 'Upon the Antiquity and Methods of Gold Mining in Ancient India', *JESHO,* vol. V (2), 1962, pp. 195-211.

———, 'Antiquity of Gold Mining in the Gadag Region of Karnataka', in M.S. Nagaraja Rao (ed.), *Madhu: Recent Researches in Indian Archaeology and Art History,* New Delhi: Agam Kala Prakashan, 1981, pp. 81-3.

———, 'City and State Formation in Early Historic South Asia', *SAS,* vol. V (1), 1989, pp. 1-16.

———, 'Patterns of City Formation in Early Historic South Asia', *SAS,* vol. VI (1), 1990, pp. 163-73.

———, *The Archaeology of Early Historic South Asia: The Emergence of Cities and States* (with contributions from George Erdosy, R.A.E. Conningham, D.K. Chakrabarti and Bridget Allchin), Cambridge: Cambridge University Press, 1995.

Appadurai, A., *Economic Conditions in Southern India (1000-1500 AD),* in 2 vols., Madras: University of Madras, 1936.

Arasaratnam, S. and Aniruddha Ray, *Masulipatnam and Cambay: A History of Two Port Towns 1500-1800,* New Delhi: Munshiram Manoharlal, 1994.

Banerjee, N.R., *The Iron Age in India,* New Delhi: Munshiram Manoharlal, 1965.

Basham, A.L. (ed.), *Papers on the Date of Kaniṣka submitted to the Conference on the Date of Kaniṣka,* Leiden: EJ. Brill, 1968.

Basu Majumdar, Susmita, 'Monetary History of Bengal: Issues and Non-issues', in D.N. Jha (ed.), *The Complex Heritage of Early India: Essays in Memory of R.S. Sharma*, New Delhi: Manohar, 2015, pp. 585-606.

———, 'Typological Studies and Typological Progression in Indian Numismatics—A Case Study of Early Medieval Kalachuri Coins of Ratanpur', *South Asian Archaeology 2010*, 2017, pp. 276-87.

Begley, Vimala, 'Arikamedu Reconsidered', *American Journal of Archaeology,* vol. LXXXVII, 1983, pp. 461-81.

———, 'From Iron Age to Early Historical in South Indian Archaeology', in Jerome K. Jacobson (ed.), *Studies in the Archaeology of India and Pakistan,* New Delhi: Oxford and IBH, 1986, pp. 297-316.

———, 'Ceramic Evidence of pre-Periplus Trade on the Indian Coast', in Vimala Begley and Richard Daniel de Puma (eds.), *Rome and India: The Ancient Sea Trade,* New Delhi: Oxford University Press, 1992 (rpt.), pp. 157-96.

Begley, Vimala and Richard Daniel de Puma (eds.), *Rome and India: The Ancient Sea Trade,* New Delhi: Oxford University Press, 1992 (rpt.).

Belshaw, Cyril, *Traditional Exchange and Modern Markets,* New Jersey: Prentice Hall, 1965.

Bhattacharyya, A., *Historical Geography of Ancient and Early Medieval Bengal,* Calcutta: Sanskrit Pustak Bhandar, 1977.

Bhattacharyya, Bhaswati, 'The Hinterland and the Coast: The Pattern of Interaction in Coromandel in the Late Eighteenth Century', in Rudrangshu Mukherjee and Lakshmi Subramanyan (eds.), *Politics and Trade in the Indian Ocean World: Essays in Honour of Ashin Das Gupta,* New Delhi: Oxford University Press, 1998, pp. 19-51.

Bhattacharyya, P.K., *Historical Geography of Madhya Pradesh: From Early Records,* New Delhi: Munshiram Manoharlal, 1977.

Biswas, Atreyi, *The Political History of the Hūṇas in India*, New Delhi: Munshiram Manoharlal, 1973.

Bose, A.N., *Social and Rural Economy in Northern India, c. 600 BC-200 AD,* in 2 vols., Calcutta: Firma KL Mukhopadhyay, 1967.

Boussac, Marie-Francoise and J.F. Salles (eds.), *Athens, Aden, Arikamedu: Essays on the Interrelations between India, Arabia, and the Eastern Mediterranean,* New Delhi; Manohar, 1995.

Boussac, Marie-Francoise, Jean-Francois Salles and Jean-Baptiste Yon (eds.), *Ports of the Ancient Indian Ocean*, New Delhi: Primus, 2016.

Bowersock, G.W., *Roman Arabia,* Cambridge Mass: Harvard University Press, 1983.

Braudel, Fernand, *The Mediterranean and the Mediterranean World in the Age*

of Phillip II, tr. S. Reynolds, in 2 vols., London: Fontana, 1972.
———, *The Wheels of Commerce,* tr. S. Reynolds, London: Fontana, 1985.
———, *The Structures of Everyday Life,* tr. S. Reynolds, London: Fontana, 1985.
Broeze, Franz (ed.), *Brides of the Sea: Port Cities of Asia from the 16th-20th Centuries,* Honolulu: University of Hawaii Press, 1989.
Bulnois, L., *The Silk Road,* tr. Dennis Chamberlin, London: George Allen and Unwin, 1966.
Chakladar, Haran Chandra, *Social Life in Ancient India, Studies in Vātsyayāna's Kāmasūtra,* Calcutta: Greater India Society, 1929.
Chakrabarti, Dilip K., *Theoretical Issues in Indian Archaeology,* New Delhi: Munshiram Manoharlal, 1988.
———, 'Chandraketugarh', in A. Ghosh (ed.), *An Encyclopaedia of Indian Archaeology,* vol. I, New Delhi: Munshiram Manoharlal, 1989, pp. 95-6.
———, *Ancient Bangladesh: A Study of the Archaeological Sources,* New Delhi: Munshiram Manoharlal, 1992.
———, *The Archaeology of Ancient Indian Cities,* New Delhi: Oxford University Press, 1995.
Chakrabarti, Kunal, 'Textual Authority and Oral Exposition: The Vrata Ritual as a Channel of Communication in Early Medieval Bengal', *Studies in History,* vol. X (2), 1994, pp. 217-41.
Chakrabarti, Kunal and Kanad Sinha (eds.), *State, Power and Legitimacy: The Gupta Kingdom*, New Delhi: Primus, 2018.
Chakravarti, Ranabir, 'Kulottuṅga and the Port of Viśākhapaṭṭinam', *PIHC,* vol. XLI, 1981, Bodhgaya session, pp. 142-5.
———, 'Bhoṭṭaviṣṭi: Its Nature and Its Collection', in B.N. Mukherjee, D.R. Das, S.S. Biswas and S.P. Singh (eds.), *Dineśacandrika: Essays in Honour of D.C. Sircar,* New Delhi: Sundeep Prakashan, 1983, pp. 203-8.
———, *Warfare for Wealth: Early Indian Perspective,* Calcutta: Firma KL Mukhopadhyay, 1986.
———, 'Merchants of Konkan (10th-12th Centuries AD)', *IESHR,* vol. XXIII (2), 1986, pp. 208-15.
———, 'Monarchs, Merchants and a Matha in Northern Konkan (900-1053 AD)', *IESHR,* vol. XXVII, 1990, pp. 189-208.
———, 'Horse Trade and Piracy at Tana (Thana, Maharashtra, India): Gleanings from Marco Polo', *JESHO,* vol. XXXIII, 1991, pp. 159-82.
———, 'Rulers and Ports: Viśākhāpaṭṭinam and Motuppalli in Early Medieval Andhradeśa', in K.S. Mathew (ed.), *Mariners, Merchants and Oceans,* New Delhi, Manohar, 1995, pp. 52-77.
———, 'Coastal Trade and Voyages in Konkan: The Early Medieval Scenario', *IESHR,* vol. XXXV, 1998, pp. 97-123.
———, 'Early Medieval Bengal and the Trade in Horses: A Note', *JESHO,* vol. XLII, 1999, pp. 194-211.
———, 'Nakhudas and Nauvittakas: Ship-owning Merchants in the West Coast of India (*c.* AD 1000-1500)', *JESHO,* vol. XLIII, 2000, pp. 34-64.

———, 'Between Cities and Villages: Linkages of Trade in India (*c.* AD 600-1300)', in Georg Berkemer, Tilman Frasch, Hermann Kulke and Jürgen Lütt (eds.), *Explorations in the History of South Asia: Essays in Honour of Dietmar Rothermund,* New Delhi: Manohar, 2001, pp. 99-120.

——— (ed.), *Trade in Early India,* New Delhi: Oxford University Press, 2001 (paperback edn. 2005).

———, 'Politics and Society in India (AD 300-1000)', in K. Satchidananda Murty (ed.), *Life, Thought and Culture in India (c. AD 300-1000),* vol. II, pt. I, New Delhi: Centre for the Study of Civilizations, 2002, pp. 58-171.

———, 'Seafarings, Ships and Ship Owners: India and the Indian Ocean (AD 700-1500)', in David Parkin and Ruth Barnes (eds.), *Ships and the Development of Maritime Technology in the Indian Ocean,* London: Routledge and Curzon, 2002, pp. 28-61.

———, 'Trade and Later Indian Powers in the Indian Ocean (*c.* AD 400-1300)', in Alok Tripathy (ed.), *Proceedings of the International Conference on Maritime Archaeology,* New Delhi: Organizing Committee for the International Conference on Maritime Archaeology, 2004, pp. 35-54.

———, 'On Board the Hermapollon: Transporting Gangetic Nard from Muziris', in Martin Brandtner and Shishir Kumar Panda (eds.), *Interrogating History: Essays for Hermann Kulke,* New Delhi: Manohar, 2006, pp. 147-64.

———, 'Three Copper Plates of the Sixth Century AD: Glimpses of Socio-economic and Cultural Life in Western India', in Ellen Raven (ed.), *South Asian Archaeology* 1999, Gronignen: Egbert Forsten, 2008, pp. 395–9.

———, 'Merchants, Merchandise and Merchantmen in the Western Sea-board of India: A Maritime Profile (*c.* 500 BCE-1500 CE)', in Om Prakash (ed.), *The Trading World of the Indian Ocean 1500-1800*, New Delhi: Pearson, 2012, pp. 53-116.

———, 'India Traders in the Early Medieval Times (1000-1300)', *Studies in People's History* II, 2015, pp. 27-40.

———, 'Vibrant Thalassographies of the Indian Ocean: Beyond Nation States', *Studies in History* 31 (2), 2015, pp. 235-48.

———, 'Merchants vis-à-vis the State Society: Reflecting on Some Case Studies from Early Historic and Threshold Times', *Studies in People's History*, VI, 2019.

———, 'Indic Mercantile Community and the Indian Ocean World: A Millennial Overview (*c.* 500-1500 CE)', in Angela Schottenhammer (ed.), *Early Global Communities across the Indian Ocean World*, Salzburg: Palgrave MacMillan, 2019, pp. 191-226.

Chakravarti, Ranabir and Suchandra Dutta Majumdar, 'An Ancient Gymnasium at Bandhogarh', *Monthly Bulletin of the Asiatic Society,* July 1992, pp. 1-7.

Chakravarti, Uma, *The Social Dimensions of Early Buddhism,* New Delhi: Oxford University Press, 1987.

Champakalakshmi, R., 'Archaeology and Tamil Literary Tradition', *Puratattva,* vol. VIII, 1975-6, pp. 110-22.

———, 'Peasant State and Society in Medieval South India: A Review Article', *IESHR,* vol. XVIII, 1981, pp. 411-26.

———, 'Society and Economy in South India: 400-1300', in Romila Thapar (ed.), *Recent Perspectives of Early Indian History,* Bombay: Popular Prakashan, 1995, pp. 266-308.

———, *Trade, Ideology and Urbanization: South India c. 300 BC to AD 1300,* New Delhi: Oxford University Press, 1996.

Chandra, Satish (ed.), *The Indian Ocean: Explorations in History, Commerce and Politics,* New Delhi: Sage, 1987.

Chattopadhyaya, B.D., 'Transition to the Early Historical Phase in the Deccan—A Note', in B.M. Pande and B.D. Chattopadhyaya (eds.), *Archaeology and History: Essays in Memory of Shri A. Ghosh,* vol. II, New Delhi: Agam Kala Prakashan, 1987, pp. 727-32.

———, 'Urban Centres in Early Medieval India: An Overview', in Romila Thapar and Sabyasachi Bhattacharyya (eds.), *Situating Indian History for Sarvepalli Gopal,* New Delhi: Oxford University Press, 1987, pp. 8-33.

———, *Aspects of Rural Settlements and Rural Society in Early Medieval India,* Calcutta: K.P. Bagchi, 1990.

———, *Coins and Currency System in South India c. AD 225-1300*, New Delhi: Munshiram Manoharlal, 1990.

———, *The Making of Early Medieval India,* New Delhi: Oxford University Press, 1994.

———, 'State and Economy in North India: Fourth to Twelfth Century', in Romila Thapar (ed.), *Recent Perspectives of Early Indian History,* Bombay: Popular Prakashan, 1995, pp. 308-46.

———, *Representing the Other? Sanskrit Sources and the Muslims: Eighth to Fourteenth Century,* New Delhi: Manohar, 1998.

———, *Studying Early India: Archaeology, Texts, and Historical Issues,* New Delhi: Permanent Black, 2003.

Chattopadhyaya, Debiprasad (ed.), *History of Science and Technology in Ancient India,* in 2 vols., Calcutta: Firma KL Mukhopadhyay, 1986, 1991.

Chattopadhyaya, Sudhakar, *Early History of Northern India,* Calcutta: Asia Publishing House, 1958.

Chaudhuri, K.N., *Trade and Civilization in the Indian Ocean: An Economic History from the Rise of Islam to 1750,* Cambridge: Cambridge University Press, 1985.

———, *Asia before Europe: Economy and Civilization of the Indian Ocean from the Rise of Islam to 1750,* Cambridge: Cambridge University Press, 1990.

Childe, V. Gordon, 'The Urban Revolution', *The Town Planning Review,* vol. XXI, 1950, pp. 3-17.

———, *Man Makes Himself,* Harmondsworth: Penguin, 1965.

Chowdhury, Abdul Momin and Ranabir Chakravarti, eds., *History of Bangladesh: Early Bengal in Regional Perspectives up to c. 1200 CE*, in 2 vols., Dhaka: Asiatic Society of Bangladesh, 2018.

Cooney, Gabriel, 'Introduction: Seeing Land from the Sea', *World Archaeology,* vol. XXXV, 2003, pp. 323-8.

Das Gupta, Ashin, *Malabar in Asian Trade 1740-1800,* Cambridge: Cambridge University Press, 1967.

———, *Indian Merchants and the Decline of Surat, c. 1700-1750,* Weisbaden: Franz Steiner Verlag, 1979.

———, *Vangopasagara* (in Bangla), Calcutta: Pratikshan, 1989.

———, *Merchants of Maritime India, 1500-1800,* London: Variorum, 1994.

———, *The World of the Indian Ocean Merchant, 1500-1800* (compiled by Uma Dasgupta: with an introduction by Sanjay Subrahmanyam), New Delhi: Oxford University Press, 2001.

Das Gupta, Ashin and M.N. Pearson (eds.), *India and the Indian Ocean, 1500-1800,* Calcutta: Oxford University Press, 1987.

Dasgupta, K.K., *A Tribal History of Ancient India: A Numismatic Approach,* Calcutta: Nababharat Publishers, 1974.

Dasgupta, Paresh Chandra, 'Some Early Indian Literary References to Tamralipta', *Modern Review,* 1953, pp. 31-4.

Dehejia, Vidya, 'Collective and Popular Bases of Early Buddhist Patronage: Sacred Monuments', in Barbara Stoller Miller (ed.), *The Powers of Art: Patronage in Indian Culture,* New Delhi: Oxford University Press, 1992, pp. 35-45.

Deloche, Jean, 'Koṅkaṇ Warships of the Eleventh-Seventeenth Centuries as Represented on Memorial Stones', *BEFEO,* vol. 76, 1987, pp. 165-84.

———, *Transport System and Communications in India Prior to Steam Locomotion: Water Transport,* vol. II, New Delhi: Oxford University Press, 1994.

———, 'Geographical Consideration in the Localization of Ancient Sea-Ports of India', in Ranabir Chakravarti (ed.), *Trade in Early India*, New Delhi: Oxford University Press, 2001, pp. 312-26.

Deyell, John S., *Living Without Silver: The Monetary History of Early Medieval North India,* New Delhi: Oxford University Press, 1990.

Digby, Simon, *War-horse and Elephant in the Delhi Sultanate,* Oxford: Orient Monograph, 1971.

———, 'The Broach Coin Hoard as Evidence of the Import of Valuta across the Arabian Sea during the Thirteenth and Fourteenth Centuries', *JRAS*, 1980, pp. 129-38.

———, 'Economic Condition before 1200', in Tapan Raychaudhuri and Irfan Habib, eds., *The Cambridge Economic History of India, c.1200-c.1750,* vol. I, New Delhi: Orient Longman, 1984 (Indian rpt.), pp. 45-8.

Ducene, Jean-Charles, 'The Ports on the Western Coast of India according to Arab Geographers (Eighth-Fifteenth Century AD)', in Marie-Francoise Boussac, Jean-Francois Salles and Jean-Bapiste Yon (eds.), *Ports of the Ancient Indian Ocean*, New Delhi: Primus, 2016, pp. 165-78.

Erdosy, George, 'The Origin of Cities in the Ganges Valley', *JESHO,* vol. XXVIII, 1985, pp. 294-325.

———, *Urbanisation in Early Historic India,* Oxford: BAR Publications Series, 1988.

Fick, Richard, *The Social Organization in North-Eastern India in Buddha's Time,* tr. Shishirkumar Maitra, Varanasi: Indological Book House, 1972 (rpt.).

Fiser, Ivo, 'The Problem of the Setthi in the Buddhist Jatakas', *Archiv Orinetalni,* vol. XXII (2-3), 1954, pp. 238- 66.

Frank, Andre Gunder, 'The Centrality of Central Asia', *Studies in History,* vol. III, 1992, pp. 43-98.

Frank, Irene and David M. Brownstone, *The Silk Road: A History,* New York: Facts on File Publications, 1986.

Frye, R.N., 'The Rise of the Kushan Empire', in *History of Humanity,* vol. III, Paris: UNESCO, 1996, pp. 456-60.

Ghosh, A., *The City in Early Historical India,* Shimla: Indian Institute of Advanced Study, 1973.

Ghosh, A. (ed.), *An Encyclopaedia of Indian Archaeology,* in 2 vols., New Delhi: Munshiram Manoharlal, 1989.

Ghosh, Amitav, *In an Antique Land: History in the Guise of a Traveller's Tale,* New Delhi: Ravi Dayal, 1990.

Ghosh, Suchandra, *From the Oxus to the Indus: Political and Cultural Study c. 300* BCE *to 100* BCE, New Delhi: Primus, 2018.

———, 'Anahilapura: Understanding Its Expansive Network during the Time of the Chaulukyas', *Asian Review of World Histories*, VI, 2018, pp. 236-45.

Ghosh, Suchandra and Durbar Sharma, 'The Port of Sanjan/Sindan in Early Medieval India: A Study of Its Cosmopolitan Milieu', in Kenneth R. Hall, Rila Mukherjee and Suchandra Ghosh (eds.), *Subversive Sovereigns of the Sea*, Kolkata: Asiatic Society, 2017, pp. 67-88.

Ghoshal, U.N., 'Economic Conditions (Post-Mauryan)', in K.A. Nilakanta Sastri (ed.), *A Comprehensive History of India,* vol. II, Bombay: Orient Longman, 1957, pp. 430-57.

———, *A History of Indian Political Ideas: The Ancient Period and the Period of Transition to the Middle Ages,* Bombay: Oxford University Press, 1966.

———, *A History of Indian Public Life,* vol. II, Bombay: Oxford University Press, 1966.

———, *Contributions to the History of the Hindu Revenue System,* Calcutta: Saraswat, 1972 (2nd edn.).

———, *The Agrarian System in Ancient India,* Calcutta: Saraswat, 1972 (2nd edn.).

Gil, Moshe, 'The Jewish Merchants in the Light of Eleventh-Century Geniza Documents', *JESHO,* XLVI, 2003, pp. 273-319.

Gopal, Lallanji, 'Textiles in Ancient India', *JESHO,* vol. VII, 1964, pp. 53- 69.

———, *The Economic Life of Northern India c.* AD *700-1200,* Varanasi: Motilal Banarsidass, 1965.

———, *Early Medieval Coin Types*, Varanasi: Benares Hindu University, 1966.

———, 'Indian Shipping in the Early Medieval Period', in Lokesh Chandra et al. (eds.), *India's Contributions to World Thought and Culture,* Calcutta:

Swami Vivekananda Centenary Celebration Committee, 1970, pp. 108-22.

Grover, B.R., 'An Integrated Pattern of Commercial Life in Rural Society of North India during the Late Seventeenth and Early Eighteenth Centuries', in Sanjay Subrahmanyam (ed.), *Money and Market in India, 1100-1700,* New Delhi: Oxford University Press, 1990, pp. 219-55.

Haider, Najaf, 'The Network of Monetary Exchange in the Indian Ocean Trade 1200-1700', in Himanshu Prabha Ray and Edward A. Alpers (eds.), *Cross Currents and Community Networks: The History of the Indian Ocean World,* New Delhi: Oxford University Press, 2007, pp. 181-205.

Hall, K.R., 'Khmer Commercial Development and Foreign Contacts under Sūryavarman I', *JESHO,* vol. XVIII, 1975, pp. 313-30.

———, 'International Trade and Foreign Diplomacy in Early Medieval South India', *JESHO,* vol. XXI, 1978, pp. 75-98.

———, *Trade and Statecraft in the Age of the Cōḷas,* New Delhi: Abhinav, 1980.

Handiqui, K.K., *Yaśastilaka and Indian Culture,* Sholapur: Jaina Samskriti Samrakshana Samgha, 1968 (2nd edn.).

Heiman, J., 'Small Exchange and Ballast: Cowry Trade and Usage as an Example of Indian Ocean Economic History', *South Asia,* vol. III, 1980, pp. 48-69.

Heitzman, James, *Gifts of Power: Lordship in an Early Indian State,* New Delhi: Oxford University Press, 1994.

Hourani, George F., *Arab Seafaring in the Indian Ocean in Ancient and Early Medieval Times,* Beirut, 1951.

Jain, J.C., *Life in Ancient India as Depicted in the Jaina Canonical Texts and Commentaries,* New Delhi: Munshiram Manoharlal, 1974.

Jain, V.K., *Trade and Traders in Western India* AD *1000-1300,* New Delhi: Munshiram Manoharlal, 1989.

Jha, D.N., *Revenue System in Post-Maurya and Gupta Times,* Calcutta: Punthi Pustak, 1967.

——— (ed.), *Feudal Social Formation in Early India,* New Delhi: Chanakya, 1987.

——— (ed.), *The Feudal Order: State, Society and Ideology in Early Medieval India,* New Delhi: Manohar, 2001.

Jha, Viswa Mohan, 'Economic Condition: North India', in R.S. Sharma and K.M. Shrimali (eds.), *A Comprehensive History of India*, vol. IV. (2), New Delhi: Manohar, 2008, pp. 261-310.

Jhanjh, Dev Kumar, '*Akṣaśālika*, *Akṣaśālin* and *Suvarṇakāra* as the Engravers of Copper Plate Charters of Odisha (*c.* 7th-11th Centruries CE)', *PIHC* (78th session), 2018, pp. 117-26.

Joshi, M.C., 'Navigational Terms in the *Nāmaliṅgānuśśana',* in S.R. Rao (ed.), *Marine Archaeology of Indian Ocean Countries,* Goa: National Institute of Oceanography, 1991.

Kane, P.V., *History of Dharmaśāstra,* in 5 vols., Poona: Bhandarkar Oriental Research Institute, 1941-62.

Kosambi, D.D., 'Dhenukākaṭa', *JBAS,* vol. XXX, 1955, pp. 50-71.

———, *An Introduction to the Study of Indian History,* Bombay: Popular Prakashan, 1956.

———, 'Indian Feudal Trade Charters', *JESHO,* vol. 2, 1958, pp. 281-93.

———, *The Culture and Civilisation of Ancient India in Historical Outline,* New Delhi: Vikas, 1972 (paperback edn.).

———, *Combined Methods in Indology and Other Writings* (compiled, edited and introduced by B.D. Chattopadhyaya), New Delhi: Oxford University Press, 2002.

Kulke, Hermann, 'Fragmentation and Segmentation versus Integration? Reflections on the Concepts of Indian Feudalism and Segmentary State in Indian History', *SH,* vol. 4, 1982, pp. 237-63.

———, '"A Passage to India": Temples, Merchants and the Ocean', *JESHO,* vol. XXXVI, 1993, pp. 154-80.

——— (ed.), *The State in India, 1000-1700,* New Delhi: Oxford University Press, 1994.

———, 'Rivalry and Competition in the Bay of Bengal in the Eleventh Century and its Bearing on the Indian Ocean Studies', in Om Prakash and Denys Lombard (eds.), *Commerce and Culture in the Bay of Bengal, 1500-1800,* New Delhi: Manohar, 1999, pp. 17-36.

Kulke, Hermann and Bharabi Prasad Sahu, *History of Pre-colonial India*, New Delhi: Oxford University Press, 2018.

Kulke, Hermann and Dietmar Rothermund, *A History of India,* New York and London: Oxford University Press, 2004.

Kuppuswamy, G.R., *Economic Conditions in Karnataka, AD 973-1336,* Dharwar: Karnataka University, 1975.

Lahiri, Nayanjyot, *The Archaeology of Ancient Indian Trade Routes up to c. 200 BC: Resource Use, Resource Access and Lines of Communication,* New Delhi: Oxford University Press, 1992.

Lal, B.B. and K.N. Dikshit, 'A 2000 Year Old Feat of Hydraulic Engineering in India', *Archaeology,* vol. XXXVIII, 1985, pp. 48-53.

Lambourn, Elizabeth, 'Describing the Lost Camel: Clues for West Asian Mercantile Networks in South Asian Maritime Trade (Tenth-Twelfth Centuries AD)', in Marie-Francoise Boussac, Jean-Francois Salles and Jean-Bapiste Yon (eds.), *Ports of the Ancient Indian Ocean*, New Delhi: Primus, 2016, pp. 351-407.

Levin, G. Bongard, *Mauryan India,* New Delhi: Abhinav, 1985.

Lewis, Archibald, 'Maritime Skills in the Indian Ocean, 1368-1500', *JESHO,* vol. XVI, 1973, pp. 238-64.

Ling, Trevor, *The Buddha;* Harmondsworth: Penguin, 1980.

Liu, Xin Ri, *Ancient India and Ancient China: Trade and Religious Exchanges, AD 1600,* New Delhi: Oxford University Press, 1988.

Majumdar, A.K., *The Caulukyas of Gujarat: A Survey of the History and Culture of Gujarat from the Middle of the Tenth to the End of the Thirteenth Century,* Bombay: Bharatiya Vidya Bhavan, 1956.

Majumdar, R.C., *Corporate Life in Ancient India,* Calcutta: Firma KL Mukhopadhyay, 1925.

——— (ed.), *The History of Bengal,* vol. I, Dhaka: University of Dhaka, 1941.

——— (ed.), *The Vedic Age (The History and Culture of the Indian People,* vol.1*)*, London: George Allen and Unwin, 1951.

———, (ed.), *The Age of Imperial Kanauj*, Bombay: Bharatiya Vidya Bhavan, 1966.

———, *The Age of Imperial Unity,* Bombay: Bharatiya Vidya Bhavan, 1968.

———, *The Classical Age of India,* Bombay: Bharatiya Vidya Bhavan, 1970.

Maloni, Ruby, *Surat: The Port of the Mughal Empire*, Mumbai: Himalaya Publishing House, 2003.

Margritti, Roxani, 'Like the Place of Congregation on Judgement Day: Maritime Trade and Urban Civilization in Medieval Aden *(c.* 1083-1229)', unpublished Ph.D. thesis, Princeton University, 2002.

———, 'Monetization and Cross-Cultural Collaboration in the Western Indian Ocean (Eleventh to Thirteenth Centuries', in Francesca Tivellato, Lear Halevi and Catia Antunes (eds.), *Religion and Trade: Cross-Cultural Exchanges in World History 1000-1900,* New York: Oxford University Press, 2014, pp. 192-215.

Marshall, P.J., *East Indian Fortunes: The British in Bengal in the Eighteenth Century,* Oxford: Clarendon Press, 1976.

Mazumdar, B.P., 'Industries and Internal Trade in Early Medieval North India', *JBRS,* vols. LXV-LXVI, 1979-80, pp. 230-56.

McPherson, Kenneth, *The Indian Ocean: A History of People and the Sea,* New Delhi: Oxford University Press, 1993.

Misra, Satish C., *Muslim Communities in Gujarat: Preliminary Studies in their History and Social Organisation,* New York: Asia Publishing, 1964.

Mookerji. R.K., *Indian Shipping: A History of the Seaborne Trade and Maritime Activity of Indians from the Earliest Times,* Bombay: Bombay & Co., 1912.

Moraes, G.M., *The Kadamba Kula: A History of Ancient and Mediaeval Karnataka,* Bombay: B.X. Furtado, 1931.

Moreland, W.H., 'The Shahbandar in the Eastern Seas', *JRAS,* new series 52, October 1920, pp. 517-533.

Morrison, B.M., *Political Centres and Cultural Regions in Early Bengal,* Jaipur: Rawat Publications, 1980 (rpt.).

Mukherjee, B.N., *An Agrippan Source: A Study in Indo-Parthian History,* Calcutta: Pilgrim, 1969.

———, *The Economic Factors in Kushāṇa History,* Calcutta: Pilgrim, 1970.

———, 'The Original Territory of Harikela', *Bangladesh Lalitkala,* vol. I, 1975, pp. 115-19.

———, 'Revenue, Trade and Society in the Kushāṇa Empire', *IHR,* vol. VII, 1980-1, pp. 24-53.

———, Presidential Address, Section I, *PIHC,* Bodhgaya session, 1981.

———, *Mathurā and its Society: The Śaka-Pahlava Phase,* Calcutta: Firma KL Mukhopadhyay, 1981.

———, 'The Place of Harikela Coinage in the Art and Archaeology of Bangladesh', *Journal of the Varendra Research Museum,* vol. VII, 1981-2, pp. 57-68.

———, *Kushāṇa Silver Coinage,* Calcutta: Indian Museum, 1982.

———, 'Commerce and Money in the Central and Western Sectors of Eastern India', *IMB,* vol. XVI, 1982, pp. 65-83.

———, *The Rise and Fall of the Kushāṇa Empire,* Calcutta: Firma KL Mukhopadhyay, 1989.

———, *Media of Exchange in Early Mediaeval North India,* New Delhi: Harman, 1992.

———, *The External Trade of North-Eastern India,* New Delhi: Harman, 1992.

———, 'The Coinage of Dvārāvati in South-East Asia and the Kharoshṭi-Brāhmī Script', in Debala Mitra (ed.), *Explorations in the Art and Archaeology of South Asia: Essays Dedicated to N.G. Majumdar,* Calcutta: Directorate of Archaeology, 1996, pp. 527-34.

Mumford, Lewis, *The City in History, Its Origins, Its Transformations and Its Prospects,* London: Allen and Unwin, 1961.

Nainar, S.M.H., *The Knowledge of India as Possessed by Arab Geographers down to the Fourteenth Century* AD *with Special Reference to South India,* Madras: University of Madras, 1942.

Nandi, R.N., 'Economic Growth in Rural Feudal India', Presidential Address, Section I, *PIHC*, Bodhgaya Sesson, 1981, pp. 25-91.

Narain, A.K. (ed.), *Seminar Papers on the Problems of Megaliths in India,* Varanasi: Benares Hindu University, 1969.

Nath, Vijaya, *Dāna: Gift System in Ancient India (c. 600* BC-AD *300): A Socio-Economic Perspective,* New Delhi: Munshiram Manoharlal, 1987.

Nilakanta Sastri, K.A., *The Colas,* Madras: University of Madras, 1955 (2nd edn.).

———, *A History of South India: From Prehistoric Times to the Fall of Vijayanagar,* Bombay: Oxford University Press, 1966.

Parabrahma Sastry, P.V., *The Kākatīyas of Warangal,* Hyderabad: Govt. of Andhra Pradesh, 1978.

Pearson, M.N., *The Pious Passengers: The Hajj in Earlier Times,* London: Hurst, 1994.

———, *The Indian Ocean*, New York: Oxford University Press, 2004.

Prakash, Om, 'The European Trading Companies and the Merchants of Bengal 1650-1725', *IESHR,* vol. I (3), 1964, pp. 37-63.

Raschke, M.G., 'New Studies in Roman Commerce with the East', *Aufstieg und Niedergang in der Romischer Welt,* vol. II (9), 1978, pp. 605-1378.

Rao, S.R., *Lothal and the Indus Civilization,* New Delhi, 1973.

———, *Excavations at Lothal*, New York: Asia Publishing House, 1973.

Ratnagar, Shereen, *Understanding Harappa: In the Greater Indus Civilization*, New Delhi: Tulika, 2006.

Ray, Amita, 'Urbanization in Early Bengal', Presidential Address, Section I, *PIHC*, Goa session, 1987.

Ray, Haraprasad, 'China and the "Western Ocean" in the Fifteenth Century', in Satish Chandra (ed.), *The Indian Ocean: Explorations in History, Commerce and Politics*, New Delhi: Sage, 1987, pp. 128-34.

———, *Trade and Diplomacy in India-China Relations: A Study of Bengal during the Fifteenth Century*, New Delhi: Radiant Publishers, 1993.

Ray, Himanshu Prabha, *Monastery and Guild: Commerce under the Satavahanas*, New Delhi: Oxford University Press, 1986.

———, 'Early Trade in the Bay of Bengal', *IHR*, vol. XVI, 1987-8, pp. 79-89.

———, 'The Yavana Presence in Ancient India', *JESHO*, XXVII, 1988, pp. 311-25.

———, 'Seafaring in the Bay of Bengal in the Early Centuries AD', *SH*, vol. VI, 1990, pp. 1-14.

——— (ed.), *Archaeology of Seafaring: The Indian Ocean in the Ancient Period*, New Delhi: Pragati Publishers, 1999.

———, 'Seafaring in Peninsular India in the Ancient Period', in David Parkin and Ruth Barnes (eds.), *Ships and Development of Maritime Technology in the Indian Ocean*, London: Routledge Curzon, 2002.

———, *The Archaeology of Seafaring in Ancient South Asia*, Cambridge: Cambridge University Press, 2003.

Ray, Himanshu Prabha and Jean Franoise Salles (eds.), *Tradition and Archaeology: Early Maritime Contacts in the Indian Ocean*, New Delhi: Manohar, 1996.

Ray, Niharranjan, *Bangalir Itihas* (in Bangla), in 2 vols., Calcutta: Niraksharata Durikaran Samiti, 1980 (2nd edn.).

Raychaudhuri, H.C., *Political History of Ancient India*, with a Commentary by B.N. Mukherjee, New Delhi: Oxford University Press, 1996 (8th edn.).

Rostovzeff, M.I., *The Social and Economic History of the Roman Empire*, in 2 vols., Oxford: Oxford University Press, 1957.

Sahu, Bhairabi Prasad and Hermann Kulke, *Interrogating Political Systems: Integrative Processes and States in Pre-modern India*, New Delhi, Manohar, 2015.

Sarkar, H., 'The Emergence of Cities in Early Historical Andhradeśa', in B.M. Pande and B.D. Chattopadhyaya (eds.), *Archaeology and History, Essays in Memory of Shri A. Ghosh*, New Delhi: Agam Kala Prakashan, pp. 631-42.

Schlingloff, D., *Studies in the Ajanta Paintings*, New Delhi: Books and Books, 1988.

Sen, Benoychandra, *Some Historical Aspects of the Inscriptions of Bengal*, Calcutta: University of Calcutta, 1942.

———, *Economics in Kautilya*, Calcutta: Sanskrit College, 1967.

———, *Studies in the Buddhist Jātakas: Tradition and Polity,* Calcutta: Saraswat, 1972.

Sengupta, Gautam, 'Archaeology of Coastal Bengal', in Himanshu Prabha Ray and Jean-François Salles (eds.), *Tradition and Archaeology: Early Maritime Contacts in the Indian Ocean,* New Delhi: Manohar, 1996, pp. 113-28.

Sharma, Dasaratha, *Early Chauhān Dynasties: A Study of Chauhān Political History, Chauhān Political Institutions and Life in the Chauhān Dominions from 800 to 1316 AD,* New Delhi: Motilal Banarsidass, 1959.

Sharma, R.S., 'Material Background of the Origin of Buddhism', in Mohit Sen and M.B. Rao (eds.), *Das Kapital Centenary Volume: A Symposium,* New Delhi: Peoples Publishing House, 1968, pp. 59-68.

———, 'Iron and Urbanisation in the Ganga Basin', *IHR,* vol. I, 1974, pp. 98-103.

———, *Indian Feudalism c. AD 300-1200,* New Delhi: Macmillan, 1980 (2nd edn.).

———, *Material Culture and Social Formations in Ancient India,* New Delhi: Macmillan, 1983.

———, *Perspectives in the Social and Economic History of Early India,* New Delhi: Munshiram Manoharlal, 1983.

———, 'How Feudal Was Indian Feudalism', *Social Scientist,* no. 129, 1984, pp. 16-41.

———, *Urban Decay in India (c. 300-c. 1000),* New Delhi: Munshiram Manoharlal, 1987.

———, 'The Segmentary State and the Indian Experience', *IHR,* vol. XVI, 1990, pp. 80-108.

Sharma, R.S. and D.N. Jha, 'The Economic History of India up to AD 1200: Trends and Prospects', *JESHO,* vol. XVII, 1974, pp. 48-80.

Shrimali, K.M., 'Money, Market and Feudalism', in R.S. Sharma and K.M Shrimali (eds.), A *Comprehensive History of India*, vol. IV. (2), New Delhi: Manohar, 2008, pp. 729-60.

———, 'Monetary History of Early India: Distinctive Landmarks', in Susmita Basu Majumdar and S.K. Bose (eds.), *Money and Money Matters in in Pre-Modern South Asia*, New Delhi: Manohar, 2019, pp. 177-220.

Singer, Charles et al. (eds.), *A History of Technology,* vol. II, Oxford: Clarendon Press, 1979.

Singh, Upinder, *History of Ancient and Early Medieval India*, New Delhi: Pearson, 2008.

Sircar, D.C., *Indian Epigraphy,* New Delhi: Motilal Banarsidass, 1965.

———, *Indian Epigraphical Glossary,* New Delhi: Motilal Banarsidass, 1966.

———, *Palpurva Yuger Vamsanucharit* (in Bangla), Calcutta: Sahityalok, 1982.

———, *Pal-Sen Yuger Vamsanucharit* (in Bangla), Calcutta: Sahityalok, 1982.

Sjoberg, Gideon, *The Pre-industrial City: Past and Present,* Glencoe, Illinois: Free Press, 1960.

Skinner, William G., *Marketing and Social Structure in Rural China,* Ann Arbor: Association for Asian Studies, 1974.

Spate, O.H.K. and A.T.A. Learmonth, *India and Pakistan: A General and Regional Geography,* London: George Allen and Unwin, 1967.

Southall, A., *Alur Society: A Study in Processes and Types of Domination,* Cambridge: W. Heffer, 1956.

Stein, Burton, *Peasant State and Society in Medieval South India,* New Delhi: Oxford University Press, 1980.

———, 'A Decade of Historical Efflorescence', in *South Asia Research,* vol. X, no. 2, 1993, pp. 124-38.

Stillman, Norman A., 'The Eleventh Century Merchant House of Ibn Awkal', *JESHO,* vol. XVI, 1973, pp. 15-88.

Stoneman, Richard, *Palmyra and its Empire: Zenobia's Revolt against Rome,* Ann Arbor: The University of Michigan Press, 1992.

Strauch, Ingo, *Foreign Sailors on Socotra*, Bremen: Hempen Verlag, 2012.

Stube, R., 'Hormuz', in *The Encyclopaedia of Islam,* vol. II, Leiden: E.J. Brill, 1916, pp. 315-16.

Subbarao, B., *The Personality of India,* Baroda: M.S. University, 1958.

Subbarayalu, Y., *The Political Geography of the Chola Country,* Madras: Tamil Nadu State Department of Archaeology, 1973.

Subrahmanyam, Sanjay, *Improvising the Empire: Portuguese Trade and Settlement in the Bay of Bengal, 1500-1700,* New Delhi: Oxford University Press, 1990.

Talbot, Cynthia, *Pre-Colonial India in Practice: Society, Region, and Identity in Medieval Andhra,* New York: Oxford University Press, 2001.

Thapar, B.K., *Recent Archaeological Discoveries in India,* Tokyo: UNESCO, 1989.

Thapar, Romila, *Aśoka and the Decline of the Mauryas.* Oxford: Oxford University Press, 1961; 2nd edn. 1996, New Delhi: Oxford University Press.

———, *Ancient Indian Social History,* New Delhi: Orient Longman, 1978.

———, *From Lineage to State: Social Formation in the Mid-First Millennium* BC *in the Ganga Valley,* New Delhi: Oxford University Press, 1984.

———, 'Patronage and Community', in Barbara Stoller Miller (ed.), *The Powers of Art: Patronage in Indian Culture,* New Delhi: Oxford University Press, 1992, pp. 19-34.

——— (ed.), *Recent Perspectives of Early Indian History,* Bombay: Popular Prakashan, 1995.

———, 'The Tyranny of Labels', *Social Scientist,* vol. XXIV, September-October 1996, pp. 3-23.

———, *Early India from the Origins to c.* AD *1300,* London: Allen Lane, 2002.

———, 'Great Eastern Trade: Other Places and Other Times', Vasant J. Sheth Memorial Lecture, Mumbai, January 2002.

———, *Somanatha, Many Voices of a History,* New Delhi: Viking, 2004.

———, 'History as Literature: The Plays of Visakhadatta', in idem, *The Past before Us: The Historical Traditions of Early North India*, Cambridge (Mass): Harvard University Press, 2013, pp. 353-80.

Tomber, Roberta, *Indo-Roman Trade: From Pots to Pepper*, London: Bloomsbury, 2008.

Trautman, T.R., *Kauṭilya and Arthaśāstra, a Statistical Investigation of the Authorship and the Evolution of the Text,* Leiden: E.J. Brill, 1971.

Toussaint, Auguste, *History of the Indian Ocean,* London: Routledge and Kegan Paul, 1968.

Udovitch, A.L., 'Commercial Techniques in the Medieval Islam', in D.S. Richard (ed.), *Islam and the Trade of Asia,* Pennsylvania: University of Pennsylvania Press, 1970, pp. 37-62.

———, 'Formalism and Informalism in the Social and Economic Institutions of the Medieval Islamic World', in A. Banani and S. Vryonis (eds.), *Individualism and Conformity in Classical Islam,* Wiesbaden: Harroswitz, 1977, pp. 61-71.

———, 'Fatimid Cairo: Crossroads of World Trade: From Spain to India', in Mariane Barrucand (ed.), *L'Egypte Fatimide,* Paris: Presses de l'Universite de Paris-Sorbonne, 1999, pp. 681-91.

Van Leur, J.E., *Indonesian Trade and Society,* The Hague: W. Hoeve, 1955.

Veluthat, Kesavan, *The Political Structure of Early Medieval South India,* New Delhi: Orient Longman, 1993.

———, 'Into the Medieval and Out of It', Presidential Address, Section II, *PIHC,* Bangalore session, 1995.

Verlinden, Charles, 'The Indian Ocean in the Ancient Period and the Middle Ages', in Satish Chandra (ed.), *The Indian Ocean: Explorations in History, Commerce and Politics,* New Delhi: Sage, 1987, pp. 27-53.

Wagle, Narendra, *Society at the Time of the Buddha,* Bombay: Popular Prakashan, 1966.

Warmington, E.H., *The Commerce between the Roman Empire and India,* London: Curzon Press, 1974 (2nd edn.).

Wheeler, R.E.M., *Rome beyond the Imperial Frontier,* London: Routledge, 1954.

———, *My Archaeological Mission to India and Pakistan,* London: Thames, 1976.

Whitehouse, David and Andrew Williamson, 'Sasanian Maritime Trade', *Iran,* vol. XI, 1973, pp. 29-49.

Wink, Andre, *Al Hind, the Making of the Indo-Islamic World,* in 2 vols., vol. I, New Delhi: Oxford University Press, 1990; vol. II, Leiden: E.J. Brill, 1997.

Yadava, B.N.S., *Society and Culture in North India during the Twelfth Century,* Allahabad: Central Book Depot, 1973.

Young, Garry K., *Rome's Eastern Trade, International Commerce and Imperial Policy 31 BC-AD 305,* London and New York: Routledge, 2001.

Index

Index to the Third Edition Updated and Prepared by Dev Kumar Jhanjh